GOD'S FIFTH COLUMN

WILLIAM GERHARDIE

GOD'S FIFTH COLUMN

A Biography of the Age: 1890-1940

Edited and with an introduction by

MICHAEL HOLROYD
&
ROBERT SKIDELSKY

The Hogarth Press
LONDON

Published in 1990 by
The Hogarth Press
20 Vauxhall Bridge Road
London SW1V 2SA

First published in Great Britain by Hodder & Stoughton 1981

A CIP catalogue record for this book is available from the
British Library.

ISBN 0 7012 0887 2

Printed in Finland by Werner Söderström Oy

CONTENTS

BOOK TWO

THE NINETEEN-HUNDREDS

BOOK THREE

THE NINETEEN-TENS

CONTENTS

BOOK FOUR

THE NINETEEN-TWENTIES

BOOK FIVE

THE NINETEEN-THIRTIES

EPILOGUE

INTRODUCTION

I

When William Gerhardie died on July 15th, 1977, in his eighty-second year, there was a good deal of speculation about an uncompleted novel, a tetralogy in one volume called *This Present Breath*, on which he was rumoured to have been working for the past quarter of a century. There were sound reasons for this speculation. Over thirty pages of the tetralogy (including, Gerhardie-style, its two concluding chapters) had appeared in Neville Braybrooke's Easter Book *The Wind and the Rain* in 1962. But when his papers came to be examined after his death, no new novel was discovered. Instead, within numerous large cardboard boxes fashioned into an astonishingly elaborate card index and re-soundingly labelled DO NOT CRUSH, was the engineering, the bits and pieces, of a complex work of fiction. Into this towering structure, on variously coloured rectangles of paper approximately three inches by five, Gerhardie had filed away sentences, notes, paragraphs, to which were added newspaper cuttings and less easily identifiable matter, all under the headings of various characters, scenes, and what he called movements of the novel. But there was no narrative and, it was sadly concluded, no novel.

The machinery for this legendary work, in which it was easy to lose oneself with fascination and bewilderment, was so vast that for some time it overshadowed a more orthodox manuscript (large enough in all conscience), which turned out to be a non-fiction book in various drafts that, because of its several titles (including *Time and Divine Discontent, God's Fifth Column, The World of Our Fathers*), at first gasp suggested an alarmingly prolific philosophical outpouring.

It was reasonable for the reading public to have expected a work of fiction. Gerhardie was best known as a novelist. *Futility* and *The Poly-*

9

glots had made his reputation in the 1920s and, together with some novels in the 1930s, such as *Of Mortal Love*, had won the high opinion of, among others, Arnold Bennett, Graham Greene, Olivia Manning, Anthony Powell, C. P. Snow, Evelyn Waugh, H. G. Wells and Edith Wharton (who wrote an Introduction to the American edition of *Futility*). Of the two Collected Editions of his Works published after the Second World War, the first had comprised all novels and the second included just two non-fiction titles out of ten. Yet his last novel, *My Wife's the Least of It*, had been published as long ago as 1938 and been succeeded by a massive and eclectic account of the Romanovs, a historical biography of the Rurik as well as of the Romanov dynasties that, written as narrative rather than a compilation, attempted to present a survey of a thousand years of Russian history. It was following publication of *The Romanovs* in 1940 that Gerhardie wrote *God's Fifth Column*.

Among Gerhardie's assets as a modern historian were his knowledge of Russia and his fluency in European languages. His education, and the first thirty-five years of his life, had been heterogeneously European: throughout his life he disliked being referred to as 'an *English* writer'. In his autobiography, *Memoirs of a Polyglot*, published precociously at the age of thirty-five, he tells of his childhood in St. Petersburg where his father, a British cotton manufacturer, settled in the 1890s. In his late teens Gerhardie had been despatched to England to train for a commercial career, but he joined the Royal Scots Greys in 1915 as a trooper. To improve his English, he had been studying Wilde, arriving at the cavalry barracks in York with long hair, a languid expression and an elegant cane – which he prudently substituted for an enormous sword bought second-hand in the Charing Cross Road. After his commission he was transferred to the British Embassy in Petrograd where he viewed, through a monocle, many stages of the Russian Revolution.

Following two years on the British Military Mission in Siberia, and having been improbably decorated by three governments, Gerhardie went round the world and then up to Oxford where he read English, wrote his first novel and a brilliant little book on Chehov. Then came a transformation. During the 1920s, in the words of Arnold Bennett, he was cast as 'the pet of the intelligentsia and the darling of Mayfair'. A caricature of him at this time by Edgar Spenceley uses this quotation as its caption, but adds in italics: *Success and How to Avoid It*. At this split-second avoidance he became an adept. He was taken up by Lord Beaverbrook (the prototype of Lord Ottercove in *Doom*) who, to assist Gerhardie, wrote a long article about him in the *Sunday Express*, though in a series (which included Lloyd George) entitled *Splendid Failures*. Gerhardie's 'failure' lay partly in his foreignness: he was never part of this literary and social world, but an intermittent visitor, receptive yet unalterable and, to its natives, a novelty. He had a sweet tooth for praise, having been treated as the fool of the family when young, and although he did not overvalue this lionisation, he was not insensitive to its removal, once his novelty had worn off. These experiences lie behind some of the most biting pages of *God's Fifth Column*, whose theme became the sabotaging of social values and worldly confidence by the Comic Spirit. "As a God's Fifth Columnist," he writes, "in breaking up with a pick-axe the evil *beau monde*, and making it unlikely that anyone should ever want to live in such a world, Proust, however unconscious of it himself, was the foreman of a demolition squad pulling down a condemned building, condemned alike by God and man, chilly, deceptive, and, behind an imposing façade, unhealthy, verminous, cruel, uncomfortable and, in the last analysis, fatuous."

For nearly a decade, it seemed, Gerhardie had floated delightfully yet, as Gorley Putt observed, 'neglected to set a course'. Much of this time was passed haphazardly abroad. *The Polyglots* (1925) was written in the Austrian Alps; part of *Pending Heaven* (1930) in the south of France; *Resurrection* (1935) draws on his experiences of living in Tunisia; *Memoirs of a Polyglot* (1931) has a revealing chapter on India and its attitude to Britain, and a section devoted to his tour of Canada and the United States ironically entitled "How to Lecture in America".

By 1931, the year his autobiography was published, Gerhardie moved back to England and into Rossetti House, behind Broadcasting House in London, where he remained for the last forty-six years of his life. Here was another transformation, moving the focus of his work from the comic agonies of procrastination to the imaginative power of time regained: "Nothing is until it is over." For more than forty years he travelled nowhere, but lived in increasing poverty, eventually without newspapers, radio, gramophone, television and, for much of the time, adequate heating. He was a hermit in the West End of London, his only link with the world an endless telephone line and the remembrance of things past. As a symbol, perhaps, of his preoccupation with the past, he reverted to an ancestral spelling of his name by adding an 'e' to 'Gerhardi'. Visiting him in the 1960s, Olivia Manning wrote:

Could a writer of such quality be buried alive here today, in the heart and centre of London? I found him in his sitting-room with the curtains drawn.

"But William," I protested. "It is such a beautiful day!"

"Is it?" he asked eagerly, but he did not go to look for himself.

The room with its purple carpet seemed at the bottom of a rock-pool, lit, as it was, by reflections from the great Louis XV mirror that

11

once hung in the Gerhardies' Petersburg mansion. I look at a photograph of an elegant, handsome, rather arrogant young man – the brilliant sought-after author of *The Polyglots*.

Reviewing *Memoirs of a Polyglot*, Desmond MacCarthy had written of Gerhardie's unusual mixture of conceit and humility, heartlessness and warmth, his subtlety springing from a kind of childishness, and his detachment sometimes expressing itself in irony, sometimes as sympathy. But, he added:

I am anxious about the future effects of such detachment upon Mr. Gerhardi's creative power. A literary artist, besides being in a sense immune from experience, must also be at the mercy of it, so that he cannot tell afterwards whether he has owed more to the naïve impulses which drove him to meet life, or to the aloofness which softly and inevitably disentangled him again. In Mr. Gerhardi artistic detachment has been reinforced by cultural rootlessness. There is therefore a danger that he may not care enough about anything except his work, to save that from becoming thin and fantastic. It seems to me rather ominous that he should already see in Proust's attitude towards experience a reflection of his own. Spontaneous response to life alone can nourish creation: he is too young to put up the Proustian shutters and regard the outside world as existing only for the sake of its reflection in his private *camera obscura*. The problem of every 'poet' (Mr. Gerhardi prefers this word in the Greek sense to 'artist') is to strike a balance between devotion to his art and love for their own sakes of the things which feed it. Where that balance lies, depends upon the nature of his talents. If he loves life too much, he will never assimilate it properly; if he lives for his art alone, he will have next to nothing to write about.

Though MacCarthy's warning seemed well founded, Gerhardie was still richly prolific during the 1930s, publishing (besides his autobiography) four novels; a study (with Hugh Kingsmill) of Casanova; a manual of detailed character-studies through self-analysis in collaboration with Prince Leopold Loewenstein-Wertheim; and, with Brian Lunn, *The Memoirs of Satan* (1932). This last book, being a fantastical history of mankind presented through the imaginary experiences of Satan who, at crucial moments in the lives of famous men and women, enters them in order to give their inside story, represents the first attempt by Gerhardie to tie his novelist's imagination to his interest in biographical history.

II

Following the completion of *The Romanovs*, he began his research for *God's Fifth Column* in the autumn of 1939, submitting a synopsis to his agent Curtis Brown early the following summer, and in November 1940 (after an interval spent composing a play on snobbery entitled *English Measles*) he started to write the book. "Methuens have been considering it since May and have now signed a contract with a tiny advance but good royalties," he told Morchard Bishop. "The book is in its first stage – two pages written . . . though lots of material collected and some eighty books read in preparation." The contract, which was backdated to September 30th (with royalties of 20% rising to 25%) was for "A Biography of the Age" comprising not less than 100,000 words in consideration for an advance on signature of £100, returnable to the publisher if the completed manuscript was not delivered by September 30th, 1941. "Everything, especially my promise to the Bank, makes hurry essential," he wrote. These details are significant since they help to explain the pressure of time and money under which Gerhardie was writing – circumstances which influenced the philosophical and economic content of the book.

An initial title had been *Artists Going into Action*, "meaning that men of action are misguided artists who express their day-dreams in action instead of on paper or canvas," he explained. He had assembled a string of historical anecdotes as evidence of this idea and was "just getting going," he wrote on December 18th, 1940, "when, blast! the War Office informs me that they are about to employ me: forms, interview, references, and all the sickening paraphernalia all over again!" Though this was a blow to the book, he soon spied out possible advantages: "once you are up against it, even serving your country . . . is preferable to starvation!" By March 4th, 1941, he reported the book as being "only half done, if as much. I feel that it might be rash to refuse an Intelligence job in the Army." With many interruptions he continued working as fast as he could until suddenly the impossibilities of his situation seemed to engulf him. "It is over!" he told Morchard Bishop on March 23rd. "All is finished. Clamp down the piano lid: my strings are broken, my keys are jammed. My instrument will play no more." This was written after the shock of hearing that his part-time secretary, Patsy Rosentiehl, to whom he had dedicated *The Romanovs* and who had typed his manuscripts with something of the devotion of a Countess Tolstoy, had been bombed out of her home. The conditions of work became increasingly difficult. Penelope Fitzgerald remembers him writing away frantically with a saucepan on his head to ward off the bombs that were flying around. Periodic aversion to this work would rise up in him as he came to realise that he could not finish the book by the publisher's deadline. "I am at once the slave of art and of finance," he complained. "The first is temperamental and would be no hardship but for the second, which is wearing to the nerves . . . It's pretty good, but could be a lot better and anyhow is not at all what I intended it to be and which it could be if I had ten years to write it in."

The Army job having fallen through, Gerhardie appears to have wrung more time from his publisher. "I am, after many vicissitudes, again getting a move on with *God's Fifth Column*," he wrote on July 12th, ". . . the whole conception of God's 5th Column, as a biography of the Age, is undergoing all the time a SUB-CONSCIOUS transformation in wisdom – a wisdom quite beyond my ordinary mental capacities and outlook; a wisdom dissatisfied to the point of disgust with much that has been set down and re-shaping it into new combinations. Just now again it seems to be shaping; I am advancing, I have launched a new offensive; and the Bank has been promised a speedy completion and the money due on completion."

From time to time throughout that winter he would describe the book as creeping at a snail's pace towards its conclusion, and at the end of January 1942 he took the manuscript to Methuen. After the hurry came the waiting. "The book is *officially* ready," he informed Morchard Bishop (to whom he intended to dedicate it). "But as it won't be published until the autumn, I will have the opportunity of condensing it, with one hand, and including several scenes I had not, through hurry, been able to include . . . [having been] forced to finish it anyhow of sheer physical necessity."

On delivery of the manuscript Gerhardie had been due a further one hundred-and-fifty pounds which, though swallowed up by his bank, released him from the worst financial worry. "The sun is shining, the birds are singing, and God is in his Fifth Column," he reported on April 11th. "At least, with *His* assistance, I have this week been able to bring a little order into the chaos, doing one death a day. Patsy will not be satisfied with less. I've done the Death of Tolstoy, the Death of Chehov, and to-day the Death of Proust. Alas! I'm substituting for much of what sounds somewhat peevish, querulous stuff of the 1940s a passionate appeal for a New World, to include as the basis of its economic market a standard unearned increment of one world-dollar a day to be received by every adult individual the world over. Though convincingly worded, my style in that chapter rings a little like that of a demagogue – a sort of Lloyd George at a by-election in Hackney! Plain words to plain men sort of thing . . ."

For another month, sympathetically goaded by Patsy, Gerhardie continued with this revision. "Oh dear, it's been a difficult book!" he acknowledged, adding with unconscious pathos, "I think it *ought* to sell. I think it might. Indeed, it *must* and will; the only thing that can prevent the sale of *God's 5th Column* is if it is sabotaged for its own secret purpose by God's 5th Column."

This is one interpretation of what then happened. In May he was offered a staff job on the British Broadcasting Corporation as a sub-editor in the Czechoslovakian section. "Another week or so and Methuen's should have *their* copy ready to set up," he calculated. "I have accepted the job."

The Proustian shutters opened and Gerhardie emerged from his rockpool to land in the European Division of the B.B.C. His career during the war was curiously successful. On October 6th, 1942, he was transferred to the Central Productions Unit for which he wrote scripts for general translation and use by overseas services. The following year he began his association with the highly successful victory-for-granted, free-for-all propaganda teaching service *English by Radio* which he pioneered and where he continued working until the end of March 1945, when it was decided to confine the scope of the series to a more elementary standard. Gerhardie then resigned "in order to concentrate more fully on his literary work".

This literary work still included *God's Fifth Column*. In a note on an incomplete manuscript now in the Humanities Research Center at Austin, Gerhardie explained that his book "was first completed in 1942, and was subsequently, after acceptance and appearance in the [Methuen] catalogue, withdrawn at my request for revision". Since his correspondence with Methuen was blown up during the war (and that with Curtis Brown more peacefully destroyed some years afterwards) there exists no record of exactly what happened. But it seems probable that he took advantage of receiving a salary for the first time since the First World War to negotiate for the return of his manuscript, hoping to give it more time and make it 'a lot better'.

Though his entry in *Who's Who* lengthened impressively during the last twenty-five years of his life, Gerhardie published no new book and seemed, after the manner of Desmond MacCarthy's prediction, to vanish. When specially pressed for money he would quarry out the battered manuscript and tinker away at his revisions, often adding to its length as he struggled to condense some of the sections. But the initial impulse behind the book, clouded by his unhappy working conditions, had faded, and as time went on he increasingly sought financial help from other sources: from talks on the radio; from the acceptance of a three-hundred-pound commission from Lord Beaverbrook to write his biography (a book, favourably noticed in some of Gerhardie's obituaries, of which almost nothing exists); and a number of ill-conceived plays with promising titles such as *The Private Life of a Public Nuisance*. Of these (since he had little sense of theatre or gift for dramatic dialogue) only two were performed: *Rasputin* in 1958 on the B.B.C. Home Service and two years later at the Vanbrugh Theatre in London; and his 'implausible comedy' *I was a King in Babylon* (or *You May Very Well be Right*) produced in 1948 by Jerome Kilty at Boston.

In 1947 Gerhardie had composed an ingenious 'Literary Credo' that, placed at the beginning of *Futility*, acts as an Introduction to his collected novels. From then on he preferred to lay *God's Fifth Column* to one side and pour his hopes into the work of fiction he called *This Present Breath*: against which God's Fifth Column appears to have exacted its revenge.

III

The Methuen catalogue of Autumn Books for 1942 describes *God's Fifth Column* as a 'deft trellis-work' in which the figures of poets and monarchs, prophets, artists and statesmen "each in his own time succumbing to the unseen agents of God's Fifth Column, weave their way in and out and across each other through six decades". For Gerhardie, the writing of history was least serious when it was most conventional, and least conclusive when it pretended to be most complete. In its depiction of chosen personalities and events, his book carries a personal philosophy: a vision of life as it is and as it should be. Uncharacteristically for Gerhardie, who valued literature less as argument than as evocation, it is a work with a purpose: if, as he says, "our wishes are our real educators", then his pages aim at redirecting our wishes to their true ends.

His *Biography of the Age* is of the age he lived through. It is shaped by his own personal experiences, and his reflections on them. Some of his examples – of British money financing the cotton mills on the Neva to the ruin of Lancashire, of the schoolmaster telling his pupils he would not teach them the day Tolstoy died – are drawn from his own early life in St. Petersburg. His dissection of English class distinctions is penned with the savage accuracy of the outsider. Lionised for a time by English society for his novels of Russian life, Gerhardie, who spoke to the end with a faint Russian intonation, never quite fitted in to the English social structure. He felt increasingly isolated when the glamour of early success had worn off. No doubt his friendship with Lord Beaverbrook, another outsider, was partly the attraction of mutual precariousness. Gerhardie's cosmopolitanism also comes out in his fierce denunciations of national assertiveness.

But more than just cultural or national rootlessness was involved. He included the family in his strictures on all forms of collectivism – "that ungodly unit of pernicious preferential loyalty" he called it. Although firmly heterosexual, Gerhardie never married. To him the family, with its exclusive demands, was a microcosm, and breeding ground, of the larger collectivisms in whose name individuals were required to sacrifice their chances of self-fulfilment. As an artist, he is completely on Tolstoy's side in describing the domestic upheavals which dogged that great writer's life; ignoring the possibility that the creative impulse needs to be nourished by ordinary experience, however distracting it might seem. Gerhardie wanted to be left alone in order to create; and he ended alone, his creative flame extinguished. His choice of the individual 'suffering unit' as his frame of reference and the loosest kind of world-federation as his worldly ideal, thus reflect the personal experiences he brought to his history.

Although Gerhardie never came under fire in the First World War, his view of history was shaped by the war. In retrospect, it appeared to him not as a struggle between good and evil, between freedom and 'Prussianism', but as a combined assault by the 'men of action' on the 'suffering units' (or individuals) of all nations. In his first novel, *Futility*, it is the comic frustration of the war, seen from the vantage point of the Allied interventions in Russia, which chiefly struck him. But in *The Polyglots*, his hero [himself] preaches in the best 'war generation' style:

> Throughout the countries which had participated in the war there is still a tendency among many bereaved ones to assuage themselves by the thought that their dead had fallen for something noble and worthwhile . . . Mischievous delusion! Their dead are victims – neither more nor less – of the folly of adults who having blundered the world into a ludicrous war, now build memorials – to square it all up. If I were the Unknown Soldier, my ghost would refuse to lie down under the heavy piece of marble; I would arise, I would say to them: keep your blasted memorial and learn sense! Christ died 1918 years back and you're as incredibly foolish as ever you were.

Later, Gerhardie came to doubt the literary merit of this passage, which Shaw, he records, had selected with unerring inaccuracy as the book's

17

best piece of writing, but the feeling is genuine, and is the theme of *God's Fifth Column*.

The suffering unit was Gerhardie's measure of the crimes and follies of rulers, and the efforts of professional historians to exculpate them. His criticism of historians was that they 'echo the generals and statesmen'; the calculations, that is, of the insane. Abstention from judgment led to the worship of power. The historian, Gerhardie wrote, in one of the discarded drafts of this book, is "like a butler, absorbed by his duty of rating the events he announces in the order of their conventional importance, while keeping any private thoughts . . . to himself". He is "too busy ushering in his facts, too replete with his ceremonious virtue" to "dwell on the disparity between their conventional and their human values". Gerhardie wanted history to be "morally accurate – accurate in the relation of what has been done to what has been suffered". It should be "*by implication*, a moral indictment of the crime against humanity". The italicised phrase is important: history's moral lessons were to be conveyed through art, not through preaching; through humour, irony, wonder and incredulity. As an epigraph to one of the versions of the book, he had quoted Horace: *Ridentem dicere verum quid vetat*? (And why should the truth not be told humorously?) To Gerhardie the clairvoyance of the comedic vision was a searchlight through the fog of earnestness generated by historians to hide the lunacies perpetrated by rulers. His humour was not a refuge, but an illumination of reality, rooted, as Hugh Kingsmill observed in his introduction to Gerhardie's *Resurrection*, "in a perception not of what is socially incongruous, humour's usual subject matter, but of what is spiritually incongruous".

For Gerhardie (who dedicated a later draft of the book to Kingsmill) it is the artists, not the historians, who are the true spokesmen for mankind, and it is through the artist's vision that he tries to bring the age into moral perspective. In his autobiography, he writes of the "immemorial attraction between the man of action and the man of thought", reflecting his own temptation by Beaverbrook. But for the thinker, this is a snare and delusion. The relationship is never reciprocal. "The fascination," he continues "supposed to be that of thought, exercised by the man of thought on the man of action, ends invariably in discovery by the thinker that what the man of action really requires him for is to vent on him his own thoughts." It is not, therefore, through their direct impact on the world of action that thinkers and artists can improve the world, but by remaining true to their artistic vocation of depicting things as they 'really are' – which, to Gerhardie, meant depicting and judging temporal events in the light of the universal and eternal.

By his terms 'Aristotelian' and 'Platonic' (introduced in chapter 77)

Gerhardie tried to formalise the distinction between the politician and the thinker, the historian and the artist. "It is by the touchstone of the Platonic conception of reason as a quality or an attribute, as against the Aristotelian conception, of reason as power, that this biography distributes its store of sympathy to the public figures of the last fifty years. The Platonic Idea is indeed the counter on which the sundry figures of the Age are thrown to find out whether they ring true." Few statesmen pass the test: to some extent Woodrow Wilson, to a lesser extent Neville Chamberlain. Similarly, he divides his team of writers into Aristotelians and Platonists: Gorky, Zola, Shaw, Victor Hugo, who were essentially terrestrial prophets; Chehov and Proust, who were poets: "the poet's value rises in the eyes of posterity; the prophet's sinks."

Gerhardie was a bit of both. The writer who comes closest to his own philosophy of history is from neither group, but is the half-poet, half-prophet, Tolstoy. He was greatly attracted by Tolstoy's insistence that the Gospels were a highly practical teaching, conforming as they did to the real needs and interests of suffering humanity, compared to which the ambitions of rulers and statesmen were the height of unworldliness: a contrast expertly drawn in the scene (chapter 23) between William Jennings Bryan and Tolstoy, in which it is Tolstoy the dreamer who is shown to be the realist, and Bryan, the practical man, who is depicted as living in a world of illusion.

Hostility to interpreting the events of his age in terms of mechanical causes and effects inevitably gives to Gerhardie's portrait of his age something of the quality of static tableaux. His historical pageant, in fact, consists of a number of wonderful death scenes, which illustrate not the connection between temporal events, but "that beautiful marriage between time and eternity". Nevertheless, the temporal treatment is not entirely static. In his opening chapter, Gerhardie describes the 'motive-power' of the Age as "the natural resentment engendered by any person, class, nation, movement or religion attempting to justify its hegemony by identifying its interests with the supposed good of others". He sees a movement of humanity against the tyranny of family, class, race, unearned privilege, established religion which he hopes will culminate in the abolition of sovereign nation-states, leading to a world-federation, and a minimum, guaranteed, unearned income for all. The agent of this transformation is God's Fifth Column – divine discontent with the human order, sabotaging men's complacency, shattering false gods. The point about God's Fifth Column is that it undermines 'all inconclusive formations', the over-earnestness or over-optimism of the reformer equally with the criminal projects of dictators and the conservative acceptance of things as they are; continually sifting the true from the false, until human society has come to rest "upon the only

19

x PREPONDERANT INFLUENCE OR AUTHORITY, ESP. OF GOVT. OR STATE.

foundation acceptable to God". The theme, like the fifth columnist himself, enters the work surreptitiously and gains force through cumulative illustration. It first appears in the shape of Meredith's Comic Spirit and then recurs in a variety of forms – for it speaks to each in his own language: in the shape of Tolstoy's incompatible wife (God's way of testing the man who wanted to love and thought it easy); as Tchaikovsky's despair (deemed wholesome for the music-maker's soul), and most outrageously as the 'homunculus' Hitler, the apotheosis of the mediocre in politics, nakedly exposing man's greed and self-seeking (the embodiment and indictment of the ape-man whom human beings had accepted as their self-image).

A. J. P. Taylor found Gerhardie's description of Lord Beaverbrook "the only contemporary account . . . of any value". As a historian, Gerhardie did not attempt to emulate Taylor's short, snappy, sentences. "The world of politics awaits its Proust," he wrote, and in his effort to fill the gap, he often felt the need to adopt the Proustian style. One reacts to Gerhardie somewhat as Samuel Beckett reacted to Proust, "exhausted and angry after an hour, submerged, dominated, by the crest and break of metaphor after metaphor: but never stupefied". There is a danger, as Gerhardie acknowledges, in cramming so much enthusiasm into a single phrase, in never being able to leave anything out. Fortunately, his methods are sufficiently flexible, his vision sufficiently coherent, to give the work as a whole a satisfactory artistic shape. He develops his themes through collocations of vivid incidents and personalities: the absurdity of Queen Victoria, empress of more than half the world, defending her hearthside rug from the footprint of Balfour; the fatuity of political speeches and ententes cordiales when put beside actual events; the comedy of Tolstoy and Gorky "conversing angrily about divine love"; the gaiety of Chehov's funeral, his coffin arriving in a truck marked 'For Oysters' and being solemnly followed by the wrong procession; the more bitter absurdity of Sir Edward Grey and Prince Lichnowsky exchanging warm handshakes as they leave the job of killing to others. The incidents and personalities are subtly linked through contrast and parallel: the death scenes of the various characters, for example, all serve as reminders of transience – and of immortality. Gerhardie varies his tone in each case so as to capture something essential in the dying person, reporting Oscar Wilde's death with wit and pathos but presenting the death of the Tsar and his family as redemptive suffering. The style usually accommodates each subject, echoing the Proustian or Chehovian rhythms and nuances, then moving to the brash or empty colloquialism of some of the political leaders: from the lyrical to the crusty. For to Gerhardie most politicians, monarchs, statesmen were 'apes of God', and his narrative of their actions serves the purpose of exposing the fatuity of national leaders. His exasperation at the rhetorical inanities and abuse of the truth-telling Word chattered out by these apes of God is deliberately expressed in their language of cliché, acting as a parody of what he saw as conventional history-writing.

About one quarter of Gerhardie's original text has been omitted. Although he worked intermittently at his manuscript for many years, he never considered he had got it ready for publication, and we have left out, or cut, chapters and parts of chapters, which seemed less ready than the others. Since it was not intended to be an academic work of history, we have not thought it necessary to supply those sources of quotations which Gerhardie himself omitted: where necessary, footnotes have been added to explain some contemporary reference, now obscure, or who someone was. Nor, except in one instance, has it been necessary to correct the historical record. Although Gerhardie despised the world of facts, he recorded them more accurately than many historians who worship them.

Michael Holroyd
Robert Skidelsky

BOOK ONE

THE EIGHTEEN-NINETIES

1

MEDIEVAL SURVIVALS

As the century entered on its last decade, Margot Tennant was twenty-six, with four more years of dashing spinsterhood ahead before becoming Mrs. Asquith. William II, turned thirty-one, had been sitting on the German throne for two years, in exultation, in excitement. Hitler was approaching his first birthday. Tolstoy had put sixty-two years behind him, and was faced with twenty more to uncoil the angry dust in. The century was petering out in flippant gestures and mighty sighs.

Mrs. Asquith, besides being so palpably her own heroine, has over-dramatised, to the delight of our ironic faculty, her entire age and sex. To read the Kaiser's autobiography, one would gather that no finer, nobler, gentler creature, too sensitive to live, ever wore a robe of purple and ermine. Hitler has dramatised himself as a man achieving a brazen divinity through roughing it among thugs. And old Tolstoy, in vainly modelling himself on Christ, discovered a Golgotha peculiarly his own.

Shortly before certain 'gallants and graces', known in London as 'The Souls', in the welcoming verse of their host, young George Nathaniel Curzon, "gathered to dine, in the year '89, in a haunt that in Hamilton Place is", the doors of a German lunatic asylum had closed on the new inmate, Friedrich Nietzsche. The afflicted mind, taking leave of the body on the threshold of the mental home, had fluttered at large, wondering where it might lodge. It entered the soft skull of one Adolf Hitler, just then seeing the light.

The Kaiser, fired by Kipling's vision of the white man's burden, was about to dismiss Bismarck whose assertiveness, he says, 'had become oppressive'. Three-years-old D. H. Lawrence played disgruntledly in a Nottinghamshire mining-village street with other miners' urchins. Nicholas Ulianov, turned nineteen and leading a double life under the more romantic name of Lenin, was being admitted, after not unjustifiable misgivings on the part of the authorities, as home student to the Petersburg Law School. Marcel Proust, a year older, a languid and

25

incredibly polite young socialite of Paris, was entertaining with exquisite sensibility selected guests at his parents' dinner table. Anton Chehov, advised at twenty-nine by an established writer that he had genius, resolved to stop pot-boiling.

In a biography of the Age, nothing that has taken place in the period covered is properly irrelevant. On the other hand, everything is irrelevant by the test of that which has been left out. Why D. H. Lawrence? Why not Picasso? But once it is conceded that this biography is intended to throw into relief the motive-power of the Age as understood by the present writer, then nobody need be included who does not, nobody rejected who does, throw that motive-power into relief. This motive-power is the natural resentment engendered by any person, class, nation, movement or religion attempting to justify its hegemony by identifying its interests with the supposed good of others.

In personal relations, undermined by the able work of God's Fifth Columnists, Henrik Ibsen and Bernard Shaw, it is the family which in our Age has suffered a reeling if timely blow to its hitherto unchallenged authority. An admirer wrote to Chehov to enquire why the family, a much revered institution, was cracking. Chehov replied that the family was a human conception, and all human things were cracking: why not also the family? In the class struggle it is the established social order, with the fable that inheritors of unearned increment and wage earners were two different races of men, superior and inferior, and never the twain shall meet, which has been reversed in Russia; subjected to a monstrous if spurious new orientation in Germany and Italy, and perhaps dented in England. In religion it is the established Churches which have been superannuated or at least depleted, circumvented or deflected by new and modern brands of godliness: Spiritualism, Theosophy, Christian Science, the Salvation Army, the Oxford Group Movement, and the like. In nationalism it is imperialism, holding up the multiplying mirror to its own face, which has fainted at what it has seen there.

When, among others, Margot Tennant was by Curzon gathered to dine, in the year '89, England was a medieval land; France had retained the mould of the eighteenth century, and in Russia what the village commune had been at the time the Rurik Norsemen took over in A.D. 810 that it was still. Austria and Italy had not even begun to digest the aristocratic sugar, lavishly coating the bitter pill beneath. Germany was honeycombed with pumpernickel Courts caked over with an elaborate etiquette-and-culture icing. It would be easy to disprove these assertions by pointing out the rise of the commercial and professional classes in Germany and England, the radicalism in France, the enlightened intelligentsia and benevolently-minded bourgeoisie in Russia. It is, however, the style of life that determines the character of a nation and of the subsequent struggle. The style of life was essentially as described.

In America alone could the revolutionary ideal of brotherhood, the new start, the sense of an outright assumption of equality as between man and man, freely manifest itself. Through the United States blew a pleasant breeze, a companionable quality of spontaneous friendliness – their heritage from that small band of pilgrims who had cut themselves adrift for good and all from the meaner servitudes of Europe. In America alone there was human courtesy as distinct from European class-courtesy. America may have her social fads, her smart sets, her old families, her strikes and lockouts, her fetishes and pretensions, some even more puerile than our own, but she has rid herself of the fetid fable, the fatuous assumption that class distinctions are inevitable.

Europe was and is, in this respect, like India, a backward continent. True, the French Revolution had long abolished the *gentil homme* – in theory, as the English Revolution, more amusingly, had turned everyone into 'esquires'. Content with this fine concession to the spirit of man born free and equal, they, however, still wanted someone to black their shoes for them.

It was, characteristically, a Russian aristocrat of old vintage, Count Tolstoy, who was struck by the incompatibility of the treatment meted out to the lowly and poor with the covenants in the New Testament, which we as Christians profess to believe. Indeed, believe with a fervour, a zest never so quick to take umbrage as when the Church is attacked on a point of form: never so elastic and broadminded as when Christianity is being depleted of all its spirit. Tolstoy discovered, towards the end of a life of intermittent debauchery, that it was not right. In a series of simple little books he proceeded to say so, to the pained astonishment of the clergy who had believed that humility in the poor was not only in this world of appearances eminently fit but also offered opportunities of advancement not to be overlooked in the next. The Gospels, argued the officers of the Church, vouchsafed the down-and-out, in return for passing discomforts, compensations in eternity, while taking a frankly gloomy view of the heavenly chances of the well-to-do. Could anything be more fair?

The English clergy in general, and the Anglican in particular, found fault with the Count's theology. When an English translation of *Wherein is My Faith?* made its appearance, it brushed softly against the velvet of the bland, lush Anglican garden-party spirit of compromise: compromise with slums and poverty and benevolent armament manufacturers subscribing heavily to selected charities: the whole subtle, humorous, inimitable paraphernalia of the established social complex so dear to clergymen. But that was all.

The Church of England, comfortable in its settled habits of reformed Catholicism, had been singing hallelujahs for joy at the astonishing persistence of the English medieval order. Squire, parson, farmer, their relationships still rooted in the feudal system, continued straining to participate in a little international usury offering the highest average return on their savings.

2

MARGOT

Margot Tennant, even apart from her representative, warmly feminine outlook on the world of her time, is herself a valuable cross-section of British society. She is an epitome, an unintentional self-satire, a comic epos, a microcosm and a self-taught method, profusely illustrated in no half-tones, for mastering the unspoken intricacies of the British social system.

Springing from the loins of a large-calibre, self-made Glasgow man of business who ended up in Grosvenor Square, and, on her mother's side, a more discreet Anglican parson stock, she was at the age of thirty sought in marriage by a middle-aged widower with children, a rising lawyer-politician, Mr. H. H. Asquith, who, though Oxford bred, wished to consign to social oblivion his modest provincial origin and upbringing in the notorious social courage of his second wife.

In her told story you have the untold story of British social life; of aspirations which are never mooted; of the bluntest of social ambitions never acknowledged even to oneself; of the steady pushfulness of crude fathers, keen blades of commerce indiscriminately on the make, producing in the course of a single generation gracious peeresses taking refuge, from the vulgar curiosity of social climbers eager for a recipe of such spectacular success, in the coy protective shyness of conscious distinction.

Unacknowledged, as though by tacit collective consent, as something too trite in an England concerned only with spiritual realities, the opportunities of accumulating social and material stock with both eyes glued resolutely – and, what is the more remarkable, sincerely – on eternal values would have surprised the cynic erroneously believing this country to be 'matter-of-fact'. It is *not* matter-of-fact. It is invertedly spiritual. We tolerate the manufacture of new aristo-cum-plutocrats because we have been taught that only treasures laid up in heaven merit social applause. In which opinion and applause the newly-favoured eagerly concur, raising saintly eyes to a heaven which will surely compensate them for their staunch endurance of material responsibilities on earth.

Thus the material ideal is kept attractively untarnished. We say that money and rank are not important, and imply that whoever thinks they *are* important has by that high standard not achieved real wealth or distinction. When he has so qualified, his treasury will swell with virtue, his proud house efface itself to a mere headquarters of good works. Those disporting themselves on the top of the world do no more with us than implement their spiritual ideals. With pain and sorrow they have torn themselves away from a cloistered and cherished obscurity to breathe the dust and heat of the common day. Some are rising statesmen who, with a sigh of nostalgia, postpone the true calling of their fine intellectual natures, their delectable contributions to English letters, until they may, without injury to the State, retire to write an account of their life and their stewardship, of their love of birds, of the science of the angling worm.

Yes, the material ideal is kept untarnished. But surely not unenvied? If there indeed be envy to compete with the rich in their sacrificial exercises in the cause of charitable works, such envy is successfully inoculated against by the false but widely credited axiom that success in Britain is an open house. Stress is laid on a half-truth: that there is always room at the top. With these two tags goes the exhortation beloved of people living on unearned increment. stand on your own feet. And, true enough, anyone may gather gold and honours, as it is open to anyone who stoops to pick up sufficient coins on the way to dine at the Ritz. Anyone can be a gentleman in his own esteem by merely ceasing to be self-conscious.

The political result of all this is incalculable. We put no one's back up either at home or abroad, for we heartily invite them to do as we do. The Anglo-Saxon community is accordingly more supple than any frankly hierarchical system: not so authoritatively inelastic as the Jesuit order, nor so formally cryptic as the Masonic, nor yet so uninvitingly exclusive as that of Zion. Most important of all, it is merely commercially – not literally, as in the case of the Totalitarian fraternity – cut-throat. It is a world at once sensitive and serene, plain and coloured, subtle and simple, too funny and too devastating for words. Lady Oxford and Asquith, who had sat on Tennyson's knee, looked out of her bedroom window with Gladstone, was consulted by old Lord Salisbury about his sons' political chances, confided in philosophically by Arthur Balfour, mournfully confessed to by Joseph Chamberlain; who broke her nose and every single bone of her body hunting, and rode her mount up into her father's Grosvenor Square house, married a prime minister, yet through it all never ceased to believe that it is the meek who shall inherit the earth: Margot Asquith, without being significant merely for all that, is not negligible despite it, and remains for all time the embodiment of the unique British instinct for making the best of both worlds.

3

THE EMPRESS FREDERICK

The circumstances that William II was half English counted for nothing in his upbringing. The Empress Frederick, his mother, the eldest daughter of Queen Victoria, was herself but half English, her father, a royal handyman, the Prince Bernhard of his day, being a German princeling acclimatised to these shores, incidentally introducing a good deal of salutary Teuton *Tüchtigkeit* into British administrative life – among other things, providing our War Office with a German-modelled General Staff to fight his compatriots with in 1914.

The inescapable aristocratic principle of 'the higher, the fewer', necessitating that anyone, before being a somebody, must have at one time, some generations back, been a nobody, is equally operative in the evolutions of royalty. Having married the Queen of England, Prince Albert of Coburg, prospectively King Edward's father and the Kaiser's grandfather, began to lord it over his relatives at home who, after all, were only Germans while he, though regarded in England as an irretrievable foreigner, in return considered himself to be an Englishman with a vengeance – indeed, the first gentleman in the land.

Before his eldest daughter, the future Empress Frederick, had kissed her father goodbye and taken her newly-wed husband energetically by the arm to lead him to the railway coach – as indeed she was to lead him throughout his life – the Prince Consort took her aside. With German earnestness he impressed on his daughter that the mere fact of her having, through her marriage, become Crown Princess of Prussia was of small account compared with that which she already was. Never – but *never* – must she forget that she was primarily Princess Royal of Great Britain and Ireland, Queen Victoria's eldest daughter.

She indeed never forgot. Everything in Berlin and Potsdam seemed to her small and shabby, not in the best of taste compared with the lofty splendours of Windsor and Osborne. Plumbing was elementary; baths a luxury. Twice a week they rolled out a tub from the Hôtel de Rome for her new father-in-law, His Majesty King William, to immerse himself in. When the Crown Princess asked for an egg-cup she created embarrassment in the royal household. A liqueur glass was supplied instead, as approximately answering her requirements. The Crown Princess was stubborn, inordinately self-assured, impatient and wilful, not on the best of terms with her parents-in-law, and she put her unrelieved surplus energy into landscape painting, dabbing on the colours with a will.

Her husband was physically fearless but morally like wax in his wife's hands. He was mild, chivalrous and kind-hearted, qualities of but little avail in a man whom a woman considers her intellectual inferior. Like her mother, Queen Victoria, she was drawn to downright men – provided she was drawn to them at all. Count Seckendorff, her court chamberlain, who, while pampering her in her hobbies, contradicted her without embarrassment, earned good marks. She succumbed to the usual royal delusion that such a man must be sincere; that his pandering to her every whim was not the fawning of a sycophant, since he was so daringly outspoken in his other judgments. Her putting up with his occasional impudence enabled her to believe that, though born to be obeyed, she was broad-minded and, unlike her mother, tolerant of criticism; while his titillation of her follies convinced her of the depth of his devotion. She was near to being in love with him, and scandal was ripe to draw the natural conclusion.

4

THE KAISER

Of such antecedents and perplexities William II with the withered arm was conceived and set down on a globe he was to kick off and set rolling on its first round of universal grief and agony. His parents both died of cancer: his father at San Remo in 1888, when William was twenty-nine; his mother, the Empress Frederick, who loathed her son, in August of 1901, only seven months after her own august thrice-jubileed mother, and in the thirteenth year of her hated son's reign. She had chosen a wife for him from a once-royal house fallen into obscurity, from which she wished to rescue it by selecting for her son a consort who, she expected, would be eternally grateful to her for the honour. The new Kaiserin, however, transferred her gratitude to her husband, whose part she invariably took in his constant quarrels with his mother.

The Empress Frederick, crown princess for a third of a century, enjoyed but a few months on the German throne before being relegated to supernumerary dowagerhood. Cruel as her fate might seem – to be compelled to surrender pride of place to her hated son on the death of her obeisant husband – she might have consoled herself by the reflection that at any rate she was spared, let us say, the fate of an Indian widow consigned to a slow death on a funeral pyre. But life is cruel, because we are incapable of contriving such reasonable consolations, and those perishing on pyres do not lessen even our toothache.

At the age of nineteen, when Germany was united into an empire under William I, the joint grandson of the first emperor of the Second Reich and of Queen Victoria began to feel that he was born to a career second to none. The sheer heraldic weight of some three dozen German dynasties above whom, at twenty-nine, he was called to reign supreme went to his head. Martial rhetoric, always second nature to a Prussian, blared forth in no apologetic under-statement. Glory was definitely German; her armour bright; might envisaged hopefully, if a little uncertainly, as, maybe, right. The prophet of American and world democracy, Walt Whitman, who had entertained hopes of the Emperor Frederick, wrote at his death in 1888, "I am not sure of Germany now. I have no faith in this young emperor, in this William. He is a proud, narrow martinet, reactionary and dangerous, the reverse of his father in all the good things for which his father stood."

The paradox about the Kaiser was that he was pro-English but anti-

Prince of Wales. He continually contradicted himself because he was both impulsive and excessively frank. You could not rely on Bismarck because he was consistently insincere. You could not rely on Wilhelm because he was sincerely inconsistent. The French called him 'William the Timid', an appellation which grated on his vanity, and he compensated himself for his feeling of certainty about nothing by showing himself to be opinionated about everything. When feeling abandoned and weak, he pushed himself to the fore, for support seizing hold of strong words. In a study of William II, Nauzanne had taken his measure, expressing a controversial opinion in perhaps the only way a self-respecting writer can avoid the reiterated effect of braying like a sheep – in epigrammatic form:[1] *"Il fallait à l'Allemagne un chef grave, silencieux, et mesuré. Le destin lui a donné un maître agréable et primesautier, mais faible et énervé. Militaire, il ne l'est que pour ses diplomates, diplomate il ne l'est que pour ses militaires."*

Interesting because of his colourful insignificance, all his life he darted backwards and forwards between St. Petersburg and London, Rome and Vienna, to consult his brother monarchs on how to keep the peace of Europe which he alone was disturbing. Vested with power largely curbed by a Constitution, itself curbed by his nominees whose principal task was to curb him, William II throws the political impotence of monarchs into startling relief. His family ramifications, too, were considerable. He was related to everybody, everywhere. Coronations, weddings, funerals saw him swing a short leg over the saddle-cloth of his white charger and, moustachios waxed to point upwards, put in a prominent appearance. Asquith records that no other monarch had impressed him quite so much as William II by the comprehensiveness of his general knowledge. But the Kaiser's own book is an involuntary double-edged self-commentary on his character and career, leaving the impression that he is, in a company hardly noted for mental brilliance, taken all in all, possibly the greatest ass of the last half century to wear a crown.

[1] Germany needed a serious, quiet and moderate leader. Destiny gave her a pleasant and impulsive leader, but one who was weak and irritable. He is a military leader only to his diplomats, a diplomat only to his soldiers.

5

FAILURE OF A MISSION

Put not, we are warned, your trust in princes or in the sons of men: for in them is no salvation. The times the German and the Russian emperors met to reassure each other that war between their two countries was mortally injurious to both their countries' interests and dynasties should have, if power and goodwill counted for anything, averted the war of 1914. But for all that the two monarchs and their statesmen and other public figures could do in the matter, they might as well have had the opposite intentions.

The Germans and Russians, moreover, did not delay their peaceful exertions till it was too late. Far from it. They began to exert themselves thirty-six years before their sustained, impassioned, spirited activities for peace broke out in the First World War.

For the benefit of readers blinded by mere prestige values, who do not think history is history unless the writer weaves a fine net of causes and effects, it might be shown that the war of 1914–18 was the outcome of the Treaty of San Stefano of 1877, parented by Bismarck who, after signing the Treaty of Berlin of 1878, remarked to his obsequious officials gathered to render him homage in the German Foreign Office, "Now I am driving Europe four-in-hand!" The result of these two treaties which, with the Russians at her very gates, had snatched Constantinople from them, was merely to sour the Russians against the Germans. Bismarck, at last tumbling to it that all he had succeeded in doing with his honest brokerage was to drive Russia into the arms of France, sent William II, then still a Prince of Prussia, to St. Petersburg to attempt to undo his own nefarious work. None understood or even dared to question Bismarck's change of policy. As the future Kaiser puts it, they all merely surmised that the Iron Chancellor now considered that the moment had come for shuffling the political cards in another way, or, as William's grandfather had put it, to 'juggle' differently.

Wicked and stupid as it seems to 'juggle' with the fates of living beings, there might be something to be said for the sheer dexterity of the game, had any of them juggled with any prospect of lasting success. None of them, however, did. Napoleon III's juggling in 1870 produced Sedan. 1870, 1877 and 1878 paved the way towards 1914. 1914 flowered into Versailles. Versailles's hot-house cultivated the prickly pear,

Hitler. Hitler brought about Sedan of 1940, completing the circle exactly seventy years from the Sedan of 1870. And so it goes on.

None of them, we are to conclude, was very clever even at his own rather silly business. They 'juggled' and died, leaving the world in a sorrier state than when they entered it. Why the ordinary, decent, serious-minded populations of the world should allow these harlequins to play bloody chess with their parcelled fields of accumulated toil is a question that must be met, alas, with a melancholy admission. The populations of the world, individually more decent than their rulers individually, are in their masses on a level with the collective irresponsibility of their leaders, who are in this respect but their own corporate personifications. The Führer represents the people, obtains his savagery from the savagery inherent in the mass, the wolf-pack; they obtain their confidence from him: mutual intoxication, in which personal responsibility is consumed in an anonymous collective self-righteousness. That, with insignificant variations, is the history of all national leadership.

So Bismarck, having juggled against Russia, had now decided to juggle in favour of Russia. Having some little time ago deprived Russia of Constantinople, he now instructed the future German emperor to offer Constantinople and the Dardanelles to Russia. Alexander II, who had had Constantinople filched from his very grasp by foreign enemies, had since been assassinated at home. His big burly son, Alexander III, a giant with a ruddy spade beard, stood four-square to receive the future Big Willy, vain flushed, unduly excitable, and with a withered arm who, in the name of Bismarck, now offered the Russian autocrat Constantinople. To this offer the Tsar rejoined: "If I want Constantinople, I shall take it whenever I feel like it, without Prince Bismarck's permission."

Gruff Bismarck had sped his future sovereign on the way to St. Petersburg with the contemptuous maxim ringing in his ears that in the East all those who wore their shirts outside their trousers were good fellows, but those who tucked their shirts inside were, as he put it in the vernacular – *Schweinhünde*. Little did he guess that to Alexander III, as gruff a man as himself, *Schweinhünd* in the Russian vernacular was a definition of the Iron Chancellor. The Tsar confessed as much to William, whom, moreover, he regarded as a lunatic. The young royal envoy, fast graduating in the art of juggling, foretold by Bismarck that one day he would be his own chancellor, encountered on his mission to Petersburg copious evidence of the Chancellor's diplomatic blunder. '*Revanche pour San Stefano*', combined with '*Revanche pour Sedan*', was how St. Petersburg and Paris were now juggling against him.

The future master of Germany had a heart-to-heart talk with an old

X Schweinehunde

Russian general who, however, in the face of abundant royal charm, expostulated in high words:[1]

> *C'est ce vilain congrès de Berlin!* [he screamed]. *Une grave faute du Chancelier. Il a détruit l'ancienne amitié entre nous, planté la méfiance dans les coeurs de la Cour et du Gouvernement, et fourni le sentiment d'un grave tort fait à l'armée russe après sa campagne sanglante de 1877, pour lequel, oui, elle veut sa revanche! Et nous voilà ensemble avec cette maudite République Française, plein de haine contre vous et rempli d'idées subversives, qui en cas de guerre avec vous, nous coûteront notre dynastie.*

The future William II returned to Berlin, like another envoy returning *from* Berlin merely half a century later, with the words jingling in his brain: 'Failure of a mission'.

6

ALEXANDER III AND HIS SUBJECTS

Alexander III was not himself troubled by any fear of a European war. At the time of an acute international crisis he summoned the Diplomatic Corps into his presence to hear an important pronouncement which, when delivered, was confined to one sentence. "While I live there will be no war in Europe," he said.

And that was all he said.

And while he lived there was no war in Europe.

At home in Russia, where he ruled with the iron hand of reaction, the

---

[1] It's this wretched Berlin congress! A grave mistake on the part of the Chancellor. He has destroyed our old friendship, sown mistrust in the hearts of the Court and the Government, and given rise to the feeling of a grave wrong committed against the Russian army after its bloody campaign of 1877, for which, I agree, it wants to wreak revenge! And there we are, together with this accursed French Republic, full of hate for you and riddled with subversive ideas, who, in the event of war against you, will cost us our dynasty.

Emperor considered that so long as class distinctions were kept rigid, and 'subversive ideas' stamped out as soon as they appeared, all was well under himself, the nation's father, dispensing a heavy-handed justice under God the Father above.

His privileged subjects had little reason to disagree with him. Identifying their own interests with the good of the country – indeed with the divine order which they fondly imagined to be hierarchical, almost monarchical – they regarded any tendency in favour of a Constitution which challenged the trinity of God, Tsar and Fatherland as in thoroughly bad taste. That the oppressed should exhibit every baleful trait of the depressed was for the privileged but another proof that the down-trodden, to yield the best results, must be trodden on. They were 'the people'. The privileged, who lived on dues and taxes they squeezed out of their peasants, in return preened themselves on their high conception of duty to Church and State, their lofty consciousness of responsibility before Tsar and Fatherland, in whose joint cause they got 'the people' to do all the most irksome, dangerous and disagreeable tasks.

'The people', though individually more homogeneous than in any other country, were considered as a race apart. Themselves regarding the gentry as some exalted but malignant race of lamas whom it was their hard fate to obey and serve, they accepted the abuse habitually hurled at them, when these refined, superior beings deigned to speak to them at all, as merely the marking, the delineation, of the gulf separating poor from rich. To them indeed that seemed to be the point of being rich: sending the poor about their business. And the peasant, exhausting his servility upon his landlord, his landlord's steward, the police inspector and the local bailiff, avenged himself upon his shabby horse, his pregnant wife.

The Tsar, Alexander III, considered that the position indeed left nothing to be desired. He believed that once a peasant, always a peasant; that the lower orders were better off without education, and that every man should remain in the state to which it had pleased God to call him; in his own case, alas! to be tsar. He even objected to his Government being called the 'Imperial Government'. He said there was no Government in Russia: there were himself and his servants who executed his orders.

ALEXANDER ULIANOV AND MINORITY RIGHTS

Another Alexander, a youth by the name Ulianov, did not see eye to eye with the Tsar on a point of private principle, from that concluding that he was in conscience bound to plot the Emperor's assassination. Ulianov defended murder on grounds of idealism, led to it by inescapable meaning, to him of an immaculate logic, to his shrewd younger brother Nicholas, *alias* Lenin, completely cock-eyed and impracticable.

Even to theorists prepared to defend murder for a rich variety of reasons of subtle shades and lurid colours, the grounds upon which Alexander Ulianov considered the assassination of Alexander III to be a glorious intellectual necessity may seem perhaps a trifle pedantic. To others, who regard murder as murder by whoever, wherever, whenever committed, the working of Alexander Ulianov's mind is merely another clinical exhibit of homicidal sophistication. One day, man may think it simpler to rule out murder wholesale than to go on splitting hairs over the degrees and kinds of permissible homicide.

Alexander Ulianov was not going to hurl a bomb at the Russian autocrat because the Tsar in his mistaken but unshakable conviction was Russia, with Russians merely for his voiceless slaves. Lenin's elder brother, Alexander, at the discerning age of nineteen, was planning to deprive his august namesake of his life because Alexander III was, on the face of it, supported by the vast majority of the population, however voiceless; whereas he, Alexander Ulianov, subscribed to minority views, intrinsically no less right than those of the majority, but unable to make themselves adequately felt save by force of explosion latent in a bomb about to be released by a sovereign independent thinking-unit.

"Terror," he nobly declaimed when being tried for his life – which, despite the force of eloquence rather than of logic, he was to forfeit, while the Emperor stayed grimly alive – "terror is the only form of defence open to a minority whose sole strength resides in its absolute conviction of possessing a moral right to its opinions as against the physical force available to opinions enjoyed by the majority." Which, when reduced to unrhetorical terms, merely means resort to murder in support of controversial views.

"We'll get nowhere with these tactics," the even younger Lenin wrote to their sister. He was at the time of his brother's execution concluding his high-school course in the small far-away provincial town of Simbirsk, carrying away the first prize awarded to him as the head of the school by the principal, who was none other than Kerensky's father. The head-master-father of the future Premier of the Revolution, unversed in necromancy, untutored in practical astrology, utterly unable to read the stars, could not peer into the years ahead when his own son, Alexander Kerensky, now a small boy, would have his term of residence at the Winter Palace curtailed by this precocious seventeen-year-old pupil Nicholas Ulianov, who indeed would chase his little boy, by then in his thirties, clean out of the country. Kerensky Senior gave young Lenin an excellent character, describing him in his report as 'very gifted, consistently painstaking and regular in his attendance'.

Lenin, intellectually contemptuous of the fallacious link in the chain of reasoning for which his elder brother Alexander laid down his life, nevertheless resolved to avenge his fate by more efficacious means. Nurtured from his tender years in revolutionary surroundings, endowed with a shrewd mind which cut through the pathetic fallacy, he made up for his realistic ruthlessness in politics, his readiness to shed other people's blood for the dictatorship of the proletariat, by succumbing to all the mawkish middle-class illusions about family ties; that is, of blood being thicker than water. He would have done well, in this respect, as a Chinese. Because his brother Alexander had been executed, though Alexander III received not a scratch, the latter's son, his namesake Nicholas II with his entire family, were as a minor consequence of Lenin's larger activities, butchered one-and-thirty years after Lenin's brother had been struck down by the implacable pedantry of his own logic.

Neither Alexander nor Nicholas Ulianov had given a thought to the well-nigh unbearable burdens of the Russian peasant, whom the intelligentsia, no better than the other literate classes, treated with a marked economy of graciousness, as though reserving this for better things. The elder brother had dedicated the best in him to an abstraction, the younger to his mother and her family, reserving his venom for the class struggle, in which peasant and worker were but so many pawns in an absorbing game of chess.

ANTON CHEHOV, JOHN MORLEY, F. E. SMITH – AND THE PEOPLE

More tender souls, incommoded by conscience pangs, dallied with social palliatives. The *muzhik*, although a Russian like themselves, of their very flesh and blood, was and must inevitably remain a beast of burden. Endowed with kind hearts, their idea was to treat him like a domesticated animal who, on suitable occasions, will eat out of their hands and for the rest rejoice in his spiritual estate of man, abide in Christ, and labour for them in docility.

Anton Chehov, who in the year 1899 became twenty-nine, was under no illusions as to the efficacy of these well-meant efforts on the parts of the *zemstvo*[1] to raise the cultural level of the peasant who was sunk into penury beyond all hope of moral recovery. Nor was Chehov a Fabian: he had scant faith in the gradual development of socialism. An artist, literally, to his finger-tips (his peasant stock notwithstanding, he had slim, beautiful hands), he believed that the only politics a writer should invoke were to protect himself from politics. He yet placed his finger on the problem, already seething, and of which our own century was to get a full double smack in the face, when he said that, were it possible to lay the burden of the most unpleasant of our physiological functions – to wit, evacuation of our bowels – upon the working classes, we should not hesitate to do so, and afterwards, of course, justify ourselves by saying that if the best people, the great sages and scientists, were to waste their precious time in each attending to his own functions, cultural progress might be seriously impeded.

This is one of those independent flashes of insight which penetrate through the tissue of delusion that befuddles lesser men, to the marrow of reality, registering, on the plates exposed to the X-ray light of intuitive divination, the offending growth. It is the faculty of independent perception – whose other name is genius – without which all sociology is like a diagnosis for cancer conducted on the surface of the skin. Chehov was a doctor of medicine. His prescription, following his diagnosis of cancer of the heart in the body politic, was simple and radical. Abolish poverty, educate all children in the same schools and universities, and so abolish classes.

[1] District Council in pre-revolutionary Russia.

John Morley, a contemporary residing in another part of Europe, pandered by implication to the very standpoint above, which Chehov reduced to a crucial absurdity. In answer to Winston Churchill naïvely informing the Liberal statesman-historian that he, Winston, was brought up by his father, Lord Randolph Churchill, never to fear English democracy but to trust the people, Morley weightily agreed, in these words: "Ah, that is quite right. The English working man is no logician, like the French 'Red', whom I also know. He is not thinking of new systems, but of having fairer treatment in this one." He thereby implied that, in his Liberal view, palliatives, not abolition of unnatural class differences, were ample to keep 'the people' as a race distinct from the upper and middle classes: he himself soon afterwards gaily rose from the middle class into the peerage as Viscount Morley of Blackburn.

It is useless, by way of demonstrating the egalitarian opportunities inherent in the British way of life, to point to an occasional trooper finishing up as Field-Marshal Sir William Robertson, Chief of the Imperial General Staff, or to the son of Sergeant-Major Smith becoming Earl of Birkenhead. Such instances, neither sufficiently rare to be ignored as exceptional nor general enough to be fair, are surely indictments, rather than vindications, of a system enabling perhaps the sixth Earl of Birkenhead to shine as Lord-Lieutenant of Derbyshire when, but for the unfair start obtained for him over other Smiths by the 'Smith of his Own Fortune', he might, if left to his own resources, be hard put to it to retire as Sergeant-Major Smith.

Lord Morley's Liberal idea of social progress boiled down to fixing a safety valve on the top of the boiler in order to let the steam of proletarian discontent escape by force of its own pressure. The absurd biological inference, unchallenged from without and nowhere challenged very seriously (save later in the Soviet Union) from within, that Blackburn lads must be racially and radically inferior to the sons of noble lords, could be drawn from the social code of every land in Europe.

9

THE CASE OF D. H. LAWRENCE

D. H. Lawrence, who was the son of a coal-miner who had worked at Brinsley Colliery since the age of seven, and a mother with social

pretensions whose ambition it was to raise her son into genteel surroundings, remained all his life, despite his fame as a writer, painfully
self-conscious about his working-class origin. As he says himself

> My father was a working-man
>   and a collier was he,
> at six in the morning they turned him down
>   and they turned him up for tea.

> My mother was a superior soul
>   a superior soul was she,
> cut out to play a superior role
>   in the god-damn bourgeoisie.

> We children were the in-betweens
>   little nondescripts were we,
> indoors we called each other *you*,
>   outside it was *tha* and *thee*.

Lawrence's father was a jolly, bright-eyed, curly-bearded man who
could dance, was clever with his hands, and could mend anything, but
did not satisfy his bleak, faded, puritanical and intellectually pretentious
wife, to whom he felt socially inferior. Mrs. Lawrence mobilised her
children in a defensive alliance against their father, whose only aggression took the form of coming home nearly drunk and, lacking ready
repartee to his wife's withering replies, banging his fist on the table. Mrs.
Lawrence thought nothing was wrong with the values of the world: in
her craving for genteel respectability she felt she was merely getting its
measure right. She sensed the secret of the English social structure,
which is that everyone 'wants to be in on it'.

Priding herself on coming from a more genteel strain, she could not
despise existing social distinctions which substantiated her claim to
superiority over her husband's standards. It is her kind of people who in
fact encourage the privileged classes in perpetuating an artificial social
order. For these are still the Middle Ages. Our modern commercial
structure is but a superficial variation of the feudal *perpetuum mobile*.
The physiognomy is the same. Its expression may be studied in the
chauffeur jumping in and out of his awkward seat merely to open the
door for his employer; in the cap-touching porter; the small-town baker
deferring to the local châtelaine; the bland New Jerusalem-cum-Oxford
parson; the unapproachable big banker and the powerful international
magnate, modern versions of the robber-barons, from their impregnable forts above the cross-roads holding up the ordinary folk who go

about their daily business – in the modern idiom, cornering the necessities of life by their manipulations of the money market. It is a habit with conservatively-minded people, too intelligent to justify present inequalities, to make out a case for privilege by invoking the nostalgic past, when the forefathers of irresponsible company directors were conscious of their feudal duties and responsibilities towards the villagers dwelling under the castle's immediate protection. Be this as it may, like all men they were primarily conscious of duties and obeisance owing to themselves. Nor does one's heart respond to the sheer goodness of human nature at the sight of the beggar's pot of gruel left outside the wall of the bishop's palace, any more than at the soup kitchen of the modern charity racket.

These are still the Middle Ages. The social staircase, far from generating resentment in the farmer or the parson, is a beacon and a magnet, and a precept to the backward 'hand'. The successful 'hand' turns farmer. The farmer, turned merchant, sends his sons to schools where they may mingle with the gentry, and himself, swelling into a big business magnate, eventually aspires to a barony. The parson, grovelling at the squire's table, slowly grovels his way towards a bishopric and a 'palace'. A land whose loftiest ideal among a population of potential gentlefolk is acknowledged gentlefolkdom, cannot wish sincerely to revolt against established authority. The nether layers of the population, bereft, like Lawrence's father, of a social sense of ambition, merely prove to their aspiring sons and wives their natural inferiority of status. *They* – the rising men agree with Mrs. Lawrence – *deservedly* remain 'the people'.

10

THE CASE OF CHEHOV

A wiser man than Lord Morley, Chehov, who said he had peasant blood in his veins and you could not astonish him with peasant virtues, nevertheless objected to this entirely artificial social division of the same malleable material into masters and 'men'. His grandfather had been a serf, his father a draper and haberdasher. His grandfather beat his father

43

with a stick, and always on the crown of the head. The father beat his son. And Chehov says he could not sincerely disbelieve in progress, because the difference between the time when they used to beat him and the time they stopped beating him was considerable.

He accordingly derided all palliatives designed to gloss over the real evil as merely mischievous and hypocritical in perpetuating an unnatural division of the same plastic homogeneous humanity. What the peasants needed was not elementary schools, but money to enable them to send their children to existing schools and universities – as he had managed to be sent himself – and thus in a single generation to wipe out an absurd and arbitrary inferiority, obviously not latent in the new-born babe but encountered in his subsequent conditions. Those who did not recognise the potential average equality of new-born babes were either insincere because biased through self-interest or, if sincere, they afforded evidence of mental inferiority irrespective of heredity.

Gradual processes were not only ineffective but also positively baleful. Side by side with the gradual development of humane ideas came the gradual growth of ideas of the opposite order. Slavery was no more. But the capitalist system was growing. And in the very heyday of liberalism, just as in the days of Genghis Khan, the majority fed, clothed, and defended the minority while itself going hungry, inadequately clad and defenceless. Side by side with the gradual emancipation of man, the subtle art of enslaving was also suavely being perfected.

11

BISMARCK, WILLIAM II, AND 'THE BLESSING OF LABOUR'

To the employer this subservience of labour to himself seemed a proper and natural state which nothing in the scheme of things need ever bring to an end. But that was not all. He expected the labourer to be feelingly beholden for the privilege of being allowed to work for his daily bread instead of – what would seem to be the natural alternative – starving with good-natured docility.

William II, when still a Prince of Prussia and apprenticed to Bismarck at the German Foreign Office, was warmly commended by his chief (and future servant) for reporting an occurrence that deeply shocked the Iron Chancellor's patriotic feelings. A German shipyard, the Vulcan Company in Stettin, was about to close down for lack of custom, while the 'Hanseatic shopkeepers', as Bismarck called them, no doubt imbued with a fine commercial sense of buying in the cheapest and selling in the dearest market, were ordering their ships from English shipyards.

Bismarck, apparently not in the least restrained in the presence of his future sovereign who was soon to sack him, fumed and stamped about the room, ringing all bells at once, sending Foreign Office dignitaries flying in all directions to countermand these orders. The impression which remained with the future Kaiser – perhaps the only humorous observation in his memoirs so overcharged with self-pity – was that under Bismarck privy councillors were perpetually vanishing in hot haste, with their coat-tails sticking straight out behind them.

The aftermath of the Prince's intervention occurred when, after ascending the throne in 1888, William II travelled to Stettin to place honorary insignia on the flags of his Pomeranian Grenadiers, and visited incidentally the Vulcan shipyard. There, instead of the pounding of hammers, he found he had entered into an atmosphere of reverential silence. With bared heads and in a perfect semi-circle, the workmen of the Vulcan works stood before him, headed by the oldest workman with a snow-white beard and a laurel wreath in his hand. In plain, pithy words, as no doubt befits a horny-handed workman, he craved permission of his sovereign, in token of their gratitude to him for being able to eat bread, to hand over the laurel wreath.

"That was in the year 1888!" writes William II. And he adds, fatuously, "In those days the German working classes knew how to appreciate the blessing of labour."

'Ah, those were the days!' is the sigh of nostalgia uttered by those who have savoured the blessing of labour from a becoming distance. It is the transitory, no less than the established, class – the transitory considering itself as already established – who, looking back, sigh for 'those days!'

But why did they not last? The usual answer, "Good enough while they lasted", however sincerely felt to be true by the few, really means, by the test of the happiness of the many, that they were not quite good enough to last.

12

PAPA HITLER AND DER DRANG NACH OBEN

The same instinct which drove the mother of D. H. Lawrence towards genteel respectability induced Hitler's father to leave his native village. He set out on foot for Vienna, propelled by a force bubbling up in him and latent in most men: the craving for self-respect assuaged by the gregarious esteem of one's fellows.

It is not an admirable emotion, this inner uncertainty only allayed by the approbation of the herd, and grandly styled 'ambition'. It is productive of mayors and city worthies basking fussily in the public gaze. It is the motive-power of party politics. It is ugly and factitious. 'The old gentleman', as Hitler respectfully refers to his father, who whistled for the future Führer when desirous of sending him on an errand, was the bastard son of a poor cottager by a farm-hand of the name of Schicklgruber. He is presumed to have married her when Hitler's father reached the age of five, in 1842. At thirteen the future begetter of Adolf buckled on his satchel and set forth for Vienna from his native woodland parish, with three gulden in his pocket. There he worked at a trade, which he chucked to strive for 'something higher'. As a village boy the position of the parish priest had seemed to him the highest in all the sentient universe. But, with the widened worldly outlook of the capital, he began to aspire to the dignity of a second-grade civil service clerk as the highest of all. Little did he know that his unborn boy would in time become the All Highest Warlord. After ascending at twenty-three to the undreamed-of heights of a junior customs officer, he returned to his native village, where he had sworn never to set foot until he was 'somebody'.

Evidently a success story. It was repeated on a wider scale by his son Adolf, who did not return to Vienna, where he had sold picture postcards to visitors in public bars and lived in a casual ward, until he was her absolute master, arrived to proclaim her incorporation in the Reich. But the newly-fledged junior customs officer could find nobody in the village who had ever seen him other than as a customs officer. Nobody who could measure his rise. He was moved from one post to another, married, begot children, including Adolf (who saw the light in the little frontier town of Braunau), and retired at the age of fifty-six, settling down on a little farm which, like his forefathers, and in the teeth of his elevation to petty officialdom, he tilled himself.

Herr Hitler senior, like Mrs. Lawrence, produced a moody, dissatisfied son, dissatisfied with his parents' inconsiderable progression on the social road and short-circuiting his own efforts. Adolf Hitler, the son of a stickler for frontier regularity, broke out into unbridled licence in international power politics; D. H. Lawrence, the son of a puritanical mother, indulged in his books in outrageous sexual licence: Lawrence, unable to satisfy a woman, running riot in print; Hitler, unable to bestraddle a horse, sending his mechanised cavalry a-gallop across the continents.

Both were the victims of a savage attack of inferiority fever kindled by a prickly pride, to which Lawrence for his part gave expression in his usual broken-backed verse:

> O I was born low and inferior
>   but shining up beyond
> I saw the whole superior
>   world shine like a promised land.

> So up I started climbing
>   to join the folks on high,
> but when at last I got there
>   I had to sit down and cry.

> For it wasn't a bit superior,
>   it was only affected and mean;
> . . . They all of them always kept up their sleeve
>   their class-superior claim.

> Some narrow-gutted superiority,
>   and trying to make you agree,
> which, for myself, I couldn't,
>   it was all my-eye to me.

His happiness perhaps would not have been affected appreciably if, instead of being born 'low and inferior', Lawrence had been born at the opposite English social scale, say, a 'George Nathaniel Curzon, a most superior person' (a line that, Curzon bitterly complained, had handicapped him throughout his career). Lawrence would then have deplored his deracination from the soil, and envied Burns his roots.

Curzon's biographers stress the tragedy of a mere line in a limerick from the adolescent pen of a fellow Oxford undergraduate estranging Curzon's personality from that popularity and affection of the populace essential to a successful political career at home. They forget that it is that very lack of popular appeal in the whole Curzon make-up which had been early espied by his fellow undergraduates and deftly caught in a limerick. It has been staunchly denied by his friends that Curzon, the unaffected, warm-hearted, high-spirited, genial Curzon was at all 'superior'. This reiterated denial reminds one of the equally staunch protestations about Marcel Proust ever being a snob – which, nevertheless, he was as completely as Curzon, who once snubbed Oscar Wilde for identifying himself with the upper classes, was assuredly 'superior'.

13

CURZON – ARTISTS OF ACTION

"Man," says Proust, "is the creature that cannot come forth from himself, who knows others only in himself, and who, if he asserts the contrary, lies." There is, however, a way of acquiring a universal sense of values by reflecting meekly on one's own inevitable limitations; of enlarging one's outlook, deepening one's insight, even begetting originality, in the contemplation of one's own and other men's sterility, the narrowness, the egotism, the abject arbitrariness of the individual's approach to life. The limitations of, let us say, Curzon so contemplated are staggering against the vista of terrain, by him untrodden and unseen despite his travels.

We are all so made that we cannot envisage anything, even a few days ahead, without our imagination contriving to produce in advance the false décor and characters necessarily unknown to us. We are all artists in the Goethean sense of "*in der Beschränkung zeigt sich erst der Meister*,"[1] since we all live by the limits of our imaginations. In this sense, Curzon, acutely aware of his own glittering future all set fair in the heart of the capital of a British Empire considered by him to be, after Providence, the greatest agency for good, but unaware of the squirming hell of slums some five miles to the east from the place where he was felicitously dining, was, like most of us, a limited artist.

It was, then, with a vision of himself as a man of letters if of political

[1] In restrictions the master first shows himself.

future, a man of a certain style, that young Mr. George Nathaniel Curzon who, according to his guest Margot Tennant, had 'a childish love of fine people', entertained the Souls at dinner at the Bachelor Club in July of 1889. Outside, window-boxes gay with flowers, frock-coated gentlemen in tall hats, high-stepping horses, splendid equipages, diffused a subtle flavour of elegant well-being in a London that had not yet lost her austerely benevolent Georgian air. The West End was disporting its light wedding-cake stucco and seasoned brick amidst boughs, trees and flowers. The Park and gardens, squares and palisades sprouting their green between the brick and mortar might have served to remind the city-dweller pining for the country, or the countryman pining for town, that a city is a collection of houses dumped in the country, not a handful of earth sprinkled down between bricks. And that mellow July the overblown gardens, according to one Oscar Wilde who, in patent-leather boots and carrying an ebony cane, sauntered down Bond Street, called in at his bankers to clip into his holder a dozen golden sovereign earned night after night by his plays, before dining out with charming young Lord Alfred Douglas – according to Oscar, a master of measured and elegant prose, the air just then was "full of the heavy odour of roses, and when the light summer wind stirred amidst the trees of the garden, there came through the open door the heavy scent of the lilac, or the more delicate perfume of the pink flowering thorn."

But, side by side with the elegance, went the dirt, the incredible clinging red mud of the primitive streets, passing hansoms besplashing pedestrians taking refuge on the far side of the pavement. Side by side with the two-baths-a-day habit of the classes exercising their bodies for pleasure, went the fantastic basement-cramped tubless condition of the servants, the 'lower orders' sweating from necessity. Compared with them, the Russian peasant living in filth, yet steaming himself out without fail once a week, even though afterwards putting on the same cotton shirt, or the flea-ridden but public-bath-spirited Arab, were models of cleanliness: the English woollen-underclothed menial until recently washing himself, very thoroughly, mark you, from the waist up only. And the slums . . . Nowhere else in the world, not in the black hole of Calcutta itself, was there to be found such a peculiar combination of inartistic sordidness and soulless squalor, such cheerfully accepted filth and fatalistic penury. London was not only the largest and richest, but also the dirtiest and meanest capital in the world – her sullenly drunken population of 'White Negroes', as he called the British wage-slaves storming the pubs at nightfall, having on his visit here in the 'fifties shocked the arch-expert in human sordidness, Dostoievski himself.

About the Law Courts and the City, where top hats and frock coats were still the order of the day, hung a mellowed evanescent Dickens reek. What had once been a subject for satire had, fortified by literary prestige, grown venerable with tradition. The social mixture had set, hardened in a certain mould with recognisable contours, only to begin to disintegrate as Queen Victoria's reign, an age not unreminiscent of the short-lived glory of Venice, Genoa, and Holland, entered on its last decade.

It was against this background that young George Nathaniel Curzon, whose "hair was straight and sleek, who dined at Blenheim twice a week", was giving his banquet. He had been ordered off to Switzerland by his doctors on account of lung trouble, and this was a farewell dinner to his friends. On each chair was a copy of a poem from the pen of this future artist of action, commemorating the banquet "set at the bidding of Georgius Curzon" and commending every one of his guests "in doggerel", as he says himself, "appalling".

14

MORE MARGOT

While there is not among the long list of decorative names of 'gallants and graces', of 'souls and spirits', one who can be said to have produced off his own bat anything remotely satisfying to spirit and soul, each of the participants was a day-dreaming artist cherishing his own vision of incommunicable beauty, imbued in addition with a certain general *Schwärmerei* for the things of the spirit and the mind.

Margot was, of course, there. She was at once Heartbreak House *and* Horseback Hall. At the time of this avowedly Heartbreak House banquet she was in the very trough of her romance with Peter Flower, a thorough-going Horseback Hall follower to hounds: a romance described by her with such painstaking care not to tread on her own corns. This chapter in her book, far from being the reckless dance of self-abandon she would like it to be, gives the impression rather of a cat stepping over hot bricks.

For our vanity is, alas, our private Golgotha. Mrs. Asquith is determined to cut a dashing, romantic, as well as sensible, high-principled, earnest, cultured, profound and charitable, but wittily incisive, wickedly epigrammatic, though sweetly forgiving, and, if mundane, also deeply-religious, at once *spirituelle* and spiritual, meditative, Christian figure. And she is satisfied that the reader will take her at her own valuation.

It would indeed be surprising if we did not find her in this assembly of sportsmen and men and women of political action assembled to convince themselves that they were also artists and creatures of thought. In her we indeed get both sides of the British apple. Impulsive, generous and compassionate, spontaneous and warm-hearted, acute in comment, "the type it reveals," as Middleton Murry wrote when reviewing her autobiography in the *Nation*, "is not very intriguing." Katherine Mansfield, perhaps a little uneasy lest her own absent Jack might succumb to the social blandishments of Mrs. Asquith basking in the fame of her autobiography, confessed in a letter penned in exile from the south of France that for her own part she didn't care a Farthing Taster whether Margot made her horse walk upstairs or downstairs or in my lady's chamber. To her, a sensitive writer, to analyse the specimen revealed was like trying to operate on a diseased *mind* by cutting open a brain. "You may remove every trace of anything that shouldn't be there and make no end of a job of it and then in her case, in the case of all such women – the light comes back into the patient's eyes and with the vaguest of vague elusive *maddening* smiles . . . Do you know what I mean? Here's, I think, the root of the matter. What is Insensitiveness? We know or we could find out by examination what it is NOT, but it seems to me the quality hasn't been discovered yet. I mean it's x – it's a subject for research. It most certainly isn't only the *lack* of certain qualities: it's a kind of *positive unknown*."

15

ARTHUR BALFOUR

"Dear Arthur", of course, was there, Arthur Balfour, "the High Priest, the heart that to all hearts is nearest", Arthur Balfour, by unanimous consent their most precious and dearest. Winston Churchill, then a Harrow schoolboy of fifteen, observed this intellectually elegant man across his father's dinner-table, protected all his life from rude impact by cushions of admiring friends in whose company he quietly scintillated, dined, travelled, staying in their delightful houses as though they were his own. Yet far from confining himself to the care of the brilliant people who admired him, Arthur Balfour accepted with courteous gratitude invitations from unfashionable people who were erudite or musical or in other ways interesting, and who invited him because he was fashionable, and he also accepted, with quite peculiar stress of gratitude and courtesy, invitations from unfashionable people who were not erudite, nor musical, nor in any way interesting, and who invited him because he was fashionable *and* erudite *and* interesting. He never threw up a boring acquaintance with whom he had an engagement for the most dazzling of parties, leaving behind him wherever he trod a trail of subtle gratification and even happiness.

He would have been, one feels, an invaluable tomb for the moral excavations of the social archaeologist Marcel Proust. As a small boy he disconcerted his Cecilian mother with a philosophical question: "Can you tell me," he asked, "why I love you so much?", betraying an early preference for reason to feeling, and soon afterwards confessing a preference for philosophy to politics. In this he was discouraged by his mother, who pointed out that if he did not go into politics, but instead confined himself to a contemplative life, he would find that by the time he was forty he would have nothing to contemplate.

Metaphysics and philosophy, unlike fiction, do not feed on variegated experience, least of all political experience, but on leisure which, while offering opportunity for disinterested reflection, rarefies and magnifies the most trivial of personal occurrences into an object-lesson from which to draw suitable inferences expanded at leisure into generalisations. Profound philosophers were either solitary men leading trivial boarding-house existences, like Kant and Schopenhauer, or unruffled princes, like Buddha and Marcus Aurelius. Had Arthur Balfour not, to please his mother, embarked on the futile road of politics only to prove himself an indifferent and repressive statesman,[1] he might have developed into a considerable philosopher; his remark "If there is no future life this world is a bad joke: and *whose* joke?" affording evidence of contemplative emotion of no mean order.

Arthur Balfour grew up bereft apparently of any emotion at all, his nervous force unimpaired, his reasoning faculties in perfect equilibrium, always fresh and unruffled after spending the forenoon in bed, and willing to equate both sides of a question for any friend or stranger imprudent enough to have his decision immobilised by seeking A.J.B.'s advice. His big reputation, says Hugh Kingsmill, was a mosaic of small

---

[1] The Irish, after their experience of him, nicknamed him 'Bloody Fanny'.

reputations. "Men of affairs admired him as a philosopher. Philosophers admired him as a man of affairs. Thinkers of plebeian origin were flattered that an aristocrat should condescend to enquire into the mystery of things; and aristocrats were enheartened by the rumour that one at least of their order was capable of sustained thought."

But, though outwardly unruffled, Arthur Balfour was not unconscious of his intellectual superiority over all his friends. In the same way and for the same reason as an established aristocracy, emancipated from the thraldom of social pretence, is reluctant to place its leisure at the disposal of the aspiring bourgeoisie congested with uneasy pride, Balfour's kindliness was not to be mistaken for acquiescence in an uncritical identification of his own powers with the congested intellectual strivings of, let us say, 'dear George', his host at the banquet. He could never accept on equal terms a George Curzon who had in him the making of a pro-consul, but never a philosopher. Arthur Balfour's placid lucidity would be irritated by Curzon's 'fixtures'.

16

THE SOULS

Curzon who, like most politicians (in Churchill's curious phrase), aspired to add to the ephemeral reputation of politics the more enduring fame of literature, faintly resented 'dear Arthur's' immaculate manner, hinting at some intellectual breeding against which Curzon's showmanship would seem forced. His ironic aside to Humbert Wolfe, some thirty years later, on the subject of Balfour's spurious Olympianism seems to suggest as much. Confronted by dear Arthur's latent but none the less unquestioned intellectual hegemony, with its ever-present threat to crush a perky intruder by the whole weight of his ironic understatement, all Souls indeed maintained themselves towards him in a safe equipoise of affectionate awe. All the Ettys and Willys, Bettys and Bingys, Tommys and Harrys, Sibyls and Hildas, Millicents and Gladyses, carefully asterisked by our Margot under their full titles as earls, viscounts, viscountesses, countesses, marchionesses, marquesses and duchesses, were there, fumbling with their copies of the welcoming doggerel, trying to find the lines glorifying their own persons and, discretion as yet the better of wine, applauding the author for compliments addressed to a neighbour.

The real writers, however, were not there. Social historians might presume that a society of self-confessed wits with artistic leanings must have included all the most brilliant artists of their time. In reality it included nobody save a coterie of more or less acknowledged social reputations: persons of established aristocracy, and persons establishing themselves as 'Souls', mutually exuding art at each other. The first, thick-skinned aristocrats bashfully allaying their doubts as to being able to uncover a soul, the second, climbers, attempting to dispel the suspicion (well-founded, moreover) that they had joined the 'Souls' to consort not with artists but with the aristocracy.

The real artists, already or later world-famous, were not there at all. One feels that Oscar Wilde, at all events, would have dearly loved to be present. As for Shaw – who, Oscar said, had no enemies though his friends disliked him – Shaw was reading to William Archer his first play, *Widowers' Houses*, and in the process of sending Archer to sleep: Archer, on waking to find that Shaw had completed the reading, observed yawningly that sleep was also a manner of criticism.

17

DIVINE SABOTAGE

At thirty-three Shaw had not been heard of outside soap-box circles, Archer's nap having discouraged his dramatic ambitions and delayed his start. If he could boast a name, it was Corno di Bassetto, a pseudonym under which he masqueraded as music critic in the *Star*.

The master of English prose whom Curzon gathered to dine in 1889 was George Meredith who, admidst the sprouting fungus of decadence, in his own words 'showed sunlight of the mind, mental richness rather than noisy enormity'. Not for him the peacocks of Beardsley or the green carnations of Oscar, who found him magnificent but unreadable. Not for him the epicure's immaculate fastidiousness of Walter Pater, nor the English dogrose nurtured on soil imported from Gautier, Baudelaire and Huysmans. Nor indeed Hardy's dour resignation to the malignancy of fate, nor Swinburne's dolorous Eros. Not for him George Moore's braggart paganism, nor Rudyard Kipling's tin trumpet. Meredith's was 'the laughter of the order of the smile'. He indeed defined the function of the Comic Spirit as doing what in modern parlance may be described as God's Fifth-Column work among men: the sabotaging of worldly confidence and complacency by the Comic Spirit, the wisdom of the world being, with God, but foolishness. Unlike the dramatising sociologist, Bernard Shaw, then merely in the making, Meredith thoroughly distrusted that most disastrous of all human enthusiasm: our insane eagerness to sacrifice the present for the purpose of furthering a hypothetical future. A perpetual sacrifice of a certainty for a perpetually deferred hypothesis is an absurdity distasteful to the Comic Spirit. As Meredith himself envisages the Comic Spirit, "men's future upon earth does not attract it; their honesty and shapeliness in the present does; and whenever they wax out of proportion, over-blown, affected, indelicate; whenever it sees them self-deceived, or hoodwinked, given to run riot in idolatries, drifting into vanities, congregating in absurdities, planning shortsightedly, plotting dementedly; whenever they are at variance with their professions, and violate the unwritten but perceptible laws binding them in consideration one to another; whenever they offend sound reason, fair justice; are false in humility or mined with conceit, individually or in the bulk, the Spirit overhead will look humanely malign and cast an oblique light on them, followed by volleys of silvery laughter." This is a satisfying statement of the work of God's Fifth Column. But the image of the Comic Spirit indulging in immoderate laughter is itself not immune to comic criticism.

18

PREDILECTION FOR MEDIOCRITY

The English public at all times are curiously addicted to respectable mediocrity. They reviled Oscar Wilde for being wittily pagan, and though he said he wished to change nothing in England except the weather, they sent him to gaol for an offence irrelevant to literature.

And then they reviled Bernard Shaw for digging up their beautiful social garden. And when Lloyd George introduced social insurance for the socially unsure they branded Lloyd George as 'the best-hated man in England'. But when later they had to write of the 'nineties, they could speak of nothing but the brilliant coruscations of the Irish Wilde; and when they searched for a name in contemporary English literature with anything of a European reputation approaching Tolstoy's or Ibsen's, they could only dig up the Irishman Shaw. And when they wanted a patriot to win the Four Years' War for them they could only drag out the 'best-hated' Radical anti-Boer-War Welsh agitator, Lloyd George. And all their respectable safety-first Carlton Club favourites went up in black smoke. And when they wanted to get someone to win the Second World War the anti-Soviet Tories had blundered us into, they brought out of cold-storage the political apostate, the snub-nosed ne'er-do-well urchin Winston, whom they had spent a quarter of a century in keeping down, and who had been anathema a quarter of a century earlier.

19

TORY DEMOCRACY

Each of us carries with him a private image of the world, with himself in the centre of the picture, and Winston Churchill at fifteen saw the world as an English playground, with himself scoring hits in every game. His father, Lord Randolph Churchill, dallied with the idea of a Tory democracy, a mild forerunner of the Fascist 'ideology'; a political creed designed to appeal to traditionally-minded persons not themselves enjoying the privileges of tradition, as a counter-blast to the liberal-radical outlook. His father's son, young Winston not unnaturally regarded England as an ideal democracy, giving every man an equal chance but being properly the concern of men of property and old traditions with, as the phrase went, a stake in the country. Himself enjoying all the initial privileges and having seen a few isolated men advance here and there from complete obscurity and every disadvantage to high places in the esteem of their fellows, he considered the English social order as one leaving absolutely nothing more to be desired. Any further advance, perhaps in democracy, was the business of a benevolent aristocracy to grant from time to time, as the occasion called, with caution and discretion and good grace.

Arthur Balfour's ideas about Tory democracy differed considerably from Lord Randolph Churchill's. The words sounded all right, but they never meant what he, Balfour, meant by them. What was democracy? It was government by the people. He was all for that; and as early as 1883 he was all for the extension of the franchise, though Lord Randolph was not, Churchill senior believing in letting only certain classes participate in the suffrage. But Balfour believed that the more you extended responsibility to the *whole* community the more Tory the result was likely to be, meaning by Tory an inclination to continuity. The case of Switzerland, where there was real universal suffrage and where the referendum was used, and always in a Conservative sense, seemed to Balfour to confirm his argument.

Results similar to Swiss, of a predominant conservatism, would have manifested themselves under universal suffrage in late Victorian England, this nation desiring nothing so much as to be a totalitarian State of natural aristocrats freely acknowledged as such by those already arrived, the whole divided into two parliamentary groups tossing elegant persiflage across the floor of the House on sundry parlour-game questions, prior to dining out delightfully at each other's houses. "I dined last night," Arthur Balfour writes to his friend Lady Elcho, "with the Asquiths, and as the fortunes of debate would have it, A. and I had rather a sharp passage in the House after dinner. Asquith was the challenger; but I felt a mild awkwardness in replying to a man in the strength of his own champagne! I did it all the same, and with considerable vigour." A far cry from the concentration camp of totalitarian politics. Party politics were a game of squash designed to ventilate the mind by opening the mental pores through a resort to vigorous exercise in the hope of postponing as long as possible the fatty degeneration of the brain.

At the beginning of the reign of Queen Victoria the territorial oligarchs had purchased another lease of power by an alliance through matrimonial channels with what in our own age is called Big Business. As may only be expected, the successful commercial class, merchants who had made money at home or in India, had been touchy about their social position and thus a little sceptical of that of the old established Tories, and accordingly violently radical, until the aristocracy recognised them. In exactly the same way as the well-oiled wheels of Arthur Balfour's intellectual mechanism might be irritated by Curzon's 'fixtures' grating upon his lucidity, so the easy-going aristocracy's natural affability contracted into involuntary coils of refusal at the solemn imitation by the rising bourgeoisie of its own unconscious rituals as though thereby hoping to remove, while stupidly accentuating, the crucial difference between them. Some Lady Dorothy X, whose small daughter had contrived a juvenile friendship in the Square garden shared by Lady Dorothy with the wife of a rich banker who had just bought a house in Berkeley Square, after reluctantly giving tea to the banker's wife whose bonnet had struck her as a trifle too gaudy and who had talked eagerly of Lady Dorothy's cousins without, however, contriving to impress Lady Dorothy, when it was all over would dismiss the episode in some such words, addressed to her husband: "I do not altogether care for her, so I don't think we'll ask them again. They are . . . well . . . not *quite* the sort of people . . ."

20

THE NEWLY RICH

Having forced recognition on the aristocracy with ties of money and blood, the merchants settled down in the conviction that, if business acumen deserved hereditary perpetuation, the family-business principle was indeed best served by the acquisition of honours and dignities enjoyable in perpetuity. The Whigs and Tories had quarrelled about the Corn Laws and Factory Acts. The progressive party was against ameliorating the horrible conditions of child-labour, not because they were more savage than the landed gentry who had matured among trees and flowers, loved dogs (but singled out foxes and hares for ill-treatment), but because, identifying their own interests with industry's, they identified industry's interests with the country's. The Tories, while seemingly taking the more humane view in the dispute, had their own settled convictions of the place assigned to the tiller of soil, believing with a fervour borrowed from the Old Testament that a man should remain in the state to which it had pleased God to call him. As their interests merged, they gradually drew together, while lavish new creations of peers from the ranks of the newly rich turned the House of Lords into a predominantly middle-class body, from the point of view of those who had been sitting there before. To those shut outside, the new peers and their wives merged into the glamorous new world of fashion indistinguishable from the old. As for the second generation, men and women being creatures of habit, and never more so than of enjoyable habits, the second generation already regarded themselves as a body of seasoned aristocrats mellowed by time. The novelty of merchants flowering into peers was met halfway by the equally daring renovation of an old English tradition of peers once again sallying forth into trade, as they had done until the Georges brought in the Hanoverian idea that a gentleman must not add by his own exertions to the profits he enjoys from other men's labours.

Margot Asquith's newly-rich father's love of art, she tells us, was exhausted in perpetually comparing his own pictures with other people's. He wanted his daughters to marry lords, and took pleasure in Margot's advancement, delighted when, taking him to dine with the Randolph Churchills, she capped her reputation for social courage by introducing him to the Prince of Wales. The well-to-do mistook their greed in collecting old masters, which they commissioned for a song and, when their investments sank low, sold to America, for culture and the love of art. The lip-service rendered to art in fashionable London society was, as elsewhere, on the plane of those cosmopolitan ladies surrounding Liszt in Weimar and Paris, whose appreciation of music was exhausted in the word uttered at the end of each piece and a long sigh: "*Charmant!*" As the Liberals and Conservatives, for aught else they were doing for the toiling population of Britain, were merely exercising in a sort of word-badminton across the House of Commons floor, so the Souls were merely playing a charade, like children 'pretending' to be cultivated.

Young Margot Tennant, chiefly because of her daring in clearing fences in pursuit of that 'anxious brown streak' Mary Webb calls the fox, enjoyed the added reputation for audacity in pursuing opinionate views in the field of literary craftsmanship. She put right the Lady Londonderry of her youth about the marchioness's misconception as to J. A. Symonds' style; clung to her opinion of Arthur Balfour's style as 'the finest', and generally encouraged the doubtful compliment of being regarded by old men with not enough gumption to detect the silly fake in the Russian as the English Marie Bashkirtsev, omitting no opportunity of benefiting old poets with her young advice: our Margot's literary sense, sharpened by thirty more years of reading, culminating by 1920 in a passionate acclamation as a great creative masterpiece of literature of *If Winter Comes*.[1] By any true artistic standards, which must of necessity

[1] The best-selling novel by A. S. M. Hutchinson, first published in 1921.

always be the highest known standard, these innocents at home, beneath the veneer of culture with which they were coated, had hardly a suspicion "*worauf,*" as Goethe suggestively puts it, "*es eigentlich ankommt.*"[2]

21

TOLSTOY

Writing of politicians, big business men, monarchs, statesmen, soldiers and sailors, however eminent, gracious or charming, one still feels one has been writing (and one says it amiably) of the apes of God, when by contrast one approaches a Shakespeare, a Tolstoy, a Goethe, a Beethoven. (At this low estimate of their human worth, our national heroes may demur: Who saved your country for you? they might reasonably ask. But who from? is the answer.)

Away from the seats of power, in the little frontier town of Braunau, famous as a Napoleonic capture during his blitz on Vienna, a piece of human dynamite, to his parents the boy Adolf, was growing up on a picture book featuring the Franco-Prussian War (in which our own Kitchener had received his baptism of fire on the German side), growing up in Churchill's words into 'an abortion of frustration and hate', while the youth Winston himself was at Sandhurst, maturing on visions of Marlborough and Napoleon for the war in South Africa due at the end of the century. Both Austro-Czech boy and Anglo-American youth were dreaming fast of military glory.

Abetted by a dynamic American mother (who, had her intellect been equal to her temperament, might have been, according to Margot, a notable woman), Winston was determined to do or die. Adolf, issued from a Czech-named wench ignited by an Austrian progenitor, was resolved to be a German or burst. Half a century later, at the apex of their martial careers, they were to characterise each other, respectively if not respectfully, as 'that abominable creature Hitler' and 'that besotten fool Churchill'.

---

[2] Of where the real importance lay.

Tolstoy had done with Napoleons, just as Adolf was deploring having been born into an age devoid of opportunity for collecting, in the first Earl of Birkenhead's subsequent phrase, "those glittering prizes which fall to men of stout hearts and sharp swords". In the longest novel in literature, *War and Peace*, Tolstoy had indulged that adolescent partiality for swaggering, booted and spurred, in escapades of gallant deed and amatory daring which appeal to the boy and youth in man. No detail of gesture, attitude, dress, bearing or equipment had escaped the small, piercing black eyes of the Russian sage. With a realism and imagination never before attempted he had thrown on to his vast canvas all that he had observed and with his innate honesty and candour himself experienced, and his uncanny insight into human beings divined. All of which he had – here was the refreshing novelty – unrhetorically expressed. As a young artillery officer he had come into close quarters with that collective irresponsibility called War. And he was no longer impressed.

In *War and Peace*, he had dismissed contemptuously Napoleon's claim to have shaped the destinies of millions of living beings, regarding him instead as the puppet dangling jerkily from an invisible thread held by the inscrutable Hand – in modern parlance, an agent – a nefarious agent – of God's Fifth Column, wreaking havoc and desolation in the hearts of men and women, sabotaging their little strongholds of smugness, their traffic of complacency. For not of such, but of a knowledge born of grief and of sacrifice, is the Kingdom of Heaven.

The term Fifth Column, not yet of course in use, originated in the Spanish Civil War. In 1936 four rebel columns were advancing on Madrid under the command of General Mola, who boasted in a broadcast that the soldiers of his four columns would be welcomed by their friends already awaiting them in the capital. These mysterious friends within the gate were humorously described by the republicans resisting the advance of the four rebel columns as the Fifth Column. And so the term Fifth Column came to be adopted by the dictionaries.

God's Fifth Column is that destroying agent – more often the unconscious agent, sometimes malevolent or maladroit in intention – of spirit within the gate of matter. Its purpose is to sabotage such structures and formations of human society, built as it were of individual human bricks, as have proved to be unserviceable for association into larger groups of suffering units because insufficiently baked by suffering to cement with their immediate neighbours.

Tolstoy, whose shrewd ironic insight into character had earned him world fame, had tired of the half-baked. Now, mature of years and honours, he was searching his heart, tearing down the intricate web of artificial conceits and desires which man had spun around him, merely to be caught in his own web.

He had simplified his own needs to the mere rudiments of existence. He wore a peasant shirt, a long shaggy beard, and made his own boots. But, burdened with a large family, an exacting wife, he could not give up his large manor house in the midst of an old ancestral estate, and the inconsistency of the outward circumstances of his life with his inner convictions saddened the old man, who preached that it was the duty of men of goodwill to give everything away.

There lived on his estate a big loud-mouthed peasant who, whenever he encountered 'the great writer of Russia's soil'[1] strolling deep in thought on his solitary walks, taunted him with his inconsistency; after which Tolstoy, considering him with gloomy thoughtfulness, put his hand in his purse and handed the drunkard a rouble. Far from thanking the novelist, fast qualifying as a martyr, the peasant derided him by alluding to the inconsiderable proportion the rouble formed of Tolstoy's accumulated royalties, and staggered off to the village inn, imprecating aloud as he went against the hypocritical rich.

These encounters much worried the old man, who found it difficult to reconcile his acute distaste for this loud-mouthed peasant with his own daily endeavour to love his neighbour as well as himself. He might perhaps have eased his heart by reflecting that Jesus Himself showed a certain distaste for the society of the scribes and Pharisees who doubted His divinity. Assailed by the four columns of the spirit in his reading, Tolstoy tripped over the fifth column at home.

Having enriched the heritage of the heart and mind with his works, dissatisfied with his success and perplexed by the unabating callousness and brutality of the world, Tolstoy, when pressed for precise moral guidance, withdrew into himself and meditated in solitude. In a woodland clearing of his beloved Yasnaya Polyana, in a birch grove where the sun-spangled leaves made patterns on the ground, he might pause wonderingly and ask in Wordsworth's mellowed words –

> Think you, 'mid all this mighty sum
>   Of things forever speaking,
> That nothing of itself will come,
>   But we must still be seeking?
>
> Then ask not wherefore, here, alone
>   Conversing as I may,
> I sit upon this old gray stone,
>   And dream my time away.

[1] So Turgenev on his death-bed had designated him: ". . . believe me, my friend, great writer of Russia's soil."

Sorting his letters, he observed one day, "They all make a great fuss about me, writing of and around me. But when I'm dead, in a year or two, people will say: 'Tolstoy? Ah, you mean the count who tried to make his own boots, soon after that going off his bat. Is that the fellow you mean?'"

Already, as a youth, he sorted out from his own experience four precepts by which men live: (1) for their own happiness; (2) for their own happiness while doing the least possible harm to others; (3) doing to others as they would be done by; and (4) for the happiness of others. In old age, his thoughts crystallised in an interpretation of the New Testament. Far from the easy-going belief popular among intellectuals that the Gospels, though admittedly fine, were beyond the moral strength of human frailty, Tolstoy again and again stressed that the kernel of Christ's teaching, as He had Himself insisted, was that it was a yoke that was easy and a burden that was light. Bitterly impatient with his sceptical contemporaries who regarded the New Testament as a beautiful but unattainable ideal, Tolstoy demonstrated Christianity to be a practicable teaching, well adapted to the average powers of mankind, not in the least beyond the moral strength of ordinary men and women. It was, he held, the only eminently practical solution of our pitiful cross-purposes; a solution limpid, luminous in its simplicity. Consider, he said in effect, the reverse of the ideals which Jesus encouraged us to apply in this our life in order that we may create the Kingdom of Heaven in our midst. Consider the martyrdom which most of us were ready to suffer, or suffered without being consulted, suffered against our will, in the cause of perpetuating injustice and cruelty and all manner of artificiality in the empirical world. Consider, he said, the unspeakable tortures suffered by, let us say, a simple Russian soldier who, obeying his Tsar instead of Christ, falls a victim in one of those perpetually recurring wars in which Russia is forever attempting to snatch Constantinople, a pseudo-religious, imperialist, Greek-Orthodox cause the poor fellow does not even pretend to understand, but in the furtherance of which he nevertheless is captured and skinned alive by the Turks. Could he not have carried the lighter cross of Jesus for a better end? What was the brunt of Christ's teaching? Simplicity of living which left one with a surplus store of energy and goodwill, which it was sheer joy to harness in the service of others who, on their side, were particularly placed in regard to you.

And the alternative? The swelling of your own little ego into a prickly pear of touchiness, whose pricks were two-edged swords wounding yourself as much as your foe. The Christian idea of immortality was buried in the very folds of a paradox: that he only regained eternal life who had divested himself of the last shred of that ego which could desire its own perpetuation.

Tolstoy had meditated on the problem of dissolving the tormenting desires of the One in the beneficent service to the Many, and, at sixty-two, he felt that the cup of human sorrow was now, as the century was entering on its last lap, filled to the brim: *Then What Are We To Do?* His soul, of a great moral teacher, at last gave a voice to his indignation – *I Cannot Be Silent*.

22

WILLIAM II AGAIN VISITS ALEXANDER III

Clergymen, no less than laymen, have been severely exercised in guessing the inscrutable purposes of Providence. We say that all our standards, all our criteria, are human, therefore no fit instruments with which to measure extra-human purposes. Admitting that the wisdom of this world is foolishness with God, even so, is it not more fitting to apply to the high purposes, eluding our comprehension, our severest rather than our flabbiest test?

To wit, the acid test of humour. For humour is in truth clairvoyance applied to this life. There is nothing this side of the veil so serious or incorruptible as humour. What is this in us that laughs, that will not stand solemnities, that *will not* be impressed by life? Is it not the noumenon of Intellectual Man? Never to be taken in – put it at its lowest – by the pious fraud of international good intentions?

Pause, then, and ask yourself, you who perhaps favour Providential intervention in the small and large affairs of men, what attitude you might reasonably expect on the part of your Supreme Being towards, let us say, the Russo-German *rapprochement* consequent on William II's visit to St. Petersburg to inform Alexander III that he had just sacked Bismarck – a communication which, the Kaiser tells us, elicited from the hitherto morose and incommunicative Tsar a quick and genial outburst of response. "He seized me by the hand," the Kaiser records, "thanked me for this token of my confidence, regretted that I had been brought into such a situation and added in exactly these words (but speaking in French): 'I understand perfectly Thy line of action; the prince for all his greatness was after all nothing but Thy employee or functionary. The moment he refused to act according to Thy orders he had to be sacked. I, for my part, have always distrusted him, and I have never believed a word of what he wrote or said to Me Myself as I was sure he was trying to trick Me all the time. For the relations between Us two, mon cher Guillaume –, (*this was the first time that the Tsar so addressed me*) – the fall of the prince will have the best of consequences; distrust will disappear. I have confidence in Thee. Thou canst trust Me.'"

I will ask the reader a question. Is this spontaneous exchange of eager confidence, sincere though it may be, between two wary monarchs and their mutual resolution not to go to war with each other, impregnable against the highest test of human critical integrity – the assaults of humour? If it is not, what reason may we have for assuming the Deity to be so impressed by this avowal of two hearts of oak as to take careful note of their assurance of non-aggression and forthwith oblige them both by removing every obstacle lying in the path of their ambition to preserve peace between their two countries, or, if possible, even the peace of Europe, always providing their own interests (a term which includes aspirations to expansion) are not affected or checked by as much as an inch? And, moreover, provided the class structure of their respective countries guarantees the existing hierarchic social order, with themselves on the top rung of the ladder? Why indeed should we expect Providence to be endowed with a critical faculty inferior to our own, and see noble drama where even the unaided human eye discerns tinsel melodrama bordering on opera-bouffe?

23

BRYAN AND TOLSTOY

For contrast, consider another scene also taking place in Russia. William Jennings Bryan, the eminent American statesman and champion of bi-metallism, is on a visit to Tolstoy with whom he discusses the great novelist's (Bryan thinks baleful) ideas of non-resistance to evil. "Do you mean to tell me," asks the noble-minded yet naïve citizen from the New World, "that if you saw your daughter being raped by a strong man before your very eyes you would offer no resistance?"

Tolstoy smiles. His piercing little eyes under the shaggy eyebrows, which seem to penetrate his visitor to the marrow of his private thought, light up with mild irony. It is the irony which sees through the foibles of a statesman deeming himself to be very hard-headed and practical, in a position to expose what he thinks are the Utopian ideas of an artist and dreamer.

"Well, well," says Tolstoy, slowly shaking his shaggy old head. "I've lived to be an old man. I have spent a full and varied life; but never once did I come across or hear of a case in which a man attempted to rape a daughter in front of her father and I will not waste my breath in discussing hypothetical questions."

In the one case you have two princes shaking hands on the impulse and, as the Kaiser observes, the Tsar remaining true to his word up to the day of his death. "But," he adds, "it became otherwise under his weak son." And it becomes otherwise every year and month under any unforeseen combination of men, the same or different men, of inter-mittent goodwill or variable opinion. Why should man expect Provi-dence to be impressed by the presumption of continuity contained in the personal avowals of representative individuals or groups of individuals whose resolutions, Providence must know, are about to be reversed by their successors? Have we not the explicit warning: Put not your trust in princes or in the children of men: for in them is no salvation?

In the second instance, we have an emanation of luminous simplicity so easily countered by mundane argument; indeed, so insecurely balanced on the border-line of childish credulity and profound philos-ophy as to suggest, like the Sermon on the Mount, inspiration emanating from a spiritual source different from our immediate experience, yet one in which we feel we have our true being. What better answer to return to an unimaginatively pious statesman than to point out that he is sacri-ficing fact to hypothesis?

Some readers may think Tolstoy's refusal to discuss an improbable hypothesis was a mere evasion, since Bryan, in pitching into the Russian's philosophy of non-resistance, was being metaphorical merely to accentuate his own argument. What, they may ask, was wrong with Bryan's question? Surely it applies to all manner of cases, personal, civil, international and religious, and is the touchstone of them all.

It is. But merely as demonstrating the fallacy inherent in the question itself. "Would you allow a great hulk of a giant to rape your daughter before your very eyes, or would you attempt to knock him down?" is the standard question of those who doubt the applicability of the Sermon on the Mount to human affairs. Accentuated merely in degree this standard question, with minor variations, is generally deemed by simpletons to be a telling way of presenting the case against non-resistance to evil. For what's wrong about heightening the degree of an argument?

But just here indeed is where the argument is fallacious. Questions, no less than answers, can be demonstrably wrong. The case of non-resistance to evil, like the whole philosophy of the New Testament, rests on *degree*, not on kind. It is never pedantic or doctrinaire like the Pharisees or scribes, but ,elastic and hopeful, believing, with a faith evoked from the unseen world of the spirit, in the law of averages showing up a preponderance of human decency present potentially among average men and women and manifesting itself in kindly behaviour when not artificially misapplied by fanatical leadership urging the moral priority of some particular end over the ugly means employed to attain it. Giants out to rape daughters in front of their fathers are too rare to serve as argument for putting the whole world on its guard, keying up humanity into a state of perpetual tension, arming everyone to the teeth against potential assassins lurking around every corner: a remedy more likely to cause the very danger it postulates. The probability of a hypothetical atrocity stands in inverse ratio to its degree. It poses as a hard-and-fast postulate in a realm of shifting sands incapable of supplying evidence of anyone's behaviour in a situation the place, time and actors of which are in the never-never land of hypothesis, perpetually out of view.

Tolstoy, accordingly, was not evasive but merely succinct in his answer to Bryan. He could have added, "No more than you – unless you choose to brag before the event – can I tell you now how I would behave in a contingency too unnatural to envisage and therefore clearly false in *degree*. I would act according to my feelings if, when and how it happens: the improbability of the situation not excluding the use of moral persuasion if the highly improbable giant should be open to this, comparatively speaking, less improbable argument."

24

WALT WHITMAN AND WORLD DEMOCRACY

In March 1892 Walt Whitman, who, as somebody observed, has epitomised his own people so perfectly that he could make no impression upon them, died in New Jersey. During his seventy-three years of life he, who set out deliberately to be the national poet of American democracy, in whose voice he sang perhaps over-lustily of their common virtues, merely found that in the chorus of collective self-praise he indeed could not be heard. The complete success of an American genius camouflaging himself in America as the average American was the measure of his failure: he could not be seen. When at last it was realised at home that Walt presumed to speak in her voice, his country, whom it was his mission to present as the leader of a world democracy, apologised for him to Europe.

Here, alongside Tolstoy, was an independent detector of 'the great fraud upon modern civilisation'. "As if," he expostulated scornfully at the heartless sophistries uttered in defence of inequalities of opportunity, "as if it harmed me giving others the same chances and rights as myself, as if it were not indispensable to my own rights that others possess the same!"

An extraordinary readiness to behave *as if* it did harm one not to be mean is the root cause of those periodic invitations cheerfully issued by our rulers to strip ourselves bare, to give our blood, our lives, our sons, our all to ward off again and again some pressing new evil rearing its head once, lately twice, every generation: an evil which, whatever the hue of its scales, is but the self-same serpent of resentment lurking under the bracken we tread, whistling with insouciance in the vast jungle of human greed.

"If America is not for freedom," exclaimed Whitman, "I do not know what it is for. By God! are men always to go on clawing each other – taxing, stealing, warring – having a class to exclude and a class excluded – always to go on having favourite races, favourite castes, a few people with money here and there, and all the rest without anything everywhere?"

The future Führer, a man, unlike Walt, of dark, Alpine stock with a suspicion of Semitic blood in his ancestry, was at the time of Whitman's death nearing his third birthday, innocent as yet of the idea of climbing on the shoulders of the Nordic myth, from there to look down upon democracy. Endowed with a perfectly magnificent physique, descended of sturdy English Quaker and good Dutch stock, Walt Whitman was a specimen of manhood that Hitler would have gladly picked out as the perfect Aryan. Compared with Walt, the Egypt-born Hess would have appeared to him a dago. But Whitman's ideology exulted in human anatomy irrespective of race. Appointing himself the bard of American democracy, he apostrophised the common people. "Grand, common stock," he sang, "convincing growth, prophetic of the future – proof undeniable of perfect beauty, tenderness, and pluck that never feudal lord nor Greek nor Roman yet rivalled. Let no tongue speak their disparagement to one who has been through the war in the great army hospitals."

Like Tolstoy himself, Whitman sickened of a society utterly corrupt, with prestige-values, its abject snobberies, its pitiful climbing and self-deception in an unending struggle to reach a delusive equality in a world of ever-changing social values. "The melancholy prudence," he laments, "of the abandonment of such a great being as a man is, to the toss and pallor of years of money making, with all their scorching days and icy nights, and all their stifling deceits and underhand dodgings, or infinitesimals of parlors, or shameless stuffing while others starve, and all the loss of the bloom and the odor of the earth, and of the flowers and atmosphere, and of the sea, and of the true taste of men and women you pass or have to do with in youth or middle age, and the insuing sickness and desperate revolt at the close of a life without elevation or naïveté (even if you have achieved a secure 10,000 a year and election to Congress), and the ghastly chatter of a death without serenity or majesty, is the great fraud upon modern civilization."

25

TCHAIKOVSKY'S DESPAIR

Through the mouth of an ageing house-painter who gilded cherubim on church ceilings and put his trust in God, Chehov spoke his own conviction: "We must labour, we must sorrow, we must suffer sickness," he said, "and he who does not labour and sorrow will not gain the Kingdom of Heaven. Woe, woe to them that are well fed, woe to the mighty, woe to the rich, woe to the moneylenders! Not for them is the Kingdom of Heaven. Lice eat grass, rust eats iron, and lies devour the soul."

Unencumbered by social injustice, indifferent to all forms of politics, molested neither by tsarist absolutism nor by the metropolitan police, financed all his life by an anonymous lady admirer conveniently electing to remain unknown, later to reside at a becoming distance and confining her demands on him to occasional excursions on horseback, Tchaikovsky might surely have escaped sorrow and sickness, his life-long labour being after all a labour of love.

It was not to be. The spirit had made early inroads into the flesh to ensure that his soul must suffer pangs in order that he might sing loud of sorrow. "*Und wenn der Mensch in seiner Qual verstummt, gab mir ein Gott, zu sagen, wie ich leide*",[1] he might have echoed Tasso.

It would indeed require a fantastic world, a Garden of Eden peopled by boys, with a barbed-wire fence to exclude all women, in particular his wife, to have lifted Tchaikovsky's cloud of melancholia. Even then his lyre would have twanged melancholy with nostalgia for the absent sadness in a paradise wanting for this lost sister of his muse.

But God's ever-vigilant Fifth Column ensured this music-maker's despair, deemed wholesome for his soul, by more direct and even ribald means. And in November 1893, after a life of intermittent attempts to fling himself into the arms of death to escape the more terrible embraces of the wife he had married out of loving-kindness, Tchaikovsky died. Some said he died from the effect of cholera after inadvertently drinking water that had not been boiled, Tchaikovsky and a *dvornik*[2] being the last two victims of the subsiding cholera epidemic in St. Petersburg. Others hinted that the draught of life had proved too bitter for so sensitive a man and that – on the principle of 'if at first you don't succeed, try, try, try again' – he had at last committed suicide.

On a summer's evening Tolstoy, sitting in the garden, listened as sounds of the *Four Seasons of the Year* wafted through the open window. Tears came to his eyes. There is a pensive Russian sadness and a question in those simple strains addressed to life: how long? they seem to ask, how much more? and, if one thinks into it deeply, really what for?

There are others, touched with the gold-dust of morn, recalling those incredibly pure lines unmarred by a naïve, pronounced romanticism, of the youthful Pushkin –

> Слыхали ль вы ва рощей гласъ ночной
> пввца любви, пѣвца своей печали?..

The virgin melodies of the earlier Tchaikovsky moved Tolstoy. Then, suddenly, he drew away, alienated by ill reports of the composer's private life. Tolstoy, who could ask stray English visitors to Russia, to wit, young Shane Leslie on his greenhorn pilgrimage to Yasnaya

---

[1] And if man is silent in his torment, there exists for me a god to say how I am suffering.

[2] Yard-keeper.

[3] Did you hear beyond the grove a night-time voice,
Singing of love, singing of its own sadness?

Polyana, "Are you a virgin?" would not be long in sniffing out Tchaikovsky's bashful introversion.

Zhukovski,[1] Pushkin, Lermontov had all duly improved on German, and especially Byronic, romanticism. Wagner avowed to have gone 'full-bloodedly' Italian with his *Tristan*. And Tchaikovsky, scratching awhile around the folklore muckheap, staggered all Europe with his full yearning melodies by embracing Chopin and all derivative Western romantics, but infusing the *penchant* of his musical heritage with such a strong dose of Slavonic melancholy, such a racket of Russian straight-forwardness, such devastating sincerity over something – this is his undoing – about which he is painfully unable to make up his mind, that the aged, asceticised, *Liebestraum*-sick Liszt would have nothing to do with him, confining his belated interest in Russian music to Borodin and Mussorgski and Lyadov.

In the early months of his last year, while the pathos of his final symphony percolated through his being, Tchaikovsky had conducted concerts in London and Cambridge, the eastern University having the grace to make him an honorary Mus. Doc. And the summer months saw its completion. Only a few days before he died, Tchaikovsky himself conducted at St. Petersburg the first, and for him the last, performance of his Sixth Symphony. Such is the critical level the world over, at all times and in all places, in all branches of art, that the work, we are told, "failed to make any deep impression during its first performance". The only way, apparently, of making a deep impression on the run of contemporary critics is by a chisel assisted by a small hammer which might, if applied with sufficient force, leave a dent in the skull.

There is no explanation, save that of musical insensibility, for so ungenerous a reception of a work which, far from gaining by repetition, makes its most powerful impression the first time it is heard. This in itself admittedly implies a criticism of its quality, apparently unable to outlast the lifetime of a single individual. And, of course, it is not proof against time in the sense that the finer sensibilities of the individual man must in his maturity of judgment reject it.

But the Sixth Symphony which, just before his death, he renamed the Pathetic, possesses a surviving quality of a different order. It is the most powerful bombardment of the nerves, of the pathetic sense, of the self-pitying strain in the individual, yet devised for a full orchestra and, as such, presumably has come to stay. It appeals to the suffering unit not yet mature, or, if mature, temporarily wearied by the struggle of life. It appeals to the self-pitying egotist in man who, like King Lear, absently

---

[1] Of whom Pushkin said that he would have been translated into foreign languages if he had not spent his life translating others into Russian.

71

and almost nobly, identifies himself with the pain of life. True, it has nothing of the spiritual equations, the release of the yearning suffering unit into a state of being in which his ego merges in a timeless unity of his being with all being. It has nothing of the spiritual purity of that unearthly little coda[1] in Mozart's *Concertante Sinfonie for Violin and Viola*, where in four swinging, awe-inspired notes the passing soul announces its diffident approach at the gates of heaven; is answered in four more by the ardent welcome soaring up from the communion of saints, to whom goes out the fervent gratitude of the homing soul returned into the fold, to be acclaimed by souls transfigured and many-throated in their single joy at the reunion.

There is nothing in the whole of Tchaikovsky on this high and simple plane. Tchaikovsky's pathos appeals to a transient despondency in this sub-lunar world as it assails us in our weaker moods. As such, however, its appeal is assured for generations.

That the music which had shattered Tchaikovsky to the depths of his being for the two years during which he composed it should have left his first audience unmoved, depressed his sinking spirits to a new low level. For one, unlike blithe Walt, really blighted by homosexuality, pursued by a wife from whose 'enseamed bed' at intervals he leapt into the ice-bound Neva, only to be forcibly retrieved by an officious yea-sayer to life and, after a spell of pneumonia, rather unkindly restored to health by the doctors, suicide by cholera as an abject climax to the fiasco of his most ambitious work would not seem entirely uncalled for. It would not seem at all unreasonable for him to follow the last bars of his *adagio lamentoso* wherein, after the prayer for the dead, the bass strings descend slowly into the nethermost pit of despair to the hollow sound of turf dropped on the coffin lid, to lay down the burthen and be covered by earth.

"Come, pull yourself together, man! What's the use of despair?" Such eupeptism, natural perhaps in a business magnate who, after a lifetime spent in cornering the market, in an interview to the Press describes life as a great adventure, would have unnerved Tchaikovsky, the music poet, as surely as the business magnate would shrink from the black despair of a man like Tchaikovsky. Yet, in the face of this despair, in the teeth of his homosexual disabilities and much critical discouragement and incomprehension, what is the balance of achievement between them – even in business?

Tchaikovsky's pessimism itself, though assisted by his disabilities, is not an unreasonable view of the physical world which, as Arthur Balfour sensitively puts it, "must strike coldly on our moral imagination, if so be that the material universe is all we have to do with". His melodies, some

---

[1] i.e. the sixteen concluding notes of the Second Movement of the Andante.

incredibly lovely, streaming out of a hundred opuses, though he himself is mute, still span the earth. "Perhaps," echoes another lyrist, Proust, "we shall lose them, perhaps they will be obliterated, if we return to nothing in the dust. Perhaps it is not-being that is the true state, and all our dream of life is without existence; but, if so, we feel that it must be that these phrases of music, these conceptions which exist in relation to our dream, are nothing either. We shall perish, but we have for our hostages these divine captives who shall follow and share our fate. And death in their company is something less bitter, less inglorious, and perhaps even less certain."

Tchaikovsky, the arch-pessimist, the lachrymose poet who records in his diary that today again he cried in the course of the afternoon and could see nothing to live for, left behind an extraordinarily rich and varied legacy of concert music, opera, ballet, piano pieces, songs, constituting, year in year out, a steady repertoire for innumerable entertainments, the subject-matter of countless solid concert-halls, radio programmes, gramophone records, national and commercial enterprises and business undertakings, his enchanting melodies still spanning the five continents and seven seas.

How shabbily in life we treat our artists!

26

NICHOLAS II, LENIN, OSCAR WILDE

In the following year, 1894, the last of the Tsars, the diminutive Nicholas II, a well-meaning young man of twenty-five with beautiful grey-blue eyes, succeeded to the throne on the death of his burly father, Alexander III, who had exchanged vows of trust with William II of Germany. Nicholas, who had tears in his eyes, was taken aback by the celerity with which his big broad-shouldered father, on whom they had all leaned for support, slipped off his burden and let it fall on his own slender frame. "I don't even know how to talk to Cabinet Ministers! Sandro: oh! what *am* I to do?" he wailed on the shoulder of his cousin and erstwhile playmate Alexander.

On the advice of his English relatives, Nicholas began his reign with the intention of showing himself to his subjects, of being *seen*. He inaugurated his new resolution by venturing one fine morning across the Nevski Prospekt to a little French shop where he bought himself a pair of gloves. This daring escapade so alarmed the police and his relatives that pressure was brought to bear on the Emperor. He must not do it again. He had tempted Providence enough: now he must immure himself from his subjects; then he would die a natural death like dear Papa.

Nicky, who did not need to be influenced in the direction of auto-cracy, since his own inclination, that of a weakly obstinate nature, ran that way, was exposed to two 'opposing' female influences, his mother and his wife, who, counselling sufficiently the same thing – one, that he should emulate his father, the other, Peter the Great – accused each other of ruining his life.

Chehov, reflecting on the vain hopes which the run of mankind reposes in new events and personalities, observed that people, while readily hoping that it would be better under a new tsar, never in any circumstances hoped for anything that might necessitate the least exer-tion on their own behalf: such as cherishing the hope that they would themselves grow wiser, more tolerant, less irritable, more patient or more sensible in the future.

Marcel Proust, twenty-three at the time of the accession, was on the point of discovering a parallel thought – to wit, that all our hopes of the future were of a material nature, pleasing either to our comfort or our vanity: we were as incapable of hoping for spiritual joys as of antici-pating evocations later released by our material entanglements.

And since our wishes are our real educators, we remain, while we dwell on this hard-bitten planet, materialists. The world, considered as an individual, is a very perverse, stupid, obdurate individual who will punish a music teacher for superficial offences against young girls, but will consider as perfectly natural, let us say, the disembowelling and castrating of men unacquainted but for a chance encounter in a national or civil war. Lenin, whose problem was how to make materialists distri-bute their material equitably, was incarcerated by a government that professed to think that equitable distribution was an outrage on society, as it may well have seemed to Society. In the same year of 1895 Oscar Wilde was sent to gaol because, in exquisite raiment and to the delicate sound of flutes, he paraded his sins before an England second only to Germany in the field of sodomy, as expressed in the unwritten curricu-lum of her more expensive public schools. Whereas Tchaikovsky's lugubrious introversion in a country uniformly heterosexual passed completely unnoticed, England was speechless with indignation that something which all knew existed should actually be hinted at in the Press and the law courts. While young Lenin was cursing his gaoler for being slow to sharpen the pencils with which he was covering sheet after sheet of subversive propaganda which the prison authorities were obligingly mailing for him to the outside world, Oscar was making mail-bags in Wormwood Scrubs, while Max Beerbohm was elegantly launching upon the London world of letters vacated by Oscar his 'New Urbanity'.

27

THE LAW VERSUS THE CREATOR OF BEAUTIFUL THINGS

Wilde was badly served by his Counsel, Sir Edward Clarke, and Oscar himself did not realise that the more brilliant and amusing and witty he became the more the jury hated him. Lord Alfred Douglas, endowed despite his slender years with better gifts of advocature than any counsel, would have secured his friend's acquittal if Clarke had had the sense to call him as a witness. If Alfred Douglas had been allowed to present his father in the proper light, as a brutal and hardly sane ruffian, the jury's image of a tender father protecting his young boy from the corrupting influence of a hardened sodomite would have been shattered, and Lord Queensberry not acquitted in the libel action which Wilde inadvisedly had brought against him.

The same evening that Oscar Wilde failed in his action against the Marquis of Queensberry he was arrested in Lord Alfred Douglas's rooms at the Cadogan Hotel in Sloane Street. In Douglas's own words, Wilde knew nothing about the Law Courts and was in the state (generally described as an ideal one by judges) of being 'entirely in the hands of his legal advisers', a position more terrible than which it is difficult for a man to imagine this side of hell. Alfred Douglas went to see Wilde every day at Holloway Prison, where Oscar was on remand, awaiting trial. Separated by a corridor about a yard in width, his visitor had to shout to him to make himself heard in the babel of anguished voices, with a warder pacing up and down the intervening corridor. Oscar was a little deaf. He could hardly hear what his friend was saying; he merely looked at him, and tears streamed down his cheeks.

Here were two friends, both of them kind-hearted, exquisitely mannered and imbued in a high degree with aesthetic sensibility. And there, by contrast, was the bloated, benignly hypocritical nineteenth-century England, which had recently hanged little boys and girls for stealing a spoon, now venting her spite against one who had dared to parade his contempt for its smug standards.

That Oscar Wilde was himself largely to blame for the predicament into which he had got himself was not so clear to him as it is to us who do not share his tastes. Had he not scared the British public by elevating his homosexual private paradise into a philosophy of life, but merely taunted them, like Shaw, with their social hypocrisy, he would in the end have earned their respect. But the British public, imagining that Wilde's aestheticism aimed at substituting sodomy as the foundation of English home life – not to say finance – rose up at him in a solid wall because it seemed to them – merchant, bishop and costermonger – that the family institution, though under fire from Bernard Shaw, was not to be re-formed, so far as they could see, with any permanent advantage to the nation, upon a homosexual basis. The unimaginative infer that any new set of ideas presented with vivacity is aimed at overthrowing the existing order, oblivious of the truth that it is itself but a reaction against uniformity, and constitutes, at most, a certain corrective: as such, contributing to the richness and variety of existence. Respectability in any case has a lead-weighted bottom: however you may upset it, it will always right itself.

Wilde, unreasonably affronted by Lord Queensberry's visiting-card describing him, with curious prudence, a cautious qualification, as "Oscar Wilde posing as somdomite," jumped into the trap. Considering that Queensberry defined him as one merely *posing* as a pervert, it might really seem as though Oscar resented the insinuation of aspiring to a title he did not possess in his own right. It was hardly necessary for him to have taken umbrage, seeing that he *was* a sodomite, at being told that he was merely pretending to be something he was not accused of being.

Here was Oscar Wilde, at the height of his dramatic success, with *An Ideal Husband* and *The Importance of Being Earnest* running to full houses, about to make him a fortune and crown his reputation as the wittiest dramatist of the age. Here he was, the brilliant debonair Oscar, rising in his box in response to calls of "Author! Author!" to explain as the clamour subsided to polite attention, "The author cannot take the curtain as he has just left the theatre." And he staked it all on a foregone chance of getting even with the ruffianly old marquis who was pursuing him into the theatre with bunches of carrots, and in other ways making his life in London unendurable.

The situation was as pathetic as it was absurd. Oscar Wilde, an unconscionable social snob who rather hoped his father's knighthood, earned in a Dublin surgery, might pass for an old baronetcy, and spoke readily of when he was at Magdalen rather than just Oxford, and had never forgotten the nasty snub administered to him by George Nathaniel Curzon caddishly enquiring upon what grounds he, Wilde, used the first person plural when referring to the aristocracy, Oscar Wilde of course had been extremely gratified to meet the eighth Marquis of Queensberry, in the very teeth of his threats to horsewhip him. Attracted by young Lord Alfred Douglas, quite as much by his name as his beauty, he was not averse for making a friend of his father, his crude ruffianry notwithstanding, because of his marquisate. Though Queensberry went about threatening to horsewhip Oscar Wilde if he caught him dining with 'Bosie', when he did come upon them lunching at the Café Royal he consented, at the invitation of his son, to leave his own table and join theirs. The famous dramatist indulged the crazy peer by pandering to his well-known predilection for agnosticism. Queensberry was a real tough who, had he not been born to become a Scottish peer, would have distinguished himself no doubt as a footpad. Not burdened with excessive intellect, he claimed to have discovered loopholes in Christianity which he delighted to expose to anyone who could be made to listen to him. Bored by his father's conversation and not perhaps exactly enchanted to see his friend so unexpectedly mealy-mouthed, Bosie left them to each other. Wilde and Queensberry seemed to be engrossed in a competitive exposure of religion as one big swindle. And Bosie, daring to hope that he had disposed once and for all of his father's objection to his literary friendship with the brilliant Oscar Wilde, at last rose and left the table.

It was past four o'clock in the afternoon, and his father and Oscar were deep in animated confirmation of what would seem to be their identical views, paving the way to a lasting solidarity. One may well imagine Wilde, gratified by having hooked a real marquis and anxious to produce the best impression, pandering to Queensberry's crudities, acquiescing with a few brilliant sallies not to appear too mealy-mouthed, and the old club bore, delighted at having secured the ear of a reputedly brilliant man, sallying forth with broad lewd doubts upon the question of the Virgin Birth.

Then Bosie had a letter from his father. He entirely withdrew, he said, his objection to Bosie's friendship with Oscar Wilde, who was a most charming and cultivated fellow, a man of genius and a brilliant talker. In this he was, said Queensberry, confirmed in his opinion by his friends Lord and Lady de Grey, who were also friends of Oscar Wilde and vouched for him in every way.

Bosie was accordingly amazed when, a month later, his father again objected to his friendship with Wilde and resumed the threat to horse-whip the playwright. Consistency had never been a characteristic of the boxing marquis. Bosie's eldest brother had been offered by Lord Rosebery a peerage and a seat in the House of Lords, from which his father, Lord Queensberry, a Scottish peer, was excluded mainly because of his loud agnosticism. Queensberry who, his heir feared, might resent his elevation, expressed himself on the contrary as highly honoured, really delighted, wrote letters of thanks to the Queen, to Gladstone and to Rosebery, but afterwards, when the thing was accomplished, travelled to Homburg where Lord Rosebery was recuperating and walked under his windows, flourishing a dog-whip to thrash him with when he came out.

It was this crazy thug whom Oscar Wilde took seriously, to the ruin of his days and years, depriving the English stage, perhaps, of another half-dozen plays even more brilliant than *The Importance of Being Earnest*, interspersed with essays as exquisite as *Intentions*.

And there, his case having gone against him, he stood in the drizzling rain, handcuffed to a warder, at a railway junction, awaiting a train which was to take him to Wormwood Scrubs. Here was the man who had defined the artist as the creator of beautiful things, who had counselled a fellow-author, complaining that his book had met with a conspiracy of silence, to join in it, who had scintillated and been a lord of language, had wronged no one, but had suddenly become the target of an entire nation's spite. There he stood on the open rain-drenched platform, hatless, a convicted felon manacled like some tethered beast, when a Victorian gentleman, momentarily forgetful of Jesus's maxim about casting the first stone, or perhaps considering that he had never sinned, came up and, to acquit his debt to decency, spat in the poet's face.

28

SINGING CAPTIVES

Lord Alfred Douglas records in his autobiography how, in consequence of a last-minute hitch over a surety in a libel-action case, he was taken –

> Into the dreadful town through iron doors,
> By empty stairs and barren corridors,

and locked up for the night in Wormwood Scrubs. "I was put on the second and top floor of the sinister and forbidding-looking iron and steel house, smelling strongly of gas, with its rows and rows of numbered cells, to which I was destined. I was in the third or hard-labour division, and I must therefore, I imagine, have been in the same building where Oscar Wilde had been confined. I thought of him as I 'went to bed' (a plank bed and no mattress), and said to myself: 'Poor Oscar, however did he manage to stand this for two years?'"

Lenin, allowed to broadcast from prison subversive propaganda which he was originally put into gaol for writing, was asking his sister for a propelling pencil and observing that, with all the food and clothes he was getting from home, he almost thought of setting up a shop in prison. While Oscar was penning *De Profundis* and living *The Ballad of Reading Gaol*, Lenin in his prison cell in Petersburg was feverishly scribbling with the propelling pencil, and little or no regard for style, at his treatise on the *Development of Capitalism in Russia*.

In March of 1897, when Oscar was coming out of Wormwood Scrubs and Tolstoy calling at a Moscow clinic to visit Chehov for a discourse on art and immortàlity, Lenin travelled at his own expense to comfortable exile in Siberia, where he employed his time in shooting bears and hares and other dumb animals, to say nothing of birds – an interim occupation which men not in any way averse to shedding human blood usually regard as a charming pastime.

After serving a sentence of two years' hard labour passed by a vindictive judge in a case normally visited, if visited at all, with six months' detention, the creator of beautiful things came out a man slightly improved in physique but broken in spirit. To use a military term, his morale had gone completely. The English Duc Jean des Esseintes could not adjust himself to the Dostoievskian role of moral and social pariah. He could not write a single play, though he sold the scenario of one, apparently to several people at once, probably on the chance that no one would really get down to writing it or, if he did, was not likely to clear the last hurdle of production. Sterile pain did not ennoble him, and all the bitter herbs did not make him whole. The spirit, employing all its fifth-column agents to seduce this worldling and win his allegiance for itself, had not weakened his adherence to the flesh in that visible world which, in the face of the dual illusion of number and time, for him, in common with Gautier, persisted to 'exist'.

Oscar dallied with the idea of becoming a Roman Catholic, but was put off by the tedium of undergoing preliminary instruction in a subject in which, though Protestant, he set up as an expert. Like Byron before him, having whipped up a storm in a teacup to prove that Victorian England was no more disposed to be associated with sodomy than

Regency England with incest, Wilde left this green and pleasant land, as it turned out, for ever. Not in the grand Byronic manner, attended by private physician and travelling in his own coach, and scanning the cliffs of Dover uttering "Fare thee well, and if for ever, then for ever fare thee well!", but unobtrusively, discreetly spirited away across the coast – a red rag to the still snorting John Bull. Out of sight, out of mind. Supplied with £800 subscribed by his friends and doled out to him by his monitor Robert Ross, he went to the little French village of Berneval disguised as "that strange purple shadow," he wrote, "who is known as Sebastian Melmoth". In anticipation of a meeting with his friend he toyed with the idea of a new name for Bosie to masquerade in, which, failing that of 'Le Chevalier de la Fleur-de-lys', was to be, he decided, 'Jonquil du Vallon'. But on meeting and probably finding Lord Alfred's nose a little out of drawing he felt, in the words of Lord Henry Wotton in *The Picture of Dorian Gray*, that his young friend had behaved very badly to him.

29

IMMORTALS MEET IN A CLINIC

In Russia it is March 28th, abroad already April 9th, 1897. The Russian Maupassant, as Tolstoy inadequately called him, is lying in a Moscow clinic, spitting blood. His consumption is taking its toll, though, were he able to read the future, he has seven more years to live. The great Tolstoy has come to see him, the Tolstoy of whom he wrote in a letter to a friend, "It seems to me that I know him well, and I understand every movement of his brows, but still I love him." Tolstoy is sixty-nine; Chehov thirty-seven.

They speak of immortality.

What did they say? Since men do not deliver themselves best in intercourse, but in solitude, what was in their minds rather than their mouths? A friend of Proust's, who wrote to him that he much preferred his person to his books, received the stinging reply that it could only mean he preferred his second-best to his best. And, of course, men of Tolstoy's and Chehov's artistic integrity do not throw away their deepest thoughts without committing them to paper.

Even two wise just men aware of each other's gifts are almost sure to botch up what should have been a memorable argument. Undue sensibility on either side (or possibly the lack of it on the part of Tolstoy) would result in a more or less uneven compromise, making Chehov feel that he was lagging behind with his own exposition in the effort of lending all his attention to the senior author, alternatively to obtruding his own thoughts at the cost of Tolstoy's.

"Life is a dream; death is the awakening," was a favourite statement of Tolstoy's.

"And what do you mean by 'die'? Man may have not five but a hundred senses, of which only the five known to us perish at death, the other ninety-five flowering into life", is a thought Chehov considered worthy of commemoration in the play he completed a few months before he died.

Tolstoy's most pertinent question was always: "Does he believe in God?" "Does," he asked Gorki, "Andreiev believe in God?" answering Gorki's rather sour "I don't know" with the acid "If you don't know that then you don't know the most important thing about him."

Chehov's answer in this respect was generally cautious and qualified. "Between there is a God and there is no God there lies a whole vast field which the true sage traverses with painstaking circumspection. The Russian knows but the two extremes, and that which lies in between does not interest him. That is why he generally knows nothing, or very little."

Tolstoy loved Chehov, and when he looked at him, his eyes grew tender as though caressing the other's face. He told Chehov that he was writing a little book about art. He had flung aside his novel *Resurrection* as he did not like it, and was writing only about art. He had read sixty books about art. Art, catering as it did for a parasitic middle and upper class which lived on the toil of the peasants, had been, he said in effect, serving up for its own questionable delectation dishes prepared from the meat of its own uselessness, cooked in its own fat of vicious idleness, and spiced with its own worthlessness. As such it had at last entered a blind alley, from which there was no outlet save retreat. Tolstoy's penetrating eye had seen the lie in everything. Service was from now to be his gospel, his artistic gospel, service due to those to whom he and his class owed their means of subsistence – the milliard-limbed *muzhik*, upon whose sea of faces the cultured classes formed but so much froth.

Therefore, he assailed his overworked, blood-spitting companion, Chehov, at whose bedside he expounded his new ideas with the vigour of the aged man enjoying uncommon rude health, therefore men of letters must write not for parasites like themselves but for the delectation of their benefactor, the *muzhik*, however rudimentary the art entailed in pleasing such a backward public.

81

Tolstoy was perfectly serious, his small black eyes blinking, now with a penetrating fire, now shyly. "Art," he insisted with vivacity, "art is not, as the metaphysicians say, the manifestation of some mysterious Idea of beauty, or God" – a contention that would have pained Plato and Schopenhauer and Santayana who, epitomising the thought of his forerunners, holds that nothing is truly possessed save under the form of eternity, which is also the form of art.

It was not Goethe's idea of art, nor Proust's, nor Ruskin's, though in echoing a universal good feeling provoked by the strings of his lyre it would tally with Pushkin's idea of his own art as expounded in his poem *The Monument* – literally a monument in verse raised to himself by the poet's own hand. It was not Chehov's idea of art. Averse to any codification of his views on art, Chehov implied clearly enough what he meant by art by making it speak out in his works – the uncommented presentation of the actual, the strange, the 'realistic', the inconclusive half, throwing into relief the absent ideal.

Chehov who, though critical of peasants and the intelligentsia alike, felt a natural predilection for the intellectual classes, in the deeper integrity of his work showed a decided preference for the under-dog. He had ceased to care for the Russian village after finishing his tales of peasant life. He found the peasants, for the most part, to be timid, irritable, downtrodden people; people whose imagination had been stunted; ignorant, with an abject, crippled outlook on life. Their thoughts were ever of the damp earth, of grey days, of black bread. They were people who cheated, but, like birds, hid nothing but their head behind the tree; people who could not count. They would not come to mow for him for twenty roubles, but they came for half a pail of vodka, though for twenty roubles they could have brought four pails. Filth and drunkenness, foolishness and deceit prevailed in the village. All that notwithstanding, one yet felt that the life of the peasants reposed on a sound foundation. However uncouth a wild animal the peasant following the plough might seem, and however he might stupefy himself with vodka, if one looked at him more closely, there was in him, felt Chevhov, that most crucial of all qualities, sadly lacking in the intelligentsia, the bourgeoisie and the rest of the gentry: the conviction that with untruth and without God you won't get through in this world, that the main thing on earth was truth, and that more important than anything in life was fair dealing.

And what of the gentry? In the remote provinces – from where, as Gogol once said, you might gallop for a century without reaching a frontier – away from the dubious control of the capital, graft was the motive power of life and the passport to everything. Searching his heart, Chehov could not remember one honest man in the small provincial town of which he was writing. Men in influential positions, contractors, builders, engineers, architects, judges, all took bribes. At the high school, so as not to get stuck a second year in the same form, the boys were sent to board with their masters, who charged their parents exorbitant sums. The wife of the military commander took bribes from the recruits called up before the exemption board to get her husband to assign them to reserved occupations. The doctors took bribes from the recruits coming up before a medical board for certifying them as unfit for military service. The local medical inspector and the veterinary surgeon together levied a regular tax on the butchers' shops and the restaurants in return for passing meat not strictly fit for human consumption. At the district school they did a roaring trade in certificates qualifying for partial exemption from military service. The higher clergy took bribes from the humbler priests and from the church elders. At the municipal, the artisans', and all the other boards every lagging petitioner was duly pursued by a shout: "Hey! Don't forget your thanks!" And the petitioner would turn back to give thirty or fifty kopecks. Higher officials of the Department of Justice who disdained to take bribes were haughty, proffered two fingers when shaking hands, were frigid, pedantic and unobliging, unduly addicted to alcohol and cards, married heiresses, and for the rest took it out in general spite.

The girls alone were fresh, fragrant and pure. Most of them had higher impulses, unfocused longings, a *Schwärmerei* for the arts and the theatre, credulous and honest hearts. But they had no understanding of life, and sincerely believed that bribes were given their parents out of respect for their moral qualities, and after they were married they aged rapidly, let themselves go completely, sinking hopelessly in the mire of all manner of petty vulgarities and inanities of provincial existence.

Nor could it be said that Chehov was at all exaggerating. With a little more self-criticism, it ought to be admitted that this picture of human cupidity, with minor variations, was repeated from Dublin to Peru. Any embittered small-townsman could tell a similar tale in France, in Austria, in Germany, as Sinclair Lewis and A. J. Cronin have told, respectively, of Main Street and High Street, to say nothing of what Upton Sinclair has revealed about oil.

Faced by such a public of readers, Chehov could not but agree with Tolstoy that in such conditions an artist's work had no meaning. The more talented he was, the more unintelligible his position. For he was working for the amusement of a rapacious and unclean animal, and, contrary to his instincts, supporting the existing order. And, angry at the thought of the unworthiness, the low cunning and the general imbecility of his readers, Chehov gave way to a mood of depression. "I don't care to work and I won't work," he said. "Nothing is any use; let the earth sink to perdition!"

83

30

THE PHYSIOGNOMY OF THE AGE

"I have seen Tolstoy," Chehov writes after this meeting. "Wise, wise eyes . . ."

But, left to his own thoughts, Chehov's critical faculty reasserted itself. War admittedly was an evil, and legal justice an evil, but it did not follow from that that he, Chehov, ought to wear bark shoes and sleep on the stove with the labourer. Something in him protested against Tolstoy's conception of life. Reason and justice told him that in the electricity and heat of love there was something greater than chastity and abstinence from meat.

And what was all this about 'Art'? He had had his fill of discussions with authors and artists as to what was artistic and what inartistic, and these interminable arguments seemed to him as irrelevant as those scholastic disputations of yore with which people wearied themselves in the Middle Ages. Now came Tolstoy who, having just gorged himself with sixty books about art, propounded stolidly that art had entered a blind alley and must retract its steps, going all humble and rudimentary to please the simple rustic, who, to tell the truth, would far rather read tales of urban vice. Nor was there anything very new in Tolstoy's conversion to apocalypticism. Old men approaching the end of their days had always been prone to see the end of the world, had always declared that morality was degenerating, art growing feeble, the world going to blazes. One might just as well propound that the desire to eat and drink has outlived its day. Of course, hunger was an old story. In the desire to eat we had certainly got into a blind alley. Still, eating was essential, and we would go on eating, painting, composing and writing, however much philosophers and irate old men might moralise away.

When he thought of the peasant, was he really any better than the gentry? The *muzhik* lived in filth, his wife lived in filth, and his children lived in filth. What he stood up in, he lay down to sleep in. He picked the potatoes out of the stew with his fingers, though the whole family ate out of the same bowl. He drank kvass with a cockroach in it without even bothering to blow it away! Was it for such a public that Tolstoy expected him to adapt his stories?

Of course, one might plead extreme poverty. But did the rich peasant live any better? He, too, lived like a pig. Only look at him! Coarse, loud-mouthed, a head like a cudgel, broader than he is long, fat, purple-faced snout – altogether a foul-mouthed fellow! His children the same. And when he had had a drop too much he'd topple with his nose in a puddle and sleep there.

Perhaps it was altogether too sanguine to entertain hopes of betterment for anyone so steeped in all manner of perversity as the human animal, Russian or other. Perhaps, after all, Tolstoy's apocalypticism was no mere passing mood, and, indeed, no edifice of lasting rectitude could be merely superimposed on foundations so corrupt as ours. Perhaps the social cataclysms, as yet buried in the folds of the next century, were the subtle work of that Fifth Column of the lingering Avenging Spirit destined to undermine and eventually bring down the whole insanitary structure, to clear at last the site for the kingdom founded on goodness, on scruple, on sacrifice, on benign simplicity of living.

"*Messieurs et Mesdames!*" with unctuous (not to say fatuous) self-satisfaction concludes a voice on Radio-Paris, "*et en voilà ici nous vous avons donné la physiognomie de la Bourse!*" One might hope that the decade trailing in after it the dour *fin-de-siècle* had presented something of the physiognomy of the closing nineteenth century, the 'Naughty Nineties', so deceptively bland looked back upon from the growing pains of the twentieth.

To its credit let it be said that the curtain did not close in on it without some attempt being made to spare its successor the mortal agonies of a belligerent legacy. The initiative was taken by the well-meaning, nominally most powerful, if intellectually most modestly-equipped, monarch on earth, the Emperor of Russia, Nicholas II, the last of the tsars. In August 1898, through his Foreign Minister, Count Muraviev, he issued an invitation to the nations of the world to meet and take counsel together as to how to ensure peace and prosperity through international co-operation. It was as though Providence, knowing the savage fate in store for him twenty years later, paused to relent, saddling instead his small store of intellectual powers with a task that would weigh down a political virtuoso like Franklin Roosevelt, but also with the most glorious opportunity for good given to man, which, if Nicky but prove equal to it, would spare mankind two appalling world wars and himself the fate of being butchered with his entire family in the Ekaterinburg cellar.

It was not to be. The only sincere acceptance was on the part of the United States. President McKinley, deeply moved by this timely overture to outlaw war, appointed a delegation of distinguished men of learning, of undisputed integrity eminently qualified for the high and noble task of statesmanship in hand if the other powers had but had a grain of good will in them and not sent instead professional diplomatists, curbed, moreover, with instructions fated to shipwreck any conference.

The conference met at The Hague in 1899, and, for all the difference discernible, they might have met in a thieves' kitchen: burglars they were in frock-coats, come to find out how they might stick to their stolen goods and, restive of prolonged peace, how not to forgo the coming century's plunder. The Hague Conference was saved from total collapse – be it said to her honour – again by America which (having earlier achieved a body called the people of the *United* States), now shamed the other nations into conceding, if nothing else, at least the shadow of a permanent court of arbitration.

Had Russia sent Tolstoy, France Anatole France, England Bernard Shaw, and Germany, say, Hermann Hesse, they could have achieved a permanent world peace by signing away with alacrity, for good and all, each on behalf of his respective country – and more power to his elbow! – that altogether fantastic 'sovereignty' which is the alpha and omega of all the inane mischief, all the useless, never-ending bloodshed in the world.

"There is such a thing," said Oscar Wilde, echoing the wisdom of Chuang Tze, "as leaving mankind alone." Men exercising statecraft as a profession, statesmen, let us say, of the Arthur Balfour type, with all their suavity of intercourse, even with all their disinclination to assume responsibilities, are incapable of refraining from what they deem to be salutary, repressive statesmanship. They know nothing, they learn nothing, and they are in consequence worth nothing except as uncles and as patriots indulging the national egotism – that is, behaving like a profligate uncle who leads his nephew astray. The story of utter bankruptcy of statesmanship on the world arena is yet to be told. The beginning of the debacle presaging the twilight of the statesmen's power was not to strike the public imagination until somewhere in the middle of the Second World War. It was in particular the pitiful spectacle of a horde of very foolish-looking old faces, who had done yeoman service in the picture Press for three generations, turning up at the railway station to greet the returning prime minister of the day, lest in the coming reshuffle following a recurrent disaster they be left out in the cold; this is what probably caused them to be identified in the public mind with the unemployed turning up at the labour exchange. It was the idea that statesmen were making a living out of politics; that the supply of them at any time exceeded the demand; that they were more or less under perpetual notice, not adapted for any other uses, and not strictly necessary to anyone save themselves. From about that period dates the impatience of people the world over to get rid of them at any price, together with a growing desire to have the bare public services and supplies run by impersonal, retiring scientists trained to weigh things with impartial precision and to measure causes and effects with detachment.

Dear Arthur, whose hand in Irish politics in the closing century was to pave the way for De Valera, and whose hand in making the peace by pandering to the senile cynicism of Clemenceau was to pave the way for Hitler, and whose early graduation and long experience in diplomacy was to culminate in an achievement which set the Jews and the Arabs by the ears in Palestine – now, at the turn of the century, spent New Year's Eve, as always, in the bosom of his adoring relatives at Whittingehame. His niece and very indulgent biographer, Mrs. Dugdale, recalls how he insisted that the nursery party be wakened up to join the elders before midnight struck. And it is perhaps fitting that dear Arthur should himself take a leading part in seeing out the old century.

It was a century which had been young when Napoleon had begun his importunities, and had grown old, though little the wiser for it, with the outbreak of the Boer War. In youth – this was the experience of Disraeli – everything seems hopeless and irremediable, but in old age men find that everything in the end settles itself – more or less badly. This might be said of an age ushered in in desperate hopes by the dedication of the 'Eroica' to a Bonaparte who was going to make Europe free, and ending in a decadence that has had enough of hope, and has folded up in elegant despair.

With his favourite niece Alison on his knee, Uncle Arthur benignly dispensed to the children and infants the mulled claret, as though appointing himself the trustee – ominous thought! – of the new generation. Then he opened the front door and let the twentieth century in.

BOOK TWO

THE NINETEEN-HUNDREDS

31

THE BOER WAR

''For behold!'' cried Max Beerbohm, ''the Victorian era comes to its end and the day of *sancta simplicitas* is quite ended. The old signs are here and the portents warn the seer of life that we are ripe for a new epoch of artifice. Are not men rattling the dice-box and ladies dipping their fingers in the rouge-pot?''

And, indeed, Queen Victoria, whose longevity, already divided into early, middle, and late Victorian eras, looked like projecting itself into the Edwardian and Georgian eras, to be known perhaps, respectively, as very late and quite preposterously late Victorian eras, was gone. And King Edward, gleefully unencumbered by nursery-strings which had constrained him for sixty years, was no longer furtive in rattling the dice-box.

There is a famous restaurant in the Strand where, if you wind your way down to the cloakroom, you may enjoy a few words with the aged lavatory attendant who will tell you of the kings who had in his time penetrated into those inner subterranean recesses to wash their hands and brush their royal hair.

''What about the Prince of Wales?''

''Yes, I knew the Prince of Wales. I used to see him here before the war.''

''Before this war? Or before the last war?''

''*No*, sir. Before the Boer War.''

''Oh, you mean the other Prince of Wales?''

''Yes, sir.''

''Were you really here before the Boer War?''

''*No*, sir. I was on the door *before* the Boer War, and have been down here since just *after* the Boer War.''

While Edward, Prince of Wales, was Prince of Wales, his eldest sister married and had a son, and when he was Kaiser, Edward was still Prince of Wales. And when his younger sister Alice married, he was still Prince of Wales; and when she had a daughter, Alix, he was Prince of Wales; and when Alix married and was Empress of Russia, Edward was still Prince of Wales; and when in 1901 he at last became king, he had but nine years of life in hand.

The Edwardians accordingly had to make haste to crowd their sumptuous week-ends with their regimented pleasures, their brass bedsteads, pink-silk reading-lamps, ribboned coverlets of swansdown, champagne and endless ptarmigan, into Queen Victoria's leavings to her son.

In reality, of course, as anyone can see, there are no such things as eras. There are no eighteen-nineties or nineteen-hundreds, except in the associations of human memory. There are no such divisions, because people's lives overlap, their individual activities overlap, and social developments and world events overlap also. The Boer War bestraddled the border of two centuries and reigns alike. These picturesquely-called Victorian, Edwardian and Georgian divisions are too arbitrary to make sense. He who does not see that the segments into which we cut up life are revelations, not of truth, but merely of our particular defect of sight, has not begun to think.

But deeper causes underlie our temporal errors. In order that we may be encouraged to err, each in pursuit of his deficient vision of the universe, God's Fifth Column cunningly camouflages itself as taking our own view of right and wrong. That unending rush and pressure of righteous assertion is what makes the mills of God turn round in Time. Whether they indeed grind slowly is a matter of personal impression. But for them there would be no Time. That they grind exceedingly fine might be supposed necessary to break up any lumps of crude unreason in an equilibrium of maximum diversity balancing the constant unity in God.

"Nature," Goethe says, "has no system. It has life; it is life and succession from an unknown centre to an unknowable bourne." So also thought Wordsworth, dreaming 'mid all this might sum of things forever speaking'. Genius, as opposed to talent which readily defines diversity, implies seeing life, art, science, history, as converging upon itself from this unknown centre. Genius accordingly suggests rather than defines: for how 'define' unity? Goethe despised mere history. "*Soll ich*," he makes Faust ask, "*vielleicht in tausend Büchern lesen, dass überall die Menschen sich gequält?*"[1]

"Day," says Spengler, "is not the cause of night, nor youth of age, nor blossom of fruit." The more deeply we live in history, the more contemptuous we become of the sheer charlatanism of forging chains of

[1] "Must I read in a thousand books that everywhere men and women had suffered torment?"

causes and effects. Goethe's writings in natural science are examples of living nature presented without formulae, without laws, almost without a trace of the causal. For Goethe, as for Plato and for Coleridge and for all men unencumbered by Aristotelian backdoor nosing into the Father's many mansions, Time is not a distance, but a feeling. "That which you please to call the spirit of the times," says Faust, "is but the Lord's own spirit, in whom the times behold their face."

God's Fifth Column speaks to each in his own language, which is but another way of saying that there is no action without counter-action: that is what the process of being ground infinitely fine between pain and knowledge, the two mill-stones, amounts to. Poor Oscar who, some time before going to gaol, propounded that the future belonged to the dandy and that it was the exquisites who were going to rule, unleashed Kipling, who said that the sin men do by two and two they must pay for one by one. A Kipling, who assured his Maker that it was enough that through His grace he saw naught common on His earth, not the least of noble sights being that "if you treat a nigger to a dose of cleanin'-rod 'e's like to show you everything he owns", tardily in life made the discovery that "we but teach Bloody instructions, which, being taught, return to plague the inventor."

And so we had the Boer War, treating the Boers to a dose of cleaning-rod to encourage them to show us what they kept deep down in the bowels of their Rand. Robert Louis Stevenson, a tubercular case not apparently satisfied by the blood he was spitting up himself, had been demanding earlier, "Shall we *never* shed blood?" Chehov, also a consumptive, bored and melancholy in his enforced exile from Moscow in the curative tedium of the Crimean coast, was entrusting his *fin-de-siècle* thought to the philosophising colonel in his exquisite *Three Sisters*: "Mankind used to be absorbed by wars, all its existence being filled with campaigns, attacks, victories. This has now outlived its time, leaving behind it a vast blank space, with nothing to fill it yet."

The blank space was filled – as of old – with 22,000 British lives, £223,000,000, with defeat after defeat, eventually to bring down to their knees 71,000 Boerish peasants after two years and a half of bloody slaughter, with a force of 300,000 British troops, and to the accompaniment of loud boos from the entire world. Whether Hitler's pitiless imagination was in need of any such precedent to allay his moral scruples in later overrunning small countries is extremely doubtful. But, as the best minds and hearts in Britain realised at the time, this ignominious adventure depreciated British moral currency, giving point to the fable of English hypocrisy, while certainly encouraging the incurably romantic Germans to take a cue in empire-building from the ruthless but successful English. The Kaiser deplored that his bespectacled Germans did not take a leaf from Kipling's 'flannelled fools at the wicket' and 'muddied oafs at the goal' who grudged 'a year of service to the lordliest life on earth', yet pocketed half the world. He dearly wished German youths would turn away from *The World as Will and Prefiguration* to pioneering, gravely dubious, though, whether there were any among his nation of officials who had smelt wood-smoke at twilight, heard the birch-log burning, or read the noises of the night.

The Kaiser and his chancellor and uncle, Hohenlohe, toasted in champagne the British Navy, and Tirpitz suggested that his sovereign should decorate the Commander of the British warship that had stopped a German merchantman, since news of it had helped to swell credits in the Reichstag for the building of a full-size German navy: 'which, being taught, returned to plague the inventor'.

The Kaiser was worried by a rising feeling in Germany against England, threatening to engulf him also, since he was, he complains with a certain relish of martyred pride, always referred to in Germany as being half an Englishman whenever his native patriotism *vis-à-vis* his mother's country was at all in doubt. The Palmerstonian John Bull, refined upon by Salisbury and Balfour and imbued with an imperially commercial sense by Joseph Chamberlain, was envied on the Continent, but was not loved. The Kaiser, explaining why he despatched the famous telegram to Krueger, introduces a foretaste of Hitler's specious Führer-of-all-Germans-anywhere claim when he says that Germany was outraged at the British attempt to overpower the Boers because they were a little nation of Dutch origin and therefore racially under German protection. He might just as well have extended his protection to the Anglo-Saxons, of whom, had his mother contrived to be the eldest son (instead of merely the eldest child) of Queen Victoria, he might conceivably have been king. The dictation emanating from England – *das Diktat*, already – must cease, said his uncle Hohenlohe. Feeling was running high in German subjects of a quasi-English Kaiser. And so he sent to Krueger a telegram of encouragement that made the English, as they read it in their morning papers, say the man was – well – a howling cad!

Russia and France proposed to Germany to make a joint attack on England to cripple her sea traffic while she was involved in the Boer War. The Kaiser claims virtue in resisting the temptation. Lest Paris and St. Petersburg misrepresented things in London, to make it appear that Berlin had initiated the idea, he telegraphed to his grandmother Queen Victoria and to his uncle Edward, Prince of Wales. The Queen's answer was a hearty thanks. The Prince of Wales, who, according to Lord Knowlys, habitually spoke of his imperial nephew in terms enough to make your hair stand on end, telegraphed astonishment. The Kaiser counts his virtues by piling on his abstentions from international crime, like the old Jewish fiddler in Chehov's story who counts his losses by totalling up hypothetical transactions that might have turned into profits had it but occurred to him to go in for them. "When England was deeply involved in the Boer War, we might have fought against England – or against France," he adds disarmingly, "which, at that time, would have been compelled to forgo help from England. But we did not do so."

How kind. Again, "While the Russo-Japanese War was in progress we might have fought not only against Russia, but against France also. But we did not do so." How considerate.

The Kaiser, primed by Bismarck, had picked up the elements of what even Goethe called English craftiness and what the rest of the world mistakenly called English hypocrisy – our habit of giving disinterested reasons for self-interested motives. The world mistakenly believed the English to be devilishly cunning, shamelessly cynical, unaware that the English are guided in most things by an altruism – instanced by the adage that honesty is the best policy – which is merely synonymous with self-interest, sometimes mislaying the sequence and identifying self-interest, if less critically no less sincerely, with altruism. The Germans, incurable romantics, went all romantic even over their Bismarckian deceitfulness which they openly advertised, and set the world against them.

The Kaiser could not refrain from boasting all over Europe about his technique in holding Lord Salisbury to ransom. Before and during the South African War England had to buy Germany off. He was delighted at his success in military blackmail, considering it cheaper and more profitable than military operations. He got the better of Lord Salisbury over China and Samoa and the Portuguese colonies. His vanity getting the better even of his prudence, he bragged to his grandmother Queen Victoria of his cleverness, and, overcome by a sense of his own responsibility as her eldest grandson, warned her that she was badly served by her Prime Minister, whom he described as 'an unmitigated noodle'.

This triumph of sincerity over discretion earned the Kaiser the unenviable name of an Englishman in Berlin and a Prussian jackboot in London; while the haughty lord, informed of the Kaiser's efforts to lower the First Minister of the Crown in the esteem of his Queen, regarded him with feelings bordering on aversion.

32

BOSTON AND PARIS

1902 saw the funeral of Zola. All day long the Latin Quarter marched in serried ranks down the boulevards of Paris. When at street corners they clashed with the Royalists, there developed something of the mutual disdain and maledictions bandied between the church processions of the Montagues and the Capulets. The whole affair which had shaken France, and indeed had shaken England even more than the Oscar Wilde affair which had merely left it speechless, had been a trial of moral strength. It had been a clash between the lilies and the tricolour, between the Army and the Republic, between nationalism and socialism. It had been a tug-of-war between principle and expediency; between justice and honour; between scruple and means-to-an-end. Church and State became embroiled, though Rome herself stayed neutral. In the whole Dreyfus Case, Dreyfus himself was, of all the persons involved in the stupendous affair, the most unimportant. And of all its ramifications and complexities he it was who knew the least.

To the Royalists it had been, they thought, a heaven-sent opportunity for uprooting the Republic. Whether Dreyfus was guilty or innocent was to the Nationalists of less account than the vindication of French military honour and the exposure of Germany, implicated, so it seemed, from the spy upwards to the Emperor William himself. To that end they thought, as any virulent nationalism – notably, the Nazis – might think, that the sacrifice of one innocent Jew was cheap enough. But the moral conscience of the world would not rest till the injustice was righted. Zola, dragged into the fray reluctantly despite himself, won immortal laurels. Banned in England as a pornographist, for whose works translators and booksellers had been consigned by English judges to long terms of penal servitude, it was to England that he had fled for refuge from his frenzied enemies, to be acclaimed here as the champion of the moral code. An inveterate materialist, he raised with his tremendous letter *J'accuse* the prestige of literature as a crusading force to new heights of glory.

While living for a time at Nice and Paris, Chehov read the papers assiduously. "Let Dreyfus be guilty," he writes to his friend, the Russian Northcliffe, Suvorin, who in and out of season ran down the Jews and championed the military, "and Zola is still right, since it is the duty of writers, not to accuse, not to prosecute, but to champion even the guilty once they have been condemned and are enduring punishment. I shall be asked: 'What of the political position, the interests of the State?' But great writers and artists ought to take part in politics only so far as they have to protect themselves from politics. There are plenty of accusers, prosecutors, and gendarmes without them, and, in any case, the role of Paul suits them better than that of Saul."

He could not help himself, he loved the military, Suvorin lamely replied from Russia, where, in his newspaper *Novoye Vremya*, he was blackening Zola's character while serialising his novels without payment. He, too, loved the military but that should not, Chehov answered, blunt either one's powers of discrimination or one's sense of decency. Even long before Dreyfus's innocence was apparent, Chehov felt dissatisfied with the verdict. Apart from the criminal law, the penal code and legal procedure, there was, he tried to drum into the thick skull of his rich and enterprising friend, a moral law, which was always in advance of the established law, and which defined our actions precisely when we tried to act on our conscience. The conscience was a surer guide than legal subtleties. If, despite steering conscientiously, continually consulting the chart and the compass, a sea captain still manages to get shipwrecked, would it not be more reasonable to attribute the result, not to the captain's incompetence, but to something else – the chart might be out of date, or for that matter the bottom of the sea itself might have changed. In the same way juries were known to feel that there were fine shades and subtleties which could not be brought under the provisions of the penal code, and that something else was required to comply with their sense of justice, and that for the lack of that 'something' they would be compelled to give a judgment in which something was lacking.

The liberal world suspended its judgment while direct evidence of Dreyfus's innocence was lacking, to be vindicated in their refusal to believe blindly in his guilt. Through all the tense stages Marcel Proust, then a young man of literary promise, described by Anatole France as the 'ingenuous Petronius of our times', detected in the whole affair, as one might expect, just that which escaped everyone else. He discovered that people who were nationalist or Dreyfusard belonged to one or the other camp for subtly personal reasons, not necessarily because their race or background determined their standpoint. Jewish on his mother's side, Catholic and French on his father's, plying his uncertain way through a Faubourg Saint-Germain almost morbidly snobbish because it was an aristocracy that had lost its *raison d'être*, he maintained with his unbribable detachment an undisguised belief in the innocence of Dreyfus. He found that many a socially ambitious woman, even married to a Jew, would profess virulent anti-Dreyfusard views to secure an entry into Royalist circles otherwise closed to her, only to encounter there a

97

young man, the scion of an ancient house fancying himself as an intellectual, openly professing Dreyfusard views to sustain his own illusions that, however long-rooted his traditions, his intellect vibrated in tune with the progressive liberal conscience of the intellectual world.

In the face of such social imponderables, it might well be politic for a young man like Proust, making his debut in fashionable society, to be openly Dreyfusard, since if he espoused the aristocratic nationalist cause it would be the intellectual scions of the *faubourg* who, singing the praises of his intellect in Society, would be the first to turn on him. Fashionably dressed but never tidy, slim, pale, with black hair that was never to turn grey, large dark eyes, heavy-lidded and of an incredible gentleness and melancholy languor of expression, the young man wended his way through the drawing-rooms of the *faubourg*. His voice, trailing and a little breathless and just hovering on the brink of affectation, was perhaps that of his own description of Chopin whom Mme. de Cambremer imagined herself to go out to meet as she left the ball behind her to hear the wind blowing amidst the pine trees, at the border of the lake, there to see suddenly advancing upon her, different from all that one could ever dream are the lovers of the earth, a slim young man '*à la voix un peu chantante, étrangère et fausse, en gants blancs*'.[1]

While Chehov, the grandson of a serf, was trying to play the conscientious citizen, building his third village school, on his passage through France collecting books, pictures and statues for the newly-built museum of his native Taganrog, Proust in Paris noted '*d'après ce que me disait la Duchesse de Guermantes, que j'aurais pu faire dans ce monde la figure d'homme élégant non titré mais qu'on croit volontiers affilié de tout temps à l'aristocratie*'.[2]

More accurately, his hope of cutting such a figure in the Faubourg Saint-Germain, vitiated by his self-consciousness, was not fulfilled until, altogether too ill to frequent society, he received at the hands of the Duchess (who in the old days, when she refused to invite him, had seemed to him to stand upon an unattainable pinnacle of social eminence and was now a little *déclassée*), belated proof of her bad memory, and confirmation of the essentially subjective nature of all social ambition, as he heard her tell a young man new to society that Proust had always been of their set.

It had been the great age of literary salons, to which, as Proust with his unfailing integrity of observation himself admits, gravitated mostly people one did not want elsewhere. The literary ladies, by mentioning in

[1] With a slightly odd and off-key singing voice and wearing white gloves.
[2] According to what the Duchess of Guermantes told me, I could have cut the figure of an elegant gentleman, untitled, but whom one would readily believe had been for ever linked to the aristocracy.

their memoirs only the illustrious personages who, but a sprinkling on
the waters of mediocrity, had over a long range of years perhaps totalled
up to a respectable dozen or two, contrived to leave the reader with the
erroneous impression of a staple level comprising all that was most
brilliant and fashionable and renowned in the society and the arts of the
day as gathered around their own persons.

Proust's unfailing discovery of the tantalising truth that no society,
however exalted it may seem from outside to the climber egged on by the
mirage of its brilliance, was either homogeneous or finite, completed
his aspirations in life. "*Und so verbragt, umrungen von Gofaht, hier
Kindheit, Mann and Greis sein tüchtig Jahr*"[1] might well be the Faustian
epitaph (edited by Mephistopheles) on Proust, who side-tracked the
futility of his own quest on to the more coarsely fibred fellow-climber,
Bloch, dismissing him with the withering question: "How has it profited
him?" Discovering for himself that positively nothing in the world of
appearances was as it seemed, he repeated the octave of deception in
love and art, in politics and vice, retarding the normal working of the
mental levers in action to a slow-motion picture of cogitation.

It is unprofitable in the case of Proust to attempt to distinguish
between fact and fiction. His characters, though drawn from life, are
composite creatures. And it is under this mixed anonymity of fiction that
he reveals a multitude of facts about himself and others that would not
face the light in their own name and place. His great epic was not yet
begun. The first of the fifteen volumes of *A la Recherche du Temps
Perdu*, the nostalgic *Du Côté de chez Swann*, was to be separated by a
gulf of seventeen years from his adolescent effort, *Les Plaisirs et les
Jours*. But in that early extravagant book, sponsored by Anatole
France, Proust had already sounded what was to be the theme of his
masterwork: the salving of value from the passing moment in creative
contemplation of experience in terms, not of time, but of eternity.
Slowly and painfully he was crystallising in himself an epos of the whole
of French life under the Third Republic. The period covered was that of
his own childhood, youth and manhood. He did not set out to represent
France or the age. He represented only that side of its life – in his case,
the unexplored depths of human nature and the human mind – which
happened to interest him. When all is said, that is what all novelists,
from Balzac to Zola, from Stendhal to Tolstoy, have ever attempted to
do. Comprehensiveness in art is generally a brick wall enclosing dead
wood. The living form is a synthesis of inclination which, as Goethe has
it, is the only synthesis worth having in a work of art. Balzac, deluding

---

[1] And so surrounded by danger, here, as child, man and old man, was spent his active
life.

others that he was giving a panorama of the whole social scheme, was also deluding himself. His *Comédie Humaine* is a panorama not of the French social fabric but of its preposterous reflection in Balzac's own magnifying eyes. So is, of course, Zola's *Famille Rougon-Macquart*.

To Proust, society was, not a romance as it was to Balzac who knew nothing about it, but another and a worse Sodom and Gomorrah, morally more wicked than that of the senses. For if anyone chooses to see a woman in a man, or a man in a woman, it is his or her own funeral. But if everyone, all the time, everywhere, is exercising his maximum guile in the interests of maintaining at the back of his mind an absurd artificial advantage of pride to the hurt and abasement of his neighbour, for fear that the latter will otherwise discount his worth, it would really seem that human beings could no more savour the innocent joy of life in civilised society than when they dwelt in caves. Tolstoy and Christ were right. As a God's Fifth Columnist, in breaking up with a pick-axe the evil *beau monde*, and making it unlikely that anyone should ever want to live in such a world, Proust, however unconscious of it himself, was the foreman of a demolition squad pulling down a condemned building, condemned alike by God and man, chilly, deceptive, and, behind an imposing façade, unhealthy, verminous, cruel, uncomfortable and, in the last analysis, fatuous.

Taken as a sickly youth by his mother (or, as in the novel, his grandmother) to a seaside hotel, he and she run into an old hag of his mother's acquaintance who goes by the name of the Marquise de Villeparisis. This is but one of several starting-points of his social philosophy which he unravels throughout fifteen volumes of the epic. When the first volume was out, Proust deplored that the critics had called him a *fouilleur de détail* fiddling with a microscope where, on the contrary, he had resorted to a telescope to perceive in one person what was indeed an entire world.

So seen, Mme. de Villeparisis alone is a microcosm of society. This lady, invariably unimportant just when considered by others important, but represented as valid just when dismissed as worthless, is an epitome of the fluctuation of social values and, above all, an illustration of the irretrievably subjective nature of all social prestige. When young Proust inquired of M. de Charlus, otherwise the Comte de Montesquiou, what exactly was his aunt, the Marquise de Villeparisis, the answer was – "*Rien!*" *But*, Charlus hastened to add, although the title and indeed the very name which had been assumed by his aunt's husband were both wholly fictitious ("which," he qualifies indulgently, "moreover, does nobody any harm") his aunt, as sufficiently proved by her being *his* aunt, was a woman of great birth who had perhaps somewhat compromised her position in society through an indiscreet past.

To what extent she has become *déclassée* is apparent to everyone save newcomers just entering the fringes of the *faubourg*, and, at the other extreme of the scale, to such bearers of great names occupying the most eminent position in the social hierarchy as also happen to be her nearest relatives. They do not frequent her salon but drop in for a cup of tea, hardly aware that their *déclassée* aunt who, to disclaim the least suspicion that she is fortifying her own declining prestige at the social expense of her fashionable relatives, sits at an easel and paints, to give the gathering a casual air of hearth and home. The newcomers, to whom, without leaving her easel, she presents her illustrious relatives as though to bear out the connection of continuity on the walls, are as completely impressed as posterity will be when it first learns of her eminence from her own memoirs. The greenhorns are naturally baffled when anyone questions the social standing of Mme. de Villeparisis whose salon, after some perseverance, they have at last penetrated, only to hear it described as second-rate, a description belied in the present by history in the ancestral portraits, as it will be by posterity unable to infer, from the accumulated great names, otherwise than that the salon of Mme. de Villeparisis was the most distinguished in Paris.

In reality she is eating her heart out because all the most brilliant hostesses in the capital who invite her nephews and nieces do not invite her. (If they had done so she would have exhausted her interest in brilliant society in life instead of absorbing her nostalgia into a book of memoirs, inevitably to inform posterity that her own salon had been the first of the epoch.) But that is not the reason for their snubbing her, the real reason being that, Mme. de Villeparisis having suffered a sharp social decline, far from wanting to sink together, the inclination of the social animal on such occasions is to keep his distance. What is more, there are other quasi-grand ladies of birth who frequent Mme. de Villeparisis's salon because they too have suffered a decline and, while visited by their own, are ignored by Mme. de Villeparisis's illustrious nieces. Each of these *déclassées* ladies has her own Duchesse de Guermantes to whom she freely refers on her visits to her co-sufferers. These social aces, who snub Mme. de Villeparisis, are in daily contact with Mme. de Villeparisis's brilliant nephews and nieces. It is indeed they who, together, compose that nostalgic *grand monde* to which the *déclassées* women can get no access and of whose brilliant functions they only read in the newspapers. Indeed, by a sort of converse law of social preservation, it is the eminently fashionable who exhaust all their energies in evading invitations to houses where their presence could raise the social value of a salon. They feel instinctively that their own eminence depends on restricting the supply in proportion to the growing demand for their presence. Though they know how much their presence is prized, they delight, on the rare occasions on which they make an appearance to enter with the utmost show of anonymity, to get lost in a crowd, to evade recognition by means of a shy, protective coyness, to refuse to be rescued from the crowd and, if possible, leave the house before the hostess has had a chance to make the most of their presence.

A kind of reciprocal game was also being played between society and the arts, nothing being so flattering to the artist as to be received by great hostesses, not as an artist, but as a man of the world. The *grande dame*, for her part, to show that she was no less matter-of-fact about art than the craftsman himself, astounded her guests, fully prepared for a battle of wits between the notorious Duchess and, say, Anatole France, to find themselves assisting at a meal of masticating silence punctuated by abrupt inquiries as to how he likes his eggs. Through this web, composed of the warp of deception crossed by the woof of self-deception, called the world, Proust, who abominated nothing so much as people who could not distinguish goodness of heart from its many counterfeit substitutes, threaded his way painfully, picking up such telltale bric-à-brac of social knowledge as that the noble participle '*de*' was dropped unless preceded by a Christian name or 'Monsieur' or a title. His retort was to insist, for the sake of consistency, on referring henceforward to Van Dyck as plain Dyck.

While young Proust had been visiting the seaside town where he met Mme. de Villeparisis, Chehov, dragging his tubercular frame from spa to spa, convinced himself more and more of how abject and threadbare was the life of the well-fed and well-to-do: how flabby and undaring their imaginations, dim and timid their tastes and desires. How much more happy than they were those tourists, old and young, who with no money to stay at hotels, put up where they could, enjoyed the view of the sea from the height of a mountain as they lay on the green grass, hiked their way from village to village, saw woods and forests at close range, noticed the customs of the people, heard their songs, fell in love with their women.

Meanwhile Proust, eleven years younger, was taking his initial dispositions in the literary drawing-rooms of Paris, suffering cruelly from the intermittences of the human heart. The famous hostesses, who went to war over their lions, dragged the lions into the fray by assuring them that they were fighting their cause. There had been such a war between Mme. de Loynes, whose lion was Jules Lemaître, and Mme. Arman de Caillavet, whose lion was Anatole France. Mme. de Caillavet, whose husband had annexed the name in the manner of the husband of Mme. de Villeparisis, rejoiced at the epigram made to Lemaître at the funeral of Mme. de Loynes: 'Don't cry, my friend. You will meet her again in another and a better *demi-monde*.'

This was the Paris early in the century, which drew to it from all the corners of the earth the artistic nostalgia of the world. It drew the spiritual exponents of the other Paris, the intellectual capital of the New World. Boston, in spite, or because, of its austere New England traditions, wore, like a man of severe sartorial tastes who, to relieve his too sombre aspect, sports light-coloured waistcoats, an intellectual cosmopolitanism that almost ran to bric-à-brac. Connoisseur of other people's esoteric traditions, the Bostonian grew a little self-conscious of his own. Cautious of their own reputations, suspicious of being 'found out', sensitive to ridicule, the descendants of Bellamy and Pumpelly, Miss Jewett and Miss Wilkins, had shed little of their inbred New England Puritan refinement, adding to it an elaborate Boston Alexandrianism at the turn of the century. This was the Boston when T. S. Eliot was still a youth, the Boston with its mandarins and cognoscenti with their scraps of out-of-the-way erudition, the adept and the proselyte, forever orientating themselves, always looking over their shoulder to measure their daily progress on the intellectual path, comparing, correcting, retracting, forever bandying prestige values.

What they did not know was not worth knowing. This Boston was the spiritual home of Henry James and William James. There was something in its atmosphere which denuded men and women of their zest for life. Unlike the earlier New England stock, who sought the lakes and forests for refreshment, the new generation crossed the ocean to spend its cash and leisure in the casinos and hotels of Europe, while the learned hierarchy sought and found nutriment for its depleted strength in visiting the ruins of Italy and Greece, or traced the literary by-ways around Fleet Street or the Latin Quarter and returned, refreshed, to their Boston royalism, Boston Anglo-Catholicism, to their scrupulous fingering of Donne, a hyperaesthetic partiality for this or that Elizabethan dramatist or poet, a few choice lines from Laforgue or Rémy de Gourmont, a quotation from Dante inserted in an essay, a dip into Sanskrit, to dissolve once more in a sad sterility, a melancholy irony, pending a new trip.

But the expatriates who came to live in Europe, far from losing because of their severance from the native scene, gained in that, with fresh eyes, they depicted their compatriots against the backgrounds of all Europe, which served to throw their Americanism into relief. The New Englanders, by becoming English, did not see the English as to the manner born, but the Americans. Henry James vindicated his Americanism in his late masterpiece, *The Ambassadors*. As, on the psychological plane, Henry James, while severing his roots, in the long run catered for the country of his birth, so his brother William, contemptuous of 'the bitch-goddess, Success', offered in the philosophic field a complete justification, with his pragmatism, to the author of *Success*[1] and a whole band of go-getters in both the old and the new world.

It is rare that the leading writers, alive and resident in the same place, know, let alone meet, one another. Henry James never met Proust, though they must have been in Paris at the same time and pursued much the same social paths, even though James's *faubourg* was not that of Saint-Germain but St. James. This was the Paris of which later, when Proust had passed to immortality, the expatriate American approved unreservedly. He approved of him, approved of his unregenerate subjectivity, in the teeth of all his own rules of objective dramatisation which, in his own case, at last degenerated into pedantry that hardly served his own end of verisimilitude.

This was the Paris that Oscar Wilde said all good Americans went to when they died, where he was dying, he sighed, beyond his means. To André Gide, from whom he had taken a promise to hold him to writing a play, he had said, some little time before, that, no, he could not do it. "I can't . . . but, believe me, one should not expect it of one who has been struck down." Gide, embarrassed by Wilde's reputation, not enhanced by drink, was careful to take a seat facing Wilde, with his own back to the people passing them as they sat in a café on the boulevard. But Oscar was hurt. "Oh! Gide," he exclaimed, "come and sit beside me . . . When I used to meet Verlaine I did not blush for him. I was rich then, happy, covered with fame, but I felt that to be seen sitting by his side was an honour, even when Verlaine was drunk . . ."

One evening he espied a man on a bridge, leaning right over the parapet as, with a melancholy look, he surveyed the water running underneath. Anxious to avert a suicide, Wilde approached him. "*Vous êtes désespéré?*"

"*Non, monsieur, je suis coiffeur.*"

When Oscar was dying he was received, Lord Alfred Douglas tells us, into the Catholic faith. Others denied the value of this last-minute conversion, for Wilde was not only largely unconscious but deaf as well. Douglas, however, assumes that Wilde understood the words of the friar called to his deathbed. The friar spoke loudly right into Oscar's ear, and Oscar was believed to have made a feeble sign suggesting assent. So he died a good Catholic.

The supposed conversion – on a different plane of extremity – is reminiscent of a German bitch, blind, deaf and half paralysed with old age. She lay in a corner all day, oblivious to the world. Only when her mistress bent down close to her and shouted very loudly in her ear,

---

[1] By Lord Beaverbrook.

'*Scho – ko – lade!*' she would turn over and twitch feebly with her forelegs, in a faint shadow of reminiscent pleasure.

Let us trust that poor Oscar's gesture signified even as much hope of assuagement from the ills of life as that, and that he could at last repeat with Shakespeare, "My long sickness of health and living now begins to mend, and nothing brings me all things." He was conveyed to his grave. On the bier there were a few flowers, two or three wreaths, of which only one bore an inscription, that of the hotel proprietor, reading 'To my tenant.'

God's Fifth Column had completed its work.

33

IN AT THE DEATH

The Kaiser was celebrating at Potsdam the two-hundredth coronation anniversary when, together with his favourite uncle, the Duke of Connaught, who was there to represent his mother, they were torn away from the jubilee to her deathbed at Windsor. The future King Edward VII, putting in his last days as Prince of Wales, was on the platform at Paddington to meet his imperial if rather dreadful nephew, and as they drove away from the station a shabbily dressed man with a solemn face exuding virtue suddenly stepped forward from the silent crowds lining the street, bared his head and boomed, "Thank you, Kaiser!"

For royalty a refinement of luxury, a titbit more palatable than the praise even of their counsellors (whose approbation is after all merely a pat on the head from a governess) is the romantic love of the humble poor, whose hearts are more than rubies in the sense that they are more numerous – accordingly the broadest of foundations for popularity, security and power. The Prince of Wales, saying exactly what he would have liked to hear said to him by another, enlarged with an effect of *And so say all of us* by adding, "That is what they all think and they will never forget this visit of yours." The Kaiser, taking it all at its face value, a quarter of a century later deplores in his exile at Doorn that English gratitude for his turning up at his grandmother's deathbed did not apparently survive the stress and strain of hostilities. How evanescent human thanks, and vows of friendship how soon defeated!

He was, however, playing his selfless part on the principle that kind-

105

ness was its own reward, and, seizing his dying grandmother in his imperial arms, to the exclusion of her next-of-kin, he did not release her until the old Queen quietly breathed her last in his grip. Then, perhaps to underline the impression that, as her eldest grandson, in leaving Potsdam he had merely come home, and as though to expend something of his self-exhilaration at having performed his duties to perfection, but with energy still to spare in his limbs, as he stood watching a carpet slowly being unrolled over the grand staircase, he of a sudden gave it a violent kick with his jackboot and sent it unrolling rapidly of its own momentum all the way down, turning back to his royal hosts with a broad grin signifying a grand-filial sense of the fitness of things in a land appreciative of all variety of sportsmanship.

Queen Victoria had intruded only into the first year and one month of the new century, and was whisked away into the astral world. Ladies draped from head to foot in black crêpe approached one another gingerly on Kensington Garden benches, speaking in mournful, lugubrious, hollow half-tones: "Have you *heard*? Isn't it *terrible! Whatever* will happen to the country *now*?" H. G. Wells, aged thirty-four, travelled to London in a railway carriage filled with people looking as though utterly cowed by fate and speaking in whispers as though there had been an eclipse foreboding the end of the world, and as they stared at him, inexplicably devoid of any spiritual or material sign of mourning, he stared back and asked himself whether he was not doomed to live in and write for a country not indeed of the blind but of the daft.

Yet, incredible as it may seem, the country survived the shock of the Queen's loss. The public get over quite well novelties they are at first alarmed about, observes Proust. The shrewdest Republican in France thought it mad to bring about the Disestablishment of the Church, and it passed like a letter through the post. Dreyfus was rehabilitated, Picquart was made Minister of War without anybody saying a word. And it might be added that the faculty of ceasing to be astonished does not abate as the twentieth century matures into middle age, handing us out such delicious titbits as arch anti-Bolshevik crusader Churchill providing Stalin with engines of war, and Edward by the Grace of God of Great Britain and Northern Ireland King, Defender of the Faith, Emperor of India, ending up as Governor of the Bahamas without causing any more astonishment in the waking world than in a dream.

That Queen Victoria contributed any more to the wealth, health and happiness of mankind when she was alive than when she had ceased to live is one of those fables beloved of writers who succumb to another fable that you can describe people, especially rulers, in general terms, such as compounded of wisdom, integrity, single purpose, steadfastness, courage, sympathy, knowledge of men, of history, of affairs, a flair for mass psychology, and so on. In reality, Queen Victoria, like all modern sovereigns, was to life what an illustration is to the rest of the book. After the death of the Prince Consort, she expressed herself as shocked that her people should expect her to emerge again from her shattered private life into the public glare: "That my people should want to see a *poor*, *lonely*, *suffering* widow draped in deepest mourning *expose* herself to the public gaze, is something *I* shall *never* understand!!" As she did not apparently expect that her retirement would cause the Empire's heart to stop beating, she could have no final illusion about her indispensability to the nation. And it is as a legendary character, enjoying a longevity on a level with famous characters of fiction, that she lives in our imagination and contributes to the richness of existence. Imposing, even moving, as a symbol of empire, a silver, gold and finally diamond-jubileed little old lady sitting under the parasol in her carriage, she becomes almost lovable in extreme old age when, chided by John Brown for looking for her shawl on which she happened to be sitting, she replied in a gentle voice to his grumbling that some day she would mislay her head, "You are quite right. I am a poor old widow who has lost her dear beloved husband and who feels very helpless."

That she was every inch a queen as compared with her guest in the royal box at the Opera, the Empress Eugénie, was clear from a detail, small but significant. Reared for a throne, the Queen sat down without looking to see whether there was a chair or not to sit down on, convinced, as unshakably as that she reigned by divine right, that a seat would be duly pushed up for her. The Empress Eugénie, every other inch an empress, rather than take the risk of finding herself sprawling in an unqueenly attitude on the carpet, first glanced round to make sure.

34

TOWARDS THE STATUTE OF WESTMINSTER – AND BEYOND

In a memorial speech in the House of Commons, Arthur James Balfour stressed the increased rather than diminishing importance of the Crown in the British Constitution. "It increases," said Arthur, blandly looking at his audience through his pince-nez, "and must increase," he added, with the gentlest of verbal emphasis compatible with intellectural self-respect, "with the development of those free, self-governing communities, those new commonwealths beyond the sea, who are constitutionally linked to us through the person of the Sovereign, the living symbol of Imperial unity."

This curiously unreasonable appeal for protection from the united *many* to the helpless *one* (rooted in the immemorial sheepishness of men) has been watered down by the Statute of Westminster to a purely sentimental meaning requiring the Sovereign to confine his protection of his people, wherever situated, to the acceptance of their own advice. The importance of this step is missed in the conventional interpretation of the Statute of Westminster, the over-obvious being repeated *ad nauseam*, and the significant in it relating to the distant future completely overlooked. The Statute is the first sign, on the far horizon, of man's emancipation from the implications of his own sheepishness in not trusting his individual good sense but pooling his collective self-righteousness in a leader.

The real portent of the Statute is the pleasant discovery that, in replacing with obvious advantage the supreme head of the Constitution of a group of nations by a figurehead, men might soon discover the advantage of replacing the executives, and finally the legislature, by similarly impotent recipients of contradictory advice – figureheads whose constitutional stoppage of decision must automatically immobilise any foreseen formation of acknowledged group evil. Finally, there will have to be a world figurehead, similarly placed, before man enters upon his full estate.

In remote days collective fear hid behind the lowest cunning of a leader who contrived to bring the worst out of his followers. Mankind has at last reached a level of critical civilisation in the independent average members of the community considerably above the level of its leaders. The future of civilisation accordingly depends on the ability of the many to dispense with the services of the few who, by their notorious propensities for leadership, demonstrate by their ambition (never honest) their congenital inferiority to the moral average of mankind.

Although conscious of the increasing rather than diminishing importance of the Crown in the British Constitution, Arthur Balfour, on one occasion at least, showed a lack of respect for the Sovereign's person. By unanimous vote the best – positively the best – mannered man on either side of the century, he was not loved by the Queen, who took exception precisely to his want of manners. Arthur Balfour, since his very birth completely at ease with every sort and condition of people, had not noticed the baleful look in his Queen as he approached dangerously near to her little fireside carpet, a sovereign island which no foot other than her own had ever dared touch. And he, unaware of the look, of growing, almost agonised horror with which she tried to stare off the final calamity, he, so full of elegant philosophical doubt, had shown no hesitation whatever in – yes, clumsily planting both his feet on her carpet.

The Queen's opinion is not available: though we know what she said about Carlyle, who, with a blunt "You'll pardon an infirm old man, Ma'am," sat down in her presence. Her words, spoken after he had left, were, "What a strange man, Mr. Carlyle!"

35

HIERARCHIES OF INTELLECT

The world of Time provides a curious lopsided mirror of the future life, responding to a different set of values, but having this in common with our waking life – a boundless faculty for accommodating, in a given space and time on the same earth-ball, an infinite diversity of private universes. Here was a Queen, the most obvious of visible emblems of consequence, cutting a line between herself and other inhabitants of the same globe, not content to be the normal head of an empire extending over five continents, but also arrogating for herself the sole right of a little carpet. There was Arthur Balfour, within a year of being the actual head of the same empire, balancing his eminence as a man of action by leaning at the other extreme of distinction on philosophic doubt.

The man of action is the coachman on his box, driving a team of horses before him merrily with his whip. The man of thought is his own horse, plodding laboriously through the sleet and mire of life. Winston Churchill, who took to rhetoric as other men take to the bottle, was puzzled by Arthur Balfour's fastidiousness in groping with the pen after the *mot juste*. As soon dawdle over the wine list! The spoken word, flown in a second from his lips, irretrievable, reported, recorded, printed and bound in Hansard, had no terrors for Balfour, who seemed to speak without preparation, conscious that, given any argument, he could develop it with precision and elegance. But when it came to writing, he was overcome by self-consciousness, or perhaps by the knowledge that, time being of no account, there was always room for improvement. He deleted, transposed and rewrote every paragraph and sentence. "He entered the tabernacle of literature," says Churchill – a sentence not without unconscious humour, coming as it does from one who identified literature with the churning out of metaphor and bombast – "under a double dose of the humility and awe which are proper."

Were there a hierarchy of literary values visible to all, readers and critics alike would not so readily fall dupes of mere prestige values – that is, reputations themselves in constant fluctuation in an erratic reputation-market. But, like the admonition addressed to the self-styled superman Faust by him whom he had erroneously conceived to be his equal, the Spirit of the Earth – "*Du gleichst dem Geist, den du begreifst, nicht mir!*"[1]

From this inevitable if diverse limitation of critical measure springs the curious chaos of 'importance', of 'seriousness', of 'value', assigned by readers and critics to mere subjects as constituting prior claims on their esteemed literary attention. For the Curzon type of mind, deeming the Empire as under Providence the greatest agency for good, romantic imperialism in the nineteen-hundreds eclipsed in 'seriousness of purpose' any other subject of the Word, save the pious prestige traditionally conceded by good patriots to the Word of God. To such readers Sir John Seely, Regius Professor of History at Cambridge and one of the principal founders of romantic imperialisms; Froude and Dilke, its loud-speakers; Rudyard Kipling, its minstrel; and Joseph Chamberlain, its impresario, romantic imperialism, must appear as the most significant and serious wielders of words.

Yet Bernard Shaw, leaning on Ibsen, who had blazed a trail with his championing of Nora's right to exist independently of her husband, and had exposed what was putrid about the pillars of society, Bernard Shaw, by letting his invective fly at the opponents of world socialism, considered himself, and was considered by readers and playgoers sharing his views, a sounder judge of literary values than Kipling who was, not to mince words, a forerunner of fascism.

If Shaw was in the forefront, while Kipling lingered in the jungle, it might be claimed for Kipling that his jingoism was in advance of Shaw's socialism, inasmuch as it smacked of Nietzsche's transvaluation of all values which devalued Shaw and Ibsen and raised Kipling to the height of a racial philosophy looking down with contempt on the slave morality implied in the greatest happiness of the greatest number. But it could be claimed for Shaw that his school was still in advance of Kipling's, Shaw

[1] "You equal the spirit that you comprehend, not me!"

having lifted bodily Nietzsche's superman (Nietzsche having helped himself to Goethe's),[1] while Kipling's claim rested on having no ideas at all, his resemblance to Nietzsche, who was profound if incoherent, being vitiated by Kipling's transparent simplicity, capable of vulgarising Nietzsche without understanding him. As, moreover, Nietzsche's own mental mechanism had not been able to withstand the wear and tear of reconciling the pretensions with the integrity of his thought, this was unsurprising.

While Shaw, holding Nietzsche's superman-baby in his arms, looked like winning the race with his *Quintessence of Ibsenism* and repeated assertions that 'high dramatic art *does* mean Ibsen', Chehov away in Russia wrote to a manager, "What do you want to be producing Ibsen for? It's an old play, and bad, old I mean in the bad sense."

Chehov, whose influence was not realised until the nineteen-twenties, was head and shoulders above the Shaws and Ibsens who called shapes into being, not to be, but to prove something. On Shaw's own confession, intellect was a stick to beat anyone with that you might fancy. Like history books, Shaw's plays were adapted to prove a case. Ibsen's dramas, while also constructed on a mechanistic causal pattern, yet exuded some nostalgia for an elusive beauty suggested even in a title – like *The Lady from the Sea*. Slow, cumbrous, prosy, the causal levers chug and clink their utilitarian message, which, if it is an art, is but a pious fraud. Yet something faintly beautiful is disengaged, some feeling of a northern shore and a yearning – for what? What Nora or Dr. Stockmann won in their fight against the family or society is of a merely utilitarian interest. Literature, though Shaw was of the opinion that the character of the combat forged its own weapon of style, is not a scuffle. Literature is not an argument, but the physiognomic charm of phenomena. It is the scenting of a world-secret contained, not in the Absolute presumed to hide the meaning of existence, but rather in the noumenon, the subject of the object. "Do not, I beg of you," Goethe pleaded, "look for anything behind phenomena. They are their own lesson."

By that he certainly did not mean the Zola kind of realism, taking a pride in the detailed knowledge of its organisation, like the regulations of a hospital or factory – "This is how we carry on here" – an initiation into the routine of an accepted self-contained life, inartistic, unchristian and unmystic. That was not Chehov's kind of realism, which, side by side with what *was*, suggested that which all hearts yearned for as the real life. "It is not sufficiently considered," said Doctor Johnson, "that men more frequently require to be reminded than informed." Despising

---

[1] Faust, who calls himself a superman, is at once the superman and the ass inevitable in a conception which impels a man consciously to raise his stature by standing on his toes.

111

the causal logical method borrowed from our ripest and strictest science, physics, which historians and would-be scientific novelists use with a superficiality that is an outrage on science, Chehov, with all his medical training, sensed the secret of literature, which was the quest for the poetry of life. Chehov neither dissected living corpses, nor probed the meaning of life. He neither despised human nature nor conceived it as his duty to pay compliments to his characters. With an unerring instinct he knew that the motive-force of literature was to express the spirit of the object by pressing the fulcrum of the lever – a tiny movement releasing enormous forces. That was art.

He was concerned with our common humanity. He did not different-iate between strong and weak, good and bad, successes and failures, suspecting that those who would have liked him to eschew misfits and write only of the strong, the sound and successful, missed his keen vision, which discerned the common denominator beneath their illu-sions when he knew quite well that by the strong and sound and success-ful heroes and heroines they would have liked him to depict in his pages they meant themselves. Of whom indeed he had been writing.

Instead he distilled beauty out of life by seeing the eternal aspect of ephemeral existence. A poet in narrative and dramatic prose, he watched the great passing stream around him, and what he caught in his mesh were images of an undying reality.

"Everything that is exact is meaningless," says Spengler. Which, if you consider this statement by asking what is the meaning, the *exact* meaning of meaning, is reasonable. It indeed furnished Nietzsche with food for thought as he refined on the meaning of the universe being, as it seemed to him in afterthought in the lunatic asylum, a moral and not an artistic unity, the precision of the meaning of the universe as an artistic unity having contributed to the test qualifying him for admission as an inmate. Life is wiser than reason. Life *is*, and so being, it has nothing to reason about: while reason is only a partial discovery of what *is* – in-complete and therefore inquisitive. And dear Arthur, with all his delet-ing, rewriting and transposing of philosophic doubt, in an effort to fix his meaning with precision, also only succeeded in defining doubt so exactly as to make it doubtful.

The combination of the most abstruse of intellectual pursuits, metaphysics, which he wore like a buttonhole, with the most powerful of occupations, the premiership, however, ensured his prestige. He was, by his colleagues, supposed to be rendering some ineluctable service to Pure Thought. But even the English, Hugh Kingsmill thought, would not have been bowled over by a Minister of the Crown who was also a metaphysician had they known that metaphysics was but Greek for supernatural, which was but Latin for God. "His idea of seeing life in the raw was to stroll across from Carlton House Terrace to the Athenaeum, where the finer minds of the Universities, the pick of our clergy, and the flower of our Bench, quivered with expectation before he opened his lips, and relaxed with a rapturous sigh as soon as he had closed them." What few understood in the nineteen-hundreds, and as few understand to-day, is that the hierarchy of intellect is not one of subject, but of vision. It was not British imperialism or international socialism which determined the significance, the 'importance', of a work of literature, but the scenting of a world secret in the physiognomy of things, the disengaging of that pleasure which, as Wordsworth says, is in life itself.

Perhaps no one of his contemporaries quite equalled Tolstoy in his ability to communicate that sense of destiny which clings to childhood, the feeling that you, and not the pious fraud of utilitarian abstractions barking at you from lectern and pulpit, are the meaning of what is to happen; that feeling of significance in the surrounding world when the infant thinks the cupboard breathes at him, only caught in later years by the perennial youth whose other name is genius, still basking in the poetry of life, a penumbra glowing with significance around the wondering soul in a still miracle of being.

The sense of such significance, successfully communicated, may be said, by its own scales of literary values, to be the only thing perhaps that literature would feel to be at all 'significant'.

36

LENIN AND THE CLASS STRUGGLE

Finding the imperial government of Russia unsympathetic to his ideas involving its liquidation, Lenin went abroad, notably to Switzerland, where he urged the Swiss workers, lamentably deficient in class hatred, to throw over their government. It is strange that political fugitives, such as Lenin and later Mussolini, having the unrivalled opportunity during their stay in Switzerland to learn how the exemplary inter-racial, supranational State is run, not only learn nothing but, after attempting without success to wreck the model State which has given them refuge, are also impatient to get home with a view to wrecking their own.

In 1902 Lenin lived in London, editing his paper *Iskra* (*The Spark*), a communist publication distributed by underground channels. A small, stocky, carrot-haired young man of thirty-two, he spent his days at Clerkenwell Green in a tiny room assigned to him by the Twentieth Century Press. Lenin and his wife, Krupskaya, lived in Sidmouth Street, off Gray's Inn Road, in two furnished rooms under the assumed name of Richter. The landlady was not a little exorcised over their identity; what troubled her was not that a man whose real name was Ulianov but who was known as Lenin, though he called himself Richter, should have a wife known as Krupskaya, but whether they were really married. In an England which admitted refugees from every quarter of the globe without a passport, identity was immaterial. English cooking caused havoc with their digestion, and Krupskaya refers in her letters to the ordeal of Nikolai Illyich. One must have an English stomach, she laments, to cope with the oxtails and roast beef, pudding and tart and what-not. Had he been a doctor, or himself immune from constipation, Lenin, with his *idée fixe*, might have attributed all the ills of mankind to failure of the digestive organs.

This was the England which, with her ships sailing around the Cape of Good Hope, to Eastern Africa, to India, China and Japan, Australia and New Zealand and the Americas, had spun a vast economic web around the world, with the commercial spider waiting in London. Nothing on that scale has been known in the ancient or medieval world. Parallel with this expansion, whose motive power was profit, a system of civil liberty had sprung up, resting on Magna Charta and developing erratically into the Petition of Right, the Bill of Rights, the Declaration of Rights, the Declaration of Independence (an American shoot off the same branch of liberty), the Utilitarians, the Positivists, the Negations of the Manchester School leading to Cobden and Bright and Free Trade, the Single Taxers, and the Fabian Society, working towards a broadening tolerance and liberalism which lasted until the Great War.

Superbly conscious of the stability and permanence of their world, the denizens of this mild land felt secure in venting freely their occasional disgust with each other's politics, so dissipating their will to action, as well as any loftier 'Utopian' ideals, in free speech and a free press, without ever coming seriously to blows. There was untrammelled free speech in the magnificent London parks, restricted only by the curious, essentially English, Old Testament idea of the prohibitive Sabbath: that something should be closed, some time, for appearance sake – in this case, the public lavatories banging their doors in the face of the public at dusk, on the assumption that the internal irrigation of human beings stops likewise at that sinful hour.

With characteristic Russian intellectual *largesse*, Lenin, overlooking the more flagrant social abuses in his own country, riveted his eyes on the unhealthy conditions he espied under the unwritten British Constitution, and predicted an early revolution in England. Having done nothing at home beyond promoting a few strikes at the British-owned cotton mills in St. Petersburg, to be comfortably exiled to Siberia, where he took a heavy toll of bird life, once abroad Lenin did little beyond predicting a revolution where it has still not occurred, to the exclusion of a revolution at home which, but a few weeks before its outbreak, he prophesied that he and his generation would not live to see. Where industrialism had reached its peak, as it had done in England, *there* inevitably dissolution claimed priority by Marxist right of way. To prove this, he cited chapter and verse from Karl Marx's 'Bible of the Working Class'. Agrarian Russia he scheduled last for revolution. A major war would, however, suffice to rend England's social structure from top to bottom.

But both Karl Marx, despite his lengthy residence in Soho, and Lenin, apparently no better informed even after his stay in a Bloomsbury boarding-house, did not grasp the central all-pervading British social fact – to wit, that, industrialism and trade-unionism notwithstanding, the style of life in England was unregenerately medieval. And this by virtue of a standardised ideal, apparently as irresistible to all as it is attainable *in abstract principle* by all: the mass-production of young aristocrats out of plebeian raw material at our model factories – the public schools. The line of demarcation between the two English nations (as Disraeli called the rich and poor) is one of vowels. The test distinguishing the young gentleman from his churl-parent is that curious ventriloquism acquired by the finished mass-product – the trade mark of his transformation at the model factory. Plebeian parents, threw their life-savings into reclamation from the encroaching proletarian sea of their own particular patch of offspring, lovingly assigned for hothouse culture, but as often as not producing dead-sea fruit. The habit of raising the chin, from the symbolic elevation letting a fluty string of words flow down the unrestricted pipe to reach the humble man who pulls his throat in, talking in a thick husky voice, swallowing his words, but instinctively considering the pulling in of his own chin as tallying with both the manly and the humble attitude incumbent on his menial station – here is the absurd, the tragic, the shamefully pathetic line of demarcation which nothing short of a uniform educational system will ever obliterate. The only solution for England, given its characteristics, lies not in abolition of aristocracy but in making everyone an aristocrat, in theory. The shortest road in education is the abolition of all schools and universities, save Eton and Oxford, all other local schools and universities being considered as their branches.

115

To the clear-headed Lenin, the self-apparent truth that educational equality meant social equality was axiomatic in his teens. He was not the son of a peasant or workman, but of a provincial schoolteacher, with nothing but his revolutionary bent to prevent him from making as brilliant a legal career for himself as, say, Sir Stafford Cripps. He was born in the middle distance, and that is where all men, he judged, should start the race. People in privileged positions mistook, and still mistake, the sorry fact of others of necessity adjusting themselves to subordinate positions, even cheerfully submitting to an acknowledged social inferiority, for positive enjoyment of their relative positions. Village hands proffering due respect to, say, a retired Anglo-Indian colonel settled in the village in his predestined niche of patronising gentry – what could be more natural and, to judge by the smiles and cap-touching of village folk, what, to them, more gladdening? Galsworthy in *The Silver Box* reproduces the flavour of a typical conversation of the moneyed classes on the subject of the dispossessed. Among the things Mrs. Bethwick, wife of a Liberal member of parliament, has to say to her husband is, "I've no patience with your talk of reform – all that nonsense about social policy. Those Socialists and Labour men are an absolutely selfish set of people. They have no sense of patriotism, like the upper classes, they simply want what we've got . . . Quite uneducated men! Wait until they begin to tax our investments. I'm convinced that when they once get a chance they will tax everything – they've no feeling for the country . . . Education is simply ruining the lower classes. It unsettles them, and that's the worst thing for us all. I see an enormous difference in the manner of servants." *The Forsyte Saga* contains the record of a caste which, while willing to impose a certain discipline of behaviour and obligation upon its own members, so that the England they have loved may remain just as they love it best, with their own hegemony un-impaired, yet consider the rest of the population as almost a race apart. To love your own country, however, is something distinct from praising only colonels, bishops, and viceroys. Well may one ask, what is this famous love of one's own country, usually taking the form of hating two-thirds of the people who live in it? It cannot be merely houses and scenery.

The grey-haired duty-conscious Lady Jeans and Lady Margarets, who knew their rightful place in the universe, kept their distance in peacetime and during the war became aloofly useful, writing letters in hospitals for wounded Tommies (who would have much preferred a blonde bombshell to do it for them), have been freely praised for their remarkable *sang froid* in facing the seemy side of life. They were, however, merely giving expression to a moral rhetoric which afflicts the Anglo-Saxon (whereas the German is a prey to martial rhetoric) enabling Lady Jean to feel good while expending her energies on the 'nation' as distinct from 'the masses'. There was, and is, of course, that legend dear to politicians, of all callings enjoying the utmost licence of irresponsibility, called 'consciousness of one's responsibility', a myth traceable to the squire's wife disposing of her surplus rags to the poorest of their tenants. To enjoy anything at all in England was invariably to bear heavy responsibility. A distant relative unexpectedly inheriting a property of several thousand acres would speak of this windfall as a trust he hoped to be able to discharge with dignity. He would speak of being gravely conscious of his responsibilities to his tenants, even as he blows away the fortune at baccarat in Deauville. It is not hypocrisy. It is not conscious self-deception. It is what it purports to be: consciousness of one's responsibility, if irresponsibly conceived.

The sheer ingenuity of the British social system – ingenuity, if one could believe it consciously invented by a lover of *status quo* – is an immaculate *perpetuum mobile* in reality far beyond the wits of any man to invent. It just came about. Diverse invaders, constituting several layers of over-lords on the one hand, and a backward rustic native population on the other, have contrived to keep alive the idea of primordial social inequality. Trading opportunities offered by an uncommonly favourable geographical situation which had placed this little isle between the old and the new world, were duly seized, without, however, either bursting the medieval mould of liege and vassal, gentleman and churl, or for that matter inducing anyone to step out of the immemorial social rut of king, bishop, baron, squire, parson, farmer, 'hand'.

The secret of English 'superiority' is to be found in the unassailable prestige which always clings to the aloof. The distinguishing atmosphere exuded by this wet little island, lying a little apart from but on visiting terms with Europe, is the moral rhetoric characteristic of shy old maids who 'like to keep themselves to themselves'. She has become an oddly valiant old maid, a sort of Miss Prism of *The Importance of Being Earnest* defending her chastity. The aloof, by virtue of the refining influences of their loneliness, are apt to be quiet and gentle-mannered if distantly censorious, as such arousing in the boisterous an abashed, reverent interest. From gentility bred in aloofness to the ready inference, drawn from a sense of one's own seclusion, that gentle ways imply the possession of virtue, is but a step, and to regard success as the outer and visible sign of an inner invisible grace is another. Where self-flattering inferences are drawn with more facility than self-criticism you get moral rhetoric, which is an attempt to persuade others to confirm something too good for us to believe ourselves.

Moral rhetoric advertising your gentle virtues, magnified by outer

117

success, swells into social rhetoric advertising your general exclusiveness. You like to keep yourself to yourself, and to such as yourself.
Social exclusiveness is its own propaganda, securing a painful leverage
on the vanity of aspirants: are they included? Are they excluded? And
why? It is another unwritten Constitution. For the most churlish of
mankind do not live by bread alone: they require also approbation. And
who indeed dispenses the most effectual approbation? The very few,
who have made a corner in approbation, and style themselves polite
society.

That is the English style. It is a style expressing itself even in urban
architecture, the characteristic being a baronial aloofness with not
enough space in which to unfold it, the flaunting of a pillared portico
denoting 'we keep ourselves to ourselves', not buried in parks but
jostling all together, the identical design of exclusive wedding-cake
ornamentation repeated all along the row, each portico fatuously projecting a stiff upper lip at its neighbours, all alike as peas. Man was not
perhaps made for style, but style for man. Yet it does not seem so, at any
rate in England, where style, changing but on the surface, dominates
everything. Style, moreover, as ably demonstrated by Spengler, is not
the product of material, of technique, or of purpose. It is the opposite of
this, a savour inaccessible to reason, a revelation of the metaphysical
order, a mysterious imperative, a facet, or what Santayana might call a
manifestation of an essence of indispensable Being, a Destiny which,
though it absorbs material elements, overrides and shapes them according to largely unknown laws of a morphology still in its infancy.

It is that which men and women wish to feel that shapes their style of
life. Americans, while they were still pioneers, dour rebels from
Europe, were, in their revolt against the established order, confirmed
egalitarians. That, sentimentally, by force of wish, is the spirit that
pervades them still. It is the morphology of America to which Americans
conform in sentiment and from which they will not be diverted even by
fact. But having settled down and begun to employ others as his servants, the pioneer created a labour problem which was to assume the
same character as masters against men as in old Europe from which the
social and religious rebel had escaped to a pioneering freedom, a freedom which, to be complete, will, in default of a full-fledged socialism to
which the spirit of individual American initiative is averse, fulfil itself in
a benevolent capitalism. Of such benevolent capitalism, assured a sustained world market by the universal endowment of the world citizen
with a minimum unearned increment to guarantee the individual against
want and exploitation, more will be found in the epilogue.

37

THE HELLA MEETING

Meanwhile Marcel Proust, soon to begin his *magnum opus*, to lay bare before us the frauds and self-deceptions of society, was continuing to take his dispositions in the drawing-rooms of Paris. The world of politics still awaits its Proust who, truly 'taking the long view', will X-ray its illusions, its vast pretensions, futile exertions, its assumed 'long views' of future circumstances and conditions which wiser men know to be incalculable. At the head of the German Government was a witty, cultivated and, for a German, suave, diplomatist brought up for much of his time in France and England, for ever 'finesseing', but who, beneath such amiable veneer, expressed his unfaltering belief in the law of the jungle. "A considerable number of people," Prince von Bülow, Chancellor of the Second Reich, complained, 'particularly in Germany, did not realise that the will to power is the mainspring and soul of any great State." All he really found to deprecate in his compatriots was their failure "to appreciate the importance of good breeding in international intercourse" with a predatory end in view.

While taking a low view of the general decency of the ordinary citizen, far ahead of the political morality of his rulers, Bülow was debasing the conception of nations to the functions of red and white corpuscles contending blindly in the blood – an impulse of which the ordinary decent citizen, who was the battlefield, was not himself conscious, unless something got his blood up for him to spill it on another battlefield and deprive the red and white corpuscles of their own. Germany, brandishing the sword, was also inculcating the will to power into a feudal half-dormant Japan, grafting on to a sleepy orient, inadvisedly awakened by the West, a militant modern 'soul'. Like the famous hostesses of the Paris drawing-rooms, who went to war over their lions, dragging the lions into the fray by assuring them that they were fighting their cause, so did political leaders the world over involve their peoples in quarrels of their own making and then call on them to see them through. Such adolescent display made a strong appeal to a boy, then at the awkward age of thirteen, who was to make himself no less awkward to the world at large when, thirty-seven years older, without a corresponding advance in moral development, he was to tell a muzzled Reichstag that if he was to mind what other nations thought fit to think of his war on Poland, then "I congratulate you! Germany might just as well give up once and for all any idea of playing at high politics in Europe!" What nation outside Bedlam and Germany *wants* its trusted stewards to play high politics? While the people worked and loved, trusted and laid by for an old age they thought they might be allowed to spend in security, the itch of diplomacy spread like eczema over the skin of life, to defeat their hopes.

Prince Bülow, in view of the Tsar's intimation that he was bringing his Foreign Minister, was accompanying the Kaiser to Hella. When Bülow boarded the Kaiser's yacht *Hohenzollern* at Kiel, Ambassador von Tschirschky, seconded from the German Foreign Office for duty with the Kaiser, wrung the Chancellor's hands in despair. The Kaiser, he wailed, had negatived all his fervent and reasoned arguments for conferring the traditional Order of the Black Eagle on Count Lambsdorff, the Russian Foreign Minister.

The Kaiser approached them, and Tschirschky discreetly retired, leaving Bülow to tackle the monarch. Bülow, who rather fancied himself as a master of elegant persiflage, made bold to remind his sovereign of Napoleon's aphorism that what children's toys were to the nursery, decorations were to politics: "*Les hommes sont comme les enfants, il leur faut des hochets.*" Moreover, Lambsdorff was as sensitive to snubs as he was vindictive. Why gratuitously offend a Foreign Minister of a great power whose friendship was a moment to Germany?

The Kaiser's reply, surprising in its violence, was that he could not 'throw away' his highest decoration. Bitterly he complained that Bülow cared nothing for sentiment, only for politics. The Kaiser's deepest, nay, most sacred feelings must go by the board to serve the political machinations of his Chancellor! Now Tschirschky understood him better. Tschirschky had just agreed that it was indeed a very good idea not to confer the exalted Order of the Black Eagle on a fellow like Lambsdorff.

Tschirschky at this moment reappeared on deck. Motioning to him to come nearer, and fixing him with a sharp inquisitorial eye, Bülow questioned him loudly whether he thought it a very good idea to advise His Majesty to insult the Russian Foreign Minister. Tschirschky coloured deeply and, in his confusion, made no answer. Bülow continued to badger his sovereign who, at last, to throw off such insufferable importunity from his servant, suddenly lifted the whole matter out of Bülow's hands. He would, said the Kaiser, sound his dear friend, cousin and trusted colleague, Nicky himself, as to which Prussian decoration he judged best for his own minister.

On board the yacht there was an elegant, rich, hilarious Austrian nobleman, Prince Max Fürstenberg, who cracked jokes and kissed the Kaiser's hand incessantly, and courted Bülow's favour, but whose presence was resented by the Russians, who asked, "What would you have said if the Tsar had brought a prominent Frenchman to his meeting with your Emperor?" Fürstenberg's ambition was to keep the Kaiser amused. Every morning he had the latest Stock Exchange joke telegraphed to him in time to regale the Kaiser at breakfast. And, a nobleman without being a gentleman, he extracted what fun he could from commenting on other people's appearance.

Fancying themselves in their new yachting rig-out, the pair of them, emperor and courtier, stood at the rail, and Fürstenberg directed his gracious host's attention to the gangway below. Both roared as they spied the tiny figure of Count Lambsdorff on high heels, in a big Russian civil service hat, accomplish an undignified transfer from a small rocking boat in a tumbling sea on to the heaving gang-plank of the *Hohenzollern*.

Lambsdorff was a bad sailor. He looked green in the face. In his Russian civil service uniform he resembled an elderly customs officer rather than a Foreign Minister. The Kaiser, encouraged by Fürstenberg's buffooneries, now saw fit to rag his Russian guest about his apparent lack of nautical skill. The Minister, keyed up for a formal reception, was embarrassed, since obviously he could not bandy jokes with a sovereign.

Then the Tsar came on board. Bülow found Nicholas II as different in appearance from his father, the gigantic Alexander III, as from the stately and tall Alexander II, his grandfather. He was short, slender, small-limbed, delicate-looking, but sound in wind and limb. He had beautiful grey-blue eyes, soulful and melancholy, long and slender hands, a soft caressing voice. But in particular Bülow was struck by the Tsar's manners.

It was, after all, over three hundred years since the obscure provincial little landowner Romanov had added his pretty daughter Anastasia as his particular quota to the total of possible brides, from which Ivan the Terrible in the finals chose her as his wife. Owing to filicide and infanticide, no issue of that union survived, the first Romanov tsar being but Anastasia's nephew's son, without a drop of the ancient Rurik blood. Still, since 1613, they had now been sovereigns of Russia. But, here again, what advantage fate bestows with one hand it withdraws with another. After the death of Peter the Great's younger daughter, Elizabeth, in 1761, the line becomes more than a little blurred. The Romanovs, indisputably Romanovs when the lineage was obscure, having become illustrious cease to be Romanovs by fact and become Romanovs by surmise and courtesy. But it was the same everywhere, more or less. It is amusing, when dealing with royal and aristocratic pretensions to a magnificent lineage, to discover that none of them had been anything to begin with, and when at last they were somebodies, were hard put to it, as in this case, to provide an authentic sprig of the original nobody. The Tudors sprang from a steward; the Bourbons from a butler; the Plantagenets from a marauding freebooter and a village wench. King David was a shepherd – not, of course, to say a Jew.

But there he was, little Nicholas II, such as he was with brains such as he had, the offspring of a bull-necked father, an irascible mother, yet, all that notwithstanding, a very great gentleman with manners of perfect courtesy and simplicity and equality to all. Had Bülow never known him by sight, he would have recognised him in a London, Vienna, or Paris drawing-room, in St. Moritz or Biarritz "as a gentlemanly young fellow, perhaps," he says, "an Austrian count or the son of an English duke". He was as considerate and courteous with his staff as if he were dealing with foreign crowned heads. He had that natural instinctive courtesy which takes the form of treating everyone alike. He wore invariably the uniform of a colonel, the rank he had reached at his father's death, and as few orders as possible.

The Tsar liked simplicity. The Kaiser liked swagger. William II was tireless in inventing medals, aiguillettes, clasps of all sorts to exchange with his dearest friend Nicky, to cement still further, he thought, their solidarity. While he bestowed these endless decorations on the Tsar, Nicky thanked him most courteously, looking earnestly at him out of his soulful eyes, and then put them away in a drawer, never to take them out save when – oh dear! again! – about to face Willy.

Again dinner. Again the Tsar had a long and serious talk with Bülow. Again they impressed on each other that unless Russia and Germany remained friendly and at peace, 'en paix et en amitié', they would destroy each other.[1] The Tsar said that no one stood to gain anything in a Russo-German conflict, save the Poles and the revolutionaries, whereas both dynasties would very likely lose their thrones.

In this he proved himself to be a prophet. Then followed a kind of children's Christmas tree: the Tsar produced a St. Andrew and pinned it on the German Chancellor's breast. The Kaiser walked among the Russian guests, distributing Prussian decorations. But Bülow noticed that Lambsdorff, the Russian Foreign Minister, who had retained a cheerful face despite the Kaiser's jokes about his lack of nautical talent, now wore a discontented, venomous expression. Lambsdorff finally came up to Bülow, like a waiter who had been scandalously undertipped and felt himself to be the butt of his comrades, and told him politely but with ill-disguised rage that Bülow's most gracious sovereign had evidently not seen fit to give him the Black Eagle, hitherto considered as the only decoration possible for a Russian Foreign Minister.

When Bülow remonstrated with his sovereign for giving the man who

[1] As Molotov and Ribbentrop assured each other in August of 1939.

shaped Russia's foreign policy a decoration which even Germans did not want to possess, as it was associated with generals who were being retired on half pay, the Kaiser said that Tsar Nicholas himself had told him that he would be 'particularly grateful' if the Kaiser Wilhelm Order, created by his true friend and cousin Willy and designed by that very same exalted Majesty's own hand, were conferred upon his Foreign Minister. The Tsar, anxious not to offend the Kaiser, whose friendship he also deemed to be of moment to Russia, had made the request he thought most pleasing to Willy, however, by jeopardising his own Foreign Minister's goodwill.

No one, adds Prince Bülow, could care less for outward decorations than he himself. Quite apart from his philosophy grounded on inward merit, he was indifferent to these baubles because he possessed (here his tone suddenly changes to one of earnest meticulousness) all the following decorations: the High Order of the Black Eagle with Diamonds; the Spanish Golden Fleece; the Russian Order of St. Andrew with Diamonds; the Austrian Order of St. Stephen with Diamonds; the Italian Order of the Sacred Annunciation; the Order of the Annunciation, and the Very Noble Portuguese Order of the Tower and the Sword; the Danish Order of the Elephant, and the Swedish Seraphine Order; the Bavarian Order of St. Hubert; the Saxon Order of the Diamond, and Turkish and Japanese, Chinese and Siamese Orders. "I have all of them, all of them!"

38

SHAW AND TOLSTOY, CHEHOV AND GORKY

Bernard Shaw sent the greater writer of the Russian soil his *The Shewing Up of Blanco Posnet*, which drew a blank from Tolstoy, who answered that he 'looked forward to reading it with interest'. Which, in authors' vocabulary, may be taken to mean that he had already dipped into the thing without much interest and had elected to write before he had to confess disappointment. In his accompanying letter Shaw stressed that virtue was ineffective because habitually clothed in pious language, and would gain by the prestige of blunt, full-blooded, pithy speech, in which vice masquerades attractively before an admiring adolescent world.

This suggestion also seems to have drawn a blank. Virtue knocked dumb by meakness drew tears from Tolstoy's old eyes, and he could not see it swaggering in jackboots.

But the letter is the key to Shaw. He is a swaggerer, and he knows it and enjoys it. A man in trepidation of most things, he takes a double step. Metaphorically; even physically, as he strides up like a conqueror before the cine-camera. He adds an incongruous flourish of defiance to his old-maid's signature; uses belligerent barrack-room terms to convey Salvation Army sentiments. When, if the truth were known, it would be an adventure for him to cross a ditch. His professed competence in pugilism is an instinctive – and prophetic – wish to turn the tables on a latent future fascism.

And there is, parallel with this inverted timidity, a curious social snobbery about Shaw, which is effectively inverted. Positively nothing could have pleased Shaw more than that Winston Churchill, grandson of a duke, should have confirmed seriously a claim Shaw had put forward waggishly, that with a baronet for cousin he, Shaw, belonged in fact to the upper, not the middle, classes. Churchill, whose claims as a writer were about as legendary as Shaw's blue blood, must have been extremely gratified, some thirty years later, to see himself described as a real writer in a Sunday article entitled 'The Amazing Winston' by G. Bernard Shaw, following on the previous Sunday's article again mentioning the baronet cousin in support of Shaw's aristocratic origin, and entitled 'The Amazing Shaw' by Winston S. Churchill. Bombast and swagger at the peak of their respective careers, riding past and exchanging salutes.

Yes, all bounce and swagger, and his own half-sly enjoyment of it, Shaw's wit is just the kind that he unsuccessfully commended to Tolstoy's attention – the use of robust expressions in defence of meek causes.

There is a Russian saying, "No matter so long as the baby is not crying." Bernard Shaw described Tolstoy as Russia's baby: it didn't matter what went on in Russia so long as Tolstoy was not crying. For if he cried, all Europe cried 'Shame!' With an international reputation as firmly established as Tolstoy's, there was not much that the authorities could do against him. To send him to gaol, to exile him to Siberia, only meant cutting off their own nose to spite their face. Twenty years later, the British Raj in India had the same trouble with a disciple of Tolstoy, one Gandhi, who was intermittently being locked up and brought out of gaol for a conference with the Viceroy, soliciting the favour of his good offices, until it became increasingly apparent that the lords spiritual had an awkward way of defying the lords temporal, all the while refusing point blank to defy anyone. "If you have a baby," Bernard Shaw said, "who can speak with tsars in the gate, who can make Europe and

America stop and listen when he opens his mouth, who can smite with unerring aim straight at the sorest spots in the world's conscience, who can break through all censorships and all barriers of language, who can thunder on the gates of the most terrible prisons in the world and place his neck under the keenest and bloodiest axes only to find that for him the gates dare not open and the axes dare not fall, then indeed you have a baby that must be nursed and coddled and petted and let go his own way.''

Not since the days of Goethe, to whom Byron addressed a letter, 'Illustrious Sir', signing himself the humble, obedient servant of one 'for fifty years the undisputed sovereign of European literature', had there been another such universally acknowledged monarch of the mind, a position not surpassed even by that of Victor Hugo or Tennyson. People collected Tennyson's pipes, he was raised to the peerage and made a fuss of by the Queen, but his fame was confined to England and, at most, America. On the day of his jubilee, Tolstoy received an address of homage couched approximately in the terms Byron had addressed to Goethe, to which many English writers had appended their signatures, notably Bernard Shaw and H. G. Wells. In Russia, of course, the jubilee was the occasion for a pilgrimage to Yasnaya Polyana, in anticipation of which event Tolstoy kept wincing for a week. Asked whether he too was going over to Yasnaya Polyana for the jubilee, Chehov said no. Tolstoy's entire life was a jubilee, and he saw no point in adding to his embarrassment on the very day on which Tolstoy might feel he had earned a day off. The day, however, arrived. The front door bell never ceased ringing. Deputies representing a multitude of cultural associations, as well intentioned as they were usually devoid of understanding, presented illuminated addresses couched in the stiffest and flattest terms, and read them aloud.

Such was his fame that when, long before his jubilee, he occasionally came to Moscow, the news having spread, all Moscow would turn out into the streets to catch a glimpse of the great man, who had perhaps only come to do a little shopping. The streets would be lined as though for a royal procession. In the station people climbed the lamp-posts and even hung from the roofs to catch a glimpse of Lev Nikolaievich. When during his illness he travelled to the Crimea, at every station students filled the platforms and cheered: "Lev Nikolaievich! Dear Lev Nikolaievich!" He stood in the carriage corridor with his hands, as was his custom, thrust deep into the belt buckled over his peasant shirt, and looked at them through the window, large beads of tears rolling down his cheeks.

When he arrived in the Crimea, putting up at a seignorial estate placed at his disposal by some rich and mighty friend, more admirers forced themselves on Tolstoy's attention, and one lady, more vociferous than the rest of the crowd, intoned, "Dear Lev Nikolaievich, I so loved your *Fathers and Children*", untroubled by the detail that the book in question was the work of Turgenev. Doubtless she had confused it with Tolstoy's *Childhood and Adolescence*. There, from his own modest villa he had just built, partly on credit, partly on what remained of the advance from the sale of his Complete Edition, Chehov too paid Tolstoy a visit. Gorky, also due at Yalta, had been notified by Chehov of Tolstoy's impending arrival: "Lev Nikolaievich, who already suffers from a dearth of intellectual intercourse, will be terribly bored here and we must go and see him often." Of all existing Russian writers Tolstoy admired Chehov most, though he did not like his plays. "You know," he said as he saw him out, "I don't like Shakespeare, but his plays are better than yours."

What troubled him about Chehov's plays was that he could not discover what they were *about*. His own plays were about right and wrong. This was simple. They were problem plays. Their problem was invariably that, though it was easy for the playgoer to discover what they were *about*, it was difficult for the characters, and more difficult still for the author, to decide what good, if any, there was in evil, and what evil, if any, in good, and who was which. The hero usually represented a great good man like Tolstoy himself, respected for his principles but derided for their incompatibility with his way of life. The puzzled inertia of the hero, his inability to strike out on a bold line of action without detriment to the interests of the people who had invested their emotions in him, remained the theme of the plays, while suspense and action were supplied by the tragic violence of the surrounding darkness through which his own light shone but fitfully.

Voltaire, Victor Hugo, Byron, Dickens, Tolstoy, Shaw, Gorky, Thomas Mann, are prophets rather than poets, who, to make the world aware of their literary merit, must battle against the established order. At all times the contemporary world responds more immediately to collateral than to aesthetic values in literature. The pure poets, such as Chehov and Proust (neither of them, through poor health, lack of money and lack of time, entirely pure), have a thin time of it. The poet's value rises in the eyes of posterity; the prophet's sinks. The prophet, however, if also a poet, such as Tolstoy, survives in so far as in the heat of the struggle he has discovered and communicated a beauty often more urgent than that of the pure poet who has despised the heat and burden of the day. The poet-rebel, like Hermann Hesse, turns sooner or later from the sheer tendentiousness of rebellion to the contemplation of innocence, admiring a solitary daisy in a field, listening to Mozart, and painting in water-colours.

Gorky noticed that Chehov spoke of Tolstoy's books with the same tender solicitude as he spoke of his own, as though little could be added by 'darkening counsel with words'. Tolstoy himself could not speak of Chehov's *Darling* without tears, comparing it to lace made by a chaste young girl in olden times, a lace-maker 'for ever'. He spoke with great agitation, his eyes full of tears, while the recipient of such imaginative appreciation (inspired criticism, Coleridge held, should take the form of appreciation, there being little point in speaking of what has left one cold), knowing quite well that never while he was alive, or even after he was dead, could he hope to receive appreciation from a more illumined or more tender source, sat there, his head bowed as in flushed embarrassment he was wiping his pince-nez. He had a high temperature that day, Gorky relates, red patches on his cheeks. When Tolstoy finished Chehov was silent for a long time. Then he said in a low, bashful voice, with a sigh, "It has misprints."

When Chehov walked on the lawn with Tolstoy's daughter, Tolstoy sitting on the terrace with Gorky drew his attention: "Look," he said, "how gracefully he treads the grass, elegantly, like a girl. What a marvellous man!"

But he could not take to Gorky. "I don't know what it is," he kept saying to Chehov, "but I can't take to Gorky sincerely." He envied in a way Gorky's origin. He himself would have liked to have risen from the bowels of the earth, to have owed nothing to anybody. Here was Gorky, a village lad, a boy lacking even such a thing as authenticated parents, an apprentice to a village shoemaker, acquiring literacy by his own unaided effort, then wandering on foot athwart and astride the broad acres of Mother Russia, writing bitterly without heed of what the authorities might do to him. Adopting the pen-name of 'Maxim the Bitter' (Maxim Gorky), in a year or two he acquired an enormous army of readers among the workers and students, a little weary of the old Tolstoy, preaching equality but still lingering, decade after decade, on his ancestral estate, and a little sceptical of the delicate consumptive coughing Chehov, coughing too, it seemed, through his diffident stories, while Gorky, arm-in-arm with his friend Chaliapin, is bestriding the banks of the Volga, singing at the top of their voices. "I am more of a *muzhik* than you," Tolstoy said, considering Gorky not without a look of envy.

"What a boast!" replied the culture-conscious Gorky, so immersed of late in European letters that he felt called upon to apologise personally for every ditch and open sewer in Russia. Tolstoy, in his peasant garb, may have looked even more of a peasant than Gorky. But when plebeians, taking Tolstoy's egalitarian principles for granted, treated him as an equal, he would astonish them by suddenly talking to them like a count addressing his serf. Tolstoy had a brother, also a count, since in

Russia a count bred as many counts as he bred sons. Alienated by Tolstoy's anti-clerical and anti-monarchist views, as Tolstoy was by his brother's stupidity, they were in old age brought together. Love shone from the eyes of the stupid brother as he beheld the visage of brother Lev, a love nourished by the recollection of their childhood and over-coming his contempt for the piffle he thought his brother wrote when he would have done far better to stick to Orthodoxy in religion and show an unswerving loyalty to the throne. His brothers had been handsome and dashing; Lev was the ugly duckling who had, moreover, failed at every-thing including the university where, for an unknown reason, he had been reading higher mathematics, at which he failed dismally, failed at everything he tried, until, suddenly, he became not only Russia's but also the world's greatest writer of the age. After that he went on failing in his private life – failing as a husband, failing as a father, as a patriot, as a Christian; turning with disgust upon his writings which, the more he renounced them, the more famous they made him. And here he was, the prisoner of his own renown.

He could not take to Gorky. Gorky's nose, that of a duck, put him off. And neither women nor dogs took to Gorky; significant that! Dogs and women in this respect had an instinct absolutely infallible. Gorky was like a theological student who had been forced into taking Holy Orders against his will. He had the soul of a spy. He'd come, God knows whence, into the land of Canaan, sniffing around everywhere, spying for something to report to his God, and his God was like a water demon with which peasant women frighten their children. Chehov, telling this to Gorky, laughed till the tears ran. Wiping his eyes, he went on, "I said 'Gorky's a good man!' but he insisted, 'No, no, I know.'"

When, having excommunicated him, the Head of the Holy Synod heard that Tolstoy was dangerously ill in the Crimea, he sent two priests in an attempt to extract a confession. He would have liked to be able to publish to the world that Tolstoy had shed his heretical beliefs and returned to the bosom of the Mother Church, confessed and received the Eucharist before his death. But the great writer refused to see the priests, observing to his favourite son, "Tell me, how is it, Sergei, that these gentlemen do not understand that even in the face of death two and two still make four?" The gentlemen returned to St. Petersburg without understanding.

One day when the incredibly wiry old man, far from succumbing to the arms of death, called for a Tartar pony to take him for a ride, Gorky, strolling pensively along the mountain road overlooking the sea, was overtaken by Tolstoy, looking, astride the Tartar pony, like a gnome under a mushroom hat. Tolstoy's brows were knitted, he seemed to be mumbling angrily to himself. Assuming that he was not disposed for conversation, Gorky obligingly hung behind. But turning his head, Tolstoy said sharply, "Where are you off to?" Accommodating the pace of the pony to the brother novelist trotting on his flat feet, he began to vent his anger on him for not knowing whether Andreiev and other contemporary writers believed in God. Conversing angrily about divine love, they came to a bend in the road where, outside the gate of a palatial estate, a group of Grand Dukes, fine strapping men indulging in expensive scent and loud laughter, stood conversing before a riderless mount and another horse harnessed to a cabriolet, completely blocking the way. Gorky speculated how Tolstoy, advancing on his Tartar pony, would solve the problem of overcoming such combined resistance of the reigning dynasty.

As they came level, the Romanovs had turned towards the gate. Tolstoy frowned angrily at their manly backs, and as the Tartar pony advanced, the two highly-bred Romanov stallions sidled nervously to the side of the road, letting Tolstoy pass in triumph. He looked at Gorky, then at the disappearing backs of the Grand Dukes. "Fools!" he said, pandering to Gorky's republican sentiments and to dissipate the last suspicion that Count Tolstoy was, any more than Maxim the Bitter, disposed to compromise with the established order. Then, lest anyone assume that revolutionary leanings in a vagabond could dispute the sedentary eminence of one who could not hope even to spend the night away from his wife without getting into hot water, "Even the horses," he added, "knew they must make way for the great Tolstoy!"

39

DESIGN FOR MURDER

Tolstoy wrote to his sovereign Nicholas II in a tone of one conscious of being, not only Russia's but indeed the world's great luminary trying to adapt himself, not without justifiable irritation, from his pinnacle of intellectual supremacy to the understanding of the poor fish who, by a fluke of fate, found himself sitting on a throne from which he weakly defended the absurd anachronism of absolute power. It has long since, Tolstoy pointed out, been taken for granted in all countries with any pretension to enlightenment that the democratic form of government was the only form compatible with the individual's self-respect, and Russia's backwardness in this respect was a source of astonishment abroad and of unjustifiable humiliation for Russian nationals everywhere.

Tolstoy, in his intellectual attack upon a Tsar who had no intellect, enjoyed advantages, which were, however, parried by the Tsar endowed with a natural advantage of not understanding Tolstoy's intellectual attack.

The political implications of Tolstoy's writing found no favour with the Russian Government, and his interpretation of the Gospels which revealed the priesthood as the modern Sadducees made his name positively obnoxious to the higher clergy. Unlike his father, Alexander III, Nicholas II was tolerant in religious matters, but he was advised that the orthodoxy and autocracy hung together on what the Bolsheviks later described as the opium of the people: the faith in twin fathers, a heavenly and a temporal. In March 1901 the Most Holy Synod accordingly issued a decree of excommunication against Tolstoy, merely setting the stage for a very spirited and, of course, brilliant reply on the very subject which occupied his mind.

Tolstoy, perhaps the greatest Christian philosopher of modern times, concentrated on the two essential principles of Christianity: priority over other loves in the love of God, which is the love of a mystic unity rooted in truth, and, next, the love of your neighbour, which means service rendered to those with whom you are in daily touch rather than to mankind in the abstract.

But, here too, God's Fifth Column was at work, setting the mills of God to grind exceeding fine, leaving no room for smugness, no loophole for self-approbation. It was to be no easy victory. Clan warfare had left its mark on the suffering unit by shifting his idealism from that single suffering unit, the repository of all feeling and being, to a preoccupation with numerical abstractions – clans, nations, territorial religions, class struggles, ideologies. Seduced by the imposing but unfeeling illusion of numbers, man had become incomplete and dissatisfied, forever craving for some mirage of appeasement on the horizon, unable to concentrate on the treasure of living at hand. Woman, too, preoccupied with a priority of love she dispensed to her own kin, paid but lip service when pretending she understood that she owed a prior love to God and her neighbours.

Those distorted priorities of loyalty, and not approval of a militant attitude, are the meaning of Christ's words when He says He brought not peace but a sword. He has come to set members of the family – which also means members of the clan, the tribe, the nation – at variance with one another. How indeed could it be otherwise if the suicidal, literally preposterous, loyalties were to be righted?

The Holy Synod did not want anything righted, believing that there was such a thing as leaving the Church alone. But Tolstoy's ideas of non-resistance to evil, running their course, could not stop at the point at which a wise and cunning Roman emperor, unable to resist the advent of pure Christianity, adulterated its message, blunted its arrow, by absorbing it into the State. From then on Christianity, having become a State religion, split with the State, and Christians were seen fighting each other in the name of the same Christ.

Christ's sword was not a symbol of patricide, fratricide and matricide. His command that we love our neighbour as we love ourselves implies that we cannot love our relations appreciably better. But the readiness to let our protective solicitude for our own families swell into preventive attacks was the root of the principle impelling us to repeat the pattern with larger units composed of clans, convictions, ideologies, in a recurring design for murder. An entirely anonymous murder, too, of other suffering units personally unknown to us: a hell on earth, the exact opposite in fact of the kingdom of heaven.

The spirit's right of way through the labyrinths of sentient flesh is in fact that sword of Christ which has not ceased to wound and kill, and shall not cease to kill or wound until the body bends its knee before the soul. Love of family, delightful in a Lenin, does not apparently prevent him from regarding with complete detachment the murder of Nicholas II's family. And Nicholas, likewise a model family man, and, in his own poor light, a Christian, has not scrupled to authorise the creation of numerous orphans by affording precedence to the State. That State which is but an unholy conglomeration of families and clans into a larger appetite for prior loyalty over God.

The old man of primitive tribes, his far descendants, the Campbells and Gordons, and Scotland for ever, the Union, and the intermediate invasions by foreigners, Angles and Saxons, have not apparently put a stop to another projected invasion, by the descendants of the Saxons who stayed behind in Germany or the descendants of the Saxons who invaded Britain. With all these implications of a misreading of the Gospels Tolstoy would have nothing to do.

Repulsed, after several decades of marriage, by his wife as a wife and a dominating spokesman of that ungodly unit of pernicious preferential loyalty, the family, the old man was severely exercised by the problem of reconciling his distaste for her as such with the love due to her, second only to God, as his immediate neighbour. The bane of Tolstoy's life, as the bane of most writers' lives, was his family. Having made the initial error of marrying, he multiplied the error by multiplying himself through his children, thus himself becoming a bone of contention. None of them remarkable, and his wife having grown into a hideous monster of clinging possessiveness, they all, while obviously knowing less about what was good for him than he did himself, pretended they knew more. Had he contented himself with possessing relatives, like brothers and sisters and nieces, he could have kept his distance and neutralised their encroachments. But he had produced his own brood, and they proved to be his undoing.

One might think that Providence, having approved of the man and his work, would now assist Tolstoy to complete his mission. But the mills of God grind finely. Providence would endure no more complacency in the man himself than in society, in the nations, in the world, in Nature, in the universe. It proceeded to sabotage the great man. Job was given boils, Tolstoy a ludicrous wife, a lunatic to torment him; an agent of God's Fifth Column, subtly armed to torment the man who wanted to love, and thought it easy.

Tolstoy's problem of how to love Christ more than his own wife was easy to him. He had no difficulty of inclination in loving Christ more. No difficulty at all – except his wife who made difficulties about being loved less, and thus would have made it quite easy for him to adhere to his inclination without further moral scruple, did he not recall the second injunction to love his nearest neighbour (which she unfortunately was) as well as he loved himself. Unable to do so, he hated himself and hated her the more for making him hate himself. It was easier to love one's enemies.

40

IT IS BETTER TO BURN THAN TO MARRY

His wife said that she did not understand the love of enemies, and insisted that there was some affectation about it. "She and many others do not understand it," Tolstoy noted in his diary, "chiefly because they think that the partiality they experience for some people is love."

Proust about this time was slowly learning the austere, if painful, lesson which all great spirits must learn before they shed the body of this death, but which is an axiom to saints: that it is not to persons but to all the world, the universal spirit, that we owe the comprehension of love.

But Tolstoy, too, experienced the difficulty of loving indiscriminately all the world. Noting down that he could love his wife at a pinch, he was defeated by his attempt to love his third son, Lev, who was positively rude to his father. "But I cannot love Lev." Another son, Andrei, he describes as one of those in whom it is difficult to believe that the divine spirit exists at all. "Nevertheless" – he makes a note to remind himself – "it does", however distasteful it must find an abode such as Andrei's "who drinks and indulges in debauchery".

His wife was now almost hideously ugly. Under the date of August 22nd there is an entry in her diary – "My birthday. I am sixty-six and am still as energetic, acutely impressionable, passionate, and people say youthful." With this assertion her husband could prepare for trouble. She looked like a lioness; he like a shaggy old lion. She continually plagued him to be photographed with her for the Press, and he complains of it in that part of his diary marked *For Myself Alone*: "Again a request to pose for a photograph as a loving couple. I consented, but felt ashamed all the time." In the photograph she holds his arm firmly with her own, as in a vice, the while gazing with dilated pupils into his eyes with a look of fierce rapacity more like that of a hungry tigress clawing her prey than of idyllic love, while he, clearly enjoined to look into her eyes, looks before him from beneath his shaggy eyebrows with a resigned, weary, sullen look.

When, to lessen the humiliation of her return after she had affected to leave him but returned the same day, he made a fuss of her, she noted down in her diary what happiness it had been for her to cling to him and *mingle souls* with him. A statement which perhaps lends force to D. H. Lawrence's glorification of men and women in their conjugal separateness. That evening he led her in to dinner on his arm. She looked exhausted and rather ashamed. And Tolstoy, to excuse himself before their daughter who did not approve of his pampering her mother, observed, "She is such a pitiable old woman. She's been laughing and crying."

He particularly wearied of her conversation. "In the morning she started talking," he notes, "first of all about her health, following that up with reproaches, and she continued talking ceaselessly, even interfering in a conversation." But her comment on the same occasion reads, "And after dinner we all had a good talk."

The great writer is not interested in *what* people say but in *why* they say it. The informative knowing writers, Kipling, Bennett, Zola, are interested in *what* people say, because they cannot think appreciably better themselves. His wife's affectations of sincerity galled Tolstoy, who was trying his best to be a Christian. "It is very hard," he notes in his diary *For Myself Alone*. "These expressions of love, this talkativeness, and continual interference. It is possible, I know it is possible, to love despite it all, but I cannot. I am no good."

The whole lot of them – wife, sons, daughters, doctors, friends and old retainers – seemed to be forever confiding their suspicions about one another in their private diaries, since become public property. The Countess scribbles morn, noon and night. Her entries are variations on a single theme: her husband, Chertkòv,[1] and her feelings. "I told Lev Nikolaievitch that I was displeased *and to some extent ashamed* that instead of taking me for a walk he had taken the whole company into the gully to hunt for Chertkòv's watch." Not to be ignored, she lay down on the bare boards of the balcony outside his bedroom, remembering, she writes, how forty-eight years ago, when still a girl, she first experienced the boon of Lev Nikolaievitch's love. It was a cold night, but it pleased her to think that she should find death in the place where she had once known love. Her husband, hearing her moving about, came out to complain that she was keeping him awake and told her to go away. Whereupon she lay down on the wet grass, in her thin dress, and hoped that she might pay him out by contracting a death chill.

Lev, who, she acknowledges, "treats me with a touching kindness", went in to his father's room, woke him up and shouted at him to go and fetch her, since it was he who had driven her out. Whereupon Tolstoy, balancing hatred of his son and namesake with a desperate resolution to love even the very last of creatures for its Creator's sake, in a mood of sullen resignation went out into the park to look for her. With the righteous assistance of Lev, he found her and carried her back, his wife bewailing aloud that "if any foreigners had seen in what a condition the wife of Tolstoy was brought in, having lain at two and three o'clock at night on the damp earth, benumbed and brought to the last stage of desperation, how surprised those good people would be!"

Her closing question echoes his title, *Then What Are We To Do?* of which her absurdly personal problem seems an unconscious mimicry. "Well, what now?" she asks. "What is to be done? What is to be done?" And she adds, with a conscious sense of a participant in a dramatic event, "It is four o'clock."

It is not perhaps astonishing that, earlier, in the Crimea, stooping over a lizard warming itself on a stone, Tolstoy asked it in a low whisper: "Are you happy, eh?" and, cautiously looking round, confided, "I'm not." An observation in a book dealing with the mentally deranged, to which

---

[1] Tolstoy's disciple and collaborator.

category he readily consigns his consort, elicits his assent. In a coarse peasant family it was the patient who suffered from his mocking relatives who had him on their hands. In sensitive surroundings it was the relative trying to protect the patient whose patience was tried to the point of making existence a mockery.

His own calvary, unseemly though it was in a man of his worth, yet fitted his peculiar faults – pride in abasement. It was but God's Fifth Column exercised to tempt a good man, to put him, like Job, through a gruelling test: through a plethora of conjugal devotion, a succession of small shocks to his dignity to shake him out of every moral complacency: to subject the spinner of large generalisations to ridicule at the hands of a crazy woman: to face the man who advocated love with – yes, love. Good at non-resistance to evil, was he? How about non-resistance to indignity – indignity carried to the point of open ridicule, a caricature of his patience, patience reduced to rank absurdity, so that the gods themselves were looking down upon the great good man and shaking with laughter?

The planners of world peace could not, it would seem, manage their own domestic peace. The situation at Yasnaya Polyana was a microcosm of the world situation, the conflict between husband and wife turning on the author's right to forgo the profits from his work. Communism versus private enterprise. Tolstoy's was the chagrin of being a best-seller! Other authors, notably Chehov, who wrote to a friend that the only way he could think of making any money was to issue *Anna Karenina* under his own name, felt chagrined for the opposite reason. But, unlike Proust who was socially self-conscious and feared most the stings of that pitiless serpent of insight, his own mind, if he made a social slip in the Faubourg Saint-Germain, Tolstoy, morally self-conscious, walked in fear lest his own guardian angel should snub him for a moral *faux pas*. "I must be careful," he writes. "Just now while out walking I twice caught myself feeling dissatisfied, first because I had renounced my freedom of will, and then because they will sell this new edition for hundreds of thousands of roubles. But in each case I pulled myself up, remembering that man has but to do what is right in God's sight."

But his wife questioned both his right of will and his right of freedom. "They talk of some sort of *right* each man has," she excogitates. "Of course Lev Nikolaievitch has the *right* to torment me by refusing to take his diaries from Chertkòv. But where does a wife's *right* come in, with whom he has lived for half a century? And where is," she asks caustically, "that *non-resistance* [for fear of self-implication omitting 'to evil'] that Lev Nikolaievitch is so fond of? Where is that?"

After tearing up into little bits and throwing into the earth-closet Chertkòv's photograph, which she had repeatedly replaced on her husband's table by her own, she states as a foregone conclusion, "Of course Lev Nikolaievitch was angry and reproached me with depriving him of freedom (*he is quite mad on that subject now*) which he had never troubled himself about or thought of before. What does he want freedom for, when we have loved one another all our lives and have tried to make everything pleasant and joyful for one another?"

In her despair reducing the problem of her jealousy to its rudiments, she becomes increasingly fantastic. "What is necessary for everyone to be happy and to do away with all my sufferings?" she asks. A question she answers herself with studied explicitness: "*To take from Chertkòv the diaries – those few black leather-cloth note-books – and to put them back on the table, letting him have one at a time to take extracts from. That is all!*" Quite simple, wasn't it? But the family feared that, if she found in them any reference to herself displeasing to her vanity, she would destroy them rather than let posterity infer that she fell short of being the ideal mate of genius. After experimenting with a toy pistol, she mused that "beholding my corpse killed by my husband", it will seem incredible to her mourning family that her life could have been saved in so simple a way: namely, by their "*returning to my husband's writing-table four or five leather-cloth note-books*". The quarrel between governments about territorial or minority rights – the Ulster question, the Danzig, the Sudeten question – is argued no better than this – with a pistol, too, in the background.

Though the sounds from her toy pistol failed to reach the ear for which they were intended, they produced on the housekeeper an impression sufficient for her to send word for the absent daughter who also acted as her father's secretary and who despised her mother. Receiving a message to the effect "Come back at once because your Mama has shot herself or something", she started for home by coach, travelling in the dark over difficult country along bad roads and returned at midnight, in a foul temper. The Countess, unaware of the housekeeper's letter, heard a carriage come up the drive and someone knock at the door. Wondering who on earth it could be at this time of night, she opened the door into the hall, where she could not see a thing, and was knocked off her feet by a combined torrent of abuse emanating apparently from her daughter and an old retainer who had accompanied her and come back in the coach to attend the post-mortem, only to find the victim opening the front door for them. Both women, the Countess notes, flung such buckets of abuse at her that she stood there, speechless with astonishment, able only to hear but not to see them. She went upstairs, the two women still screaming like two hyenas behind her. "At last," records the Countess, "I lost patience and became terribly angry. What had I done to either of them? For what was I to blame?"

At this stage, however, she qualifies her innocence. "Unfortunately," she says, "I began to shout too, and said that I would drive them out of the house and would sack the old retainer next day. But those malicious creatures were not easily quieted, and next morning, having packed their things and collected horses, dogs, and a parrot, they drove off to Sasha's house at Telyatinki." And she adds, "They themselves were to blame. It was they who grew angry and behaved badly."

Meanwhile the great old man was observing in his diary that as regards moral improvement he felt himself to be but a child, a pupil, and a poor pupil of little zeal. His wife was to be pitied, but he found it hard. "Lord help me!" he adds. The Countess's indulgence of her own whims, which permitted her to exhibit her jealousy in screams and tantrums without at all abating her volume of emotion in front of the servants, did not apparently reduce her sense of fitness as regards the limits of emotionalism to be permitted in the servants' hall. "There has been," she writes, "a nasty and scandalous affair among the servants. Our old cook was violated by the man-servant Filka (the one who muddled up the errand and fetched Chertkòv in error). He fought with her and with the Circassian footman. Screams. Hysterics. I have sacked them all!"

But she had forgiven, she notes, the participants in her own midnight drama. Her daughter and the old retainer, accompanied by their team of horses, dogs, and the parrot, returned to Yasnaya Polyana to resume the home life, from which Tolstoy, however, soon sought release by a visit, in Chertkòv's society, to a distant friend.

From there it was the Countess's mission to dislodge him by feigning illness which she hoped would bring her husband back. With the help of the housekeeper who, as distinct from the old retainer, one gathers was a yes-woman, she ('we' in her version) drafted a telegram in which her husband's return was not so much solicited as made dependent on his moral qualities, difficult to ignore in one so morally self-conscious. Moreover, the standard of conduct expected of him in this crisis was not above that of the average ordinary decent husband who would normally conceive it as his duty to return without delay to his wife's sick-bed.

Tolstoy's reply, however, when it came was couched on a note of inquiry. He was not, his telegram implied, unwilling to return at once, but, unless they considered it absolutely necessary that he should do so, it would be more convenient for him to return tomorrow. To this he requested a reply.

The amended draft of the telegram sent in the housekeeper's name, read: "Think necessary."

Tolstoy returned but was not, his wife complains, gracious.

The life at Yasnaya Polyana, turbulent on the human side, was not tranquillised by nature. His wife's entries contain references such as

137

"Finished my work on *Sebastopol* and read the proofs of *On Money*. It is pouring with rain and is windy." Or "In the evening I mastered myself and worked on *Childhood*. Torrents of rain and wind." Into such weather she drove him out, as an alternative to spending a pleasant afternoon at Chertkòv's, to wear down his restlessness on horseback, herself following him in a cabriolet lest he escape her vigilance. "It seemed to me," she writes, "that he looked round continually on purpose, and rode always faster and faster in the hope that I should at last grow cold and desist. But I did not turn (and caught a chill which I still have) but followed him till we got home. We had by then covered seventeen versts."

She proposed, as she says, to her husband that if he wished to understand her jealousy of Chertkòv he should read his old diary of 1851 concerning his love for men. At that he became terribly angry and shouted, "Go away!" and, she writes, "ran up and down the room like a wild beast. More suffering!" she concludes.

"To-day," he notes, "I felt a strong desire to write fiction but realised the impossibilty of concentrating on it with this struggle within me and this persistent feeling about her." That the inquisition to which the old moralist was being subjected at the hands of God's Fifth Column was not, however ludicrous its form, to be despised is apparent from the afterthought: "But of course that struggle and the possibility of victory in that struggle is more important than any possible work of art." His closest friend and collaborator, who despised the Countess's idea that art was more important than self-improvement, evidently shared Tolstoy's opinion, himself not lagging behind with an occasional turn of the screw. "A letter from Chertkòv," notes Tolstoy, "containing reproaches and accusations. They tear me in pieces. I sometimes think I ought to get away from them all."

His getting away did not exceed riding around the estate with his wife on his heels in a cabriolet, and after one of these rides, frozen and exhausted, he tumbled on to his bed without taking off his cold riding boots, and lost consciousness. He was late for dinner. Going up to his room to fetch him, his wife found him unconscious and kicking about in a violent fit of convulsions. Rushing back into the dining-room and sounding the alarm, she got all the diners – sons, daughters, doctors, visitors and in-laws – to rush upstairs. They threw themselves upon the great man's twitching and kicking body. Some held his legs, others his arms. Hot-water bottles were filled, mustard-plasters applied to his calves, eau-de-Cologne to his head, smelling-salts to his nose, blankets wrapped round his legs, coffee and rum poured down his throat, while his wife promptly administered an enema. The old man, his shaggy brows knitted in concentration, a frown on his great brow, his jaws

138

moving, was making strange low sounds resembling the mooing of a cow. Still delirious, he began to shed pearls of wisdom that would have delighted Gertrude Stein herself. "A company," he repeated, "a company . . . about three . . . a company . . . about three . . ."

They waited with bated breath for the revelation from across the Great Unconscious.

"To write," he said at last, and was handed a pencil and writing-pad. He covered the writing-pad with his handkerchief and drew the pencil over the handkerchief. His face was severe and damnatory, as before.

"It must be read!" he said, and he repeated several times what he had presumably been writing over the handkerchief: "Reasonableness . . . reasonableness . . . reasonableness."

His wife, in a state of abject contrition, kneeled at his side imploring divine intervention for postponing the judgment she felt she had brought down on herself. Hastily crossing herself with small movements, she whispered, "Not this time, dear Lord! Not this time." She vowed that never again so long as she lived would she torment him with her jealousy, if only he were spared to her this time. She embraced his legs in an attitude of dumb adoration while he, still delirious and mooing like a cow, kicked about vigorously.

Her contrition was sincere and complete, but did not apparently prevent her from taking advantage of his unconsciousness to abstract his diaries. Her children caught her fiddling with his keys and just about to get away with his portfolio. She was saving it, she protested volubly, from Chertkòv.

The morning after the next, this amazingly resilient octogenarian – he was eighty-two – was already up for breakfast, drinking quantities of white coffee and eating so many rusks and rolls with a good appetite that he alarmed his wife. And in the afternoon he went riding.

Two days later, having forgotten all her good resolutions, she was frothing at the mouth because Chertkòv was coming over in the evening for a talk with her husband. "When through the open casement," she writes, "I heard the sound of a vehicle on springs, I had such terrible palpitations that I thought I should die on the spot. I ran to look through the glass door to see how they would meet, but Lev Nikolaievitch had just drawn the curtain. I rushed into his other room, moved back the curtain, took a pair of binoculars and looked to see whether I could detect any particular expressions of love or joy. But he knew that I was watching, and merely shook Chertkòv's hand and assumed an expressionless face."

The interview was but short. This again she tried to cut down by conspiring with the doctor to order her husband an evening bath. While the men were talking she spied on them from another room and noticed, she says, that Chertkòv leaned nearer to show Lev Nikolaievitch something. "But," she writes, "I hurried up the bath and told Ilya Vasilievitch [the man-servant] to say that it was ready and would be getting cold." After which Chertòv got up and the two men reluctantly parted.

Lev Nikolaievitch, she notes, had become gloomy again. "Chertkòv was here. Very simple and lucid," is his entry for that evening. "He left soon after nine o'clock. Sonia had another hysterical seizure."

In the morning she realised that to have admitted Chertkòv into her house had been an effort beyond her strength. "I cannot endure him at all. He is simply the Devil!" Again they had a brush of words. She notes that her husband's kindness has not lasted long. Her entry, reading, "He shouted at me again" is corroborated in his own version, confined to his diary *For Myself Alone*, with "I asked her rather warmly to leave me in peace."

"*What* husbands there are!" she exclaims.

41

POPE, KAISER AND PARIAH

1903 was the peak year for the Kaiser. It was also the year when Hitler touched bottom in Vienna. They had both come there, William II on a royal visit to Francis Joseph, Hitler to try to pass into the Academy of Painting. In the spring of the same year the Kaiser, accompanied by the tallest officers he could muster, paid a visit to King Victor Emmanuel III of Italy, notoriously short of stature. Even so, the giants were not of uniform height, each outsize officer in turn humiliating the next. When they were all gathered at the station and ready to start, there arrived, last but the reverse of least, the very, *very* tallest officer in the German Army, Colonel von Plüskow, nicknamed in Paris 'Plusquehaut', who dwarfed all the rest.

What effect they had on Victor Emmanuel, who disliked '*prepotenza*' in people, can only be imagined. Since the King, who was self-conscious about his size, did not refer to the giant escort of his guest, one can only surmise that the humiliation was strictly subjective. The King's 'inferiority complex' on this point was reinforced by another. He resented the seignorial airs of the House of Habsburg, till fairly recently their over-lords, and bitterly deplored the studied insolence with which Francis Joseph had neglected to return the visit of the late King Humbert. This was a slap in the face, not only at his late father and himself, but also at the whole of Italy. "A slap in the face!" repeated the King, looking up at Bülow. In the circumstances the visit of the German Emperor, even with his bodyguard of giants, was a salve to an old wound, though he was well aware that the Kaiser detested Queen Elena – the only one in Rome for whom Francis Joseph entertained the least respect.

With the ninety-three-year-old Pope, Leo XIII, the Kaiser got on very happily. The Pope treated him to a speech in which he saw William II as another Charlemagne, and himself as another Pope Leo III, at whose behest Charlemagne had subjected the whole civilised world of his day to the Cross. Pope Leo XIII entrusted the modern Charlemagne with the holy mission, described by him as 'the same' as that entrusted by Pope Leo III to Charlemagne, of extirpating root, stem and branch socialist and – he added – atheist ideas – a mission the Kaiser em-braced with a grin of enthusiasm. It was also a mission which the skulking fourteen-year-old boy Adolf was to consider essential – so far as the socialist element was concerned, Hitler's idea being that before Germany sprang on Europe she should first kill off her own socialists. There seems to have been, in 1903, what statesmen like to call a wide margin of agreement between Pope, Kaiser, and future Führer. The Kaiser, in his answering speech to the Pope, expressed himself as strangely moved that a Pope of ninety-three should speak such exalted words to so young a monarch as himself. At the time, the Kaiser was thirty-four and young only in relation to the Pope, on whose behalf he enjoined God to prolong His apostle's life: a request, at ninety-three, savouring of a taste for miracles. Intoxicated by his own words, the Kaiser argued (as though having to convince some intractable opposing power, whereas his difficulty was to convince himself) that earthly majesty was dust, since God's was the kingdom, the power and the glory. But though the Pope was the acknowledged representative on earth of an admittedly superior spiritual realm, the Kaiser in referring to the 'mutual co-operation of Kaiser and Pope' gave precedence to him-self.

From Rome the Kaiser returned to Germany, and took as usual the leading part in the autumn manoeuvres, telegraphing to the ex-cavalry-man, Chancellor Bülow, that he had won the mock battle and carried off the laurels, adding, "I hear that the impression made was a very deep one." To make sure he won the day, the Kaiser would send an aide-de-camp to the opposite camp to spy out all he could about their intended movements. In this way he remained invariably the victor.

After the manoeuvres came a visit to Vienna. The Kaiser had been shooting in Hungary, where he had caused mass slaughter among the beautiful stags herded together for him to unload his *kaiserliche und königliche* gun into. While shooting deer with the Tsar at Spala the Kaiser was told that many splinters of wood had been found in the intestines of the deer. The poor animals, insufficiently fed, were driven to stripping the bark off the trees to alleviate their hunger. The Kaiser's concern about wood in the stomachs of animals he was about to pierce with lead irrespective of where it struck them, is interesting. His host on this occasion, the Archduke Frederich, was married to an insignificant mediatised princess entertaining lofty matrimonial ambitions for her daughters. They were pretty. When the heir presumptive, Archduke Francis Ferdinand of Saràyevo fame, began to pay frequent visits to her house her hopes rose steeply. But when she noticed a gold bracelet with the Archduke's miniature on the wrist of her maid-of-honour, a mere Countess Sophie Chotek, her faith in human gratitude was rudely shaken. Her poor daughters! And happiness had seemed so sure!

Her sense of fitness was not catered for by the news that the Emperor-to-be of Austria had married her maid-of-honour morganatically in the teeth of every obstacle, because he loved her. Nor did it please her to hear that the former countess was to be transformed into the Duchess of Hohenberg. Now as the hostess of the German Emperor on his way to Vienna, she impressed upon his Majesty the impropriety, as it struck her, of the heir to the throne of Austria shackling himself with a morganatic wife when (this she left implied) he could have made any one of her daughters his future empress.

Bülow joined the Kaiser's train at Vienna-Neustadt. William II greeted his Chancellor with the words: "Of course I shall take no notice of Franz Ferdinand's wife." The German Ambassador at Vienna argued with his sovereign against this decision, which would turn the future Emperor of Austria into an enemy. But the Kaiser only grew more irritable. "Why," he cried, "if I give way here, I shall find my own sons one day marrying maids-of-honour or perhaps even the chamber-maids!"

In this he proved prophetic. Prince Oscar, his fifth son, ten years later married the Countess Ina Bassewitz, who had to be artificially inflated to the rank of Princess of Prussia to make her worthy of his imperial and royal highness. Even so, the Kaiser who, though capable of bursts of kindness, was not Nature's gentleman, received the bride's father, Count Bassewitz Levetzow, who was the Prime Minister of Mecklenburg, with the ungracious words, "This marriage is not very welcome to me." The father replied, "Nor to me either."

But on the train journey to Vienna in 1903 the prospective devaluation of the Hohenzollern currency was but in horoscope. Bülow, realising that the Kaiser's vanity would prevent him giving way in the presence of a third person, whispered to their Vienna Ambassador to leave the carriage, and tackled the Kaiser anew. They were already passing through Baden. Bülow argued that he would be the last person to shackle Germany's future to that of Austria. But why gratuitously antagonise her future Emperor?

They passed Mödling. "Your Majesty," said Bülow with the insistence born of despair, "you are not there to prevent people of rank all over the world from marrying beneath them. Nor is Austria your concern. You have to consider only German interests. These would be grievously injured if you offended the heir to the Austrian throne."

The Kaiser still protested volubly, vehemently. The train was entering the Vienna terminus. From the windows could be seen the green Austrian plumes. Already the strains of '*Heil Dir im Siegerkranz*' burst upon them, when Bülow made a last appeal to his sovereign. "Your Majesty: it is now in your power, and your power alone, either to make a permanent friend or life-long enemy of the future Emperor of Austria. Which is it to be?" The Kaiser gave Bülow a look that was half angry, half mischievous. The train pulled to a halt. Old whiskered Francis-Joseph was on the platform to greet William II. After the Kaiser had embraced the ancient Emperor of Austria, kissed him, as is the custom between brother sovereigns, on both his whiskered cheeks, he approached the Archduke with the friendliest of airs and with enquiring charm asked, "Pray, when may I have the honour of paying my respects to your wife?"

The Archduke blushed crimson with pleasure, bowed low and kissed the Kaiser's hand. The same afternoon William II called on Ferdinand's wife, future Duchess of Hohenberg. The Archduke waited upon the Kaiser on the doorsteps of his house and led him humbly and dutifully to his wife. German Kaiser and future Austrian Kaiser were satisfied: Ferdinand with Wilhelm; Wilhelm with himself. Saràyevo alone put a term to a friendship which might have lasted a lifetime.

There was, that autumn, another visitor to Vienna. A fourteen-year-old boy called Adolf Hitler had just arrived to seek admittance to the Academy in the Faculty of Arts. Having submitted specimen drawings and paintings, he was awaiting the result, the while catching a glimpse of the glittering equipage of life prancing past him in old Imperial Vienna. His eyes were greedily glued on the fate-favoured German Kaiser in his golden eagle-topped helmet. For in his secret heart Adolf would have dearly loved to play the glory game himself. If there is anything interesting about the paranoic Hitler it is his career, his starting from scratch. As soon as he could read, Adolf had pored over his father's encyclopaedia with its colourful Prussian uniforms, containing a description of the Franco-Prussian war, of the victorious Prussian uhlans entering Paris through the Arc de Triomphe, while his native Austrians had apparently had no part or share in the military glory. The Holy Roman Empire of the German nation had degenerated into the double monarchy, the decrepit Austro-Hungary, its Slavonic appendage proving top-heavy for its strength. There, across the Bavarian frontier, was the young Second Reich, glowing with health and energy and youth; and here, now, driving past was the glittering monarch, a symbol of the strength and bright-eyed glory of its martial destiny!

So it seemed to Hitler, who could not see the world, nor follow history, save in this crude reading. If Hitler had any fault to find with Kaiser Wilhelm it was his mistaken tenderness to socialists in Germany. But young Hitler's strictures in this respect were groundless. In a letter of December 31st, 1905, addressed to Bülow, the Kaiser ends as follows: "First shoot the socialists down, behead them, render them impotent – if necessary per blood bath – and then war abroad! But not before, and not *à tempo*." General Kessel, entrusted with the Berlin Military Command, testifies to having been ordered twice in *en clair* telegrams from the Kaiser to open fire on the people in the streets. Kessel ignored imperial orders, and praised the Post Office for its discretion.

Old whiskered Francis-Joseph received Bülow with the graciousness only natural in a dynastic ace welcoming the First Minister of a territorially superior, if genealogically inferior, Crown. Of the Russian Foreign Minister, the little high-heeled Count Lambsdorff, of whom the Emperor William had spoken with open derision, the Emperor Francis-Joseph spoke with cordiality, even affection. To Queen Elena of Italy, whom William detested, Francis-Joseph alluded in the tender language of an old gallant speaking of an exceedingly charming and pretty woman. But about her husband, little King Victor Emmanuel of Italy, Francis-Joseph grumbled. He found him, well – ambitious, perhaps altogether a little too . . . active. It had been easier to deal with his predecessor, the old Humberto.

42

LENIN AND USURY

While the countryside slumbered under a blanket of snow, in the towns the *muzhik*, graduating in the factories as a proletarian, exchanged his grievance as a social pariah for a revolutionary's esprit de corps, and learnt for the first time the reasonable if ugly slogan 'Proletarians of all lands, unite!' The new century was crystallising into national camps of masters scrambling for the world's trade, and of workers' camps within each nation resenting the terms on which they were bidden to work for the masters: the masters snarling and brandishing their sundry national colours threateningly at the masters of other nations, but in the name of the whole nation; the men vaguely threatening the masters of their own nation in the name of the whole working class of all nations.

Lenin, having reached the age of thirty at the turn of the century, was studying ways and means of getting the predatory patriots to commit hari-kiri. He discovered suicidal trends in capitalism gone raving mad in imperialism. The workers in England who produced the goods which in a sane order of society they should be able to acquire, could not afford to do so, and the manufacturers, despairing of their surplus products, were tempting foreign countries, who pleaded lack of money, to take them off their hands by lending them the cash with which to buy them. The foreigners then took the credits and the goods, and for the most part the British manufacturer never saw either again. When the workers at home pleaded for higher wages to enable them to buy the home goods they sorely needed, the British manufacturer argued that higher wages increased his costs which sent up prices, which meant scaring the foreign customer off the goods, and even the credits.[1]

This avarice was dignified by the more elegant name of International Finance. That it was a short circuit just where financiers thought they were taking a long view is clear from this example, typical of many others: a Lancashire factory producing cotton-spinning and weaving machinery, and being a satellite firm financed by the cotton industry at home, would offer long-term credits to induce Russian merchants to set up cotton mills all over Russia, with a view to supplying and replacing British machinery over many years. With what result? Russia, enabled to meet her own requirements in cotton goods, ceases to import Lancashire textiles, and the British cotton industry, forced through loss of its

[1] This account owes more to Gerhardie than to Lenin.

Russian market to curtail its output of textiles, reduces its normal order for replacement of machinery from the satellite firm, the Lancashire factory supplying Russia with machinery and financed by the Lancashire cotton mills, now both registering a sharp decline in their shares. The factory, to make up for its loss of custom at home and to justify its existence to the parent firm, augments its inducements of supplying machinery on long-term credit abroad, and the cotton industry at home reels under the fresh blow to its textile exports.

While England had no competitors in the field of foreign loans because she was the sole industrialised country, the system, however weird, of offering foreigners money that they might relieve her of her surplus goods, seemed to work. But by the time England had, through these blandishments, supplied other countries, notably Germany, with machinery, before long Germany also found herself with surplus goods and begging other lands to borrow her money wherewith to take off her hands the very goods her own work-people could not afford to buy.

When this happened, foreigners in mechanically virgin lands discovered that money was indeed going cheap. All they had to do was to be good enough to accept some machinery with it, which they were generally glad to do. The result was that rural countries where you could still dump machinery were becoming alarmingly scarce, and England and Germany, whose workers were going short of things at home, began to compete with each other for the high privilege of dumping goods and credits abroad.

And not only England and Germany: Great Britain and the United States both competed for the privilege of supplying the capital city of imperial Russia, St. Petersburg, with an electric tramway system on credit, and where the credit and the tramway were dumped there they are still.

A new era had opened with the twentieth century. Abroad, a frantic competition was unleashed in underselling goods and credits to get rid just as fast as might be of the fruit of the labourer's toil at home. And, to get ahead of the rival competitor abroad, a desperate struggle was waged at home to keep down the wages and send up the hours of the workers producing these 'surplus goods' they could not themselves afford to buy. This new era, glorified by the name of International Finance, deemed too intricate, almost ineffable, for human understanding, was, fundamentally, the cause of the Four Years' War (which also no simple self-respecting soul any longer pretends to understand). And it was likewise the cause of the Second World War, and it will continue to be the cause of world wars until a sane, simple, rational, honest and non-interest-bearing money system is put on the market, enabling the people at home to acquire the things they produce.

"We certainly," wrote the Kaiser, "did all that was possible to meet England half-way, but it was useless because the German export figures showed an increase; naturally we could not limit our world-commerce in order to satisfy England. That was asking too much."

The Kaiser complained that, even quite early in his reign, England everywhere opposed German aspirations, adding naïvely, 'even such as were justified'. The Kaiser's trashiness and naïve sincerity show up diplomacy for the silly game it is. When you set against the Kaiser's negotiations for a coaling station, say, Tolstoy (assumed by simpletons to be childish) in his limpid exposition of non-resistance to evil, the sheer absurdity of the preoccupation of these wily apes stands out in all its unattractive nakedness.

The Kaiser calls the British Ambassador to witness, and reports him as saying that "Germany, a young, rising nation" – she seems to enjoy eternal youth – "a young, rising nation turned directly to England in order to acquire territory with her consent" and was cold-shouldered, which "was certainly more than England could reasonably ask", that surely England who "already owned almost all the world, could cert-ainly find a place where she might permit Germany to establish a coaling station", and that he, the British Ambassador in Berlin, "was unable to understand the gentlemen in Downing Street", and that, failing British consent, Germany would naturally occupy under her own steam such places as were suited to her ends, "because, after all, there was no law against it".

A strange British Ambassador! At any rate, not one answering to the definition, which so shocked Nicholas II, of an ambassador as a man sent to a foreign country to lie and deceive another nation on behalf of his own.

When Germany acted as advised by the British Ambassador and occupied Kiao-chou, and the British Government instructed its envoy in Berlin to protest energetically, "when the English Ambassador," writes the Kaiser, "assumed this tone he was referred to his conversation with me."

He could live neither with, nor, it would seem, without us. England, owing to her dependence on sea communications, lived in fear of poten-tial and hypothetical rather than actual danger, such as the contingency of Constantinople passing into Russian hands, which once made the British Empire tremble on the brink of war. It was presumably the fear of Russian warships (which in those days would founder if you blew at them with a good pair of bellows) that, however, was the hypothesis on which we were ready to stake a painful certainty. Then it was the naval expansion of Germany: again a known evil cheerfully accepted for a hypothetical good. All this exertion was to maintain a highly precarious balance of power. On this balance, kept in unsteady equilibrium by frock-coated gentlemen with immaculate manners, hung all that vast commercial edifice: all depending on, all capable of being wiped out by, one false diplomatic step.

43

THE DEATH OF CHEHOV

If for men of genius writing were not so exhausting a race between them and their creditors, they might survey with a wider benevolence the whole field of contemporary artistic output, subscribe to all current reviews in every part of the world, and keep abreast of all the latest publications in every branch of art. The subtle torture of writing stories on time! Is there a calvary more absurdly uncalled for?

In addition to this, Chehov was besieged by requests: to find in his Crimean exile accommodation for a sick *littérateur*; to intercede with the Rector on behalf of a student expelled from the university; to help with a centenary celebration, lend a hand in an epidemic, lend money to the wife of a deceased author, and a hundred other requests. To the widow, who asked him for three hundred roubles, he did not reply for a long time, later writing to justify his silence by the natural disinclination to refuse a request. He did not have three hundred roubles, nor one hundred roubles. What he had received of his advance he had spent, and was again heavily in arrears. Indeed, though he had sold his collected works for seventy-five thousand roubles,[1] the money paid in instalments had been quickly swallowed in repaying old debts, and he was trying to raise a small sum on an I.O.U.

Nor did his fame bring him much happiness. For twenty-five years he had been reading criticisms of his work without alighting on one valuable comment, one word of helpful advice. Only once had he been impressed, when a certain critic, Skabitchevski, wrote that he, Chehov,

£7,500.

would end by dying drunk in a ditch. What irritated him were the critics who compared him with other authors, even the classics. You could harness anyone to anybody, he said angrily, and if, instead of harnessing his play to Goncharov, they had harnessed him to King Lear, the critique would have been just as pretty and readable. He caught himself getting more and more irritated by his time and surroundings. However, to despise people because they were not heroes, was, he reasoned, unreasonable.

Such sentiments as the last suggest unlimited good nature. To sustain them, however, is to make a severe demand on the nervous system. And Chehov, contrary to the general belief, was, except in his letters and his work, a capricious creature. People would be constantly arriving while he was trying to force himself to work. "I write slowly," he said, "with strain . . ." There he sat at his writing-table, giving away, he felt, the honey of his life into space. Another pull at the front-door bell, and another, a third, a fourth: more visitors coming round for a heart-to-heart chat, to present the writer with the boon of their inner life's history. In an early story of his he depicted a famous dramatist to whom a middle-aged lady, despite his protests, insists on reading her play. Throughout the long session he punctuates her reading with urgent pleas that he has a train to catch, without making the slightest impression on the lady-dramatist carried away by the stilted eloquence of her own dialogue. Unable to sit through the tedium of her reading, he seizes, about the middle of the fifth act, a heavy bronze paper-weight and with both hands, with all his might, brings it down on her skull. To the maid who rushes in, he says, "Bind me. I have killed her. Call the police." There is a new paragraph of one sentence:

"The jury acquitted him."

Chehov's irritation was not unnatural. Imbued with a perfect simplicity and good nature, ready to enjoy a similar simplicity and good nature in others, he was instead confronted with a puerility of pretensions and affectations only too vulnerable to his insight, but which his clairvoyant kindness of heart was loath to expose for fear of wounding their authors. There is, however, a limit even to a sage's enjoyment of the irony of being thought a simpleton by fools. So his instinct was to retire from this too incessant contact with the poor actors of life, which Shakespeare calls a stage, or, in conjunction with each other, 'this great stage of fools'. And it was in his solitude that Chehov pitied rather than despised ordinary people who could not be heroes.

Visited one day by an elegant woman, apparently unable to draw the natural inference that a writer capable of seeing through his own characters must also be able to see through a simulacrum modelling herself on one of them, he listened to her as she ranted, "Life is so boring,

Anton Pavlovich. Everything is so grey: people, the sea, even the flowers seem to me grey, grey . . . and I have no desires . . . my soul is in pain . . . it is like a disease."

He considered her, keeping a straight face. "It *is* a disease," he said with conviction, "it *is* a disease: in Latin it is called *morbus fraudulentus*."

What perhaps Chehov hated most was earnestness masquerading as seriousness of purpose. The earnest is an unsuccessful attempt at being serious: unsuccessful because of a missing ingredient – the comedic vision. To try to be serious in earnest is like putting a coin in a pocket with a hole in it. Of all the snares that simpletons most readily fall into, earnestness may claim the most victims. The grimly unhumorous has a lot to answer for, Hitler being a morbid example. What a fuss was being made, for example, in the realm of drama, of Granville Barker, who wrote of the virtue of leading one's own life, of how a marquis's daughter, having wed a labourer, starts the morning of her married life in a cottage. This earnestness came on the heels of Ibsen extracting power from such over-obvious statements as "The strongest man is he who is ever alone."

It was Chehov's peculiar merit that, far from confusing the serious with the earnest, his work was a constant unwinding of the cocoon of earnestness spun around our private lives and culminating in the winding-sheets of national earnestness which have turned us into mummies, helpless in the face of 'grave situations fraught with the most dire seriousness' for whole continents of people who, having done nothing to merit such news except infer mistakenly that politics were a sober, serious and responsible pursuit, find themselves suddenly confronted by the absurd necessity of pitting their human frames against high explosives dropped on them, with no special ill intent, from the air.

Comedy is God's Fifth Columnist sabotaging the earnest in the cause of the serious. Earnestness is but the toll we pay to Time to be allowed to pass through. Into a platitudinous professor Chehov compressed all the earnest humbug inherent in the academic world. Without any intention of irony the retired professor of Art History quotes the well-worn lines

> Sow but the wise and the good and the lasting,
> Sow: mighty thanks everlasting
> the Russian people will render you!

addressing himself to the younger generation who have voted him a complete humbug. A retired professor of art who, while living on the toil of his connections by marriage, had written innumerable books about art without a glimmer of insight into his subject! As he takes his leave of them all, the professor is once more completely himself, self-confident, urbane, as though unaware that his is an exploded reputation. "I value your observation" is his comment on a fatuous compliment from a fawning old fool. "Goodbye. Goodbye, everyone!" he says cordially, extending not without condescension his hand to the house doctor, to whom he says, "Thank you for your pleasant society." To the younger people, who regard him as a parasite, a spinner of stilted and meaningless words, "I respect your way of thinking," he says, "your enthusiasms, your transports, but allow an old man to include in his parting message just one observation: deeds, not words, gentlemen! Deeds! Talking is not enough." A bow to the company, and he goes out.

Gorky in the end carried his career of literature to material heights never reached by Chehov, finishing as the recognised doyen and virtual dictator of Russian literature, with a town and streets named after him. Though talented, and sometimes powerful, he was, artistically, a very small kettle of fish compared with Chehov, of whom, although a professed admirer, he has no real understanding. The producers, Stanislavsky himself, overpraised by posterity, did not seem to understand that Chehov's plays were poems. *Three Sisters* is a poem; *The Cherry Orchard* a poem. When Chehov turned up in Moscow for a rehearsal of *Three Sisters* the actors assailed him with questions. What was this and that character supposed to be like? He was amazed that they should ask him. "But it's all in the book," he said, "it's all there. It's in the stage directions. It transpires from the dialogue." It astonished him that a completed play should need any more extraneous explanation than a completed story which, but for the author's presence, might fail in its effect. It was a poem. But as he listened to their rendering of it, it became increasingly clear to him that they did not understand it was a poem; in confusion and bewilderment he fled from the rehearsal. They had been dragging it out, making the whole thing absurd by infusing it with the overflow of their own natures; they were guilty of that very same offence of which Shakespeare, in the person of Hamlet, indicts the players. It occurred to Chehov that between what he had himself envisaged and that which the actors were making of it there was so wide a gulf that his responsibility of authorship would hardly stretch to cover this ridiculous attempt to attribute to him intentions he could not have entertained even when deserted by his muse.

But it didn't matter. Here he was back in Moscow, for whose streets, cafés and lights he had pined while marooned on the tedious Crimean shore, where he had languished at Yalta, irritated by a swarm of trivial people. In Moscow one was never lonely even when alone among a crowd of strangers in a restaurant. In Moscow you knew nobody, but

151

you were not lonely. If it was raining, you could still sit at a window, watch the busy life outside. There were, failing other things to observe, cabs in the streets. In Moscow there was life.

So, at any rate, he had thought while bored at Yalta. And he had made his three sisters, pining away in a far province, brood on it, yearn for it: "To Moscow! To Moscow! To Moscow!" How wastefully tedious was the passage of time; while you sighed, golden moments slipped away through your fingers. Outside, the band was playing so gaily, so bravely, and one longed to live! Time will pass, we shall have gone for ever; they will forget us, forget our faces, voices, and how many there were of us . . . The band was playing so gaily, so bravely, and it seemed in a little while we should know . . . why all this. A day would come when all would know what all this was about, why all this suffering; there would be no mysteries. Truth would be found; man would escape from the continual, oppressive dread of death, even from death itself.

He took his leave of this sub-lunar world with *The Cherry Orchard*, a shower of laughing tears. The Russo-Japanese war had broken out, peasants were called up, women howling in the villages. But he wrote gaily to a friend, "Are you going to the war? I'd like to." Knowing himself to be very ill, he visualised such a trip as full of interesting human material were he to join up as a doctor. Though defining the writer's task as one of stating a problem correctly as distinct from attempting to solve it, Chehov, as though to salve his civic conscience, readily allows a note of dissatisfaction with society to slip into his work. "We have fallen behind at least two hundred years, we have nothing yet at all, no definite attitude to the past, we only philosophise, complain of melancholy, or drink vodka. It's clear enough, isn't it: to begin to live in the present we must first atone for our past, settle with it, and one can atone for it only by suffering, by uncommon, unabating effort . . . They call themselves the intelligentsia, but say 'thou' to servants, treat the peasants like animals, learn badly, read nothing serious, do nothing at all, of science they only speak, in art understand very little. All are earnest, go about with stern countenances, speak only of what is serious, but live like savages . . . Show me where are those crêches, where those reading-rooms, of which we hear so much? Where are they? They exist only in novels. In reality there aren't any at all." To relieve such passages of their moralising tone, he places them ingeniously into the mouth of the most indolent and feckless of his characters, in this case the 'eternal student' who had got stuck at the university. And Chehov comments to Gorky, "This Russia of ours is such an absurd, clumsy country!"

At *The Cherry Orchard*'s première Chehov received an ovation, so warm and spontaneous that he could not get over it for many a week. The lyrical pathos of the concluding scene of the play left the audience

152

breathless with emotion; there was an unnerving pause of silence when the curtain fell, only to be succeeded by long, tumultuous applause which would not cease till the author himself, dumb with embarrassment, overcome beyond being able to speak, was dragged on to the stage by the actors and actresses. Chehov had now been writing for twenty-five years. He had become almost an institution. The great public, who had never seen him, were touched to the point of being shocked when they beheld a frail shell of a man, prematurely old at forty-four, whom they had always associated with a cynical new-generation iconoclasm.

"O if there were a life in which everyone grew younger and more beautiful," is a wish set down in one of his notebooks. His was the pathos permeating life with the fleeting nature of our existence, on this earth at all events, through which human beings, scenery, and even the very shallowness of things, are transfigured with a sense of disquieting importance. It was as if his people hastened to express their worthless individualities, since that was all they had, and were aghast that they should have so little in them to express, since the expression of it was all there was, and life at once was too long and too short to be endured.

His lungs, in the meanwhile, were giving out, and it was clear to those who saw him that his end was not far off. The hearty reception exhausted him; with relief he returned to his home at Yalta in the balmy air of the Crimea. His health was shattered, and at the beginning of May 1904, dangerously ill, he travelled to Moscow, and on arrival took to his bed and was laid up till June. In June he set off with his wife for a cure to the Black Forest, and settled in a hotel at Badenweiler. He wrote to his sister that he was hourly adding weight and steadily getting better and stronger, and he may have believed it, for he had already begun to make inquiries about the steamers returning to Russia, when, on July 2nd, he died.

Why did Providence strike down at the height of his powers this rare being, in the middle of his forty-fifth year? Priding himself on his ability to manage deftly the external appurtenances of the world, readily accepting (as one does in matters for which one has no real aptitude) the compliment from a woman friend that he knew how to live, he had long found the business of living an irksome struggle, his exacting genius having exhausted his slender strength. Nine years earlier he ended a long quasi-autobiographical story on a weary sigh: "Perhaps one will have to live another thirteen, thirty years . . . And what will one not have to go through in that time?" He was mature. He did not have to be changed for the future life, did not have to be converted – as, for instance, a house is 'converted' into flats. He had long prepared his transcendental mansion in a realm where hearts, not hands, build their abodes. He was

153

ready, and he went. He had not been feeling appreciably worse that evening, and he was telling his wife of a funny plot that had occurred to him for a new story, those trivial humorous stories he loved most, about a grand banquet to which distinguished foreigners, ministers and ambassadors had been asked, only as they were waiting for dinner to be served to be told by the hostess, to whom the news had that moment been broken, that there would be no dinner – the cook had bolted . . . There was the dinner-gong. He was laughing his delicious silent laugh, alternately urging his wife to go down to dinner and enlarging on his plot. They were staying in a big hotel and he was, of course, laid up in bed. Suddenly he was taken ill. His wife, about to go down to dinner, grew alarmed, sent for a doctor, who came up and found the patient rapidly slipping the moorings of life. To this German doctor Chehov, himself a doctor of medicine, of which fact he liked to remind other doctors and facetiously insist that medicine was his wife, literature his mistress, said earnestly, as from one medicus to another, "*Ich sterbe.*" In an attempt to revive his heart the doctor quickly ordered champagne. Chehov took the glass, drained it, remarking with a smile to his wife, "It's a long time since I had champagne", turned over on his other side as if to go to sleep, and died quietly without another word.

Fate, as though entering into the gaiety of his spirit, responded with a touch which might have been a plot for a short story jotted down in his note-book. His coffin arrived in a truck marked 'For Oysters', and was followed for a time by the wrong funeral procession. The remains of a certain General Müller, killed in the Russo-Japanese war, had arrived from Manchuria at the same Moscow terminus. Chehov's procession was for a time headed by a military policeman on a fat white horse and a military band and followed by General Müller's relatives. But the mistake was discovered, and Chehov's mourners, an intellectual rather than military set, found their corpse. Gorky was among the followers. He overheard a Moscow lawyer in front talking loudly of the cleverness of performing animals, punctuated from behind by fragmentary exclamations from a woman of fashion: 'He was so *wonderfully* witty . . .'

And, deep in the earth, his own words perhaps at last came true: "Those who will come one or two hundred years after us, and will despise us for having lived our lives so fatuously and so tastelessly, they, it may be, will discover a way to be happy; but we . . . You and I have but one hope. The hope that when at last we rest in our coffins, spectres, perhaps even congenial ones, shall beguile our dreams."

"As I shall lie in the grave alone," he had once jotted down in his note-book, "so in fact I live alone." Before he died he might have added in the words of his complementary if mutually unknown spirit, Proust (explicit where Chehov was implicit): "I understood the meaning of death, of love and vocation, of the joys of the spirit and the utility of pain."

How had Chehov understood it, how conveyed it? By that magic of style which Matthew Arnold calls *creative*: creative of a dynamic contemplation, at once evocative and real. It is that eternal aspect of things which, as Santayana has it when he speaks of Platonism, summons spirit out of its initial immersion in sensation and animal faith and clarifies into pure spirit. While the existence of anything is fugitive, its essence, stripped of belief and anxiety and habit, is an indelible variation of indispensable Being, an eternal form of the fleeting. "Life as it flows is so much time wasted and nothing can ever be recovered or truly possessed save under the form of eternity, which is also the form of art." Here, then, is the magic dynamic of art, at once reality and justification, the secret essence of Chehov's understanding insight, that warm and humble, calm and rich, glorious 'disillusion', the mingled vision and experience of life *as it is*, not inflated by the illusion of hope or shrunk and distorted by fear, but accepted in its own infallible proportions. It is the raising of Time into the light of eternity, into the glowing amber of the spirit, to become the life incorruptible that God and men alike can love:

Essentially all this is crude and meaningless, and romantic love appears as meaningless as an avalanche which involuntarily rolls down a mountain and overwhelms people. But when one listens to music, all this is – that some people lie in their graves and sleep, and that one woman is alive and, grey-haired, is now sitting in a box in the theatre, seems quiet and majestic, and the avalanche no longer meaningless, since in nature everything has a meaning. And everything is forgiven, and it would be strange not to forgive.

'Strange not to forgive': not cruel, callous or vindictive, but – strange. 'Strange' being the operative word, the key that unlocks the mystery of the kingdom with the knowledge that life *is*, and that no detail of its infallible proportions may be denied save at the peril of dying blind to its perfection, a perfection beyond reach of the slander, of good and evil dwelling, lamb by the side of lion, in that Kingdom of God, intimated in the parables of Jesus, "where everything is forgiven and it would be strange not to forgive".

And there was beauty, too, in the infallible proportions of light and shade cast by the hand of that supreme artist, life, revealing old Tolstoy, still alive, and never before able to see any merit in Chehov's plays, asking angrily, "But what's the *point*? What's it all *about*?", now noticing it all and laughing till the tears ran down his cheeks at a short

155

story produced at a village school as a dramatic sketch, showing an old peasant who had all his life along with other villagers unscrewed nuts in the sleepers on the railway track and, when condemned to prison as a deliberate malefactor, unable to square the cock-eyed man-made justice with divine justice which must surely take account of the innocence of his bewildered heart, gives the judge a piece of his mind. And though in his lifetime Chehov had been praised, notably for the wrong things, nobody, he once complained, had noticed . . . the first snow. Now they noticed.

44

KING EDWARD AND THE ENTENTE CORDIALE

Where romance outshone the reality, Goethe succumbed with good grace to persistent biographical inaccuracies respecting his love affairs, remarking that where a certain tradition has taken root it should be left alone to blossom and bear fruit. And one would not wish to disturb the legend of Edward the Peacemaker forging the Entente Cordiale, were it not that, like all acrobatic computations for balancing world peace on the point of a needle, it was at least as foolish as it was wise, as beneficent for the Edwardians as it proved disastrous for two Georgian generations. One wonders how much longer Foreign Offices will make play with offensive combinations for defence, whose dolorous stupidity is that they call forth defensive combinations for offence, in which power to take offence is so mixed with the power of giving it that all sense of right and wrong is lost.

The King was not personally responsible for a change of orientation in the foreign policy of Great Britain. Lord Lansdowne and Paul Cambon, the French Ambassador, initiated a rapprochement. A difficult operation in the case of two nations who were hereditary enemies and entertained for each other little more than mutual contempt, fortified by idiomatic derision of the other's ways. The mutual misunderstanding between the English and the French became totally baffling after the Entente. The King merely carried out his Foreign Secretary's instructions, and with complete success. His visit was the visible pledge of tentative support depending on eventualities to be determined when and if they eventualised, and as he was a king and the French had been without a monarch for thirty-four years they elected to be frigidly polite – which is the unwritten definition of *cordiale*. We are 'cordial' with people with whom it is in our interest to establish close relations which our natures preclude from being either intimate or sincere. King Edward's good sense was revealed during the frigid silence which greeted him as he drove through Paris on his arrival. "They don't seem to like us," said his companion. "Why should they?" said the King. But he liked French ways and French cooking. And when on the fifth day of his stay he drove to the station through Paris, the crowds, this time, cheered him.

As diplomatic relations between States are on a level not of their moral teachers and philosophers but rather of their most refractory urchins ripe for the reformatory, two fine gentlemen, both cultured and respectable, the Marquis of Lansdowne and Monsieur Paul Cambon, made a deal over other people's property. France coveted Egypt. "Covet not thy neighbour's wife" is the moral precept which our common religion enjoins us to honour. But Egypt was not England's wife, but the Turk's mistress, and we had by arrangement with her lord possessed her with some indication of mutual satisfaction. France was bidden to sate her passion with another Arab virgin. On condition that she recognised our liaison with Egypt as respectable, we indicated our willing consent to her forcible seduction of Morocco, if indeed French virility proved equal to the task. To that delicious understanding – that initial *entente* foreshadowing more to come – King Edward raised his hat as he drove through the streets of Paris.

King Edward had the reputation of being a great gentleman, who, to spare the feelings of the maladroit, adopted his own table-manners to synchronise with theirs. Legend has it that, when a guest of his ate peas with a knife, the King, rather than embarrass his companion, did like-wise. And since the Edwardians ate more than was good for them and the King's nerves were overstrained by the demand on his graciousness, his composure and affability bear out the impression that his sins were not mortal sins of the heart. On the surface he was irritable enough. One day at dinner he seized a melon and threw it on the floor to relieve the shock to his nervous system caused by Prince Edward, eventually Duke of Windsor, dropping a fork. Another night, inadvertently staining his shirt with a streak of spinach, he plunged his hand into the bowl and smeared a fist-full all over his starched front, watched with keen interest by the future Edward VIII. The King, a moment later, rationalised his action: he would have had to change his shirt anyway, he explained.

Edward VII, who liked to swing a loose leg in Paris, disliked nothing so much as being associated with two other kings, Leopold of Belgium and Carlos of Portugal who, because they also liked swinging a loose leg in Paris and were kings on a smaller scale, liked to think that they were three royal *boulevardiers* together, familiarity breeding that contempt which might bridge the gulf between them. King Edward, already burdened by his own reputation, did not wish to be saddled with theirs, and on his visits to Paris avoided the two kings. Before going to one theatre he made sure that Carlos and Leopold had gone to another, and was vexed when, one night as he entered his box, he saw that they had again changed their plans and were sitting in the stalls. To avoid them he did not leave his box, and at the end of the performance stayed behind half-an-hour to make sure that the two kings had gone home, only to find King Carlos waiting for him in his carriage outside the theatre door.

Those were the snobbish days still, even King Edward, on the subject of some recent marriage, observing to Lady Randolph Churchill that if the family of the bridegroom had not much money, it was to their credit that they had come over with the Conqueror. Young Lady Randolph's family had not come over with the Conqueror. As a Miss Jerome, she had recently crossed the Atlantic to insinuate herself into the serried ranks of the Marlboroughs, with the old duke the chief objector, since she was not even a dollar princess. Out of the bitterness of her own experience, she asked the King, who at the time was perhaps her only friend in England, whether he did not sometimes wish somebody would do a little conquering on his own.

Those were the days when, as one poet has it, "the labouring classes could scarce live a day, if people like us didn't eat, drink, and pay." They were the days when the parvenu could not but ask, "in the park and the streets when I look at the number of persons one meets, what e'er in the world the poor devils can do whose fathers and mothers can't give them a *sou*?" He rode, and he drove, and he cared not a damn, "the people look up and they ask who I am; and if I should chance to run over a cad, I can pay for the damage, if ever so bad." It was but that winter he came up to town, and already was getting a sort of renown; found his way to good houses without much ado, was beginning to see the nobility, too. The refrain goes, "So needful it is to have money, heigh-ho! So needful it is to have money." "Oh dear," he sighs as he contemplates his aristocratic hosts, "what a pity they ever should lose it, since they are the people that know how to use it; so easy, so stately, such manners, such dinners, and yet," he observes, "after all, it is we are the winners." He owns that "high-breeding is something", but concludes that "well-bred or not, in the end the one question is, what have you got." And as his thoughts turn towards the landed gentry with a view to founding a family of his own, he sings, "and the angels in pink and the angels in blue, in muslin and moirés so lovely and new, what is it they want, and so wish you to guess, but if you have money, the answer is Yes."

It was the time when men on the make insinuated themselves into the social graces, and German Jews like Sir Ernest Cassel became bosom friends of the King, and built their strongholds in Park Lane, presently to breed an aristocracy indistinguishable from the old. The King, like most kings, had empirical tastes, his interest in art being perfunctory to the point of politeness. Mrs. Asquith explains that royalty, handicapped from an early age by the acquiescence of sycophants, does not favour the company of men and women who speak their minds without fear or favour, being inclined to think of them as rather ill-bred. Royalty generally fell in most readily with conventional views, preferring soldiers and sailors to statesmen, the 'strong man' to the suave, a Kitchener to a Curzon. Originality made the least appeal to them, any man, unless he be a soldier like Roberts or a sailor like Fisher, who goes against the herd, appearing to Royalty to be 'a crank'.

When King Edward, who spoke of his nephew the Kaiser in a way to make Lord Lansdowne's hair stand on end, paid a royal visit to Berlin to 'cement' with Germany, there was in his honour a banquet followed by a very formal ball, in which a stiff minuet was danced by German officers and their wives, graciously watched from the four thrones by the two monarchs and their consorts. After half an hour of it, the King, leaning over to the Kaiser, produced in the German monarch a twinkle and a grin followed by agitated gestures to a page dressed up to look like little Lord Fauntleroy. All the while the dancers, gravely describing the intricate figures of a stately minuet, watched out of the corner of their eye the four thrones. Presently a huge footman appeared, carrying on a tray a decanter and a syphon which, with a low bow, he held before the King. Gravely Edward VII measured himself out a generous whisky with a splash of soda, and drank. Nothing like this had been witnessed at a German Court before. From next day, says E. C. Bentley who witnessed the entire scene and describes Bülow in the tights of his hussar uniform, looking like an apple on matchsticks, *der Visky-Soda* had become an institution.

It was the time, when appearances counted for more than content, when Max Beerbohm, who was a wit, a dandy of the intellect, blushed crimson because someone had said they'd seen him on a bus, and Sir Herbert Beerbohm Tree lolled in a cab, having furnished the driver by way of address with 'Round and round', and, when pressed, exploded, "Do you think I'd tell a fellow like you where my beautiful home is!" And Bernard Shaw, answering the call for 'Author', addressed his speech to the one dissentient voice piping, against the storm of unanimous acclamation, shrill abuse from the gallery, "My dear fellow, I quite agree with you, but what are we two against so many?"

45

TANGIER

The honesty of international politics is that legendary honesty (*d'ailleurs peu probable*) said to exist between thieves, and in this sense also exactly like it – that is, largely a fable. Though many of the ministers and ambassadors adhere to a high standard of person honesty, (if, through stupidity, a lesser intellectual honesty), it is almost an international tradition to indulge in the most thinly veiled diplomatic dishonesty. All is permitted for the Fatherland! Lying is being smart; stealing double smart. In much the same spirit as was later rendered more familiar by Hitler, the French Government in 1905 despatched a mission to Fez to 'protect' Morocco. This, in the teeth of a deal made in the thieves' kitchen dignified by the name of 'The International Obligations of the Treaty of Madrid', aroused resentment among the other 'signatories' loudly deploring such demonstrable lack of proverbial honour among thieves. The Sultan of Morocco, himself by no means above suspicion, hoped to set his despoilers by the ears by appealing to Germany. In diplomatic language he enquired: Would the German Government be good enough to inform him whether France in staking her claims was authorised to speak in the name of Europe?

The German Government was only waiting for this chance. Aware that England and France had made a deal over Egypt involving British consent for France to take Morocco – *if she could* – the deal resulting in a loose and tentative alliance called *Entente Cordiale*, Bülow, now under the cloak of protector of the weak and injured Sultan of Morocco and, moreover, as the champion of – a term never amiss – the sanctity of international agreements, meant to win a diplomatic victory: in plain words, to teach France a lesson not to think herself too smart just because she thought she had England behind her.

The Kaiser, who had earlier scorned Britain's advances, felt jealous to see John Bull consoling himself in the arms of Marianne. He reproached France for her infidelity to himself who had always secretly loved her. But just as he had begun to woo her, Bülow and hidden-hand Holstein, arguing that a monarch's function was to do the nation's will as interpreted by his servants, ordered their master off to Morocco. There, at Tangier, he was, in Bülow's words, to thunder threats against France.

The Kaiser at first resented tutelage running counter to his own view. But once he bestrode a white horse, he revelled in the role of protector of Islam. The day was March 31st, 1905. To his own alarm and against his better judgment, he had alarmed England shackled to France and never so dangerous as when frightened. The balance of power was upset. War seemed likely.

Bülow, pleased with himself, demanded under threat an international conference of all the signatory powers of the Treaty of Madrid, to challenge the too cordial entente by which, in return for French recognition of British occupation of Egypt, we presented a benevolent English eye to French ambitions in Morocco. The Sultan, informed that his welfare was apparently in the hands of contending European powers, was alarmed by his friends no less than his foes. France, a lover of precision, would not trust her fate to the hypothetical ambiguities of the Entente Cordiale. She could not rely on England's potential promises in an undefined contingency – still undefined in the face of an actuality. Russia was sunk in the mires of Manchuria. The only certainty lay in surrender to German threats. The French Prime Minister, Rouvier, threw over his Foreign Minister, Declassé, a sop to German vanity.

The international conference at Algeciras, into which Germany bullied the other powers, turned for her from a diplomatic victory into a diplomatic defeat, as Great Britain, backed by Russia, Spain and France, turned the scale against Germany. Defeated at the council table, it might be concluded, Germany was taught a useful lesson: threats did not pay. But such is the insidious work of God's Fifth Column, that no benefit was to accrue to mankind from any ascendancy of will over will, least of all collective will. In the empirical world all exertion not rooted in love is as blind and anonymous as the waves bearing down one upon another, with no one the gainer. The diplomatic defeat suffered by Germany at Algeciras had the tragic consequence for all that when, in July 1914, Sir Edward Grey invited the Great Powers to a conference which might have avoided war, Germany, with the diplomatic defeat at the Algeciras Conference still fresh in her memory, rejected the suggestion out of hand, recalling how, after she had scored a diplomatic victory by threat before the conference, she was outvoted at the council table.

When the conference had restored French prestige, the European position had crystallised itself into two sharply opposed camps: Germany, dissatisfied with Austria's tentative support, insisting on a closer alliance; France, purged by terror, strengthening her army and turning more eagerly to England, and a little later quietly resuming her penetration into Morocco.

Six years later, on the occasion of the unveiling of the statue of Queen Victoria, the Kaiser took the opportunity of asking King George whether he considered that the French methods, as he put it, were still in accordance with the Algeciras Agreement. "The King remarked," writes the Kaiser, "that the Agreement, to tell the truth, was no longer in force, and that the best thing to do would be to forget it; that the French, fundamentally, were doing nothing different in Morocco from what the English had previously done in Egypt; that, therefore, the English would place no obstacles in the path of the French, and would follow their own course; that the only thing to do was to recognise the *fait accompli* of the occupation of Morocco and make arrangements for commercial protection with France."

But this is running ahead. Hidden-hand-Holstein (who struck the Germans at home as being as sinister a figure as the Kaiser and Bülow, seeking to give expression to the plots which Holstein hatched in the Wilhelmstrasse, appeared abroad) couched his reasoned conclusions in a report summing up the position briefly as follows: Germany could either come to some commercial understanding with France concerning their mutual exploitation of Morocco, or Germany could bully France by pursuing a policy, which succeeded, over Tangier, to the point of forcing France to sack her own Foreign Minister, and only broke down at the conference table. The first alternative, "given," he writes, "the peculiarities of the French", seemed hopeless. Moral: continue the second policy of threats, while avoiding the conference table. Result: the Great War.

After Tangier there was an Agadir, and the Kaiser naïvely records that when from Agadir he called at Gibraltar, where previously he had been accustomed to be received with open arms, he found, coincident with a stern leading article in *The Times*, that his reception at the hands of the Governor and the British naval authorities was woundingly chilly.

46

THE YELLOW PERIL

The international goodwill of sovereigns, since it was precisely the sovereign nature of their States which made for international ill-will, was among the most ludicrous manifestations in the comedy of the Age. A supra-national organisation of society would provide a far more graceful and useful activity for monarchs, each personifying, not the power but the grace and cultural reciprocity vested in a country for which, let us say, the King of France might stand as a symbol, not merely of that which the spirit of France has given to the world but also in acknowledging from the throne what she has received from the cultures of other countries.

Instead, each sovereign wore for preference the uniform of one or other militant arm designed in self-defence or, 'taking the long view', in defensive attack, to deliver a punch at the solar plexus of another nation. The entirely ludicrous Willy-Nicky interviews never ceased, and sometimes even King Edward, in obedience to Whitehall, would steam up the Kiel Canal in his yacht *Victoria and Albert*, have the Kaiser to breakfast, and afterwards indulge in a private chat with Bülow. This they did, puffing over the remains of their breakfast at their long fat cigars, while the Kaiser obligingly paced the deck out of hearing. Then the Kaiser would ask his Chancellor what King Edward had said. And Lord Lansdowne or Sir Edward Grey afterwards questioned the King what Bülow had said. The point of it all being that in the end it apparently had not mattered what anyone had thought or said at any time: there was still a war to regale all their subjects. Not the least comical aspect was that, while the ministers were the servants, they were also the masters of their sovereigns to whom they assigned tasks commensurate with their abilities, patting them on the head when they interpreted their servants' wishes with diligent accuracy, taking them to task for their unconstitutional behaviour when they showed a will of their own. Of the three sovereigns, the Kaiser seems to have been the most fatuous, the Tsar the most obtuse, and King Edward the most innocuous.

The Tsar, not very friendly towards England, whose politics he distrusted, of whose army he was contemptuous, and whose monarchy he considered undignified, was in addition pained by the morals of his wife's uncle, King Edward, and deplored on top of it all the King's personal friendships with Jewish financiers. Nor did the Tsar care much for France. He wanted her money, he said, to build a railway, and would not let his distaste for French republicanism stand in the way of raising a loan in Paris.

It was, however, the small French citizen, the subscriber to this imperial loan, who got let down by Russian republicanism. The Tsar quite liked the Kaiser, but found him tiresome in the long run. The Kaiser could rarely contain himself for the zest, egotism, vanity, excitement and loving-kindness which all bubbled up in him at once. He generally seized the smaller Tsar by the arm and marched him up and down the deck of the *Hohenzollern*. The Tsar, who was not by nature demonstrative, felt foolish in the grip of Willy, and smiled helplessly.

Arm in arm, the two sovereigns came upon Bülow. "Do you know," the Kaiser laughed happily, "what Tsar Nicholas and I have decided to call ourselves? He is to be Admiral of the Pacific; I, Admiral of the Atlantic! Isn't it *wonderful*?" Bülow, gauging English reaction, but always the courtier, replied that he was sure the title 'pacific' expressed perfectly the Emperor of Russia's well-known desire for peace. The Tsar, disengaging his arm from the Kaiser's, seized Bülow's hand with a kind of precipitate Russian sincerity, looking into the Chancellor's eyes with a melancholy gaze expressive of a Ukranian spring evening. He agreed, he said, with all his heart. But Bülow, as soon as he had the Kaiser to himself, lectured his sovereign and got him to promise to drop this dangerous nonsense, and the Kaiser promised he would be good. No sooner had the Tsar left in his own yacht, the *Standard*, for home waters than the Kaiser signalled a parting message, reading: "The Admiral of the Atlantic bids farewell to the Admiral of the Pacific." After an interval back came the reply from the Tsar: "Goodbye."

Bülow at once pledged everyone to secrecy. Whether the Russians observed the same discretion was at least doubtful. The whole story was out in the British press, public opinion up in arms against the Admiral of the Atlantic who was already General of the world's strongest army and as such clearly a public danger.

The Russo-Japanese War not only revealed corruption in the Russian army and navy, but also, more important in retrospect, it now reveals to us what political judgment is worth at its best at any time, on a long view. *The Times*, attributing the Japanese victory to "the whole training of the Japanese in the great fundamental principles of human conduct," asked whether Japan's moral precept "may not well give this country pause and set us considering whether there were not greater ideals than buying in the cheapest market and obtaining the greatest average return upon capital".

To what greater ideals we have encouraged the Japanese with our applause may be gathered from Pearl Harbour. The *Daily News* announced Admiral Togo's victory at Shushima as 'complete, overwhelming, almost unexampled'. The panegyric of this very Liberal organ knew no bounds. Japan had dealt a blow at the hated Russian autocracy. Those who periodically attribute qualities and faults to the nationals, respectively, of their allies and enemies find themselves in frequent need of reversing their psychological estimations of national character. Today Russia is a socialist republic, Japan an aggressive fascist power. The ecstatic transport of the *Daily News* of 1904 rings strange to our ears. "Togo's victory," ran the leader, "recalls the noonday of British naval triumph, and challenges the greatest deeds of Nelson himself . . . The balance of naval power is suddenly shifted to an extent which we can hardly appreciate . . . By the Battle of Shushima Russia has ceased to count, and instead we have the Far Eastern seas once and for all controlled by a Far Eastern navy." *The Times* did not lag behind in enthusiasm. "The Russian fleet is practically annihilated" was the first message of the great Admiral, and all that subsequent information can do is to eliminate the qualifying adverb.

No wonder the Tsar was lukewarm about England. When the Russian Baltic Fleet had sailed for the Far East, in a fit of panic the Russians fired on British trawlers, in the sincere belief that they were Japanese torpedo boats of whose presence they had received false information – apparently from German sources. Only the reluctant regrets of the Tsar, extracted belatedly from him against his will, averted war with England, and Nicholas II, humiliated by this forcible extraction of apologies he should have offered freely, flew into the arms of the Kaiser and proposed a tripartite alliance with Germany and France against Anglo-Japanese 'intolerable arrogance and insolence', as he put it. The Kaiser despatched a draft treaty confined to their two countries, saying that when that was signed it would prove an irresistible magnet to France. In the meantime, the Kaiser urged the Tsar to stage a little military demonstration on the Perso-Afghan border to frighten the overbearing English. The very idea, however, frightened the Tsar.

As evidence that peace in the world cannot be solved on a basis of international alliances, one need only consider the draft treaty signed by the Tsar and Kaiser at Björko in July 1905, and repudiated by the Russian Foreign Minister because it ran counter to the Franco-Russian alliance, even though the Kaiser (though not perhaps Bülow) would have been willing, in exchange for a Russo-German treaty, to waive his claims in Morocco. It is clear that diplomatic cleverness is not in the long run necessarily more beneficent to the world at large than is diplomatic stillness. Two fools, like the Tsar and the Kaiser, had in this instance contrived a wiser document than their clever scheming ministers had been able to devise. Who knows but that a Russo-German alliance might have done no worse, and perhaps better, than a Franco-Russian one? One thing is certain: nothing can for long succeed on sovereign lines. God's Fifth Column will always sabotage it.

The Yellow Peril, of which first the Kaiser and then, after he had lost the war, the Tsar became increasingly conscious, is in truth a generic term that might well be applied to all the governments of Europe. It is their artificial panic at being got the better of which precipitates unwilling populations into war. The 'long view' in politics, God's Fifth Column has for long been trying to instil into the minds of men, is a synonym for shortsightedness, inasmuch as the wisdom of the world is foolishness with God. Since, however, politicians and journalists continually advocate either a firm stand or a statesmanlike compromise in pursuance of what they like to describe as a long-term policy, it should surely have occurred to our rulers that the Japanese, given their insular background, would make themselves as awkward in the East as we in the past have made our presence felt outside this island. Here we were: a stream of lowland Saxons bottled up on a small island, with not a few ingredients of native Celt, Roman and Norman French, a few currants and some yeast to make the cork pop: and the fine mixture not un-naturally spurts to the other end of the world, and in time overflows one-fourth of the habitable globe. Japan, too, had its native 'Celts' and diverse invaders, but whatever they may say to the contrary, it is clear enough that they are mainly Chinese. The old English caste system had its parallel in Japan. The Samurai, with their rigid discipline imposed on themselves in the interests of making Japan a land fit for the Samurai to live in, was not unlike its English counterpart recorded in *The Forsyte Saga*. The Japanese, bottled up on their little island, with their minds steeped in feudal values, indifferent as the English to all the doubtful world which isn't English, do not seem to care what the Chinese or Burmese think of them. Given such parallels of geographical position, what sense, one might ask (assuming that there was any initial sense in awakening them out of their Oriental stupor) was there in British support and encouragement of Japanese ambitions running contrary 'on the long view' to American interests? This is no criticism of any nation in particular, merely more evidence of the complete futility of planned diplomacy for a future completely incalculable when sovereign nations contrive to balance themselves by holding on to someone heavier than the rest, and overbalancing the lot.

The Tsar sought the Kaiser's opinion about the Yellow Peril, which, the Kaiser tells us, he was glad to give him, though it was really the Kaiser who, by way of supplying an answer to the Tsar, sought the Russian answer to his own question whether Russia might eventually range herself on the side of Japan, and together with her attack the whole of Europe. The Kaiser's answer took the form of saying that, if the Russians regarded themselves as one of the cultured nations of Europe, they would rally to the defence of Europe against the Yellow Peril, but if the Russians looked upon themselves as Asiatics, then they would unite with the Yellow Peril against Europe.

The Tsar, to intrigue the Kaiser, asked him which course he thought Russia was going to adopt. The Kaiser who, with customary tact, had suggested that the Tsar might conceivably turn out to be an Asiatic after all, now in his reply supported this view, which made the Tsar jump to his feet. It was outrageous to be told this by the descendant of a man who was a mere Elector of Brandenburg at a time when his own ancestor,

Peter the Great, was the fourth tsar of his line, not to say successor of the Rurik dynasty going back to A.D. 862! The Tsar, for once, was really outraged. He had, even on his visit to Japan as a youth, described the Japanese in a letter home as ridiculous yellow monkeys apeing European ways, and the fact that a Japanese policeman detailed to guard him had struck him on the head with the flat of his sword had not endeared the yellow race to the white Russian Tsar. He and his house were Europeans, and he would look upon it as a matter of peculiar honour to defend Europe from the yellow men.

In that case, said the Kaiser, the Tsar must alter his military dispositions by removing his troops from the Prussian and Austrian frontiers and altering his railway lines to converge from west to east, unless one was to draw the conclusion that the Russian military command were planning for precipitate retreat.

To this the Tsar did not reply. As Sazonov testifies elsewhere, silence from Nicholas meant that he had not been convinced. It was the mildest form of protest against which a sensitive man, well aware that the Tsar never expressed his disagreement with anyone in a form hurtful to another's pride, was powerless. The Kaiser, scarcely to be described as sensitive, felt he had been overruled. Sazonov recalls how, having expressed his astonishment that the Tsar should have spoken without a trace of irritation of a former minister who had for years pursued him with such envenomed malice, Nicholas, looking the soul of honesty, said, "That note of personal irritation I have long since succeeded in muting in me completely. Nothing is helped with irritation; more, a sharp word would have sounded more hurtful from me than from any other person in Russia."

The Kaiser's conclusions on the Yellow Peril shower such pearls of unconscious irony upon the present situation,[1] show up so completely the futility of mankind entrusting its hopes of peace and happiness into the keeping of sovereign nations, that they are well worth quoting. "Had Japan ranged herself," writes that monarch in exile, "firmly and unequivocally on the side of the Central Powers, from which, in former times, she had learned so willingly and so much: had Japan adopted soon enough such an orientation in her foreign policy and, like Germany, fought by peaceful means for her share in world trade and activity, I should have put the Yellow Peril away in a corner and joyfully welcomed into the circle of peacefully inclined nations the progressive Japanese nation, the 'Prussians of the East'." As an example of national self-righteousness and the innate human capacity to regard oneself as a lamb at the mercy of wolves, the Kaiser's approbation of the word 'Prussian',

[1] i.e. The Second World War.

in our own associations a word of ill-odour, is delightful. "Nobody," he concludes, "regrets more than I that the Yellow Peril had not already lost its meaning when the crisis of 1914 arose. The experience derived from the world war may yet bring this about." The Kaiser no longer seemed to know where the Yellow Peril was coming from, if not from Prussia, the Japanese of Europe, herself. And, most significant of all, his royal relatives appeared to prefer the Yellow Peril to the Kaiser. Nevertheless, he pursued with good will the poor Tsar even on his rare visits to his consort's Hessian relations. The Kaiser, who liked to show off before his equals and mistook this pleasurable feeling for disinterested love of 'his dearest friend and cousin Nicky', could not contain himself for impatience. The Tsar, who was in Germany on holiday with his wife's relations and could afford to buy anything he wanted, was irritated by the Kaiser's numerous invitations to partake of gala banquets.

He appeared, however, but only after much coaxing and a little irritably, in the company of his brother-in-law, the Grand Duke of Hessen, but only for a few hours, in Wiesbaden, where the Kaiser was waiting for him, all aglow with loving-kindness.

William promptly returned the visit in Wolfsgarten. He positively persecuted his Russian relatives with goodwill. Bülow had to meet the Tsar's Foreign Minister to cement further sentiments of amity. In the evening there was dinner at the castle, the Tsar being the host. All this, to stress again and yet again their mutual solidarity, their absolutely indomitable resolution not to go to war with each other – ever – and whatever happened.

Bülow had primed the Kaiser, and the Russian Foreign Minister had primed the Tsar. Again the sovereigns exchanged sentiments of amity, passionately confirmed identity of interests and purposes in remaining at peace. But, since Bülow felt he could never be certain of his restive and spirited pupil, he had instilled in him a maxim culled from Luther, testifying to the wisdom of keeping one's mouth shut. He even copied it out for him. Silence was golden, he implied, but in the mouth of the Kaiser absolutely beyond price.

Even so, the Kaiser had let himself go a bit at the end of the dinner. He recounted on his return, not without pride, having convinced the meek-eyed Tsar of the godlessness of the French Republic, the fecklessness of French ministers, and the double-dealing of the English. The Tsar seemed agreeably impressed and smiled bewined agreement when the Kaiser had said to him, "France is a sinking nation with a decided downward trend. The blood of its murdered King and nobility is on the nation which is being destroyed by atheism." The two monarchs mingled agreement over their wine. Yes, no good could befall a nation that killed its kings. On that point, more eagerly than on any other, they were, as their ministers testified, '*complêtement d'accord*'.

Not content to leave it at that, Bülow himself informed the Russian Emperor that for his own part he had been deeply impressed by some lines of Bismarck, who wrote that in the event of another European war all the three dynasties, the Romanovs, the Habsburgs and the Hohenzollerns would lose their thrones. At that Nicholas grasped Bülow's hand and shook it with much warmth, the while looking into the German Chancellor's eyes with his own soulful Russian grey-blue, so expressive, melancholy orbs, "*J'en suis convaincu aussi que vois.*"

47

THE LIBERALS

Hilaire Belloc sang

> The accursed power which stands on Privilege
>   (And goes with Women, and Champagne and Bridge)
> Broke – and Democracy resumed her reign:
>   (Which goes with Bridge, and Women and Champagne).

Arthur Balfour, the brilliant prime minister of what Disraeli once called the Stupid Party, was defeated in November 1905, and the Liberal Government of Sir Henry Campbell-Bannerman, himself the weakest link in a brilliant chain, as Lord Hugh Cecil wrote to Margot, was formed. The baleful memory of the Boer War, which had split the Liberal Party into two wings, could not keep them apart now that the magnet of power drew them together. Asquith, Grey and Haldane represented Liberal imperialism: Sir Robert Reid and John Morley an attitude of non-resistance to the forgotten evil of the late South African War; Lloyd George and John Burns militant pacificism. Grey and Haldane had wanted their imperialist friend Asquith to lead the Government, but their combined efforts, assisted by King Edward's advice – "You know, Sir Henry, we're not as young as we were!" – proved insufficient to push Campbell-Bannerman into the Lords. For a few days, besieged by threats of resignation from his leading colleagues, he

169

hedged, pleading for time until his lady had returned from Scotland. Back at 10 Downing Street, her verdict was, "No surrender!"

It must have always been pleasant to be a Liberal – a rich plantation owner, like Augustine St. Claire in *Uncle Tom's Cabin*, professing a mild leaning towards Liberal principles in regard to the more drastic treatment of domestic slaves, luxuriously indolent in the contemplation of the nobility of his own nature as expressed alike in his Liberal professions and his handsome features; or a Turgenev landowner, faintly exercised over questions of conscience and principle, while basking in his serf-appointed estates mortgaged to the hilt for card debts. Tories and Liberals dined and hunted together, while disagreeing in principle. The Cecils were particularly warm friends of the Liberals, Lord Hugh Cecil sending Mrs. Asquith little notes to congratulate Margot on the successes of her Party or to apologise for some misdemeanour by a member of his own. Hugh and Robert, like most Cecils declared to be incredibly brilliant from their first birthday, disappointed the high expectations aroused by their political debuts, not so much in capacity as in subject, both brothers developing an absolutely unrivalled technique for arguing about the equity of marrying your deceased wife's sister, some point of dogma around the Authorised Translation of the Bible, the omission of a line from the marriage services, or a verse from the Prayer Book.

In 1906, the Liberal Government, hoping to manage without the Irish votes to keep them in office, ejected Home Rule from the Party programme. Soon enough the Liberal Party was to be shackled by one ankle to the eighty Irish votes in order to keep themselves in office. Abroad, the Liberals got shackled by the other foot to despotic Russia, forfeiting all independent action in foreign politics. Even though free of a formal alliance with France and Russia, England could no longer, as of old, throw her weight against any potential aggressor without straining her loyalty to them. A balance of power proved even more difficult of achievement when several nations were herded into rival groups than when each operated on his own account. Germany, tied to Austria, became involved in the vindication of her weaker partner's troubles and ambitions. England, only nominally and morally aligned with France and Russia, found that the adage 'united we stand, divided we fall' meant sinking, the three of them together, into a morass of quibbles and insincerities, each capable of precipitating the whole edifice into the welter of war. Germany, made to espouse Austria's grievances, and Britain those of France and Russia, each found herself preparing, on behalf of her satellites, to fly at the other's throat.

In a memorandum penned by him in 1906, the Foreign Secretary, Sir Edward Grey, unconsciously testifies to the utter futility of his own or anyone else's conclusions about the 'best policy' for keeping the world at peace: "There would, I think, be a general feeling in every country that we had behaved meanly and left France in the lurch. The United States would despise us, Russia would not think it worth while to make a friendly arrangement with us about Asia, Japan would prepare to re-insure herself elsewhere, we should be left without a friend and without the power of making a friend and Germany would take some pleasure in exploiting the whole situation to our disadvantage . . . On the other hand the prospect of a European War and of our being involved in it is horrible."

1906 was the year when Marcel Proust, unaware that there was anything more ludicrous about foreign politics than the intricacies and entanglements of dynastic and feudal considerations, into which Comte Robert de Montesquiou had fatuously volunteered to initiate him at a price, had begun his great novel. Without being himself aware of being a God's Fifth Columnist, with an intellectual pick-axe he was demolishing the rotten plaster, the porous bricks and crumbling cement of fashion-able and other moribund society. Arnold Bennett met him and found him "a dark, pale man, with black hair and moustache; peculiar, urbane, one would have said, an aesthete; an ideal figure, physically, for Bunthorne." Proust continually twisted his body, arms, and legs into strange curves, after the manner of Arthur Balfour. It was Arnold Bennett's impression that Proust, far from being self-conscious, was well aware of himself. He was treated as a considerable lion, though his reputation rested at the time on a single book, *Les Plaisirs et les Jours* written as a youth. Proust sat at the hostess's own table and dominated it with his conversation, while everybody showed a special interest in him. He was just beginning to unfold the detailed mental evolutions and vicissitudes in society of a group of people of whom, though it is boring to read, one cannot stop speaking whenever a few Proustians gather together.

48

HITLER IN THE DOSSHOUSE

When Asquith moved to No. 10 Downing Street, while Margot's wealthy father volunteered to pay the rent for their Cavendish Square house, and D. H. Lawrence moved to the Davidson Road School, Hitler moved to a casual ward in a Vienna dosshouse. A widow's pampered child, his mother dead, he had found himself in early adolescence, to his intense surprise, loitering inartistically among the rejected scum of the south-eastern capital, where he had hoped to make his mark as a painter, or at least as an architect. Instead, he discovered himself to be one of the humiliated, the insulted and injured – a Dostoievskian character; very definitely the 'have-not'. Twenty years divide him from the time when he will be able to say to the party treasurer who had complained that the party's chest was empty, "Schwartz! To-morrow morning I must have one thousand marks", remarking next morning to a satellite marvelling at Schwartz's resourcefulness, "Where he got it doesn't interest me!"

Like D. H. Lawrence, born surly because he could not get back to the womb, he had sallied forth out of a respectable lower-middle-class home to see his artistic aspirations shattered and himself debased to association with Vienna's down-and-outs. Imbued with a latent sense of respectability, as the son of an admonitory official, however modest and now in his grave, his one desire was to be least like him. If he was no artist, and had neglected the chance of emulating his peasant father who had lifted himself out of dire peasanthood into a cosy niche of petty officialdom, who *was* he?

Proud he was, that was certain; but why? Of what? Unable to pretend to being even nature's gentleman, he espied, he says, the aristocratic principle in nature. Thirty years hence, on the eve of gaining supreme power, he was branded by 'the old gentleman', that East-Prussian pillar of respectability, President Field-Marshal Paul von Hindenburg, as 'that Bohemian corporal' – a term signifying everything that is racially, nationally and militarily doubtful.

The waif and stray refusing to grow up, refusing to work, demanding all or nothing; in default of *all*, remaining stubbornly the outcast, the pariah, the untouchable, wanting to play the glory game, sulking on his bunk in the dosshouse because nobody would play soldiers with him, in the bespectacled professorial and commercial modern world. Such was

Hitler. A borderline case *par excellence*. In looks, birth, race, class, education, gifts, temperament: everywhere the scales were tipped just a little against him. In none of these aspects, taken separately or as a whole, could he succeed. His vanity exposed to all these agonising frontiers of inferiority, his was not a mission of service to all mankind, but rather of making all mankind serve his own ambition. Utterly unserviceable himself, it was, in the long run, amazing though it seems, more simple for him to carve a completely new world to fit the manifold handicaps of his complicated incapacities than by training, like his father, to adapt himself to fill one particular niche in the existing world.

That, he knew, he could never achieve, because he was not fully awake and because universal goodwill was not his first consideration, but merely a by-product of his personal ambition. Rather was he a kind of astral projection, accidentally grown rigid, of the lowest common denominator of mediocrity, the 'little man', by some fluke, some unexpected materialisation, finding himself engulfed by the disconcertingly, the inescapably solidified realisation of his vaporous daydreams. It is as though what is now the fashion to describe as 'escapism' had taken solid shape. His very face, a frozen, twisted, fractured face, bore evidence of the sudden transformation. There is a strain about it, a stress, a struggle. It is a *Mein Kampf* in itself. It is a face cast in the despondent mould of the despised and injured, the groveller, the ne'er-do-well, suddenly attaining his paradise of fulfilment. But a face is not plastic and cannot adapt itself, without notice, to such a sudden change of roles.

Theosophists speak of a state of gratifying wish-fulfilment which awaits us when we slip off our mortal coil. Had Hitler died at the conclusion of the war, he would have spent that recuperative interval in realising his wishes to become Führer of Greater Germany. That he has realised his wishes on this hard-set brittle planet is so extraordinary that it strikes one as unnatural, and Hitler himself has often likened his movements in the field of action to those of a sleep-walker. It is as though the souls of would-be Führers, destined, after a period of wish-fulfilment, to be, in their second incarnation, invoice clerks on earth, have, in collectively resisting a repetition of this dismal prospect, imbued him, their peer, with all the concentrated spirit of their inflated dreams: the essence in him which propels him forward causing him, with astral disregard of solid obstacles, to pierce his way through to the attainment of his heart's desire.

He had no birth, no breeding, no education. So he said, "I'm for race." Ignoring his mother's Slav origin, born on the wrong side of the Austro-German frontier, he cried to the four winds that he was a GERMAN, and clamoured for the beginning of a new pure-blooded aristocratic race. But he had no class to boast of; so he said, "Abolish class distinctions"; all Germans from now on were to be equal. He had no acceptable nationality; so he said the country of his birth was to join the country of his adoption to make him a German. "I have brought," he said, "my home home." He had no race – and, he recognised there *was* no such thing; so he said, "Let there be race! From now onwards!" He had no profession; so he invented one, made a place for himself right at the very top of eighty million Germans. He had no culture; so he invented his own brand. He had no mind, no intellect; he was practically illiterate; so with his secretary's assistance he wrote a book to say that he despised education, and forced everyone to buy and read it – which, incidentally, solved his other handicap of having no money. In his attempt to be an architect he failed in his entrance examination; so he placed himself in a position where he could get palaces built for himself to his own design. He had no sense of accuracy or of history; so he decreed that his own accession to power was henceforward to be the chief study of every school curriculum. He had no well-founded right even to his name, his father having but tardily been adopted by his grandfather whose illegitimate child he had been; so he decreed that his name should be on every lip as a greeting.

A Dark triumph of the sinister Unconscious; a vindication of the psycho-analytic age, and an illustration of the habitually misused term 'wish-fulfilment', which should really mean what it says: actual fulfilment of a cherished wish.

If Hitler, as he sat listless on his bunk in the casual ward of the Vienna dosshouse, sharing a chunk of bread with his mate, Hanisch, had told Hanisch where he, Hitler, would be twenty-three years hence, to say that Hanisch would not have believed him is perhaps the best example of an understatement.

49

DEATH OF KING EDWARD VII

The passing of monarchs is fraught with commotion in this world. Whether their arrival in the next is greeted with silver trumpets is a matter for speculation. Assuming the entirely subjective nature of afterlife, a monarch making his entry into the *couloirs* of his defunct state would, by force of habit, still imagine himself to be surrounded with royal pomp and thus at the very least be as firmly and smugly embedded in accustomed royal prerogatives as a lunatic who thinks he is Louis XIV.

King Edward, though he had only reigned nine years, had grafted himself on the public imagination by his long martyrdom as Prince of Wales. All during the Diamond Jubilee he deputised for his mother at the longest and most tedious of religious ceremonies. And having had his fill of the hymn 'Eternal Father, strong to save', "It's all very well," he grumbled as he came out, "about the Eternal Father. But what about my eternal mother?"

Now, on his deathbed, he provided an emotional outlet for a generation brought up in an era of seeing giants against a background of puny events. Mrs. Asquith, as she freely confesses in her diary, was keyed up to a pitch of almost hysterical excitement. In her own record of the emotions through which she passed at his death there is an unconscious suggestion that she enjoys strong emotions. Her personal life, starved of occasions to which her slightly melodramatic and self-dramatising nature so willingly responds, she seems to fasten on any public occasion with a sort of grim alacrity of emotional satisfaction. Having sent her Premier husband, cruising in the Mediterranean aboard the Admiralty yacht suggestively named *Enchantress*, a wireless message, reading, "Advise your returning immediately. The King seriously ill: all London in state of well-founded alarm: Margot", she felt, as she says, shattered, and during her luncheon party at 10 Downing Street K. of K.[1] jarred on her fine sensibility by walking up, as it were jack-booted, to the window and observing aloud, amidst general silence, that the flag was still flying at the Palace.

That evening she met Sir Edward Grey and Sir Charles Hardinge. Both looked white with sorrow, and they did not shake hands. The King, who had earlier sent for his bosom friend, Sir Ernest Cassel, was now unconscious. Sir Edward Grey, driving Mrs. Asquith away in a taxi, said, "This is a very big moment; these things have to be, but it has come as a terrible shock in its suddenness."

When Mrs. Asquith was in bed, where she lay stunned and cold, the head messenger came in, followed by his wife in her nightgown, and demanded the latest news. But at midnight he walked in, this time himself the messenger of death, and, with the pleasurable feeling of self-importance with which grave news, however sad, invests the bearer, he advanced well into the room before he spoke. Stopping at the foot of the bed, he said, "His Majesty passed away at 11.45."

[1] Lord Kitchener of Khartoum.

175

Mrs. Asquith, abandoning herself to the luxury of unrestrained grief and the vision of herself as a tragic actress, cried out loud, "So the King is dead!!" and burst into tears.

Next morning Sir Ernest Cassel came to see her and they cried together on the sofa.

At dinner that night Winston Churchill, beguiled by a future holding even more for him than his past, made the company wince at his perhaps too precipitate attempt to close a chapter by proposing to drink to the health of the new King. There was a touch of mellow reproof in Lord Crewe's voice when he answered, "Rather, to the memory of the old."

Asquith returned three days later. Next day he saw the new King, George V, and, as he says, was moved by his modesty and common sense.

Some years later, when King George's sons had come of age, somebody told the King that all his life he had modelled himself as a parent on His Majesty. Mindful of the excellent example set by his sovereign, he took care to treat his own sons, not like a father, but as though they were all brothers together – just like the happy royal family. King George listened with interest. And when the man had finished speaking, he said that his father had always feared his mother; he in turn had feared his father all his life, and he believed in making his sons fear him. Discipline and fear were the right relationship between a father and his sons.

The death of Edward VII, the Peacemaker, whom William II called 'the Encircler', brought the Kaiser to London, where he was received by the entire royal family at the railway station "as a token," he says, "of their gratitude for the deference to family ties shown by my coming." King George drove with his cousin to Westminster Hall, lighted merely by a few rays of the sun filtering through the narrow windows and making marvellous play with the precious stones on the crown and the insignia resting on the gorgeous coffin, and here, over the dead body of his uncle, "My right hand," says the Kaiser, "and that of my royal cousin found each other quite unconsciously on our part, and met in a firm clasp." That night one of the Kaiser's English relatives assured him that his handshake with the King was 'all over London', and that the people were deeply impressed by it and took it as a good omen for the future. "That," said the Kaiser, "is the sincerest wish of my heart."

Some six years later King George V, receiving at Buckingham Palace an escaped British pilot from Ruhleben, imparted to him, not without glee, that the prospect of reciprocating the Zeppelin raids by our dropping a few bombs of our own on Berlin was at hand. "And that won't please the Kaiser, what!" he added, with a happy chuckle.

The Kaiser, in whose grip King Edward's mother had her last tangible experience of our world of sight and sound, was, of course, making much of his presence at the funeral of his uncle, following closely on horseback with "my friend, the Duke of Connaught".

The military boots reversed astride the riderless charger were led in procession, a custom which at King George's funeral prompted a little girl to ask, "Mummy, when we die do we all turn into boots?" Mrs. Asquith relates that when she, so familiar with horses, approached him, his defunct majesty's mount, by way of registering his opinion of the dauntless rider to hounds, stretched out his fine neck and showed her all his teeth.

This masterpiece by an anonymous hand sounded the note of popular reaction to the death of King Edward:

> The will of God we must obey
> Dreadful – our King taken away
> Greatest friend of the nation
> Mighty monarch and protector.
>
> Heavenly Father, help in sorrow
> Queen-Mother, and them to follow,
> How to do without him who is gone
> Pray help, help, and do lead us on.
>
> Greatest sorrow England ever had
> When death took away our dear Dad;
> A king he was from head to sole,
> Beloved by his people one and all.
>
> His mighty work for the nation
> Strengthening peace and securing union,
> Always at it since on the throne
> He saved the country more than one billion.

A Duke of Norfolk, as ever, leads the procession, as it winds slowly, first through the loftier parts of London, then up the increasingly more sordid Edgware Road and Praed Street, until it alights at Paddington. The Kaiser, riding through London behind the bier, noted with approval the splendid turn-out, the matchless bearing of the Brigade of Guards in their perfectly-cut tunics, all members of the future British Expeditionary Force described by him in the war to follow as 'contemptible': a term, 'The Contemptibles', which the B.E.F., as is the English habit, adopted as their own pet name. Nine kings of Europe and not a few crown princes followed the Kaiser's lead astride his steed, including the Archduke Ferdinand of Austria (who had married the maid of honour) unconsciously rehearsing his own funeral.

At Windsor, to Chopin's 'Funeral March', the procession of kings and queens moved into the St. George's Chapel, tightly packed with an audience of mourners. King George walks with his mother. Following comes her own Danish sister, the Tsar's mother, for twelve years now a dowager empress, and, behind, the Kaiser and the Duke of Connaught.

Lord Esher reverently relates that when earlier he came in to condole with Queen Alexandra, she showed him the dead King stretched on the bed clad only in a night-gown and, with a light almost of triumph in her eyes, she said, "Now at least I know where he is . . ."

But at this moment, with all eyes upon her, she was left standing, as she had been in life, still beautiful, widowed and alone, before the slowly sinking coffin. Suddenly she knelt, covering her face with her hands.

The Kaiser at the new King's request, stayed in Buckingham Palace. He talked with the widowed Queen Alexandra of bygone days stretching back to his childhood when, as a little boy, he had attended her wedding. The newest generation was sprouting up around them, and King George drew a guest's attention to his youngest son, Prince John (since dead), who had come into the room: "Here's John. Watch him make a bee-line for the plum cake." A lady-in-waiting relates how little Prince George, later Duke of Kent, plucked Prince Henry, later Duke of Gloucester, into the background, there to impart to him some comic news, over which they struggled valiantly to suppress their happy chuckles. But on this occasion Prince George was only old enough to cry because he could not eat his breakfast porridge. "Lumps!" he said tearfully, when asked why he wouldn't eat it. The Kaiser, as usual throwing his weight about, took the opportunity of snubbing King Ferdinand of Bulgaria, who had aroused the derision of Nicholas II in newly calling himself 'Tsar'.[1] Always anxious to earn the praises of his Chancellor, William II also took the opportunity presented by the funeral to tell Monsieur Pichon of the wishes communicated to himself by Bülow regarding German interests in Morocco, which Monsieur Pichon – he could hardly do less – 'readily' undertook to bring to the notice of the Quai d'Orsay.

Such is the comedy of pomp and power.

---

[1] There were tsars in ancient Bulgaria, long before Ivan the Terrible (1534–84) assumed the title.

50

TOLSTOY DIES

"The sirteenth century," the Chauve Souris comic, Nikita Baleiev, used to say in an appalling Russian accent, "was unlucky. Shall I tell you why the sirteenth century was unlucky? It is because all the people who lived in the sirteenth century – (pause) – arr – (pause) – now – (pause) – dead."

The same ill-luck applies to quite a number of centuries, the death-rate of this biography alone being appalling.

Parallel with the royal drama, another, of a sovereign of a realm not of drums and flags but of the mind and heart, and of his far less gracious if not less jealous consort, was taking place, culminating in the sage's death towards the close of the same year. "I am doing," Tolstoy wrote in a letter he left behind for his wife from whom he was at least escaping, "what old men of my age often do – withdrawing from the world to live out my last days in peace and solitude." Ten days later he was dead.

There is in this final flight, desperate, yet strangely comforting, as though auguring retreat to another and a better life, an echo of Tchebutikin:[1] "I leave to-morrow, perhaps we'll never meet again, so here's my advice. You know, put on your cap, take a stick and go . . . go and keep on going, go without looking back. And the farther you get, the better."

"Still very depressing," Tolstoy confides in his diary, "and I am unwell. I feel that I am to blame, and that is good." Having spent forty-eight years with his wife and provided her with liberal offspring, of whom nine survived infancy, he was desperately dull. "Help me, Father! Source of the life of the spirit, sole origin and beginning of life, help me at least for the last days and hours of my life here, to live only before Thee, serving Thee alone. Yesterday when writing to Gàlya [Chertkòv's wife] I realised for the first time my guilt in everything, and naturally felt a wish to ask forgiveness. And as soon as I felt that I experienced complete joy. How simple and how easy! How it frees one from wanting human fame! How it lightens one's relations with people! Oh, if only this is not a self-deception and endures!"

A day came when Sofia Andreievna thought she would startle her husband into compunction by herself volunteering the incredible sug-

[1] *Three Sisters*, by Anton Chehov

gestion that he should go to see Chertkòv. But he, to whom to read another's intentions was easier than to dissimulate his own, merely observed with ill-suppressed irony that he had been expecting her to say that for some time. And there was another storm. Why, he said, talk about it? Stop playing the fool was all she need do.

This was a counsel of perfection, easier for him to give than for her to follow. And, ten days before he died, he fled. His secretary-daughter was in the secret. Rising before dawn, quietly, stealthily, lest he be heard, he let himself out of the house and, in terror of his wife, always a light sleeper, he hurried the coachman who was harnessing the horse. While the Countess slept, he drove through the gate and down to the station, where he took the train, breaking his journey at a monastery. There, surrounded by a tender esteem but a little uneasy at heart for the pain he knew he was causing his wife, he spent the night, continuing his journey, a journey without plan or destination, in the morning. Full winter had set in, and he was travelling third class with no other thought but to mortify the flesh, to expose his old age, having taken the plunge, to the elements. Too long had he tortured his spirit while mollifying the body, too long had he swallowed charges of inconsistency between his preachments and his comfortable way of life. He had reduced luxury to simplicity. It had not been enough.

When the Countess read his letter, she wilted. "My God! What is he doing to me . . ." She did not finish reading, but ran away into the park at a half-run, making straight for the pond. More than once she had stood in it up to her waist, while she sent the servants to inquire how Lev Nikolaievitch was taking it. But something about her unnatural half-run this time told them she was serious, and, having allowed her a long start, they set out in hot pursuit.

It was the secretary-daughter, who hated her mother, who shouted to one of the guests, "Follow her – you who have boots on!" while herself running to put on her galoshes. The Countess was advancing rapidly down the lime-tree avenue, making for the pond. The guest, at first concealing himself behind the trees, then made a dash for her, but was told by the daughter, puffing up behind him, not to run so fast. Moderating his pace, he was overtaken by most of the household staff: Semën Nikolaievitch the cook, Ilya Vasilivitch the old valet, Vanya the footman, all were running, and the secretary-daughter flew past impetuously like a steam-engine, her skirts rustling. The Countess had already reached the edge of the pond when, glancing round, she espied pursuit. This made her hurry. Slipping on the wet planks of the little bridge, she fell with a thud right on her back, and then, crawling and catching at the planks with her hands, rolled over into the water. The secretary-daughter, slipping on the self-same spot, sprawled on the planks and rolled over into the pond after her mother, as did the guest. Meanwhile the Countess, throwing up her hands, was sinking, and presently disappeared. Diving after her, the pair of them lugged her out, soaked and heavier than ever. The men clasped hands to make a chair and carried the Countess home in procession.

It was Tolstoy himself who, without sampling a pond, contrived to develop pneumonia from merely travelling in winter in a draughty and unheated railway coach. Taken out at a wayside station and put to bed in the station-master's house, a week later he held out his hand to one of his married daughters and said, "And now it's the end . . . and it's all right." His breathing grew more faint, but presently he sat up and said to them in the voice of a prophet, "But I advise you to remember one thing: there are a multitude of people in the world, and you only consider one Lev . . ." On these words he lost consciousness, but so strong was his constitution that there was still life in him, and he came to. His face was bluish, his nose had sharpened, and he breathed very rapidly, tormented with unceasing hiccups. The doctors were injecting camphor and giving him oxygen. He had intermittent heart attacks with severe spasms. The author of many a deathbed scene depicted with imaginative realism, he was now at once actor and spectator at his own.

Meanwhile, his wife, arrived on the scene but excluded by combined medical and family opinion from forcing an entry, lived in a railway carriage standing on a siding, making the most of the interviews she freely accorded to journalists, and posing for cameramen and cinematograph operators, a small army of whom had by now gathered at the little wayside station of Astapovo to 'cover' the sensational death of a world-famous figure. Asked why her husband had left home, she replied that he had done so as a sort of advertisement, to attract attention to himself. Once she got as far as the steps of the stationmaster, Ozolin's, house, asking that her young daughter should come out to give her news of his condition, pleading with her that all she wanted was to be 'in on it'. Just to be allowed to go as far as the ante-room. The daughter heard a buzz and saw two cinematograph operators grinding away just as her mother was slipping through the front door. "You are keeping me from him, but at least let people believe that I have been with him!" she wailed. She talked largely to the priests sent by the Holy Synod, leaving them a wide loophole to say that her husband, having repudiated all his errors, had with contrite heart returned to the bosom of Mother Church.

In his delirium he was muttering, "I will go somewhere where no one can interfere with me." And in a loud tone of conviction he moaned, "To escape . . . I must escape!" Tossing about, with loud and deep groans, he was trying to rise from the bed. Having sat up, "I'm afraid," he said, astonished. "I'm dying . . ." Twice he sighed, "It is hard." A single candle was alight in the room, standing behind his head. Recognising his favourite son, he called, "Serëzha!" Sergei at once knelt so that he might hear him better. His father said something which seemed to make a sentence. But the son could make nothing of it. The house-doctor had caught a few words which, with the piety of medicine attending on literature, he had at once noted down. They were: "Truth . . . I love much . . . they all . . ."

Towards midnight he began to toss about. He breathed rapidly, loudly, his voice was husky, his hiccups increased. Three doctors were at his bedside. After an injection of morphia, to which he had objected, he calmed down. They gave him something to drink, and he even took the tumbler in his hand and drank. Doctors came in and went out. For three hours he slept, wandering in other worlds, on short leave from this, whence he was due to be discharged. The door into the adjoining room was ajar. There, as though in the grandstand, sat relatives arrived for the last scene. In the sick-room, lighted by a single candle, at the pillow-side, sat Chertkòv. And from the bed came a difficult, regular breathing of an immortal soul about to relinquish its tenure in the world of Time. Two hours dragged by, and at two o'clock in the morning, at the house-doctor's suggestion, they called the Countess.

She had been married to him nearly half a century, had borne him a dozen children, had copied out *War and Peace* fourteen times in her own hand, had edited and re-edited all his editions, managed his estates, acted as his literary agent, and had, because she wanted to serve God and Mammon by reconciling her husband's spiritual with his natural instincts, forfeited her position as the first of her husband's lieutenants and counsellors to the late newcomer Chertkòv, who pursued an uncompromising spirituality on a large unearned increment. Led into the room as a last concession, and only because her husband was safely unconscious, she stood and looked at him from a distance. Then going quietly up to his side, she kissed him on the forehead, sank to her knees, and murmured, "Forgive me!" The doctor who suggested that she should come, now asked her to leave, for fear that Tolstoy might open his eyes. She complied, but not at once, lingering a little by his bedside. Then she retired, taking her place in the grandstand in the adjoining room among the minor relatives. There she remained for the next four hours. But ten minutes before the end she went up to him a second time, knelt by his bed, and said something. But he had by then settled his accounts with the empirical world, and it was certain he could neither see nor hear her.

At three o'clock in the morning, the effect of morphia having begun to wear off, he began to move and groan. But he did not again regain complete consciousness, though when someone held the candle near his eyes he made a wry face and turned aside. The visible world clung tenaciously to him. After five o'clock in the morning his breathing became slower and fainter and, suddenly, ceased. One of the doctors said aloud, "The first cessation!" Two more cessations followed, and finally a slight rattle. Came the last sigh, and there was a silence, broken by one of the doctors observing professionally, "A quarter to six." The house-doctor went up and closed the unseeing eyes.

The four brothers, including Lev whom he could not love, and Andrei in whom he could not credit the presence of the Holy Spirit, carried their father's coffin, while cameramen and cinematograph operators were scrummaging for position for the best angle, and feverishly turning their handles. The coffin was laid in a luggage van on a siding and coupled with their coach to a passenger train, uncoupled again at a junction, coupled to an express train on the Moscow–Kursk line, and railed home to Yasnaya Polyana.

A bishop remained stubbornly if self-consciously seated when the senators rose in a body to honour the passing of one long since acclaimed as his better by no less a master than Turgenev himself, who on his own deathbed had pleaded in a letter to the younger man, "My friend, great writer of the Russian soil!" to forego prophecy and return to literature. And Nicholas II, priding himself on his sense of proportion, noted down in his diary that in his view too much fuss altogether was being made over the death and funeral of Tolstoy. But in a Petersburg school the master told the boys that today he would not teach. A man towering above his fellow men, a great genius of the human spirit who had lived in their midst and survived, an almost legendary figure, into their own decade, had just passed away, a writer unique in power and comprehension, renowned in his lifetime as an immortal the world over, but the special pride and heritage of Russia, an artist miraculous in the simplicity of his touch, a wonderful man . . . Like some great wounded beast, feeling his end was near, he had made for the woods to die there, alone, away from all . . . There would be no Russian literature lesson that afternoon.

BOOK THREE

THE NINETEEN-TENS

51

AMERICA TAKES A HAND

It was again America who, in 1898, having salvaged from the wreck of The Hague Disarmament Conference a permanent international court of arbitration, in 1908 pressed a court of justice on a diplomatic Europe mentally still floundering in the period before the wars for the Spanish Succession. And then, in June 1910, the United States, emboldened to hope that its own example in establishing a Federal Republic capable of absorbing any number of independent sovereign states might not go unheeded by Europe, launched a plan that would have spared a trusting mankind two suicidal world wars. An international force consisting of the combined navies of the world was to keep all nations permanently at peace. That was the proposal.

The resolution was adopted unanimously by the House of Representatives. It was adopted without a dissident voice by the Senate. It was acclaimed by the Press and the whole American people. It was eagerly signed by President Taft who, knowing something of the Machiavellian spirit of Foreign Offices, sent two of his personal friends, Mr. Elihu Root and Dr. Nicholas Murray Butler, to Europe to sound out the responsible statesmen before they had a chance to sabotage the plan.

Dr. Butler consulted Sir Edward Grey. He had conversations with Philippe Berthelot, the permanent head at the Quai d'Orsay. He went to Berlin and saw Bülow and the Kaiser himself. He went to Vienna. Mr. Root travelled to The Hague, to Paris, to London. Then they made their report to the President. What would Woodrow Wilson not have given to be, in 1919, in the position in which President Taft, commanding the unanimous votes of both Parties in both Houses, found himself in 1910!

And what was Europe's answer to this friendly initiative of wisdom from the New World? The American proposal was received with exquisite politeness. "*But*," said the Ministers of State, our diplomatic longheads, "not yet." Four years, this was, before the first calamity burst upon the world but was to leave them as it found them, cheerfully clinging to their old opinion – "Not quite yet; wait and see."

"They waited," says Dr. Butler, "and they saw."

The First World War over, H. G. Wells wrote his *Outline of History* in which he warned, "Drop your fatuous sovereignties or it will happen again."

And it happened again.

"Against stupidity," Goethe exclaims in despair, "even the gods themselves struggle in vain!"

That to a body of men intent on finding a solution for preventing wars the obvious idea should not have occurred to extend their accepted principle for exchanging the incurably disabled to include the incurably insane – to wit, statesmen who get a war going – argues a queer incapacity for sustained thought. Even to stop a war that has already started, nothing more revolutionary than an extension of the existing convention for exchanging prisoners-of-war need be invoked. Taking all Cabinet Ministers in rotation, beginning with the head of the Government and his opposite number in the enemy country, each in turn is invited, under the auspices of the International Red Cross, to meet his opposite number in the enemy camp and, failing to agree on immediate peace terms, each is duly interned in a neutral or the other's country, and the process repeated all down the scale, until the list of ministers and, after them, of members of the legislative bodies having been exhausted, some trade-union leader, worker, artist, doctor, dentist or musician must at last be found in each belligerent country who is willing to come to terms with his opposite number.

Such a method would not exact any greater hardship from statesmen than they themselves are willing to impose on generals who, when they fall into enemy hands, submit to captivity as a matter of course and do not expect to be released till hostilities are over. The answer – that such a method would not prove acceptable to statesmen and that nothing but the killing off of a substantial portion of the population itself can be decisive – would argue that men were no better than ants reacting in a purely automatic fashion without even enough brain-force for the little initiative and mother wit required to break out of the rut of a suicidal convention.

Why should there be new methods of waging war and not new methods of making peace? If unable or unwilling to rescind all frontiers and nationalities and merge all the earth's resources in a world republic, statesmen confessed their impotence to prevent future wars, there was still the alternative – the one available to a child who can in an emergency stop an express train by pulling the communication cord – to stop a war that had already started. If it was not beyond the wits of the various national representatives assembled at The Hague to agree, first upon a court of arbitration, then upon a court of justice, followed by various conventions for humanising war, surely they might have set a new precedent for the automatic exchange of statesmen between enemy countries at the outbreak of hostilities in order to immobilise a war at the outset. But it was not apparently given to them to draw this logical conclusion. They might be capable of agreeing on reducing, by international treaty, poison gas to an agreed potency, or limiting the use of submarines to specified areas. But neutralisation by exchange of their own poisonous nuclei would have seemed to them almost obscene. The normal course, to their minds, in a diplomatic impasse, was to burn their nation's boats and urge their nationals to wade ashore to safety through a sea of blood.

America's timely counsel of common sense went unheeded by Europe, with two world wars to follow as the price of Foreign Office sagacity.

52

COLONEL HOUSE AND WALTER PAGE COME TO EUROPE

Next, President Wilson sent his friend Colonel House to sound the statesmen and monarchs of Europe for a possible indication of a change of heart. After a military banquet at Potsdam, attended in force by old Prussian war horses, who could not make out what sort of a colonel Colonel House was, since he wore no uniform, let alone carried a sword, House had a lengthy audience of the Kaiser. The banquet had been to mark some anniversary of a severely Prussian character, and the generals resented the presence of an American civilian to whom their Kaiser appeared to be devoting too much time in the midst of their celebrations called to extol, not peace but rather the spirit of victory. The Kaiser, not to be overheard by his Prussian Blimps, had taken House aside. And while Woodrow Wilson's friend was broaching the subject of an enduring world peace, the Kaiser was developing his pet theme – the Yellow Peril. There they stood on the open terrace, surrounded at a respectful distance by Prussian veterans, some of the 1870 war – the Kaiser banging his palm with his fist and in turn wagging a stern warning forefinger at Colonel House to drive home his own points about the Yellow Peril – moustachios waxed to point up, old Prussian war lords drawn up in a semi-circle, moustachios, walrus fashion, pointing lugubriously down. The Kaiser banging his palm, then vigorously wagging his forefinger: bang! wag; bang! wag; old purple-faced generals of the Prussian guard the while watching suspiciously from afar, rolling a slow, captious eye from their emphatic sovereign back at one another. This went on for some time.

In the face of all his imperial assurance, they, in the simplicity of their soldier hearts, still felt the man was a bounder. When during a banquet the Emperor raised his glass to a distinguished old general, addressing him, as a mark of special favour, familiarly in the second person singular by his Christian name – '*Du, Moritz!*' – the general, rising noisily to his feet and drawing himself up stiffly to attention, his face inscrutable in its marble lack of expression, recited his full names, rank, title and regiment, in some such manner as this – '*General-Lieutnant der König- lichen Preussischen Pferdartillerie, Graf Fritz Walter Egon Moritz von der Vogelweide zu Hauch*', and sat down noisily, having taught his sovereign not to take liberties with a Prussian officer. The Kaiser was always being reminded that the dignity of the throne was not, in the opinion of his subjects, identical with the person who occupied it.

In this respect it was the blameless monarch, King George V, who was most successful in fusing the two. Walter Page appreciated this happy mixture of common humanity and royal dignity which he espied in King George, who reminded him, as he was presenting his credentials, of a fact of which all American ambassadors were painfully aware – that he was hard done by. It was a shame that a rich country like the United States could not provide her Ambassador with an official residence. Next, Walter Page saw the King in full regal panoply of pomp and circumstance. The brilliance and opulence of the throne room impressed Ambassador Page, as later the style of life in Buckingham Palace impressed President Wilson. The King and Queen and the royal family sat on a raised dais. To the one side of them sat the wives of the diplomats, to the other the duchesses, decked out in jewels by the ton. The queue of débutantes had to wait till the initial ceremony was over. First the ambassadors came in and bowed and the King shook hands with them. Next came the Ministers of the Crown. They bowed – but were not shaken hands with, because the ambassadors represented foreign sovereigns and were here as guests, whereas the Ministers were merely servants of the Crown.

In front of the King stand officers in resplendent uniforms, turbanned and bejewelled Indian princes, and all around stand ambassadors, courtiers and pages holding up the Queen's train. When the Queen and

King move, two courtiers back before them, one carrying a gold stick and the other a silver stick. The queue of waiting débutantes moves forward. They curtsy to Their Majesties and pass on and out of the presence.

The presentation over, a stand-up supper was served. In a smaller room the King and Queen and members of the royal family walked around and talked to the members of the diplomatic corps. At a sign they all troop back to the throne room, and, preceded by the backing Goldstick and Silverstick, Their Majesties come in, hand in hand, and bow to the ambassadors, then to the duchesses, then to the general group, and they go out. The show is ended.

No less than by the style of the Court, Walter Page was impressed by the English butler, notably his own, who performed his complicated functions without a hitch, ministering to His Excellency's guests from the moment of arrival to the last minute of departure when, having first given them a drink and a cigar, he called their carriages and banged the door on them.

The Kaiser likewise comments with approval on what he calls English 'externals', showing, as he says, that in a country under parliamentary rule more importance was attached to pageants of an almost medieval magnificence than in the case of 'the young German Empire'.

A plague on young empires! Only jackanapes like the Kaiser and Kipling and Hitler can interest themselves in young empires. An empire does not endear itself until – as *'das liebe, heil'ge Röm'sche Reich, wie hält's nur noch zusammen?'* – it is, like old cheese, due to crumble to pieces.

But the Kaiser also admired the Russian Empire – and the Russian Army. In November, 1910, he managed to get the Tsar to come to Potsdam and bring his new Foreign Minister, Sazonov, to 'cement' with the new Chancellor, Bethmann-Hollweg, and his Foreign Minister, Herr von Kiderlen. "The result of the conferences between the two statesmen," the Kaiser bleats his clichés, "seemed to promise well for the future. After they had exchanged views, both harboured the hope of the establishment of favourable relations between the two countries."

But it did not end even there. Royalty, the visible sign of national sovereignties, exerted themselves to the last: even so, they still plunged into war. In 1912, more solidarity. Kaiser and Tsar met at Baltic Port. Their two yachts anchored side by side. The Tsar had his children on board. The monarchs vied with each other in hospitality and good will. They inspected each other's squadrons and took meals in turn at each other's table, doing themselves pretty well. Royalty may not exercise much influence on events, but they never lack for either deference or champagne.

The Kaiser admired the Russian regiment drawn up in his honour. He liked the look of the strong young soldiers with their bold mien accentuated by the way they all wore their caps cocked jauntily over one ear; their sun-burnt, martial faces. It was his last visit to Russia. The Kaiser deplored the fact that the Tsar's decisions were invariably reversed with every new visitor who made a strong impression on him. He was not, like his father, Alexander III, a strong man who, having made up his mind that he would not go to war, abided by his own decision. With the Tsar it was always the last man who was right. And inevitably he could not himself, the Kaiser regrets, always be that man.

That year, too, there was a furtive attempt on the part of the British Government to negotiate an offer of neutrality, conditional upon certain limitations in German naval construction. This mission, sponsored by Haldane, alarmed at his 'spiritual home' having become a 'powder magazine', however, finally fell through, as Sir Edward Grey was afraid of jeopardising the existing tentative understanding with France and Russia. The German war party was offset, on the other hand, by the growth of a pacific socialism and a pacifist Chancellor. It was Sir Ernest Cassel, a friend of the late King Edward, a millionaire of German-Jewish extraction, who went to Berlin and presented a verbal note which aroused in the Kaiser and Bethmann-Hollweg a degree of astonishment. "It was interesting," says the Kaiser, "to watch the play of expression on Bethmann's face as he was told about the matter."

The Kaiser, half an Englishman, volunteered to write the answer in English, but complained that his Chancellor subjected his grammar and style to much torture, "owing to his habit of probing things philosophically, and to his methods of profound thoroughness, which caused him to be most particular with every word, in order that, having been studied from every angle, it should afford nobody cause for criticism later on." Which, we may add, did not prevent Bethmann-Hollweg from deploring, two years later, that we should attach importance to a mere scrap of paper. The Kaiser's English, though fluent, was hardly better than his cousin's, the Tsar's wife's. He was capable of writing to Nicky, "Should you like to sign it? It would be a very nice souvenir for our *entrevue*." On the other hand, as far back as the first year of Bülow's chancellorship, the Kaiser was able to give him proof of uncommon insight into English psychology. Above all, he insisted that there must be no playing the diplomatic game or 'finessing' with an Englishman. For once the Englishman had become suspicious, there was nothing more to be done with him, despite the most honeyed words and obliging concessions. As indeed Hitler must have found out after he had not only made us suspicious, but also positively frightened us into declaring war on him.

But on his visit to London in the previous year to attend the unveiling festivities of his grandmother's memorial, the Kaiser was still the principal guest. Amid salutes and greetings, the statue was unveiled, revealing the Queen, in white marble, seated upon her throne. And the march-past began, the immaculate troops faultlessly wheeling in the circular space around the statue. At a gala performance to celebrate the occasion a curtain painted by a lady, "executed", the Kaiser notes, "with much dash and enthusiastically acclaimed by the audience", depicted King George and the Kaiser, life-size, on horseback, riding towards each other, exchanging military salutes.

Then the war began.

53

1914 or ALICE IN WONDERLAND

"How *did* it . . . how *could* it have happened?"

When on August 4th, 1914, Mrs. Asquith, who had heard her husband tell the House of the British ultimatum to Germany, came home to Downing Street, she went to bed, and there, alone between the sheets, she pondered this question.

It is a question which the unsophisticated heart – and beneath her protective veneer Mrs. Asquith is a compassionate, warm-hearted being – may well ask. But ask whom? Ours is such an Alice-in-Wonder-land world, with the goal-posts moving all over the place as the game is played, with good intentions souring into evil, and evil turning to good. It is a world of crooked mirrors and distorting acoustics. Put your question. Back comes the answer in a parody of your own voice. Whatever you wish to believe, that you will hear yourself speak: in the brain chamber of each one of us is quartered our private ministry of propaganda to keep up the ego's morale.

But Alice, pardonably dazed in Wonderland, says she is seeking information. She has set out on a *fact*-finding mission. "What brought about the First World War?"

"The assassination of Archduke Ferdinand of Austro-Hungary at Saràyevo," flashes back the answer. The steel jaws of the monster official historian snap to like a mouse-trap; the implication being that if facts you want, facts you will get, nothing but facts, but, inevitably, never *all* the facts. For facts to be relevant must be susceptible of demonstration as causes of events. But who, apart from God, is able to produce *all* the causes? And what use picking a few choice causes to string on a pet theory?

Alice, in the sincerity of her heart, cannot reconcile a shot fired off at Saràyevo with four years of pitiless slaughter of millions of innocent men on land, on sea, under the sea, and in the air. "Were there any other reasons?"

"Any number!" echoes her brain-box. "Take your choice –according to allegiance or opinion."

None of the answers satisfied Alice. Alice's questions are prompted by feelings at once real and ideal. But the world cannot answer in kind because the world is not real and ideal, but merely actual and abstract. Alice is aware that she is running up a rapidly descending staircase, and all she can do, while getting out of breath, is to pick up her feet in the same place over the shifting moment. Let her stop, and the moving staircase will drag her down into the grave.

But that is not all. There is the added unreality of numbers. For they have pulled a hood over her head so as to render her oblivious, not merely of B and of ten million Bs, but even of what she herself saw but a moment before or might see a moment after. Bemused by this garish fun-fair world, Alice is almost ready to believe that, here, anything, of course, might start a brawl.

There was the Kaiser, himself as garish a figure as you could wish to find at any fun-fair. Tinsel suited him, who had never stepped out of his kindergarten, where he had once played with his future consort Augusta Victoria. She, who had admired him in the nursery, admired him when he played at being Kaiser. He had not developed his emotions, merely letting his impetuosity overrun the atlas instead of the nursery floor. And she had nothing in her to develop, save jealousy of her husband, supreme lord of Germany and of her own emotions. Her love for him, as the courtier Eulenburg said, was "like the passion of a cook for her sweetheart who shows signs of cooling off", the Empress forcing herself upon the beloved unwilling affections.

When Europe was on the brink of war, the Kaiser was still playing a sort of floor-game with lead soldiers and cannon. In the political field he was trying hard to emulate Bismarck who "could juggle with five balls of which at least two were always in the air" – a trick, the Emperor adds sadly, regrettably beyond his own powers. At this time, when peace hung in the balance, everybody in France and Russia and Britain blamed one man. But for the Kaiser, everyone thought, all could be settled peacefully.

When what everybody prayed might happen to the Kaiser at last did happen to him and he was a fugitive from his own people, it did not occur to him that he had merited anything but praise in surrendering, to save further bloodshed, his diadem of empire for, he thought, a martyr's crown. An exile in Holland, he would have given much to have followed a different course in the crucial days of July 1914. Time hanging on his hands, he took up with himself the belated question of war guilt with which the Allies, not unnaturally, had saddled Germany, and expressed a reasoned feeling for relegating this question to an international tribunal; a method he had marginally annotated as 'Rubbish!' when Nicholas II in July 1914 had telegraphed his view that the conflict should be relegated for arbitration to the International Tribunal at The Hague.

The war over, four million dead, and himself listed at the top of war criminals, the ex-Kaiser wrote, "A real clearing up of the 'question of guilt', in which surely Germany would have no less interest than her adversaries, could be accomplished only if an international, non-partisan tribunal, instead of trying individuals as criminals, should establish all the events which led to the world war, as well as all other offences against international law, in order, thereafter, to measure correctly the guilt of individuals implicated in every one of the nations participating in the war. Such an honest suggestion was officially made by Germany after the end of the war, but, so far as I know, it was partly refused, partly found unworthy of any answer at all."

Yet on July 27th, 1914, Sir Edward Grey announced in the House of Commons that he had made a proposal to Germany, France and Italy to hold a conference with Great Britain, but that, although France and Italy had accepted, no reply had been received from Germany. "This," Mrs. Asquith says, "is a complete answer to the Kaiser's contention that Germany did not want war."

The Germans, being riddled with martial rhetoric, refuse conciliation to prevent a war when all other nations are clamouring for an immediate conference. Germany begins a war arrogantly, spurns mediation, but halfway through, realising she has bitten off more than she can chew, suggests peace-conferences to end bloodshed. The English, riddled with moral rhetoric, begin a war with the utmost reluctance, suggest conferences and plead common brotherhood to avoid it, generally to no avail; but once they embark on it, see it through to the end, remain deaf to all appeals for humanity, brand the enemy as a moral leper, nay, vermin that must be exterminated to make the world clean. But having muddled through to victory, they shake hands with the enemy, who, they now declare, is not a bad sort.

195

54

NATIONAL SOVEREIGNTIES ARE POWDER MAGAZINES

Having been outwitted at the international conference, called at their own instigation, over Morocco, the Germans preferred, this being with them a matter of pride, to blackmail the other side into a diplomatic defeat. They would not have a conference. The Tsar who, in the teeth of Horatio Bottomley's perhaps one and only piece of sensible advice – "To hell with Serbia" – thought he was in honour bound to prevent Austria from trampling little Serbia, would have readily agreed to negotiate the matter with Austria. And the Kaiser telegraphed to Nicholas II to the effect that he was doing his utmost to persuade Vienna to agree to 'frank negotiations'.

It would not require much persuasion on the part of Germany, since any threat to leave Austria in the lurch would have exposed her to the wrath of Russia. But the balance-of-power principle – a supposedly steadying balance rocking like a drunkard – may have induced the Germans not to risk antagonising their principal ally. The Kaiser's telegram crossed one from the Tsar advising conciliation, and in another, answering Willy's first, Nicky urges in his make-do English, "It would be right to give over the Austro-Serbian problem to The Hague Conference. I trust in your wisdom and friendship." To which the Kaiser, as already mentioned, pens the marginal comment "Rubbish".

Each monarch is particularly nervous of the other's advisers. The Kaiser replies to the Tsar's second telegram, warning him not to mobilise his army if he does not wish to precipitate irreparable disaster. Though nominally more powerful than the Kaiser who, by nature more meddlesome, is curbed by his Constitution, the Tsar, through ignorance and vacillation, is in reality quite as much a slave of Russian cross-currents and cross-purposes as the Kaiser is of German. Each monarch has some ministers or generals who want a war and suspect their opposite numbers of stealing a march on them by precipitating mobilisation – when protested against always defended as being sincerely preventive.

Ruminating on the past, the Kaiser at Doorn quotes the Russian Foreign Minister Sazonov's statement: "The German Emperor's love of peace is a guarantee to us that we ourselves can decide upon the moment of war" as conclusive evidence of Russian war-guilt. The mediocre Sazanov or the profiteering Suhomlinov might well contemplate trapping their sovereign into a 'preventive war' with Germany or Austria. In a crazy international system of offensive defence, a statesman or general planning for 'preventive war' would be shocked to hear himself described as a war-monger, when the description answering most nearly to his own conception of himself would be that of a long-term pacifist. That is why, reading guilty men describing themselves in their memoirs invariably as men of peace, historians shift the blame from one to another, and for the most part in vain.

Nicholas II, along with other rulers of Europe, was merely guilty of acquiescing in an idiotically precarious international order of quite obsoletely and unnecessarily 'independent' States, so touchy about their 'sovereignty', so nervous of attack, so provocative in defence of what they considered their safety, that any of the statesmen, had they but the brains, could surely have foreseen the folly of trusting these inflammable structures called Sovereign States to the accident of any lighted match, such as Saràyevo – merely one out of a box, any one of which was just as sure to set alight the powder magazines of Europe.

55

THE TSAR'S DAUGHTERS

Only six weeks before the outbreak of the war the Tsar, convinced of the self-adjusting international mechanism of the system ensuring at all times the balance of great powers, took his family on a yachting trip to Rumania. The idea, but tentatively mooted, was to affiance his eldest daughter, Olga, to the reigning king's grandson, Carol, second in succession to the throne. On board his yacht *Standard*, the Autocrat of All the Russias was approaching Constanza, Rumania's port on the Black Sea, where the old King Carol and his consort Carmen-Silva and their family were awaiting the imperial family of Russia.

Olga's three young sisters are evidently in the know. For when, after the usual presentations and a Te Deum at the Cathedral held by the Bishop of the Lower-Danube, the two royal families at last sit down to a banquet, the younger girls are constantly bending towards their French-Swiss tutor, Pierre Guillard, and with their laughing eyes indicating their eldest sister. She is sitting, dutifully and sensibly, beside Prince Carol, and is answering his questions with her usual friendliness.

Fate, however, this day decreed that, in order that the future King Carol should have for a son a particular Michael, the womb of another woman, a particular Helen of Greece, was required to achieve the necessary results. And God's Fifth Column accordingly was exercised to sabotage the match between the Russian and Rumanian royal houses. In this way, we must presume, births are conditioned – *if* indeed we choose to believe (as we need not) that the final generation on earth thus conditions all the earlier matches.

The banquet for eighty-four guests and the Te Deum were an attempt to bribe destiny. But destiny will not be bribed or deflected from its course. The King rose to welcome the Emperor, speaking French with a strong guttural German accent. The Tsar, in a soft and melodious voice, rose in his turn to render thanks to the King. But none among them suspected that fate had placed a veto on this matrimonial prospect. The girl was destined, four years hence, to be murdered in a cellar at Ekaterinburg. Young Carol was marked for a chequered career.

Both families were there in force. Crown Prince Ferdinand's beautiful wife, the future Queen Marie of Rumania; her cousin, the Russian Empress Alexandra, both, among other things, granddaughters of Queen Victoria – they were all in some sprawling way related, representing the involved, meandering, consanguine, tainted pedigrees of royalty.

The Tsar's three younger daughters could barely conceal their boredom. And the attitude of their august father was one of tender commiseration: poor dears! *Of course* they felt bored! He too felt nothing but unalloyed tedium in official exchanges of civilities. And when, an hour later, the imperial yacht lifted anchor and steamed away for home in the direction of Odessa, they all felt happy and wanted to laugh and play pranks. As yet the Archduke Ferdinand is a living man, enjoying life in the arms of the Duchess of Hohenberg, the Kaiser on his northern holiday, the English countryside a quiet paradise, the London Season in full swing, and a summer peace reigns everywhere in Europe.

By next morning the engagement was off. Or, at any rate, indefinitely shelved. Olga did not want Carol. She preferred Russians to foreigners. She had danced with one or two terribly fascinating naval aides-de-camp of her father's. The whole of Russia was her garden. What was she to Carol? And what was Rumania to her?

56

POINCARÉ VISITS NICHOLAS II

July 20th, and a battleship, not inappropriately named, *La France*, casts anchor in Kronstadt Bay. On its deck appears a small dour-faced civilian, and the Emperor of Russia comes aboard to greet his distinguished visitor and ally, the President of the French Republic. The Marseillaise, a suspect tune run to ground in Russian factory districts and presaging the overthrow of the monarchy, blares forth from shining regimental brass. The Emperor and the President depart together and arrive in Peterhof, Russia's show-place, spouting fountains in imitation of Versailles; and the President of the Republic, a word of evil omen in absolutist circles, is escorted to his suite in the Great Palace.

Again a banquet. Four days of ceremonials. Monsieur Guillard informs us that the President produced an excellent impression on the Tsar. But it does not seem to matter what impression any personage produces on any other personage. Four years hence, on a certain date in 1918 when Poincaré, still President, will be seen conferring the baton of a Marshal of France on General Foch – providing the curious spectacle of one disagreeable man kissing another – the Tsar, a charming man, will be seen sitting for hours in a chair without moving, transfigured by a religious quiescence described by his gaoler, a commissar in Siberia of the Union of Soviet Socialist Republics, as 'idiotic indifference'.

Poincaré stays four days with Nicholas, partakes of banquets, has his fill of ceremonies, and confers on the nine-year-old Alexei, the heir to the throne, the Order of the Legion of Honour, a decoration instituted by Napoleon I, who murdered and pillaged during his invasion of Russia a hundred years earlier, apparently without his Order having lost anything in the esteem of his victims' descendants. And this is because they also belong to predatory nations practising murder and arson, without prejudice to subsequent friendly relations: a result showing that the maximum sacrifice exacted by Sovereign States from their subjects is generally for something not sufficiently serious to warrant even a post-mortem grudge.

Poincaré finally commends Monsieur Guillard as an admirable French tutor, and, having showered his largesse of flattery, leaves an excellent impression on the Emperor, who stresses the, to him, agreeable fact that the President of the Republic is not at all a diplomatist. Raymond Poincaré, who, five years later, was to reduce the jerry-faced Lord

Curzon himself to tears of impotence, the Tsar found a pleasant companion, a remarkable man of a high order of intelligence and – as he adds absurdly – "*which is never amiss*, a brilliant talker". In high hopes of a permanent international peace ensured by Franco-Russian collaboration, to that end the Tsar sped back the President of the Republic on his water-route to France.

Then the bomb exploded at Saràyevo.[1]

57

THE KAISER'S ARGUMENT

The German Emperor in his *Memoirs* provides – not unexpectedly – the German point of view. His explanation, more plausible than convincing, nevertheless constructs the framework for Germany's refusal to come to terms before the outbreak of the war. In France, he points out, the idea of revenge had been sedulously cultivated since Sedan, while Germany had no reason for staking what she had won in the Franco-Prussian war of 1870. Russia, in a state of continual internal ferment, might be expected to welcome a national war as a sort of safety-valve to release the rising steam of a brewing civil war, to say nothing of her ambitions for an outlet through the Dardanelles. England, he fancied, might welcome a war to squash German commercial and mercantile expansion. England, France and Russia together were suspected in Germany of fostering the encirclement and overthrow of Germany. Germany's anxiety to forestall their moves was the explanation of her diplomatic tactics and her reluctance to be out-manoeuvred, as she had been at the Morocco conference.

The Kaiser's line of reasoning, curiously ineffective, resembles Hitler's later pronouncements with which we have grown painfully familiar and which so distressed Neville Chamberlain, who called in vain from the Führer for 'well-marshalled arguments' to substantiate his claims. William II's argument contains the same large air-pockets, and

[1] In fact, the assassination of Archduke Franz Ferdinand at Saràjevo had occurred before Poincaré's visit on June 28th, 1914.

apparently admits as legitimate veiled threats to attain his predatory demands. In view of the grouping of three very strong powers against him, the only political course open to Germany, the Kaiser argues, was to defer Germany's claim to a share in the apportionment and management of the world to which, he says, her ability entitled her, until such time as Germany had secured so great an economic, military, naval and political ascendancy as to be able to attain her aim by mere threat of force. "The aims of the Entente," he writes, "could be attained only through a war, those of Germany only without a war."

Proust, whose sacrifice in the world war did not exceed the strain of coming up at forty-five before a medical board which rejected him, might have described in a dictionary of national biography his part in the Great War in two words: 'Seriously inconvenienced'. A fervent patriot, he had no doubt of the justice of the French cause, nor of the guilt of any. But the logic of passion, he recognised, even in the service of justice, was never irrefutable by one who remains dispassionate. To remain blind to what was false in the claims of the person called Germany, to see justice in every claim of the person called France, the surest way was, not for a German to lack judgment and for a Frenchman to possess it, but for both to be patriotic.

58

IMPOTENT POWER

Patriotism is not an evil, provided it is quiet. But a peaceful nostalgia for one's own land is better. It is competitive patriotism which is a bore and a general nuisance, being unblushing self-approbation anonymously multiplied and hurled at the throats of other similarly swollen fools.

The Saràyevo incident now followed into a symbol of mass suicide. For one murder the world's outraged sense of justice exacted four million murders. The name itself – Saràyevo – reaching western Europe through the German Press, fastened itself on the English and Latin imagination in a German spelling, so perpetuating its mispronunciation. The German 'je', correctly designed to reproduce the Slavonic sound 'ye', became the doubly absurd 'Sarajèvo'.

The diplomatic chancelleries got working in Petersburg, Berlin, Vienna, Paris and London. On the evening of Wednesday, July 29th, as Mrs. Asquith was resting before dinner, her husband came in and, contrary to his usual habit of walking up and down as he spoke, stood still, a habit denoting in this seasoned Yorkshireman unusual mental perturbation. He told his wife that he had caused precautionary telegrams to be sent to every part of the Empire that they must prepare for war.

The Tsar from his Peterhof Palace was sending telegrams to Tiumèn, an obscure town in far Siberia, where Rasputin was recovering from a wound inflicted on him by a jealous peasant woman. The Empress associated herself with the text of these telegrams which, indeed, she is likely to have inspired. "We are frightened by the war that threatens. Do you think the war is possible? Pray for us. Help us with your advice."

From his bed in the hospital at Tiumèn – the same God-forsaken Tiumèn where, less than four years hence, in a peasant cart, escorted by Red soldiers with drawn swords, the Tsar and his consort, with one of their daughters, would be taken to entrain, on their last stage of martyrdom, for Ekaterinburg – from the same Tiumèn Rasputin answered that they must at all cost avoid war, in order to prevent the most terrible catastrophe befalling the dynasty and the country.

Mrs. Asquith, as she records, was 'thrilled with excitement' at the information conveyed to her by her husband.

"Has it come to this!" she exclaimed.

At which he nodded, we imagine with the ponderous gravity of the monumental fellow whom any man eight years Prime Minister must feel himself to be.

At the House that afternoon there had been rumours of resignations in the Cabinet. Whether anyone resigned or not mattered little to him, Mr. Asquith told his wife, so long as Crewe and Grey remained. He, Asquith, did not intend to be caught napping.

Britain, only superficially divided over the Boer War, and not at all over Wilde, was about to have its own Dreyfus Case, rending the whole country in two, with the likelihood of a civil war, over Ulster. Riddled with moral rhetoric, the country, like all rhetoricians, had been luke-warm over cases of palpable injustice, but got heated over what was a mere impasse in a game of political chess, because, as in the Dreyfus Case, the honour of military gentlemen was impugned.

The Ulster dilemma was insoluble. In resisting the very Crown forces (themselves averse to coercing her), Ulster was at once stressing her loyalty to the Crown and rebelling against the King's conscience in the constitutional if suspect keeping of the Liberal Government who, for the privilege of keeping it in their own hands, had sold their political conscience for eighty Irish votes. But had the Liberal Government agreed to a general election, they would have been disloyal to their Irish members who had put them into power for the purpose of getting their Home Rule. And had Ulster confined her action to mere protests, she would have been forcibly included in Home Rule, which to her was all that was most opposed to home. Yet in disobeying the Crown Forces, even in the cause of her loyalty to the Crown, her action, loyal but unconstitutional, established a precedent for the other side, who till now had been constitutional if disloyal.

On Thursday, the 30th, Mr. Asquith told the House that he proposed to put off, for the present, consideration of the second reading of the Amending Bill. He hoped that by a postponement of the discussion the patriotism of all parties would contribute what lay in their power, if not to avert, at least to circumscribe the calamities which threatened the world.

Great Britain on the brink of a civil war with most of her smart friends on the opposite side, Mrs. Asquith was cut as she came into the Speaker's Gallery. But curiosity triumphing over political virtue, the twittering peeresses assailed her as in one voice: "Margot, but whatever *can* this mean?"

And Mrs. Asquith, obviously elated at having it straight from the horse's mouth, an advantage that seemed to rebuke their irresponsibility in cutting one who dwelled in the stable, replied with a high sense of dramatic pathos:

"We are on the brink of a European War."

59

PREVENTIVE MOBILISATIONS

Next day, Friday the 31st, the Prime Minister returned from an interview with business men in the City. He delivered himself of his views upon the great pundits of our business world in the following terms to his wife, always the most intimate recipient of his confidences: "They are the greatest ninnies I have ever had to tackle. I found them all in a state of funk, like old women chattering over tea-cups in a cathedral town."

In the House of Commons, the weighty Asquith delivered himself of these weighty words: "We have heard, not from St. Petersburg but from Germany, that Russia has proclaimed a general mobilisation of her army and her fleet; and that, in consequence of this, martial law was to be proclaimed for Germany. We understand this to mean that mobilisation will follow in Germany, if the Russian mobilisation is general and is proceeded with."

When he received the Kaiser's telegram warning him of the most dire consequences unless Russia recalled her order for mobilisation, the Tsar was taking a warm evening bath. He got out without completing his ablutions, hurriedly wiped himself, threw a dressing-gown over his shoulders and passed to his study. From here he engaged in telephone conversations with his Minister for Foreign Affairs, Sazonov. To him the Self-Upholder of All the Russias conveyed his orders to countermand mobilisation.

It is not clear whether Sazonov did or did not want a 'preventive war' with Germany. No sooner had Nicholas got back into his bath than he was called to the telephone. His War Minister, Suhomlinov, was speaking. It was the same Suhomlinov who, a little later in the war, was tried by a military tribunal for profiteering in military supplies, now urging with all the sincerity of which he was capable that to countermand mobilisation after it had started was, in a country of Russia's size and unwieldiness, merely playing into the hands of the enemy, who would then steal a march on them. The argument, whether sincere or not, is at least plausible in a country in which, as someone says in Gogol, you can gallop all your life-long without reaching any frontier. The Autocrat's reply to his War Minister on this most crucial point of the crisis was, we gather, admonitorily inconclusive.

Mr. Asquith ended his speech in the Commons with the words: "In these circumstances I should prefer not to answer any questions until Monday."

A. J. Balfour's niece and biographer, Mrs. Blanche Dugdale, stresses her uncle Arthur's public spirit in actually forgoing, 'against every normal habit', his regular week-end in the country and roughing it in Carlton House Terrace, a close neighbour of the German Ambassador and within sight of 10 Downing Street, the Admiralty and the Palace, riveted to town by the swift drama of events. "He let," says Hesketh Pearson, "his tennis and his golf go hang, and did his bit by breathing the air of the metropolis for a fortnight at a stretch."

60

PREVENTIVE ULTIMATUMS

Now one might think that, after the many visits to each other's capitals and the repeated assurances that neither wanted war, the two monarchs might have brought their combined good-will to bear heavily on the side of peace. In actual fact, what happened? They both got frightened. Liddell Hart[1] quotes General von Chelius's report from St. Petersburg: "People have mobilised here through fear of coming events with no aggressive purpose, and are already terrified at the result." On the margin of his telegram the Kaiser had written "Right; that is the truth."

"But," writes Liddell Hart, "the Kaiser, now equally frightened and willing, could not stop his own military machine. For Moltke was insistent that 'the unusually favourable situation should be used to strike'." He pointed out that France's military situation was nothing less than embarrassed, and that Russia was anything but confident. "If," says Liddell Hart, "three men can be singled out as the main personal causes of the war, at this time, they are Berchtold, Conrad and Moltke."[2]

And one may add that if, despite thirty years of mutual royal and diplomatic visits of sincere good will, any given three men at any given time may find it possible to drive a whole unwilling world to slaughter, then there is something very wrong with the organisation of the world.

The time-limit of the German ultimatum expired on Saturday, August 1st, at noon. But the German Ambassador, Count Pourteles, did not make his appearance at the Ministry of Foreign Affairs, and hopes again rose.

In the meantime the Tsar, his wife and daughters were at evensong in the little church of the Alexandria Palace at Peterhof. Monsieur Guillard, meeting the Emperor a few hours earlier, records that he was struck by the expression of utter weariness on his face. "His features were drawn, the colour sallow, and even the bags under his eyes, which appeared when he was tired, seemed to have grown considerably." The Tsar, having saddled his Orthodox God with the task of undoing an

---

[1] *A History of the World War, 1914–1918.*
[2] Leopold von Berchtold, Austrian Foreign Minister; Conrad von Hoetzendorf, Austrian Chief of Staff; Helmuth von Moltke, German Chief of Staff.

expired ultimatum, prayed fervently, prayed with all his heart, his whole being filled with a simple and trusting faith. The service ended, Their Majesties with the Grand Duchesses returned to the Farm Alexandria. Being endowed with a number of gorgeous palaces, they always preferred a small house or a farm such as others, not favoured with opulence, inhabit of necessity.

The clock was nearing seven in the evening when Count Pourteles appeared at the Ministry for Foreign Affairs and was shown into Sazonov's room. In his hands he held Germany's declaration of war. But suddenly his face puckered, he wept, and put his arms around Sazonov's shoulders.

When the Emperor with his family returned to the farm after the service, it was about eight o'clock. Before going in to dinner, the Emperor entered his study just in case any telegrams had arrived in his absence, and picked up a telegram from Sazonov informing him that Germany had declared war. This, in view of his ardent solicitude for divine intercession, somewhat puzzled the Tsar. While he stood there, wondering about the well-known strangeness of the ways of Providence, the Empress sent in his second daughter, Tatiana, after him to inquire why he wasn't coming in to dinner. The Tsar said he was coming. Following his daughter, he entered the dining-room where his wife, with the conjugal eagerness hardly falling short of Mrs. Asquith's, at reading the expression on her husband's face, inquired what was the matter. He, looking very pale, and in a voice betraying that he was upset, revealed that the worst had happened. The Empress looked at him wide-eyed, and burst into tears. The youthful Grand Duchesses in their turn began to cry.

At dusk London news-vendors were shouting "Germany declares war on Russia!" and that night the Benckendorffs were dining at 10 Downing Street.

61

MOLTKE: MASTER STRATEGIST – AND MORE TEARS

The Russian Ambassador, Count Benckendorff, insisted that it was not the Kaiser but the German war party who wanted war. Mrs. Asquith said yes, it *was* the Kaiser. He was the big man in Germany against whom neither his son nor any party could prevail. Benckendorff said no, it was not the Kaiser, and Mrs. Asquith said yes, it *was* the Kaiser! At which the pair of them, Ambassador and wife, screamed together, "No, no, it was *not* the Kaiser!"

There had been a suggestion from Sir Edward Grey that, while there was any chance of agreement between Russia and Austria, Germany and France should hold their hand. Prince Lichnowsky, the German Ambassador in London, making the most of it in his eager desire for peace, had telegraphed to Berlin: "This would appear to mean that in case we did not attack France, England would remain neutral and would guarantee France's neutrality."

The German Emperor and his Chancellor, Bethmann-Hollweg, saw their chance. The Kaiser said, with an eye roving from Moltke to a map of Europe, "We march, then, with all our forces, only to the east?" He seemed to have forgotten his many Willy–Nicky reassurances.

But Moltke shook his head. The strategy he had perfected over many a year of intensive military study called for simultaneous targets east and west. He had to march on France as well as Russia because he had worked it out that way, and could not change his plans under, say, another ten years' notice. "Could military folly go further?" asks Liddell Hart, an expert on that brand.

The Kaiser, himself no mean hand at manoeuvres, seemed nonplussed by his Chief of the General Staff's assertion that two enemies were better than one. "Your uncle would have given me a different answer," he said bitterly.

Moltke, as he himself testifies in his memoirs, replied, "This is impossible, your Majesty. The advance of armies formed of millions of men is the result of years of painstaking work. Once planned, it cannot possibly be changed."

On August 2nd, Mrs. Asquith called to see her friends, the Lichnowskys, at the German Embassy in Carlton House Terrace. She found the Ambassador's wife that Sunday morning lying on a green sofa with a dachshund by her side and crying her eyes out, while the Ambassador was walking up and down the room in great agitation, and wringing his hands. On seeing Mrs. Asquith he caught her by the arm and cried in a hoarse, high voice, "Oh, Mrs. Asquith! Dear Mrs. Asquith! But vy dis Wahr! Vy dis Wahr! Oh! Say der is surely not going to be Wahr!"

Prince Lichnowsky, says Mrs. Asquith, had a pointed head and might have stepped out of Goya. In addition to a peevish voice he had bad manners with servants, when, one might imagine, his voice sharpened into shrill notes of injured severity. Princess Lichnowsky was a woman who did not make the best of her good looks, allowed her figure to run to fat, wore black socks, white boots and crazy tiaras. Edith Wharton recalls somewhere her first meeting with Princess Lichnowsky who, on learning that Mrs. Wharton was a writer, inquired in a high, singing voice, "Do you write . . . just so, or *mit* a *Pör* – pose?" Some years after the war, an English acquaintance visited Princess Lichnowsky in Germany, and to him she confessed a certain nostalgia, almost homesickness, for London with its easy ways and incredible politeness in bus conductors who thanked you when they handed you a ticket, and the sensible English taxi-cabs you could get into without either doubling up or disarranging your tiara. Now, on that tragic August morning two days before the British ultimatum to Germany, when Mrs. Asquith said goodbye to the Ambassador, tears were streaming down his cheeks.

Herr Ballin, the German shipping magnate, on a visit to England at this juncture, records his impression of German management of the crisis. "Even a moderately skilled German diplomatist," he wrote, "could easily have come to an understanding with England and France, who could have made peace certain and prevented Russia from beginning the war." To this there is a comment from the editor of Ballin's memoirs, who adds, "The people in London were certainly seriously concerned at the Austrian Note, but the extent to which the Cabinet desired the maintenance of peace may be seen, as an example, from the remark which Churchill, First Lord of the Admiralty, almost with tears in his eyes, made to Ballin as they parted: 'My dear friend, *don't* let us go to war.'"

62

THE DIRECTING BRAIN: THE EMPRESS

At Petersburg, now russianised into Petrograd, the Emperor appeared on the balcony of the Winter Palace, the people thronging the immense cobbled square below. At the sight of him they sank on their knees and burst into that musically most satisfying of national anthems 'God Save the Tsar'.

Here it was, as undeserved as it was spontaneous and as strong as it was fleeting, for harassed rulers always the most prized of civil virtues – national unity crystallised round themselves. As if at a signal, all the local worthies became patriotic. In intent, purposeful-looking processions they marched, united by a feeling that all the shortcomings inherent in the scheme of things, which had hitherto prevented them from being happy, were due to a malignant cancer, now to be eradicated, a cancer which – the Russian newspapers left no room for doubt – was the German Reich. Slavonic wrath was unanimous. A small gentleman, who had behaved with marked restraint for nearly a lifetime, beholding his *vis-à-vis* in the train reading the *Petersburger Zeitung*, a paper catering for the Tsar's German-speaking subjects (but read also by many an Orthodox Russian for the excellence of its financial page), now snatched the offending rag from the stranger's hands and flung it on to the floor. The Germans, it was already being rumoured, diverted themselves by throwing returning Russian baby passengers out of express trains. Who but a moral outcast would, in the circumstances, read the *Petersburger Zeitung*?

Pierre Guillard, the Tsarevitch's tutor, records with satisfaction on August 3rd that the Emperor, the day before, had given a solemn vow at the Winter Palace not to conclude peace while even one enemy remained on Russian soil.

Having taken this vow before the whole world, Nicholas II, says Monsieur Guillard, underlines the character of this war: "It is a struggle to the end, a struggle for existence."

But they all say that. One has yet to hear a ruler announce a war as a light recreation, a delightful costume-party enabling his subjects to get out of their drab and dusty town clothes into tight uniforms and becoming nurses' apparel.

The Empress, usually tongue-tied, seemed to have opened her heart to the tutor. She expressed her utmost indignation at the news that the

Empress Dowager had been stopped on her way to Petersburg, having to return to Berlin in order to proceed to Copenhagen. "How could he, a monarch, have stopped the Empress!" she exclaimed, unconsciously betraying the limitation of her indignation, apparently confined to monarchs slighting empresses. "How could he come to this!"

It did not occur to her to ask how could the whole pack of them, tsars, kaisers, generals, ambassadors, prime ministers and foreign secretaries, come to this, to involve well-meaning credulous mankind in this humourless unnecessary slaughter.

"He has completely altered," she went on, really meaning that her opinion of her cousin was susceptible to change, "since the time that the war party, which hates Russia, has acquired an overpowering influence over him; but I am convinced that he has declared war against his will." That 'hating' Russia also shows her adolescent state of development. It was not that they hated Russia, but that they loved Germany too well, which was at the bottom of it all.

The Empress Alexandra Feodorovna, not endowed with clairvoyance or clairaudience, could not have seen the Kaiser's roving eye as it turned greedily from Moltke to the map of Europe spread before him, when he thought that France and England could be bribed out of the war and he gave voice to his pleasurable surmise: "We march, then, with all our forces to the east?"

As an example of the way in which high politics get mixed with emotionalism, of how the wife of the man who had his share in precipitating a war that might have been avoided had he kept his head, a wife reputed to be the 'directing brain' of that absolute monarchy, the Empress went on, "I have never liked him for his insincerity. He has always played the fool, and he is so vain! He has always reproached me that I wasn't doing anything for Germany, and he did all he could to separate Russia from France. But I never believed that this could be to the advantage of Russia. This war he will never forgive me!"

It is, alas! in hands like these that we are still, and shall remain until the anachronism of sovereignties is lifted clean out of the largest muddle of our lives, and the very term 'international relations', now in the hands of feeble-minded wives and their not much wiser husbands, kings, generals, presidents, prime ministers, dictators, is eliminated and the whole question placed on a completely automatic footing of production and distribution – the whole question of 'international relations' being transformed into one vast but indivisible problem of world housekeeping, properly the sphere for the organising genius of woman.

63

SIR EDWARD GREY

The German ultimatum to France gave her eighteen hours in which to decide, without mobilising, that she would stand back and let Germany and Austria together deal a quick blow at isolated Russia. Germany had already mobilised, ostensibly against Russia alone, actually for a two-front war.

Moltke was to have his two-front war. But to put a good diplomatic face on an evil intention, the Wilhelmssstrasse instructed its Ambassador in Paris to make French neutrality impossible of acceptance by demanding the handing over to the German Army of the fortresses of Toul and Verdun to fortify by deed a word of neutrality.

It is not unlikely that the more intelligent Germans regarded such crippling neutrality imposed on France as preferable to Moltke's complex two-front war. A neutrality which, one can imagine, was enough to make French generals foam at the mouth. The Germans also made it clear that if, meanwhile, France mobilised, Germany would at once make war on her.

News percolated to Paris that Britain was in the process of defining her indetermination not necessarily not to go to war.

On August 3rd Sir Edward Grey made his famous speech in the House of Commons. It was one of those typically British statements of fair play, seemingly careful but really shockingly haphazard which profoundly satisfy the dour English instinct, but which make foreigners, particularly the French, think we are not all there. The logical French thought that Sir Edward was muddying the clear waters of what, in this case, for them resolved itself into a transparently lucid question: "*Pour ou contre?*" The Foreign Secretary, however, hinted that he had gone dangerously far in his interpretation of Anglo-French cordiality by affirming conditional limited naval support for France in contingencies themselves contingent on hypotheses, the lot subject to approval or reversal at the hands of Parliament.

It is not easy for some men to do their thinking on their feet, and Sir Edward Grey's crippled and curiously infelicitous sentences could not have made it easy for Members to follow his argument. "I want," he said, "to look at the matter without sentiment, and from the point of view of British interests, and it is on that that I am going to justify what I say to the House." Immediately switching over to pro-French sentiment, he continues, "If we say nothing at this moment, what is France to do with her fleet in the Mediterranean? If she leaves it there, with no statement from us, she leaves her northern and western coasts at the mercy of a German fleet coming down the Channel, to do as it pleases in a war which is a war of life and death between them. If we say nothing, it may be that the French fleet is withdrawn from the Mediterranean. We are," he said, breaking off his thought, "in the presence of a European conflagration; can anybody set limits to the consequences that may arise out of it? Let us assume that we stand aside in an attitude of neutrality, saying, 'No, we cannot undertake and engage to help either party in this conflict.' Let us suppose," he resumed, once more switching off the current of his thought, "the French fleet is withdrawn from the Mediterranean, and let us assume that the consequences make it necessary at a sudden moment, in defence of vital British interests, we should go to war: nobody can say that in the course of the next few weeks there is any particular trade route, the keeping open of which may not be vital to this country. We feel strongly that France was entitled to know . . ."

One wonders why this broken-backed attempt to do his thinking on his feet, instead of reading a prepared statement, should have been held up as a model of lucidity.

Then came the qualified commitment: "In these compelling circumstances, yesterday afternoon, I gave the French Ambassador the following statement:

I am authorised to give an assurance that, if the German fleet comes into the Channel or through the North Sea to undertake hostile operations against the French coasts, the British fleet will give all the protection in its power. This assurance is, of course, subject to the policy of His Majesty's Government receiving the support of Parliament, and must not be taken as binding His Majesty's Government to take any action until the above contingency of action by the German fleet takes place.

This curious delay to the eleventh hour in formulating terms and conditions that should have been foreseen and stated a decade before recalls a station-master who, asked what time the train was due, answered dourly;

"That depends."

"What does it depend on?"

Taking out his pipe, "That again depends."

Continental nations simply do not understand hesitant statements hedged in by a string of qualifying clauses: what Mr. Neville Chamberlain was pleased to call, in contra-distinction to Hitler's predatory bellowing, 'well-marshalled arguments'. One can imagine the French Ambassador sitting down to draft his telegram to Paris – "Sir Edward Grey has assured me that . . .", a sudden flush of confusion suffusing his cheeks as his mind's eye beholds his telegram arriving at the Quai d'Orsay. A Quai d'Orsay confident that, to honour the pledge of cordiality underlining the Entente, England has sprung to her feet like one man to stand by republican France reluctantly implementing her promise to the Tsar of Russia. And – instead? Oh shame! These twice-qualified assurances of naval protection in a hypothetical contingency are hurriedly deciphered, then placed before the Foreign Minister of France.

'*Ah mais!*'[1] Expansive Gallic gestures signifying that this was August 3rd, not April 1st. An exchange of quick, excited colloquies – '*Enfin! ce n'est pas amusant!*' '*Ah, mais je vous crois bien!*'

Sir Edward Grey goes on, "Things move hurriedly from hour to hour. French news comes in, which I cannot give in any formal way, but I understand that the German Government would be prepared, if we would pledge ourselves to neutrality, to agree that its fleet would not attack the northern coast of France."

Nothing apparently of the western coast of France. This clumsy omission is typical of German diplomacy in a delicate crisis when every hour is vital.

"I have only heard that shortly before I came to the House," Grey adds, and there is in the hurry with which he dismisses this aspect, instead of taking it up and telegraphing to Berlin "You say nothing of the western coast of France," a suggestion that, like Moltke who could not reconsider his strategy, Grey's brain could not at short notice reshape the speech he had prepared to deliver to the House. So instead of taking it up with the Germans that they should include the western coast of France, in addition to the northern, as the price of British neutrality, which would be exactly equivalent to the scope of his guarantee to the French Ambassador that the British fleet will keep the German navy off the coast of France, he dismisses it all with – "But this is too narrow an engagement for us," side-tracking suddenly, "And, Sir, there is the more serious consideration – the question of the neutrality of Belgium," thus at one go wiping out all the relevance of his long argument about the coasts of France.

It is perhaps too much to expect that Members of Parliament gathered in force would follow intelligently this jerky sort of reasoning. If anything emerges clearly, it is diplomacy itself, shown up for the hazardous, utterly pernicious and precarious thing it is, offering common ground

---

[1] The equivalent of the German *Na! aber!*

for every sort and kind of deliberate, accidental and unintentional misunderstanding through ruse, shortcoming and cross-purpose – a common ground, in short, for everything but common safety. Sir Edward Grey's speech, prepared before the German offer not to attack the northern coast of France altered the very premise of his argument, was delivered by him as it stood, mainly because of the labour expended in preparing it. Rather than scrap at the last minute the bulk of his speech, he reveals how his diplomatic mind (the best in Europe, by the way: which might give some idea of the worst) has been playing blind man's buff with contingencies and contentions based on a hypothesis largely disposed of when, at the end, he suddenly confesses that the Germans had as good as met him halfway, brushes this aside as of no importance, and starts on a new trail, thus dismissing as irrelevant to his new argument the brunt of his speech about the undefended coasts of France. The response of the House to such muddled presentation cannot be intellectual: excited emotion, a sense of impending big events, of great issues in the balance: that is all they can be expected to have gathered.

What dismal nonsense it all is, this double-crossing through Foreign Offices and embassies four times quadrupled simultaneously in four main capitals alone. Unsubstantiated argument, half-house reasoning, one-sided guarantees, telegrams incompletely worded: "It would appear . . . if I understood him aright": world peace hangs by such threads. Telegrams conveying insincere proposals setting traps; daring civilians, unfitted to keep the peace, threatening to unleash huge armies drilled for murder; timid generals, military men who, one would think, were trained to know no fear, dithering with panic and cutting short by hours, by minutes, the time in which well-meaning statesmen, having to stand and speak as though they were actors, must put together an argument sounding like the least of several dismal alternatives somehow to get their countrymen, brought up on caution and trusteeships, to throw their all into the melting-pot, to offer freely the lives of the beings most dear to them; the former, grudgingly, with hesitation and evasions; the latter, as a matter of course, cheerfully, with gestures of emotional largesse: "Take my sons, but let me keep my money."

What had they been doing before? Could they not have agreed before on an automatic deflation of every possible variety of an inevitable crisis blowing up at intervals from the gas generated naturally by hetero-geneous opinion? Could they not have dropped their ridiculous pre-tence of 'sovereignties' – a sheer nuisance even to kings? What were Foreign Offices for but to keep the nations at peace? Who asked these sorry adolescents to be playing power politics?

It is, of course, perfectly understandable that England did not want

Germany to defeat France. But, even more than that, England did not want (even though at that time we did not yet possess sufficient data to distrust her) to have Germany perched on her very nose across the Channel. Surely all this could have been settled at leisure, before a crisis?

Now a note of self-pity crept into Sir Edward Grey's voice. "How hard, how persistently, and how earnestly we strove for peace last week, the House will see from the papers that will be put before it; but that is over." A touch of Neville Chamberlain here, whom he resembles in many ways.

The Germans, when to their fatuous astonishment they found they were at war with England, credited it all to the Machiavellian cunning, the predatory instincts of Sir Edward Grey, whose darkly-compressed aquiline features seemed to them to be verily those of a bird of prey, a sinister vulture pecking at Germany's vitals. They did not know that he was a man of singularly upright character, if rather wooden intellect. He was a company director of the Great Western Railway, from which he drew increments due more to his prestige than actual, or indeed any, work. He was a man of a religious bent, deep if inarticulate feeling, and a love of nature, though, like Neville Chamberlain, he was addicted to the vice of fishing, a pursuit which Sydney Smith describes as "running an iron hook into the intestines of an animal; presenting this first animal to another as his food; and then pulling this second creature up and suspending him by the barb of his stomach". Is it not strange that such a fiendish occupation should generally be indulged in by quiet, kindly men, whose companion love of bird life is confined to the birds they do not shoot on the wing?

64

THE RIGHT TO LEND

But Grey, exercised by his own diplomatic view of European powers, could have no idea of what was really happening in the larger world. Without claiming that Lenin was in exclusive possession of such knowledge, it is not unprofitable to present his point of view in order to amplify the current idea of the antagonisms involved and to suggest that there are more things in heaven and earth than are dreamed of by a Sir Edward Grey.

Lenin read the signs with a different interpretation from that of either Germany or Great Britain. Goethe speaks somewhere of the 'right to err', this being a prerequisite to a right in his time not yet contested internationally – the right to lend. To Lenin that was what the whole quarrel was, in fact, about. The moneylenders had been getting away with it because, while the borrowers were scattered over the entire surface of the globe, the lenders were co-ordinated, on the principle that unity is strength. But lending, to be profitable, required an extended field over which to conduct such operations. England, hitherto in a position of lending predominance, had found increasing competition in this field from Germany, challenging everywhere England's place as the principal usurer. Competition, having reached beyond a war of words, became, as inevitably it must, a war of swords.

Far-fetched as this may sound when one recalls how innocent of any such intention were the great bulk of British and German wage-earners, the theory is no more absurd than other conventional assumptions based on military, naval or dynastic considerations of supremacy, of whose deeper implications the average citizen is as innocent as of the intricacies of international finance. Why should there exist this overwhelming motive to lend money abroad, seeing that the average farmer or hard-pressed father of a family in any quarter of the globe would find it hard to raise an overdraft of ten pounds? The will to lend is the will at once to spend your money and keep it. That is what living on the interest on capital really means. And here it is that international usury sees its main chance. It is therefore not as unreasonable as at first it sounds that the war between Germany and England was a war inevitable between two nations both wanting to have their cake and eat it.

That there were other, nobler emotions, such as the impulse to protect weak little Belgium from the strong big bully, Germany, was evident. That France was fighting with a dwindling birthrate against a neighbour with a mounting population who had already once snapped up two disputed provinces, was another among a number of contributing motives. That Russia hoped to put an end to a precarious international situation by plunging headlong into it may have been yet another. And that Germany, believing herself to be encircled by enemies, hoped to give her fine army the opportunity of breaking through a tightening circle, was not the least of a chimera of delusions considered sufficient for disembowelling men in their prime.

And so it began. With a yelp and a laugh, an Austrian painter of twenty-five, resident in Munich and answering to a name not yet in use

216

as a greeting, jumped to the colours. The day war had become certain beyond peradventure, he had sunk on his knees and thanked the Deity for this belated sign of His grace.

During his youth, he later confessed, nothing damped his 'wild spirits', as he calls them, so much as the thought that the world had elected "not to erect any more temples of fame except in the sedate fields of business and officialdom". He felt chagrined at the idea that his life would have to run its course "along peaceful and orderly lines". Gone apparently were the times, such as the Wars of Liberation, when a man after his own heart, like Stein, might make himself heard of outside his own parish. By the side of Lenin's diagnosis of international competition for the right to lend as the root cause of the Great War, Hitler's lament that 'glorious wars' should have given place to uninspiring international competition between nations increasingly assuming the appearance of commercial undertakings, is characteristic.

65

TWO SCRAPS OF PAPER

The continental war had begun. England was making up its mind. On August 4th Mr. Asquith announced that the German Government had delivered to the Belgian Government a Note proposing friendly neutrality, entailing free passage through Belgian territory, and promising to maintain the independence and integrity of the kingdom and its possessions, at the conclusion of peace; and threatening, in case of refusal, to treat Belgium as an enemy, a proposal categorically refused by Belgium as a flagrant violation of the law of nations. The British Ambassador in Berlin had been instructed to protest against this violation of a treaty to which Germany was a party in common with Great Britain, and he requested an assurance that the demand made upon Belgium might not be proceeded with, and that her neutrality would be respected by Germany. An immediate reply was asked for.

Meanwhile, Belgium having declined 'the well-intended proposals' of Germany to seduce her with blandishments, Germany, 'deeply to her regret, had seen herself compelled' to violate Belgian territory near

217

Aix-la-Chapelle. Prince Lichnowsky, on the morning of August 4th had the unenviable task thrust upon him from Berlin to "dispel any mistrust that might subsist on the part of the British Government with regard to German intentions". Evidence of their innocence was borne out, the argument ran, by the obvious fact that Germany could not profitably annexe Belgian territory without making territorial acquisitions at the expense of Holland, the latter supposition being ruled out by Germany having solemnly pledged her word to Holland strictly to respect her neutrality.

One would have thought that Germany, having openly violated a similar earlier pledge given to Belgium, could hardly expect the world to take her second pledge more seriously than her first. The British Government was being asked to attach importance to one 'scrap of paper' when just about to be reproached by Bethmann-Hollweg for attaching importance to another. The excuse, unsubstantiated, was that the German Army could not be exposed to French attack across Belgium, which had been planned, the Germans said, 'according to absolutely unimpeachable information', adding the familiar 'it being for Germany a question of life or death'. It seems that it is always a question of death for persons capable of dying to sustain the life of a national abstraction in no danger of being extinguished, if at all, for more than a generation at a time.

Mr. Asquith, a master of parliamentary effect, paused after communicating the contents of the German telegram and then said in a slow, loud voice, "I have to add on behalf of His Majesty's Government: we cannot regard this as in any sense a satisfactory communication." Loud cheers. He then told the House that the British Government, in reply to this telegram, had repeated the request made the week before to the German Government, that they should give us the same assurance in regard to Belgian neutrality as was given to us and to Belgium by France. "We have asked," said Mr. Asquith, "that a reply to that request, and a satisfactory answer to the telegram of this morning – which I have read to the House – should be given before midnight."

This was the British ultimatum.

Then followed the rather prosaic reading by the Speaker (all the Members of the House being uncovered) of a message from the King:

GEORGE R.I. – The present state of public affairs in Europe constituting in the opinion of his Majesty a case of great emergency within the meaning of the Acts of Parliament in that behalf, his Majesty deems it proper to provide additional means for the Military Service, and therefore, in pursuance of these Acts, his Majesty has thought it right, and so on.

Mrs. Asquith relates how, when these proceedings were over, she went down to the Prime Minister's room, and her husband remarked on Lord Morley's letter of resignation, saying that he would miss him very much: he was one of the most distinguished men living.

For some time they did not speak. She left the window and stood behind his chair.

"So it is all up?" she said.

He answered without looking at her, "Yes, it's all up."

He sat at his writing-table, leaning back with a pen in his hand. She got up and leant her head against his: they could not speak for tears.

66

BERLIN AND LONDON

It is also the afternoon of August 4th in Berlin. The officers of the Admiralstab, not a calm race like the French but a hysterical one, as the French are erroneously reputed to be, are apparently on pins and needles. "We sit in our offices at the Admiralty," writes Captain von Rintelen, "and our nerves can hardly stand the strain of waiting any longer." The door opens and Captain von Rintelen is ordered by his Chief to drive at full speed to the Wilhelmsstrasse and return with some important document without losing a minute.

Arrived at the Foreign Office, Rintelen observes, sitting on a red plush sofa, Sir Edward Goschen, the British Ambassador in Berlin, and Mr. James W. Gerard, his American colleague. Sir Edward is looking depressed and is talking in a low voice about matters connected with the handing over of British interests to the good offices of the American Ambassador. Captain von Rintelen realises what is at stake and, as he says, 'his knees tremble' as the whole world-historic significance of this little incident opens up before him.

Then Herr von Jagow, the Minister for Foreign Affairs, enters the room and hands the captain a sealed envelope.

The Captain clicks his heels, bows, first to Jagow, then, with unfailing German punctiliousness, to the two ambassadors, and, as he says himself, hardly knows how he gets down the steps. Such excitement! Then he dashes across half Berlin in a car, the policeman at the cross-roads having been previously instructed to stop the traffic for him, in order to deliver to the waiting naval staff the Foreign Office document authorising the Admiralstab to instruct the Fleet that Germany was at war with England. One would have thought that a direct telephone call from the Foreign Minister to the Admiralty Chief would have spared precious minutes and a great deal of fuss.

At 10 Downing Street Mrs. Asquith joined her husband in the Cabinet room. Mrs. Asquith, when she writes of tense moments, chooses simple words, with complete effect. "Lord Crewe and Sir Edward Grey were already there and they sat smoking cigarettes in silence: some went out, others came in; nothing was said.

"The clock on the mantelpiece hammered out the hour, and when the last beat of midnight struck it was as silent as dawn.

"We were at War.

"I left to go to bed, and, as I was pausing at the foot of the staircase, I saw Winston Churchill with a happy face striding towards the double doors of the Cabinet room."

67

'IN A STATE OF WAR'

It was twenty-five years almost to the month before Winston again confessed to sunshine in his heart when another ultimatum remained unanswered on September 3rd, 1939.

He was not, however, the only one to be happy. The Tsarevitch's tutor, Pierre Guillard, met the Tsar in the Palace park on Wednesday morning, August 5th. He, too, looked very happy and told him that, on account of Germany's breach of neutrality, England had come in on the side of the right. Besides that, Italian neutrality seemed assured.

All traces of weariness and fatigue had left the Emperor's face. Gone were the bags under his eyes. He walked jauntily. "We have already," he said, "won a great diplomatic victory. After that there will be a victory by force of arms and, thanks to the support of England, it will come sooner than one may expect. The Germans have the whole of

220

Europe against them, except Austria. Their impudence and despotism in the long run will bore even their allies; look at the Italians!"

But Chancellor Bethmann-Hollweg – according to Jules Cambon, '*un homme très mediocre – en même temps bourgeois et courtisan, combinaison mauvaise*' – maintained that England was only taking part in the war for appearances, and that if the Germans did nothing to provoke her England would remain a sleeping partner of France and Russia, both of whom Germany might despatch at leisure. But that was not the opinion of the German Admiralty who, whenever the German Foreign Office received optimistic telegrams from their London Ambassador, Lichnowsky, received pessimistic wires from their Naval Attaché in London, Captain van Müller, full of the worst forebodings.

On that morning of August 5th, when the Tsar in his park was conversing jauntily with his son's French tutor, twelve hours after the formal delivery of the declaration of war; when, as Rintelen says, nobody expected any further telegrams from the German Embassy in London, there arrived a wire from Prince Lichnowsky, reading, "The old gentleman [Asquith] has just declared to me, with tears in his eyes, that a war between two peoples who are related by blood is impossible."

On the margin of this telegram the Kaiser annotated in his inch-high megalomaniac's handwriting, "What an awakening the man will have from his diplomatic dreams!"

Sir Edward Grey travelled with Prince Lichnowsky, who had been handed his passport, to the coast to see him off aboard. And there, instead of showing the red tooth and goring each other's side – a job they left over for others who had never even met – the two kid-gloved men, whose realms had quietly agreed to 'consider themselves to be in a state of war', parted with the warmest of handshakes and tears in their eyes.

68

'CURIOUSER AND CURIOUSER –'

Now at this point we may expect Alice, pardonably confused by the strange ineptitudes of Wonderland, to pose a question. Why, why, why, she asks, if all these men in key positions were crying their hearts out at being saddled with a war that nobody, save one stupid statesman and two wicked generals, wanted, why in reason did not all the others, admittedly the bosses of their evil counsellors, put down their feet and resolutely refuse to go to war about it? And, finally, why did not Providence, to whom they had appealed in no half-hearted way, answer their prayers instead of fulfilling the wish of the war-mongers?

Says Chehov, "So long as a man likes the splashing of a fish, he is a poet; when he knows that the splashing is nothing but the chase of the weak by the strong, he is a thinker; but when he does not understand what sense there is in the chase, or what use in the equilibrium which results from destruction, he is becoming silly and dull, as he was when a child. And the more he knows and thinks, the sillier he becomes."

But Alice is not to be snubbed. This babe-in-the-wood innocence in the face of phenomena, taking nothing for granted, is a symbol of the impotence of divinity trying to speak and make itself understood in a maturely imbecile jungle of overgrown material life.

Tolstoy, on the theory that a chain of events precedes each war, any link in which, if broken, would have prevented that particular war (or, conversely, any missing link may have produced a new chain of events perhaps likewise leading to war), absolves the individual from direct responsibility of causing cataclysms of consequences which, in their aggregate, far outweigh in importance the significance of persons.

Our Alice, then, undeterred by Chehov's snub about the inevitable infantile silliness which blights first and last questions, asks whether God in that case is bad. To this we might reply at once that, if God were bad, he would have no need to restrain himself by creating a world that was merely half-bad.

The problem of evil, we attempt to tell Alice, probably rests on free will: unless man had been endowed with free will there would have been no point in creating our world. For if we could get ourselves to believe that it amused the Supreme Being to make a puppet world in order, at intervals, to knock it down, we would have to conclude that little things pleased little minds and that God was not the real God, but some intermediate earth spirit over whose head we must then appeal for atonement to the God in our hearts, at one with the God beyond Time and evil.

"But," she asks, "have we really *got* free will?"

In answer, we have to admit that when we look forward to asserting ourselves in the future, our free will seems to be at our disposal; so that, while not hindered by other people's free will, we can, for instance, elect to sit down or remain standing. But when we look back, even such a relatively free decision of our will appears to have been suggested, timed, influenced and severely circumscribed by an aggregate of other,

222

mostly anonymous, free wills, and all our past to have been rooted in necessity or predestination.

"Is that because we don't all will sufficiently the same thing?" asks our Alice, nearly putting her finger on what is so odd about Wonderland.

Because we don't will the same thing at the top of the spiritual, but will the same thing at the bottom of the material scale: that is why. And we proceed to open out the thought. Man who, by divine dispensation, enjoys free will, should, of his own free will, concur in the working of divine dispensation whereby only the absolutely free spirits, concurring in unity and called the Communion of Saints, can enjoy absolute freedom of will. For where selfless love is unanimously desired of their own free will for its own sake as the supreme experience of timeless *being*, there is no clash of wills, but complete free will. To concur with all one's soul is to sing with the morning stars: to know in one's heart why the Sons of the Morning in their praise of the Lord are shouting for joy. It is to ascend to the topmost rung of the spiritual ladder suspended from heaven and dangling down to earth.

In the material world, on the other hand, in an effort to sate the hunger of the shifting moment in possession for possession's sake, will impinges on will in a lust of *having*, ranging from the amoeba flowing round its prey, incorporating it and oozing on, to a millionaire exulting in the ownership of a rare Rubens while eating his heart out for a Rembrandt that has eluded his grasp. All of us are floundering in the glue of accrued consequences oozing from a collective free will of our own making, which we please to call necessity; this points to a return from the highest to the lowest form of life: again the amoeba flowing round our individual free will, incorporating in it the blind collective free will, becomes necessity or predestination, and oozing on after unborn victims.

The Kaiser and the Tsar, Poincaré, Asquith, Sir Edward Grey, tried their poor best, but they got absorbed by the amoeba they had all more or less helped to breed of their aggregate collective free will, with the accent on '*My* country right or wrong'. I was the amoeba, not men whose free will it had incorporated in a collective will for the same thing, which was making the war. None had caught on to the swinging trapeze which the angels suspend to us in the hope of lifting one or other of us out of the bog of Time.

"Do we get bad, living in Time?"

Alice's is a pure-hearted thirst for knowledge, and it devolves on us to search our stupid adult hearts in attempting a sincere reply. We are perhaps the backward boys of Paradise, sent here 'to do time' in order to make progress towards a timeless life lacking reformatory conditions. For we must either go up or come down the scale of spiritual intuition. We are God's Borstal boys and girls.

"But, by the love of God," asks a bewildered Alice, "where is the love of God?"

The answer is that it percolates through matter where it gets the least encouragement. For it takes two to make a meeting. God is love. But man, steeped in time, is not, in static situations, capable of love; he must part, he must lose and yearn and grieve; he must learn to love without reciprocity, suffer unjustly: not for some utilitarian end, but because love is its own reward, love not limited by time and space, but love eternal. If God is love, love moves in the heart as the poetry of life. Eternity, knowing not change, is in love with time. Time, knowing not constancy, is unable to contemplate itself. It is the fragrant and fleeting that eternity is in love with; for she has no cause to be in love with the permanent, which is herself. That a girl at the Gare de l'Est is saying goodbye to her soldier sweetheart who entrains for the front; that now she is walking, gulping down her tears, to her place of business where she is a seamstress; that, above, the sun is shining through fleeting clouds with a benignancy as though withdrawn from human sorrow: in this there is more meaning, though one would be hard put to it to provide a rational explanation, than in German or Allied war aims. And the blending of the surrounding indifference with her poignant grief when news is brought her of his death: in the delicate hue of light and shade, in "that subtle, almost elusive beauty of human sorrow", which, as Chehov says, "men will not for a long time learn to understand and describe and which it seems only music can convey", there is a meaning hidden in the crucifixion of the sentient being and a revelation hovering on the brink of resurrection morning with its tidings that he for whom we mourn has overcome the fear of death and the myth of death.

If there were no such thing as time, eternity would perpetuate a state of coma. Eternity acquires meaning only in the living moment, each of which it catches on the wing. Without eternity time runs into the dustbin. Without time eternity would contemplate a handful of dust. Time, not to succumb to the tedium of repetition inherent in its succession of staccato moments, resorts to fluctuation. Sorrow must be followed by joy, and joy by sorrow; wars by peace, and peace by war, to provide eternity with a rich variety of spontaneous gesture to snap in motion. There is nothing more pure than eternity's unalloyed love of fleeting time, nothing more ardent than time's nostalgia for eternity: of like nature is the love of God for man, and the love of man for God.

That beautiful marriage between time and eternity, we impress on Alice, is the secret spring of the universe. That is why Alice's hare, who ran (though he did not know he was in a hurry) to fulfil God's dual purpose, was angered by her very pertinent question which, however, strove to assign to his movements a utilitarian motive. That is why hares run, why wheels turn, trees grow, birds fly: because eternity is in love with transient things, and because transient things wish to find their souls in eternity.

We cannot think of any other reasons for human calamities, wars, nature's cataclysms, called acts of God, violent dislocations of complacent human life which, if left unattended by man or God, dry up like mud or putrify like stagnant water. We surmise that since God has imbued man with free will, He cannot in principle intervene save through the implications of man's own free will. As God contemplates man wading knee-deep in the consequent necessity compounded of the aggregate free will of his kind, He may wonder a little whether the reading of antecedents making up the sum total of his situation may not perhaps suggest to the collective free will an effort to extricate the individual free will from a situation savouring painfully of predetermination, and casting unjustifiable aspersions on the good will of the Deity itself. Since any movement in life provides the camera of eternity with as good a variety of snap shots of living moments as another, why indeed should the Deity be unduly exercised over our collective problems? Backward souls learn the truth by trial and error as surely as gifted beings perceive it through intuition and insight, and since eternity cherishes the movement of the tortoise no less than that of the hare, why should Providence care?

"But does God," Alice asks, shocked, "just sit and do *nothing*?"

Indeed, no. Our own backwardness, our common frailty, is His cryptic Fifth Column. Without our knowing it, it succeeds step by step in making us see the divine, unchangeable, unshakable, irremovable truth, that is no less there because we are blind and cannot see it: that God is love. But God is no respecter of nationalities. His Fifth Column is in all of us: in our selfishness, in our failure to redeem history, in making national heroes of Charles XII, Marlborough, Peter the Great, Frederick the Great, Napoleon, Hitler – each serving as a model for the next – wherever self-love or self-interest is at war with spiritual love, everywhere, always: God's Fifth Column penetrates the fraud of piety, of prestige values, undermines our worldly self-confidence regardless of our own ideas of what is due to us in justice. Siegfried Sasson's war poem

> God strafe England
> God save the King
> The warring nations shout:
> God this, God that
> And God the other thing.
> "Good God!" said God,
> "I've got my work cut out!"

perhaps misses the point: God has not got his work cut out. Whether we return to the light by devious and tortuous ways, like Beethoven, or by sunny short cuts, like Mozart, it is all one to God, whose universe would not be a universe if its working were not automatic. Tortured thinkers like Dostoievski and Nietzsche, whom the world deems more profound than mellow poets like Goethe and Wordsworth beholding the truth from a mountain peak, are but cave-dwellers whose profundity is the distance of one having sunk into a cavern and required to climb out to see the light.

"But what of the horror, the torture, the gashing and wounding of the war of life?" asks Alice. "Is there no pity in God?"

The Second Person of the Trinity takes care of that, generally according, in response to fervent prayer, a little overdraft on the suffering unit's account – soon to be squared again – but affording temporary relief in the form of a little clearer knowledge of life, until the end, when, it is whispered, all is well.

Indeed, the King and Lord Kitchener both invoked the Deity to speed the troops to battle, but whereas the King, betraying feeling, wrote, "I pray God to bless you and guard you and bring you back victorious", commending each of his soldiers to the clemency of the Second Person of the Trinity, Lord Kitchener, with the brusqueness of one who had read the Old Testament in the spirit of the King's Regulations, quite obviously meant Jehovah when he finished his admonitions with an abrupt, "Fear God."

He also rather damped the spirits of troops expecting romantic adventures in foreign parts by issuing a warning: "In this new experience you may find temptations both in wine and women. You must entirely resist both temptations, and, while treating all women with perfect courtesy, you should avoid any intimacy."

When Mrs. Asquith left the House after her husband's speech – he had asked for and got a vote of credit for one hundred million pounds to carry on the war – she ran into Lord Chaplin, the father of the later Lady Londonderry, who said to her that he was proud to be seen with her because her husband was the most remarkable man living, adding artlessly, "He and Grey have started this war in a memorable way."

69

FREE WILL: TWO CAMPS OF NECESSITY

Though in the days before the war the Emperor and Empress treated Monsieur Guillard with a certain reserve which probably made him feel the distance between emperor and tutor, now that war had crashed upon them they confided in him with an eagerness and abundance as though they had just alighted on their long-lost cousin. The Emperor's talk, startling in its simplicity considering he was the fount of all information and action, reminds one of Nathaniel Gubbins's[1] Sweep commenting on the week's big news over a quart of bitter: "Well, cor sufferin' blimey, what do you think of little old Itler's chances in Russia now?" punctuated, you can almost hear, by the tutor's uncommunicative responses, not unlike Nathaniel Gubbins's own acquiescing interjections: "Not much." – "I do." – "That's right." – "It will and all." – "Too true." The perfect confidence between emperor and tutor never, however, descends to a level of genial familiarity existing between the Sweep and Mr. Gubbins, which generally ends with "Though you might as well 'ave one for the road," said the Sweep.

"Thank you," I said.

"The skin orf your nose," said the Sweep.

"The skin orf yourn," I said.

"Cor luvaduck, what a life, eh?" said the Sweep. "Cor sufferin' wars."

"Cor," I said.

"The Duma," said the Tsar, "has shown herself to be at the height of events and has proved herself to be the real voice of the nation."

To which one fancies the tutor saying, "It has and all," I said.

"Because," said the Tsar, "the whole of the Russian people have understood the insult flung into the face of Russia."

"They have and all," I said.

"Now," said the Tsar, "I have full faith in the future."

"That's right," I said.

"Myself," said the Tsar, "I have done everything I could to avoid war."

"Too true," I said.

[1] Nathaniel Gubbins was a humorous columnist on the *Sunday Express*. He later moved to the *Sunday Dispatch*.

"I made every effort," said the Tsar, "to find a solution compatible with our dignity and our national honour."

"'Ear, 'ear," I said.

"You will never believe," said the Tsar, "how happy I am to have got out of this terrible uncertainty."

"Not arf I don't," I said.

"I have never before," said the Tsar, "gone through such agony as I did these last awful days before the war."

"Too true you ain't," I said.

"Now I am convinced," said the Tsar, "that in Russia there will begin a movement similar to the one which broke out during the patriotic war of 1812."

"It will and all," I said.

Mrs. Asquith, in parting with Sir John French, before he went out to take command of the British Army in Flanders, asked him to give her any trifle that would remind her to pray for him, and herself gave him a small silver-gilt saint which he put in his capacious khaki pocket. French, on his side, reciprocated by cutting the *A.D.C. General* badges off his horse-cloth. Though no doubt his affection for Mrs. Asquith was genuine, still, it never does any harm to keep in with the Prime Minister's wife. In the same spirit the Grand Duke Nicholas, Supreme Commander-in-Chief of the Russian Armies, before leaving Peterhof presented the Emperor with the first trophy of the war – a machine-gun captured from the Germans on the frontier of East Prussia.

Mrs. Asquith records that, going in to her husband's dressing-room, she found him reading *Our Mutual Friend*. He told her he was going to read all the Dickens novels, as they took his mind off the war – colleagues and allies alike.

Though the Tsar thought that Turkish neutrality was assured, the Turk soon began to give trouble in Egypt. Already during the hectic days of July the Young Turk Party had been secretly negotiating with Germany, and a German-Turkish alliance had in fact been signed on August 2nd. Quite soon we were reaping our full harvest of troubles in the Eastern Mediterranean. Churchill was ready to send a swarm of flotillas into the Dardanelles to torpedo the *Goeben*. Greece was thrown into confusion; Serbia was overrun; Bulgaria, joining up with the Turks, added herself to the number of our enemies, and when Rumania, alone of the Balkan bunch, hesitatingly declared herself our friend, she was soon punished for it by the Germans exacting total retribution.

Mr. Asquith declared himself disgusted with the optimism of the Press and the credulity of people who believed in great Belgian victories. All that the Belgians had really done so far was to throw out the whole of the German time-table. The War Office, which during the Second World

War was to be criticised anew as the most inefficient of Government departments, was even more inefficient in the First World War. And when Asquith writes that "the poor old War Office, which has been a by-word for inefficiency, has proved itself more than up-to-date", one may wonder what it was like in the Boer War. Asquith's remarks about the war, like the Tsar's, who was his real opposite number in Russia, suggest a strange remoteness from it all, as though both just hoped for the best. They don't, either of them, quite know what they are doing. One does not gather the impression of a directing brain, but of just another member of the general public sitting perhaps in the front row of the grand circle.

August 17th, synchronising with Asquith's disgust at the optimism in the British Press, saw Their Majesties of Russia in Moscow. In a long cavalcade of carriages they drove to the Kremlin through enormous crowds of people who filled the immense squares and streets. The reception was quite as enthusiastic, and it is saying much, as that accorded to Amy Johnson herself on her return from Australia in 1930. People even hung from the trees like birds in order to catch a glimpse of their sovereign. It is astonishing what they will turn out to see. All Moscow's countless churches boomed and pealed in an acclamation of joy, and from the mouths of millions poured that finest and noblest of all national anthems, that soaring, rapturous but controlled Russian hymn, 'God Save the Tsar'.

There is something faintly inane about this ovation accorded to a comparatively brainless man because he has got his country into a sorry mess. Granted that he was but human and, though complete autocrat, the slave of his own limitations, he it was, if anyone, who was in the position of a God capable of making it otherwise. If any proof be needed that statesmanship is not conducted on the highest principles of wisdom as embodied in Christianity or esoteric philosophy, but is fifth-form, here it is. The morons acclaimed the befuddled little officer as a saint, and sincerely thanked him for having brought them bloodshed. In some thirty months they will execrate him for the same reason.

The war is set. The Tsar's civil and military subjects bring out of their moth-eaten stores of history all the suitable shiboleths. The journalists burnish up old clichés. The clergy sample the relevant saints. Solemnly, purposefully, the Tsar walks up the steps arm-in-arm with his ill-omened Alix.

Now slowly he descends, still arm-in-arm with his *malade imaginaire* consort, walking over the drawbridge towards the Ouspensky cathedral. Attended by the Metropolitans of Kiev, Petersburg and Moscow, and masses of other higher clergy of the Orthodox Church who, in common with their brethren of other godly brands the world over, are never at a loss to consecrate bloodshed, he proceeds to Tchudov monastery, where the whole epauletted, aiguilletted company prays at the coffin of Saint Alexei.

Yes, granted, it is not an ignoble sight, temporal power prostrating itself before spiritual. The sincerity with which the Tsar dedicates himself to a will and wisdom other than his own, even though fitting and, in his case, more than urgent, is moving. But – O God! it is the same dreary old story. The difference between men and sheep seems to be that men, unlike sheep, need not be led to the slaughter but are carried there on the wings of their own enthusiasm.

A week later news reached London that the Germans had taken Namur and that the British Army was believed to have been cut off. Kitchener had cursed and sworn over the telegram. At 10 Downing Street a party of ministers gathered in subdued excitement, as is usual on election night at the home of a prominent public man considered to be the fount of information. News percolated through that a despatch from Sir John French had arrived at the War Office but could not be traced, as Kitchener, who could not be found, had disappeared with it. Kitchener had been dining with Arthur Balfour, but it was doubted whether even he could keep dear Arthur awake after eleven o'clock. A flush of anger suffused the cheeks of an otherwise imperturbable Prime Minister, who rang bells and demanded that Lord Kitchener be traced and the despatch brought to him at once. "Tell them," he said in a state of exasperation, "to find Lord Kitchener at once; this mustn't happen again – I must have the despatch *at once*; do you *hear*?"

This is what you can do as prime minister. This man, not favoured by birth or money, worked his way up by way of school and Oxford, study and scholarship – to be a barrister; from the Bench to Parliament; from there to this. And from here he could say '*at once*' with impunity.

This was his power.

But he could not prevent war: that was his impotence. A man of character, of judgment, well-grounded in classical scholarship, a solid, ponderous but unassuming man. And, in matters of the utmost gravity to each of his fellow citizens, in the one matter which affected them most, a matter of life and death to those they loved most, he, the seasoned statesman of Britain, was as helpless and befuddled as the autocrat of all the Russians.

In London, Mrs. Asquith, motoring, as she says, with 'Henry', a week later, saw a street poster – "300,000 Germans Against Our Men". Asking her husband if this were possible, she received the reply, "Yes, they are three to one, if not more, against our poor fellows." Statesmen, it would seem, were not regulating our affairs, but merely holding a watching brief on behalf of our interests, informing us at their convenience of the extent, with details, of our casualties in the conflicts which they, not we, had brought about.

When one reflects upon the safeguards taken by solicitors on behalf of a ward in Chancery, whose money is protected by trustees, is invested on the best advice with every known device of caution and circumspection to prevent some adventurer from getting round the ward in Chancery even after she has come of age, the reckless gamble with which a man of Mr. Asquith's solid qualities is prepared to stake the British Empire, stake her whole existence and the lives of millions of her citizens on no better than the even chance of, say, red instead of black turning up on the roulette, statesmanship becomes too fantastic for sober contemplation. To say that Mr. Asquith and Sir Edward Grey were having a flutter would not be an exaggeration. "Yes, they are three to one, if not more, against our poor fellows." Again, one asks oneself, had they no idea of what they were letting us in for? Why did they not legislate for a better settlement than the insane acrobatics of balancing on the tip of a pole passed from hand to hand of six hysterical great powers?

70

THE PERPETUUM MOBILE

A national war develops like a personal quarrel, with that important difference that those who are called to face the greatest danger, to perform the most unpalatable, the most gruesome tasks, to suffer the most wracking pain and galling mutilation, or to mourn the heaviest loss, carry the most poignant memories, do not easily synchronise their feeling with the more impersonal body of opinion that places its consistency of principle above the suffering of others.

And, of course, they all paid their visit to the Western Front to see the sights. Margot Asquith came, lodged with the King and Queen of the Belgians, ran up and stood excitedly on the top of a hillock, exchanged cigarettes for a Belgian soldier's cartridge-belt and lanyard. Dear Arthur came, gazed wonderously through his pince-nez at the shells bursting in the distance, remarking on their aesthetic aspect. Curzon came, expressing casually his incredulity, as he observed some Tommies bathing in a pool, that "the lower orders should look almost exactly like ourselves".

Those were the people who in *The Silver Box* were branded as bad, envious, dangerous to society. They had nothing – not a stake in the country or a particle of profit in the Empire. They had been 'kept in their places' by those who had certainly something to fight for. But just as certainly those who had something to fight for were a small minority. So they turned to those others, whom in peacetime they hardly honoured to call even their fellow countrymen, and now told them they were Englishmen, and 'Who died if England lived?' And the poor mutts, who had never had anything in their lives to be proud of, were caught on the bait of their starved pride. And valiantly they went forward to be slain like cattle by others just like them, who too had never had the spare cash for a trip across the North Sea to make one another's acquaintance, and, given the chance, would have been the first to chum up.

71

THE UNPREDICTABLE AND INCALCULABLE

Writers do not stand up well to tyranny. Bernard Shaw had been lampooning the British Government about the war. But when he saw that the temper of the nation was in no mood for persiflage, he wrote a recruiting play. In regard to the genesis of the Second World War, his prophecy was that Hitler, as he was not born in Prague, would not wish to annex Czecho-Slovakia. H. G. Wells first waxed hot about the war; then in the middle of it got Mr. Brittling to return his German tutor's fiddle to his Pomeranian parents with a covering letter that the time had come to bury the hatchet. After the war he wrote a novel with a conscientious objector for a hero, and the soldier, Bulpington Blup, presented as an ass and a cad, only to pontificate again in 1941, "This war is justified." D. H. Lawrence, described by Middleton Murry as the man to suffer more agony than anyone else in the war, dispelled his half-hearted attitude in the midst of it by writing to a correspondent, likewise a non-combatant, "Kill Germans – in millions." He came to the point when he did not care how many million Englishmen were being killed. "What is death in the individual!" he wrote to Lady Ottoline Morrell. "I don't care if sixty million individuals die."

"It was," observes Hugh Kingsmill, "the hypothetical death of the sixty-million-and-oneth individual which shocked him, and he told Lady Cynthia Asquith that he would be mortally indignant if the war cost him his life, or even too much of his liberty." The most significant feature of the world in mid-war was that the chaos of conflicting blindnesses during the war proved, on the whole, a surer prediction of the chaos which followed the war than any single reasoned prediction. Walter Page, the American Ambassador, at first took the same aloof and slightly admonitory attitude to the British part in the war as did Mr. Kennedy, his successor during the first years of the Second World War. "But, Mr. Page: what else could we do!" expostulated King George, who also took comfort in confiding freely in Walter Page as the only independent highly-placed Anglo-Saxon who was not also his subject. "Seeing the difficulties of a limited monarch, I thank heaven for having been spared those of an absolute one." Meanwhile the Tsar still thought that the war was merely vindicating the pledge of unabridged autocracy he had given at the Uspensky cathedral at the time of his coronation.

God's Fifth Column speaks to each in his own language. Having regard to the paradoxical results obtained, one could hardly, in enlightened retrospect, say what anyone at the time was fighting *for*, or even against: at most one could say that he was fighting. After the sacking of Sackville Street during the Rebellion of Easter Week, our imaginative Kitchener had posters put up on the ruins to encourage recruiting, in which he pointedly asked Irishmen whether they wanted to see the horrors of Louvain repeated in their own homes; while Englishmen in London showed their customary forbearance by joining in the chorus of "When Irish Eyes are Smiling" at the Coliseum. In President Wilson's idea of making the world safe for democracy when he came into the war, after the Tsar had ceased making the world safe for autocracy, and Lenin considered the world safe only in the keeping of the dictatorship of the proletariat, and General Kornilov alone in the trusteeship of the military caste: in all this jumble we have a sort of crooked mirror which reflects the incalculable muddle of future cross-purposes.

For, indeed, who would have foretold that all these conflicting aspirations (of which the Japanese annexation of the German concession at Tsing-Tao was only one of a hundred imponderables) would result in Black and Tans overrunning Ireland; the Ku Klux Klan rising at the end of a war that had made the world safe for democracy, in order to stamp out the 'Red Scare' and to champion racial inequality in the United States; in Churchill prosecuting a White Guard war against Bolshevism, later to save it from Hitler. Who would have thought that the Kaiser would reach a position when, in Churchill's words, "the greater part of Europe, particularly his most powerful enemies, Great Britain and

France, would regard the Hohenzollern restoration they formerly abhorred beyond expression, as a comparatively hopeful event and as a sign that dangers were abating".

All the paradoxes presented before us in slow motion in 1914 were by 1940 considerably accelerated by that Ironic Hand which Meredith calls the Comic Spirit, and whose other name is God's Fifth Column, to demonstrate to us how similar causes, slogans and motives rooted in unrighteousness merely cancel themselves out before our very eyes. *Now* would we see our folly? Indeed, how often and how quickly must the Ironic Hand turn the handle for them to enable idolatrous gulls to see for themselves what all the corporate idealism of the angry dust amounts to?

When current results lagged behind expectation, the civilians, whom General Sir Henry Wilson called 'the frocks', sacked the generals. Sir William Robertson, who had risen from a trooper in the Scots Greys to become Chief of the Imperial General Staff in London, went to France to relieve General Sir Herbert Smith-Dorrien of his command. "'Erb, you're for 'ome!" That was all. The French general Franchet d'Esperey, on taking over his new command, summoned his staff and addressed them in some such words: "Gentlemen, from now on any man who falls back without orders, or any member of my staff, whatever his rank, who fails in his work, will be shot out of hand." He did not tell them what they were to do to *him* if he, in turn, fell down on his job. It was not considered good taste in the last war to shoot generals whose inefficiency resulted in the death of thousands of their troops, but commanders-in-chief confirmed death sentences for sentries overpowered by sleep, even if no one lost his life through it. To achieve results cancelled out within twenty-five years, drastic measures, of course, were necessary.

Hitler, a runner in the Great War, widened the application of the death penalty in his own war to include generals and even ministers, stopping just short of authorising, in given circumstances, the shooting of the Führer. Could this pseudo-intellectual, this simulacrum lance-corporal of 1916, sitting dejectedly on his bunk with his head in his hands, groaning and sighing, have for one moment believed it possible that, some twenty-five years later during the Battle of France, he would issue this order to his generals, "I, Adolf Hitler, will shoot with my own hands any general who fails to advance according to schedule"? Hitler was a runner in a Bavarian infantry regiment entrenched near Neuve Chapelle when Major Winston Churchill, recently relieved of the Admiralty and unwilling to sink to the indignity of accepting, from Mr. Asquith's hands, the Duchy of Lancaster, decided to have a spell at the Front, and arrived to take up his duties at a cluster of dug-outs opposite, nicknamed 'Ebenezer Farm'. His battalion noticed an appreciable increase of offensive activity on the part of the enemy, disputed by Churchill as being due to his presence. He was known and hated in Germany at least as much, he said, as Tirpitz was known and hated in England. If the Germans really knew that he was in the trenches they would have given expression to a much more determined effort to eliminate him. To this, it might be added, that could the British have seen into the future and have guessed who was the lugubrious fellow moping in the trenches opposite, they would have considered no expenditure of ammunition unjustified in the hope of eliminating the prospective author of World War Number Two.

Churchill's brief spell at the front was marked by a steady flow of visitors from Whitehall who crossed over to France to see their friend. Birkenhead in due course visited Winston for some political back-chat about what was happening behind the scenes, and, having neglected to procure the proper credentials, relying on his tongue to get him through anywhere, spent the night under arrest. Beaverbrook 'observed' for the Canadian Government. The ex-pacifist Lloyd George, who had grimly set his teeth to fight on to a finish, and oust Asquith, was nervous of the whizzing shells and bullets, and sea-sick in crossing the Channel. When one day Churchill, having donned his more martial-looking French-blue helmet (which he preferred to the shallow English tin hat) saw shells dropping in the distance, the sight gave rise to emotion, as always with this author, running to rhetoric. "Here we are," he said, turning to Captain Dewar Gibb, "here we are, torn away from the Senate and the Forum to fight in the battlefields of France."

Lord Kitchener was an imposing shop-window with little behind it. Used to giving orders, he was out of his depths in the Cabinet room. His colleagues contrived, against the advice of the men on the spot, to send him out on a mission to Russia in the hope that during his absence some headway might be made at home. As soon as he was drowned off the coast of Scotland he was lamented as a great loss to the nation. Asquith, said to be his only friend in the Cabinet, in a measured panegyric in the House staked a claim to some special Christian Elysium for the departed tongue-tied soldier, suggesting in rhetorical language, in which politicians clothe even their genuine emotions, that his Maker would be signally pleased to greet so fine and upright a soldier and gentleman.

But if neither Kitchener nor Haig could see anything in the tank, it is only fair to exonerate their short-sightedness on an exceptionally long view, could one but credit them with the capacity for taking it. The French invented the tank, almost simultaneously with the English, in 1915, in order to be defeated by it twenty-five years later at the hands of the people against whom they had sharpened their wits. How did it profit them? It was a case of Kipling's 'bloody instructions which but return to plague the inventor', so much so that Churchill, who also had had a hand in getting the tank put over, twenty-five years later rushed over to France, vainly trying to save her from the consequences of tank warfare with an offer of full union with Great Britain. God's Fifth Column is no respector of nationalities. All destructive engines of war it turns into boomerangs. The Allies having invented the tank, the Germans lost the Great War for lack of tanks, and we had to face another war because they acquired a superiority in tanks in 1939. Similar boomerangs return in diplomacy. Our very innocent out-manoeuvring of Germany at the Algeciras Conference in 1903 made her unduly stubborn in 1914, and plunged the world into war. Nothing lasting or worth while can be achieved on the road to (Churchill's favourite word) Armageddon.

The quarrel between Lloyd George, who held that war was too serious a matter to entrust to soldiers, and Sir William Robertson who, though he had himself never led even a troop into action, dismissed all statesmen as 'poltroons', became acute when Lloyd George succeeded Kitchener as Secretary of State for War. Northcliffe, who modelled himself on Napoleon, having conceived a high idea of the military mind, declared at a luncheon that General Sir William Robertson, the leader of the 'Generals' Party', should not only rule the military but also preside over all the Cabinet Ministers as well. Having failed to keep Lloyd George out of the War Office, Robertson was intriguing to push him out. Lloyd George, wishing to get rid of Robertson, was inducing him to go to Russia, in succession to Kitchener who had got drowned on his way there. Robertson flatly refused to go. In the Coalition Government, already in an advanced state of decomposition, maggots were agog, forces at work, to remove Asquith, who wanted to stay at the helm, if only because he had been there since 1908. These forces variously divided themselves into factions clinging to Asquith in support of Robertson and his generals, and factions working to push Asquith out in support of Lloyd George against Robertson. In all this there was quite as much resentment and hatred and hope of settling old scores as was being mobilised against the common enemy, the elimination of whom was merely a job needing to be done, all the real quarrel being about how best to do it, but, over and above this, who was to give orders and who take them.

Running counter to other currents, there was Northcliffe, scheduled to go mad six years afterwards, when, journalist to the end, his last order to his editors was the triumphant wording of a poster, his final, biggest scoop – NORTHCLIFFE MAD. He was not so mad then, when conscious of his madness, as he was mad now while imagining that he was sane. Into the War Office he strutted. Lloyd George's secretary, realising that Northcliffe's support in the larger intrigues then already afoot was not to be despised, at once flung open the door into the magnificent room occupied by the Secretary of State for War. But Northcliffe, refusing to see Lloyd George himself, instead shouted at Lloyd George's secretary. "Tell him," he roared, "that I hear he is interfering with strategy! If he goes on, I'll break him!" and he strutted out again.

When, two weeks later, Asquith fell and Lloyd George became prime minister, Robertson was dismissed. The war over, but his megalomania unsated after telling the country how to win it, Northcliffe thought his country wanted him to go to Paris to tell the Big Four how they were to make the peace. His services were not, however, by Mr. Lloyd George, judged indispensable to His Majesty's Government.

Meanwhile the newspapers reported the daily progress of the war. 'Last night's communiqué' was for long a variation on the theme – "British lose a yard of trenches. A zeppelin chased. British regain two yards of trenches. Two zeppelins chased." If this seems, by blitz standards, a modest progress, it did not in common sense compare unfavourably with the final result of the First World War, when, having won the war and touched the Germans for one thousand million pounds' worth of assets, America, and to a lesser extent ourselves, lent the beaten foe over two thousand million pounds, which they sank in preparing the Second World War.

On the social side, the nostalgia of the private soldier for a private paradise droned on through the war in such popular ditties as

> Sergeant-Majors will be navvies,
> Privates own their motor cars;
> When this bloody war is over . . .

did not materialise, both private *and* sergeant-major finding it hard to obtain jobs even as navvies.

Those were, as Osbert Sitwell says, heroic days, in which men had forged for themselves a language in keeping with their deeds. A queer, stern, concentrated tongue, it seemed, which went after this fashion: "Doncher believe it, old bean . . . about one pip-emma . . . there was a blasted crash down the bloody chimney, and out of a blinking cloud of soot came that mingy blighter Bundle. My word, that was Tootaloo for Bundle – a fair tinkety-tonk, I assure you. We did have a Christmas-and-a-half, I can tell you. Well, chin-chin, cheerio, so long, old boy."

The language forged in the Second World War by, let us say, members of the R.A.F. is incomprehensible to the layman. It is, however, in all wars and on all fronts and in all fighting services, invariably a language reducing lethal terms to a kindergarten babble, a language gently humorous, devoid of all malice. It is on the home front, notably among

237

elderly ladies, still more if they are spinsters, that the language of vengeance spits fire from the nostrils. On the home front in the last war, there was 'unshakable determination', or what the Germans on their side called 'iron will', to pursue this thing – in the teeth of the law of life decreeing that all stresses and protrusions in the end merely cancel themselves out – to the bitter end.

The combination of fatuous idealism with the profiteering spirit contrasted sharply with the easy-going tolerance to mankind at large, not excluding the enemy, on the part of the men facing the brunt of the danger and discomfort. According to a German account, German womanhood volunteering for service in the military hospitals behind the Front waited impatiently for the romance of tending the wounded, long in coming on the Eastern Front. At last the glad news trickled through: the wounded were coming! The nurses had polished the linoleum floors till they shone like mirrors, beds were made, food cooked in excited anticipation of the romantic wounded. Each nurse dreamed she would encounter her intended. How she would tend him! How gratefully he would respond! She would bandage his wound, a nice wound, preferably on the arm, painful but not disfiguring. He would come to after the anaesthetic and raise soulful eyes beaming with silent gratitude and recognition. Their looks would meet, and then . . .

Runners were now reaching the hospital. The wounded were coming! The nurses, all gathered together, peered through the window. They can just discern a grey streak moving in the distance. Yes, a detachment of men is winding up the road. The wounded at last! As they approach, the nurses can distinguish their figures: bitter disappointment fills their virgin hearts. Now the wounded are filing through the gate. They are tramping up the steps, leaving traces of their muddy boots on the shining linoleum. A week's growth disfigures their sweaty, dirty, for the most part, ungainly faces. Their uniforms are in rags, running with lice. They scowl and look morose. Sullen, dejected by their ugly wounds, they spurn all ideas of romance, '*riechen fürchterlich und wollen aufs Klosset*'[1] where they queue up, splash the shiny linoleum, then tumble into bed and call loudly for food.

Charles Ricketts spoke of a letter from a servant caretaker who had been in a château occupied by the Prussians, relating which pictures had been hurt, what furniture had been smashed, how much wine drunk and wasted, together with other details. The postscript to the letter was "I had forgotten to tell Madame la Vicomtesse *que j'ai été violée quatre fois*."

How gay and lighthearted was the life at the British General Head-

---

[1] 'smell atrociously and demand to go to the lavatory'.

quarters in France. Philip Gibbs gave us a touching picture: the band playing rag-time and light music while the warriors feed, waited upon by little W.A.A.C.'s, with G.H.Q. colours tied up in bows on their hair. All these generals and ribboned staff officers indulging in bursts of lighthearted laughter. "Such whisperings of secrets, of intrigues and scandals in high places! Such callous-hearted courage when British soldiers were being blown to bits, gassed, blinded, maimed and shell-shocked in places that were far, so very far, from G.H.Q."

It was not considered quite the thing between enemies to bomb one another's headquarters, let alone G.H.Q. Churchill describes the atmosphere in which the plans and orders to advance regardless of cost in lives were hatched in tranquillity. "We sit in calm, airy, silent rooms opening upon sunlit and embowered lawns, not a sound except of summer and of husbandry disturbs the peace; but seven million men, any ten thousand of whom could have annihilated the ancient armies, are in ceaseless battle from the Alps to the Ocean. And this does not last for an hour, or for two or three hours; it lasts nearly a year." Compared with Cannae, Blenheim or Austerlitz, Churchill found the Great War to be a slow-motion picture. The tests were evidently of a different kind. Whether they were 'of a high order', he had not made up his mind. "It is certainly too soon to say that they are," he concludes.

The Russian Front presented a less concentrated picture. Instead of the neat symmetry of opposing trench-lines, there was a good deal of what mechanics call 'free play': long pauses, then perhaps a rifle cracking in the wintry air. Glittering staffs of the Supreme Commander-in-Chief, and Chiefs of Commands, and aides-de-camp, and visiting ministers, and of course the monarch in residence or away.

By the end of 1916, just after the collapse of the Asquith administration, the Germans first made overtures for peace. The popular belief that Lloyd George, the Boer War pacifist, was a more spirited war leader than the Liberal Imperialist Asquith was, like most beliefs centred around leading personalities, beside the point. All leaders at all times, whether called Charles XII, Peter I, Frederick II or Napoleon, have been saved from disaster, or not saved from disaster, by so narrow a margin of good or ill luck that the personal factor can have but a small place in a sea of incalculable forces multiplied by incalculable factors, of which the one reliable fact is uncertainty.

By December 1916, Ludendorff had to confess that Germany had lost the war. If the war did not end then it was because we would not make peace with the Kaiser. And in a war you can't just stop playing and walk off the court without being pursued by the victor. From 1917 onwards the Germans, as again in 1942, were fighting the war in a kind of sorrowful, exasperated "Stop it, I say!" spirit of a bully kicked along by two bigger schoolboys after he had meanly attacked a small boy. The big boys exhort him not to be 'yellow', and from time to time he turns and hits back. But his heart is not in it. Ludendorff, who had planned everything meticulously to the last detail, found that Germany could not contemplate an offensive, having to keep her reserves available for defence. "There was no hope of a collapse," he writes in his *Memoirs*, "of any of the Entente Powers. If the war lasted, our defeat seemed inevitable. Economically we were in a highly unfavourable position for a war of exhaustion. At home our strength was badly shaken. Questions of the supply of food-stuffs caused great anxiety, and so, too, did questions of morale. We were not undermining the spirits of the enemy populations with starvation, blockades and propaganda. The future looked dark, and our only comfort was to be found in defying a superior enemy and that our line was everywhere beyond our frontiers."

Asquith, ill at Walmer Castle, wide awake in bed on a December evening and brooding on the sudden end to an eight-year-old tenure of the premiership, was told that Germany had put out feelers for an early peace. "How I wish I could believe," his voice welled up in the dark bedroom, "that someone would have the wits to keep this door ajar."

It is a singular feature of war that those who have had the least to do with bringing it about have usually borne the most savage punishment, while it is but rare that an armaments manufacturer himself suffers from the machine he feeds for his own gain. One is half inclined to accept Tolstoy's theory that consequences, more potent in their amalgamations than causes, retrospectively condition the course of events, mere chronology being no concern of eternal God. Conversely, could one imagine the Great War ending at Christmas 1916, would the Russian Revolution have been averted? Would Liberalism, instead of Communism and Fascism, have been the order of the day? Or was it a historical necessity that unrighteous class-distinctions were ripe for dissolution and that both Communism and Fascism, with all their savagery, had to be in order to serve that purpose? If the war was to last another two years, was to mow down, wound and blind many more millions without settling anything at the end of it, unleashing in its trail revolutions, dictatorships, unemployment, poverty-in-the-midst-of-plenty, and at the end of it all another world war: could all this sum of things be attributed to the accident of a purely human agency? Or was it in fact no other than God's Fifth Column doing its inevitable work of grinding the lumps of human egotism into pulp?

When William II understood that the chances of Germany emerging victorious were small, he had a word with Cardinal Nuncio at Berlin. The Nuncio grasped the Kaiser's hand impulsively and said, "*Vous avez parfaitement raison! C'est le devoir du Pape, il faut qu'il agisse, c'est par lui que le monde doit être régagné à la paix. Je transmettrai vos paroles à Sa Sainteté.*"[1]

Meanwhile the British armies, which had, even at the end of 1915, formed but a sixth of the Allied Front, had become the major factor on the Western Front. In addition, the Royal Navy remained the supreme factor it had always been. Sir Douglas Haig, owing his promotion from Commander-in-Chief of an army corps to that of an army, thence to that of the B.E.F., to no outstanding merits of his own but rather to a dismal lack of competition, carried on the business like a butcher in charge of an abattoir. The slaughter, which the generals called 'attrition', must be kept up from dawn to dark. Haig's only duty, as he conceived it, was to work out percentages to total up in the course of months or years in favour of the Allies. When in August of 1918 he worked out that the Fourth Army had taken 21,000 prisoners at the cost of 20,000 casualties, five per cent seemed to him a sound return on his investments. Sir Douglas Haig was one of those immaculate English gentlemen of Scottish blood who, together with their perfect manners, quiet courtesy and irreproachable code of honour, combine an unimaginativeness too fantastic to be quite credible. He believed in neither the tank nor the aeroplane, asserting that his cavalry would bring him all the intelligence he wanted. Himself intermittently assailed by his boss, Mr. Lloyd George, for his terrible blunders, Haig sent down the military scale a ceaseless chain of instructions to attack the enemy without regard to cost in lives, the greatest crime in his eyes being disobedience to orders, even when the men on the spot knew that orders were based on error springing from obvious ignorance of conditions, and the compliance meant sending men to certain death without gaining the slightest advantage. It was too subtle for Haig to appreciate that there were circumstances in war when initiative on the spot must take precedence over blind obedience to orders issued in ignorance. Obey and die was the first and last wisdom of this kindly, modest, self-deprecating and immaculate knight who, like King Francis I, was without fear and without reproach.

As soon as he opened his mouth the action seemed to cut off the current from his brain, and he could neither refute Mr. Lloyd George's voluble arguments nor substantiate his own. He could never finish a sentence, while Allenby's finished sentences could not convey his meaning. Whether they understood each other is at least doubtful. But it is said that each General, however inarticulate, was always perfectly understood by his own staff officers. In this connection one is reminded

---

[1] "You are completely right! It's the duty of the Pope, he must act, the world must be restored to peace through him. I will convey your words to His Holiness."

of Chehov's saying: "The stupider the peasant, the better his horse understands him."

Haig rated everything and everyone by his one adage – "A sincere desire to engage the enemy". It was the one sincerity that seemed to him material. Lacking it, all officers, however high of rank, were relieved of their post. As far back as 1912, during a sham fight at some cavalry exercises, Haig observed to Churchill as he pointed to a certain brigadier lacking this sincerity, "This officer," he said, with a look of recriminatory significance lighting up in his placid eye, "did not show a sincere desire to engage the enemy." The phrase stuck in Churchill's mind. At the height of the war, finding himself at the side of Haig at dinner, Churchill, speaking of a certain naval episode, mischievously repeated the expression. Haig's dead eye lighted up with a flash of understanding assent. He turned to Churchill eagerly. "A sincere desire to engage the enemy," he said. How well he understood it!

There is a picture of the immaculate Haig with a kind of helpless unmilitary gesture of a lifted protesting gloved hand at a gruff reluctant Lloyd George, who seems to consider Haig with singular lack of enthusiasm, while Haig looks as though pleading with the Prime Minister for more and still more British manhood with which sincerely to engage the enemy. Haig's pleading expression seems sincere, almost pathetic, and for so stubborn and taciturn a Scot, his gesture strangely eloquent, while the volatile little Welshman, to whom words come like Ariel to Prospero, with his hands deep in his overcoat pockets, looks taciturn in the extreme, as though asking Haig to account for the lives he had sent him before. What had he done with them? Poured them down the Somme drainpipe, eh? 'Tiger' Clemenceau, his hands behind his back, has the dour expression of one not so much concerned with Lloyd George's economy in supplying British lives or Haig's liberality in disposing of them, as with France's own rapidly dwindling manhood.

'Attrition' must go on.

72

LENIN CHANGES PLACES WITH NICHOLAS

Chehov, a long way back, predicted the revolution. "While we intellectuals," he wrote in his journal, on coming home late with a headache

from one of those interminable Russian discussions on the degeneration
of everything, "while we intellectuals are rummaging among old rags
and, according to the old Russian custom, biting one another, there is
boiling up around us a life which we neither know nor notice. Great
events will take us unawares, like sleeping fairies, and you will see that
Sidorov, the merchant, and the teacher of the district school at Yeletz,
who see and know more than we do, will push us far into the background, because they will have accomplished more than all of us together. And I thought that, were we now to obtain political liberty, of
which we prattle so much, while engaged in biting one another, we
should not know what to do with it. We should waste it in accusing one
another in the newspapers of being spies and money-grabbers, we
should frighten society with the assurance that we have neither men, nor
science, nor literature, nothing! Nothing! And to scare society as we are
now doing, and as we shall continue to do, means to deprive it of
courage; it means simply to declare that we have no social or political
sense in us. And I also thought that, before the dawn of a new life has
broken, we shall turn into sinister old men and women, and we shall be
the first who, in our hatred of that dawn, will calumniate it."

And this is what indeed did happen to the first revolution, Tolstoy,
however, having long ago prophesied the coming of the second. "That
danger is growing every day and every hour. The workers' revolution
with horrors of destruction and murder threatens us, and only for a while
have we managed to postpone its eruption." People whispered that it
would come, it would come, it would surely come.

At last it came. The long-despaired-of Russian Revolution.

It took Lenin by surprise. He could not have credited, if told on New
Year's Eve of 1917, that before the year was out he would have exchanged his dingy Zurich lodging for an apartment in the Kremlin. Later
in January he had lectured to a body of Swiss socialists, expressing his
opinion that he and they of the older generation would not live to see the
coming revolution. When the news reached him he rushed out into the
street to buy a paper. As there was nothing in it, he hurried along to the
lake shore, there to read the confirmation of the rumour, earlier brought
to him by a friend, in a news bulletin posted on a board. It seemed it was
true. A provisional government had been set up in Petrograd consisting
of twelve members of the Duma. It said, among other things, that
political exiles would now be welcomed back to Russia. Dazed, he
boarded a tram and got back to his lodging to think it over.

Nicholas II, who was soon to exchange his throne for exile in Siberia,
was no less astonished by events that overtook him than was Lenin
himself, about to exchange exile for the uncrowned monarchy of
Nicholas. The Revolution overtook the Tsar at the imperial supreme

243

headquarters at Moghilëv. "My brain," he had noted in his diary, "is resting here. No Ministers. No troublesome questions demanding thought." At the front he felt at home. He was shielded all round from the bombs of urban revolutionaries by the entire strength of his own armies, re-inforced by those of the enemy. When a telegram arrived from the President of the Duma, Rodzianko, advising him that the last hour was come when the fate of the country and the dynasty was being decided, the Tsar merely observed, "This fat-bellied Rodzianko has written me some nonsense to which I will not even reply." His dinner over, he caused a telegram to be sent to the military governor at Petrograd, commanding him to suppress "from to-morrow all disorders on the streets of the capital, which cannot be permitted when the Fatherland is carrying on a difficult war with Germany".

When his wife, who had always urged him to emulate the drastic brutality of Peter the Great, now stressed in a telegram that she and her children were surrounded at Tsarskoye Selo by hostile Red troops and urged that "concessions are necessary", he, generally prone to be weak, took a strong line and refused out of hand all concessions. He telegraphed that he was well, was returning to Petrograd, adding "Lovely weather."

When General Russki's army, which he had ordered to march on Petrograd, joined in with the revolutionaries, and the Emperor's own train was stopped on the way and was turned off to Pskov, he relented, and telegraphed to the President of the Duma, "Will now make the necessary concessions." To this the reply came: "Too late." And he abdicated without leaving his train.

The day before his inevitable return to Petrograd a brief ceremony took place. The brilliant staffs assembled in the big hall to await the appearance of their Emperor. He appeared. There was a curious expression on his face, a strange flicker of a smile, half grin, half stare. His mouth seemed strangely twisted. It was as if he were conscious at once of the pathos and the foolishness of his position. But when he spoke, urging his successors, in well-worn words, to prosecute the war to a finish, his voice was firm.

Then he was driven to the station, where he entrained. He was informed that the train of his mother, the Dowager Empress Maria Feodorovna, bound for Kiev, was due in, and some minutes later he left his train and entered his mother's. The Empress Mother, a sister of Queen Alexandra, had in her time frequently urged her son (who because of his diminutive stature compared with that of his giant father, Alexander III, seemed to her unequal to the task of ruling Russia without his mother) to be firm when her son showed signs of wanting to be conciliatory, and to be conciliatory when he wished to show he could be firm. Now she cast eyes at him, eyes full of woe, saying only too eloquently that if *only* he had listened to her, things would not have come to such a pass. For an hour they were closeted in the private saloon of the Empress Dowager and no one knows what was said by the meek-eyed Nicholas or by his Danish mother who had reared him for the Russian throne.

When their tête-à-tête was interrupted, the intruders observed an embarrassing scene. The Empress Mother was sobbing bitterly, weeping freely and without restraint, and her son sat silently with averted gaze fixed guiltily at the carpet.

When Maria Feodorovna's train went past the stationary train of the Emperor, he looked at her for the last time through the window.

When the Tsar's train moved out of the station, his late Chief of Staff, now Commander-in-Chief, General Alekseiev, raised his hand to the salute. But when the last coaches containing the representatives of the Revolution, who, unknown to the Emperor, had installed themselves in the rear of his train, passed level with the Commander-in-Chief, he took off his cap and bowed low to his new masters.

Lenin was packing up his revolutionary writings that had nibbled at and finally undermined the pillars of the throne. He welcomed his brother exile but arch-enemy, Martov's, plan to strike a bargain with the Germans for facilitating their return to Russia. The Allies, had argued the Menshevik protagonist, would be sure to refuse them all facilities. It was not in their interests to encourage disruption in Russia by facilitating the return of extreme socialist elements bent on stopping the war in a country they were egging on to make a last stand. But where the Allies stood to lose, Germany stood to gain.

The Germans readily agreed, making counter conditions for the eventual return of an equivalent number of German internees. Lenin countered the counter-proposal by the condition that his train was to be sealed between the two German frontiers. Martov finally backed out of travelling home with Lenin for fear of contaminating the purity of his Menshevik reputation on arrival. He left a month later. Lenin travelled with his St. Paul, Zinoviev, who was, in the 1937 purge, executed on his own extracted confession of sin against the Marxist Holy Ghost as interpreted by Stalin. Lenin's party consisted in all of thirty exiles. He walked up and down the corridor as the train chugged across war-time Germany and sang songs out of tune. At the Finland station in Petrograd he was met by Chkheidze, the Soviet Menshevik leader, who received him in the imperial waiting-room. The dashing Marshal Voroshilov, who had yet to win his baton and even his spurs, presented Lenin with a bouquet of roses. Chkheidze made a speech of welcome, outlining the Soviet's watered-down policy of moderation, which was to support the

Kerensky government in its stand against the German Army. They all hoped that Lenin would fall into line.

Lenin's answer was to take the bouquet and turn his back on them. Instead, he made a speech to a crowd of soldiers, urging them to lay down their arms and help themselves to the land of the landowners. The soldiers were more averse to war than the townsmen. With a shout they hoisted Lenin on to the roof of their armoured car and went careering all over the town. At every halt Lenin made popular speeches, subversive of everything their leaders stood for. So they came to the mansion of the ballet dancer Kshesinskaya. She had once been the mistress of Nicholas II who, as a Grand Duke, had fallen in love with her and was sent, that he might forget her, on a cruise to Japan, where a Japanese policeman detailed to protect him had, in a fit of religious zeal, while Nicholas was inspecting a Buddhist shrine, struck the Russian heir-apparent on the head with the flat of his tin sword. Later, as emperor, Nicholas provided the dancer with this mansion, now to be the Bolshevik headquarters.

Trotsky arrived a month later, having on his way from the United States been interned in a prison at Halifax, Nova Scotia, pending investigation by the British authorities whether, as they readily presumed to be the case, Trotsky was *persona ingrata* with the Russian Provisional Government. Kerensky, who would have gladly kept Trotsky out, was not in a position to display intolerance. Political intolerance savoured of the old regime, and was unpopular with the Soviet of Workers', Soldiers' and Peasants' Deputies. Considered soberly, Lenin owed both his fame and his accession to power to his long years of voluntary exile. While things were brewing in Russia he lived abroad, out of touch with underground workers at home. Few had seen him. He was a legendary figure. His absence from the scene of cross-currents and personal contacts, which tend to compromise reputations, had left him an addict to his own clear-cut theories. Before he got to Russia, the February Revolution had already taken place. Before he returned to Petrograd from his Finnish exile, the October Revolution had been handed to him on a platter by Trotsky.

Experienced lecture-managers in their more candid moods advise authors that obscurity is their capital, public appearances their doom. Film stars liking to be alone and making one film in three years have sustained their popularity against stars who live their private lives in public. Lenin, glamorous through obscurity, was asked for his authoritative opinion whenever the men who had borne the heat and burden of the day were at cross-purposes. Far from apologising for his detachment, Lenin on arrival confined himself to berating those already on the scene for having sold the pass in his absence. A recluse, his advantage was that he could take the extreme view, while keeping himself out of the clutches of the established order – whether the monarchy, the Provisional Government of Prince Lvov, or later that of Kerensky.

The old Liberals, who had seemed so daring when they were the fringe of the opposition against the autocracy, now discovered that they had become the new Conservatives of the extreme Right. The Foreign Minister, Miliukov, a university professor of history, the hero of iconoclasts and anathema to the late Imperial Government on account of his Liberal views, now as Sazonov's successor found himself insisting on the Allies honouring a secret understanding that, as the price of her exertions, Russia was to have Constantinople. But there was a snag. The Soviet of Workers', Soldiers' and Peasants' Deputies controlled the Government, and the professor and Prince Lvov, in the eyes of Tsarist generals dangerous radicals, were dangerous reactionaries in the eyes of the Soviets. When Kerensky succeeded Lvov as Prime Minister and placed the scion of a beet-sugar millionaire, Tereschenko, young, handsome and modelling himself on an Englishman, in the chair of Miliukov and Sazonov, foreign affairs did not seem to the Soviet to be appreciably more democratic than heretofore. Kerensky, as a Social Revolutionary, was a shade more 'Red' than the Constitutional Democrats, Lvov and Miliukov. But Sazonov, who had always considered the Emperor a blameless knight, was about to be despatched to London as the new ambassador of the Russian Revolution.

The Soviet, gratified by its sense of power in controlling the Provisional Government, seemed quite happy in championing a policy agreeable to the masses, or damping a measure savouring of reaction. When a Peace Conference was announced to take place at Stockholm with a view to liquidating the war by international agreement, it seemed to such Bolsheviks as Kamenev and Stalin to be an obviously beneficent and desirable move. Everyone in Russia, from the soldiers upwards, was heartily sick of the war, and there was general agreement in favour of sending Russian delegates to the Stockholm Conference. The Social Revolutionaries were in favour; the Mensheviks were in favour; the Government itself was in favour; and a future Prime Minister of Great Britain, James Ramsay MacDonald, was so eminently for it that he proceeded to the Conference himself, until discovering at the port of embarkation that British seamen, reasoning that peace by negotiation while Germany remained unbeaten was a treasonable activity, refused to take him there. Russian soldiers, told to fight with sticks while some of their Generals had been selling their arms, had had enough of the war, interpreting as a treasonable activity not its cessation but its continuation. It could serve, they thought, no one save the interests of German or British capitalists who wished to rule the world.

Lenin, contrary to what the others expected of him, called his colleagues rank idiots for favouring the Stockholm Conference. Could they not see that they were merely playing into the hands of capitalists, in whose interests it was to stop the war in order to resume international exploitation through capital? Fortunately there were few capitalists intelligent enough to realise that peace at any price was their main interest. But because capitalists were fools, was that a reason why Bolsheviks who, with his eminent exception, were just as stupid, should play into their hands? By sabotaging the Stockholm Conference and inducing the asinine Kerensky to continue the war, capitalists would be playing into the hands of the Bolsheviks.

And this was what did happen. Kerensky, failing to persuade the Allied Governments to make a general peace, succumbed to American pressure. It did not seem to the United States Government logical to conclude peace with an enemy upon whom they had only recently declared war. Popular feeling against the enemy, slow to rise, had grown into a snowball, while in the countries exhausted by three years of fighting, hatred of the foe was rapidly melting and contempt for their own authorities was on the rise. The American Government succeeded in persuading Kerensky to lash his unwilling Army, now regarding its own officers as Enemy Number One, into an offensive against the German Army, for whose 'other ranks' the Russian soldier was animated by feelings of fraternisation rather than annihilation.

The inducement for an offensive was an American loan to the Russian Government, congenitally short of cash, of seventy-five million dollars. It was a sum of money which, in the Second World War, the British Government expended in the course of a little more than a day. But the bargain was clinched. Appointing himself Supreme Commander-in-Chief, Kerensky sent the order to the armies for a general advance. He clothed his insipid idea in rhetorical terms. "Soldiers!" ran his proclamation, "you are the freest warriors in the world. I summon you forward," he called from the rear, "to a fight for freedom, not as to a feast but unto death. We revolutionaries," he added charmingly from the sanctuary of the Winter Palace, "have the right to death."

The Germans, previously unable to reach the Russians because the Russian lines were out of range of the German guns, now waited for such of the Russian soldiers as were inspired by Kerensky's rhetoric to advance, literally, not as to a feast but unto death. News rang through the upper layers of Russian society living their normal life in the capital that the Russian Army was on the offensive. Staff officers made speeches in concert halls: the Russian Army had taken to the offensive. The news quickly percolated to London, Paris and Washington. The steamroller – hurray! – had been set rolling once more. All it had apparently lacked were a few dollars with which to grease its wheels.

When, however, the steamroller came within range of the German guns, the guns went off and the steamroller folded up.

It was the end of the war for Russia. Meanwhile, Trotsky, after an abortive rising in the capital, had been put away in prison. Lenin, always more discreet, had hidden himself away in Finland. The most interesting thing about Lenin was that he was never about when anything was happening. After things had happened, when nobody, not the least Lenin himself, understood what was afoot, he tendered advice which sometimes was taken and sometimes was not taken, with results approximately cancelling themselves out, to prove that he was, on the whole, as often right as he was wrong.

The protesting middle classes – which, in the crystallisation later to take place in Italy and Germany, might be termed conveniently the Fascist elements – then played their last card. A Cossack general who, in Imperial Russia, had enjoyed the cryptic reputation of subscribing to some independent views of his own which, while not disloyal to the autocracy, included no one quite knew what loyalty besides, named Kornilov, a small, wiry man with a dark Tartar face, seeing himself cut out for the part of the Russian Bonaparte, undertook unsuccessfully what Mussolini later accomplished successfully. The march on Rome was anticipated by the march on Petrograd. Kornilov came to within reach of the capital's outskirts. But there was something inveterately 'Red' about the city of Peter, soon to change its name to Lenin, and as Kornilov's troops approached the barricades his army melted at the fringes. It was the month of August. The pavements of the capital felt hot under the soles. The first White Guard attempt to freeze the revolution had dissolved of itself. Kerensky, scarcely knowing why, discovered that he had come out of it the victor.

But his victory had sown the seeds of his defeat. The hitherto moderate Soviet, appalled by the reality of a Counter-Revolution knocking at the gate, now inclined towards the Bolshevik faction. The peril from the extreme Right was best averted by a landslide to the extreme Left. Kerensky, pleading, as all governments do, that he was the golden mean, appeared a dangerous visionary. Deputies from every regiment at the front came to the capital to demand the speedy liquidation of the war. With Trotsky in prison and Lenin, as always at a moment of crisis, in voluntary exile, the Bolsheviks were no better prepared for a rising than any of the other parties. It was merely the coincidence of the presence in Petrograd of the Soldiers' Deputies from the front which ensured the success of the Bolshevik rising. The Soldiers' Deputies, speaking in the name of the entire retreating Russian front, made it clear that they had come with the object of putting a stop to the war still going on in the shape of German pursuit. Discovering that the small Bolshevik faction was the spearhead of social recrimination, which had largely spent itself in the other parties too inclined to be satisfied Liberals, the Soldiers' Deputies placed their services, militant on the home front, pacifist in the face of the German enemy, at their disposal.

Trotsky had advised the sailors from Kronstadt, the most bitter element in the Russian fighting forces, to use Kerensky as a gun-rest for shooting Kornilov, before turning on Kerensky. This they now did, arriving overnight in the capital, sailing up the Neva in their destroyers. Lenin had turned up at a committee meeting held at the flat of a Menshevik leader, Suhanov, whose Bolshevik wife had placed her dining-room at their disposal while her unsuspecting husband was away. Lenin, a pantomime figure, spectacled and beardless and wearing a wig to escape recognition but attracting undue attention, wrote out a resolution in a child's exercise-book. With two dissentients against ten, it was adopted. Then, as always, he disappeared and was not seen again till the day when, the Second Revolution having become a reality, Trotsky obligingly informed him that he, Lenin, was now the virtual head of the Russian Republic.

The Bolshevik programme, as such, was not only unpopular in the Soviet, but also had not been, on Lenin's interpretation, either accepted or quite understood even by such confirmed Bolsheviks as Zinoviev, Kamenev and Stalin, who in the excitement of events could not be expected to attach the same importance to the consistency of his doctrinaire principles as the Zurich exile, Lenin, did himself. Lenin was feared by men of more moderate opinions because he was consistently and uncompromisingly extreme. Impressed by the reputation of one all had heard of but few had seen, they were, now that they saw him, disconcerted by a suspicion that, in addition to being extreme, he was also not a little insane. Lenin's was the same kind of insanity as Hitler's, which succeeds in rationalising his insanity by an appeal to the patent inconsistencies and contradictions of more normal people who have not, unlike the paranoiacs, thought out their theories to their logical conclusions.

Once again Lenin appeared disguised in a yellow wig, with spectacles and, though beardless, a few days' growth already sprouting on his face. He sat quietly in the corridor outside the debating hall in the Smolni Institute, formerly an extremely conventional school for girls. When two deputies, passing through, stared at his unnatural yellow wig, Lenin not wishing to be recognised, immediately left. He retired to a room in a house nearby and lay down on the floor, covered with blankets and cushions. There, a little later, Trotsky joined him. Both lay side by side on the floor and discussed the trend of events. Meanwhile the debate in the Smolni went on. Martov, the Menshevik leader, who was anathema to Lenin, preached the gospel of moderation. Kerensky had fled from Petrograd, escorted by an American Embassy limousine flying the stars and stripes, but some other ministers still lingered in the Winter Palace, which, defended by the Women's Battalion, had partly surrendered, some of the soldiers having broken through to the cellars and finished dead drunk on the stores of Imperial wines. Martov was in favour of negotiating with the remnants of Kerensky's Government. Trotsky was outraged at such a suggestion. Leaving Lenin lying on the blankets, he strode out and, his pointed red beard thrust forward, made his way to the rostrum, from which he thundered against Martov, ending his speech, "Go where you belong," he roared, "into the dustbin of history!"

The fatuousness of rhetoric inseparable from politics the world over is reflected in Martov's reply. Feeling indignant, he could not rationalise his feeling. "Then we will go!" he cried, his emotions overcoming his sense as he elbowed his way out of the debating chamber.

The debate continued till six o'clock in the morning. Next day it resumed. Lenin did not join it till late in the evening. Kamenev had been speaking when Lenin, now wigless and de-spectacled, came up and took his place at the rostrum. As he stood there, his hands grasping the lectern, cheers rose from the delegates. Most of them had never seen him. He had been the incarnation of revolutionary intransigence, as inaccessible to his unexiled fellow-workers as he invariably was to established authority by way of evading arrest. Now here he stood before them in his shabby baggy Zurich suit, small, bald, stocky, and blinking at them through the tobacco smoke with his little Mongol eyes. Cheers rose, subsided and rose again while the thick air made him feel ill and fearful that at any moment he might ungraciously reciprocate their greeting by vomiting on them instead. With an effort he controlled the revolutions of his rising stomach, and as the cheers subsided to an attentive silence, he cleared his throat and said quietly, "We shall now proceed to build the Socialist Order."

73

THE EXECUTION OF THE ROMANOVS

"One day," said the political prisoners to themselves as they started on the long track to Siberia in the good – or evil, as the case may be – pre-revolutionary days, "one day *you*'ll be taken there."

And now he was being taken there. There had been a great hurry and flurry in getting away and leaving the home in which they had spent nearly twenty-five years of their lives. It might have been the parting scene from *The Cherry Orchard*. As they were leaving, the Emperor, snubbed on a previous occasion by a revolutionary officer who would not take his proffered hand, said shyly to the colonel in charge of the palace guard that it might be dangerous for the colonel to be seen shaking hands with him. But this colonel turned out to be an old-timer. "It's a high honour, Your Majesty." They shook hands. A beautiful fair-bearded real Russian face with grey-blue eyes as honest as the day looked into his own, says the colonel, and he felt a lump in his throat.

As they reached the train on a siding, they met with ill omen. The Empress, in climbing the raised steps of the railway coach, fell over on to the floor and hurt herself. To see them off was their new friend, the Prime Minister, Aleksandr Feodorevitch Kerensky. On the long railway journey the Emperor is, as always, making daily entries in his diary. His comments have the curiously uninterested ring of a diarist who has in childhood acquired the habit of setting down a few random observations each day to please teacher, who thinks it good exercise. He sets down the time the train stood at this or that station, sometimes adds a comment as though for the benefit of the railway or the general public. He reports the walks they took at this or that siding, mentions who came along, who stayed behind; tells of what they had for lunch, but that Alix had a headache and refused a second course. In this way, as though travelling for their own delectation, they arrived at Tobolsk, and were led under guard, walking like convicts, down the middle of the cobbled street – Emperor, Empress, four daughters, one son – to the governor's residence, where they were installed behind a high wooden fence. Nothing could detract from their dignity, of which they were unconscious, nothing humiliate them, as they were not aware of having done anyone any harm. The whole of Russia was still their garden; the whole people, apart from some misinformed spirits, must, they felt, still love them.

They had but another eleven months to live. Until the Bolshevik revolution in November, their life in Tobolsk ran a smooth, tolerably peaceful if rather indigent course. The Empress mended the Emperor's trousers, over and over again, and darned the girls' stockings and turned their coats. But they still had their own palace chef with them, their family physician, their French-Swiss tutor Pierre Guillard, an aide-de-camp, Prince Dolgorukov, and a few attendants. Local nuns and merchants' wives brought them all kinds of delicacies to sweeten their exile. The ex-Tsar was discovered sitting in the guardroom, playing draughts with the soldiers. He spent the mornings with his son, teaching him

Russian history, and notes in his diary that they had just finished Peter the First. The girls staged little comedies, and the Tsar copied out their parts for his daughters Olga and Maria from Chehov's one-act farce, *The Bear*. Chehov had lain thirteen years in his grave and could never have guessed that one day the inaccessible autocrat would turn copyist and transcribe with that small hand of his, which had signed not a few death-warrants, the lines of one of his most trivial pieces.

With the fall of the Kerensky Government, the friendly sentries were changed, and the inmates were shorn of most of their staff. The Tsar chopped wood in the yard, to the derision of the sentries. But, like the former lot, they all ended by taking a liking to the simple charm of their exalted prisoners now down on their luck; they relaxed the new irksome rules and grew increasingly friendly.

Then came disconcerting news. They were to be moved again: rumour had it, to Moscow. Lenin and Trotsky – so said the Tsar – were going to use all their wiles to get round him to put his signature to the Treaty of Brest-Litovsk. Without his signature the treaty struck him as quite obviously invalid. When Prince Dolgorukov suggested that it might be the Emperor William who had insisted, as the first condition of granting an armistice, that the Tsar be handed over to him, Nicholas said, looking very grave, that if so he was quite sure that this was in order to humiliate him. When Dolgorukov explained that he meant the Kaiser was trying to save the Tsar and his family, Nicholas said, why, this was worse still: it was an insult!

William II, who loved George V and loved Nicholas II, was loved by neither Nicholas II nor George V. He was perhaps cleverer than they who, by dint of a becoming modesty, hard work and a disdain of histrionics, attracted more sympathy. Besides, the Kaiser's cleverness was so feeble that it would have passed unnoticed in any but a royal person. The Tsar's reluctance, at this lowest ebb in his fortunes, to be saved by one whom he had never liked even in the days of equality, becomes understandable.

A mysterious agent – a commissar by name Yakovlev – had arrived from Moscow with orders to remove the Tsar and his family without disclosing where he was taking them, his chief anxiety being apparently to get his charges past obstructing local authorities querying his instructions. At Tiumèn they boarded the train for Moscow, but were stopped at Ekaterinburg by the local Soviet, who would not let the Tsar out of their custody. He never got to Moscow.

In tracing motives, one is apt to overstate the force of intentions. The Moscow Central Executive may at first have only intended that the Ural Soviet should resist the extradition. The German request may have been a pious hope that the Soviet Government would 'see their way clear to releasing', etc. The decision to execute the family may not have been taken till the very eve of the fall of Ekaterinburg to the Czech legionaries who were fighting the Bolsheviks all along the Trans-Siberian railway. Even then the Ekaterinburg Soviet may have acted without reference to Moscow. The documents available are not at all conclusive.

However that may be, Ekaterinburg, where they arrived in the last days of April, is the journey's end. They were taken to a house requisitioned from a merchant, by name Ipatiev, and the commissar in charge signed a receipt for them which reads like a bill of lading:

1 ex-tsar Nikolai Romanov and
wife Alexandra Feodorovna
1 daughter Maria Nikolaievna.

Presently the rest of the family, with the Tsarevich, who had been detained by his illness, joined them, at which reunion there was much rejoicing.

The Emperor and Empress, as they had never done in their days of supreme power, now, in those closing weeks, enter the tender realm of the imagination. They were now being exposed to every indignity they had been spared before. The Tsar bore everything without complaint. Only once, provoked beyond endurance, he muttered, "Till recently we had to deal with gentlemen. But now – the devil knows what . . ." The four daughters, between the ages of twenty-two and fifteen, slept all in one room on the floor. Sometimes in the middle of the night drunken guards would stagger into the bedroom, wake them up and make them play the piano and sing with them, changing the words of the song to give it a ribald meaning.

One by one all their staff was taken away from them. There remained only the house surgeon, two men-servants and a maid. Food was now brought from a workers' soup kitchen. The Tsar lapsed into a state outwardly bordering on apathy. So the weeks went by, and they had reached midsummer. Twelve days before the end, Ipatiev House was taken over by the local Cheka, and the Russian soldiers were replaced by a detachment of Letts speaking an incomprehensible tongue and impervious to the winning charm of the Russian imperial family. The man now in charge of the house was one Yurovski, head of the local Cheka, a man who, before he became the Tsar's executioner, had been a dentist, a watchmaker and a male nurse.

The last two weeks of the family are of the stuff of expiation, of redemption from sin in suffering, almost a break with life in Time. They seem no longer of this world, but to be conscious, as those not far removed from their end are conscious, of the future life hovering about them and ready to receive them. They forgave all their tormentors. With no less a sincerity than the virgins of old, the four girls, cut off in their prime from the visible world which had beguiled their dawn, only to turn mercilessly upon them, embroidered all their hopes of sweetness and purity into a dreamy pattern of the life to come. Olga, the eldest, copied religious poems. Tatiana yearned for a quiet nunnery in which to end her days. The Tsaritsa and the younger girls sang psalms and said their prayers together.

Three days before the night which ended their existence, a priest and deacon of the Orthodox Church were called in to celebrate Mass. In the course of the liturgy recur the beautiful words from the funeral service: "Lay to rest with the saints." The deacon, to the consternation of the priest, began to chant these words, which he should have slurred over. An amazing scene then followed. The whole family with their attendants, eleven people in all, as though by a sign, fell on their knees, praying fervently. They all looked wan, worn and spent, their faces thin and transparent, and the Tsar's blond beard of late showed streaks of grey.

On the night of July 16th, soon after midnight, they were awakened and told to get ready. There were disorders in the town. An anarchist rising was expected. So they were told. They were to be conveyed to a place of safety. And indeed, only a few weeks afterwards, Ekaterinburg fell into the hands of the Whites. They dressed hurriedly and gulped down their tea. There was some rattling noise outside, as though of a lorry back-firing, then the tramp of soldiers entering a first-floor room at the back, the sound of the butts of rifles coming down heavily on the wooden floor at the 'Order arms'. The house was built on a slope, the front of the first floor being level with the street, while at the back the ground floor opened on to a yard. Dressed and ready to start on their journey preparatory to entering on another stage of their exile, the family filed into this room in which chairs had been placed along the wall.

One can see them entering in a row. The Emperor and Empress sit down. He has his invalid son of thirteen on his knee, as if posing for a photograph. The maid Demidova places a cushion at the back of the Empress's chair. She also holds a pillow, in which are hidden some of the most treasured family jewels. Olga, the eldest, is now twenty-two, a young girl with a pronounced Slavonic type of features and a contralto voice. Tatiana is just twenty, a dreamy, romantic girl who, if things had gone differently, might easily have married her second cousin, the Prince of Wales, and been Queen of England. Maria, the Tsar's third daughter, now seventeen, is the beauty of the family. She has that slight plumpness which, when it wears off, will leave her a perfect beauty in face and limb. She is also the most healthy and level-headed of the four sisters. The last, Anastasia, named in honour of the first Anastasia Romanov who married Ivan the Terrible and started the Romanovs on their royal trail, is a little frail and mischievous and given to practical jokes.

There they stood and sat as though in a waiting-room, when Yurovski came in and informed the Tsar that he would now bring in the escort to accompany them on the journey. In marched eleven Lett soldiers armed with revolvers, rifles and fixed bayonets, who ranged themselves along the opposite wall. Presently Voikov, of the Ekaterinburg Soviet, came in with a paper in his hand. Facing the Tsar he began to read in a solemn voice a declaration signed by the local Soviet to the effect that the Tsar and his family had been condemned to death. Before, however, he managed to come to the crucial sentence, Yurovski impatiently snatched the paper out of his hand and said, addressing the Tsar, "Nikolai Aleksandrovich, your relatives abroad have been trying to save you, but they have failed, and I have orders from the Ekaterinburg Soviet to shoot you and your family."

The Emperor, who stood up, supporting his son with one hand, was visibly taken aback. "What?" he asked. The Tsar was obviously more horrified on his family's account than on his own. The same moment Yurovski raised his revolver to the Tsar's forehead at close range and fired. The Tsar fell to the floor.

This was the signal for the carnage which followed. The eleven Lett soldiers, ranged along the opposite wall, each took aim at one of the eleven prisoners. Apart from the seven members of the family, Dr. Botkin, the two men-servants and the maid Demidova were included in the execution. Evidently the Revolution was no respecter of persons. The Empress fell down, as she writhed in convulsions clutching at the feet of her invalid boy who, though the most delicate of them all and addicted to haemophilia, took longest to die. The maid Demidova, who held the pillow with the jewels inside, ran screaming hither and thither along the wall, avoiding the bullets fired at her and screening herself with the pillow as though it was a shield. They rushed at her with their bayonets, and she fell to the floor. Olga, Tatiana and Maria lay dead. Anastasia, the youngest, barely fifteen, had fallen in a swoon, and when she recovered she saw ten bodies lying around her. She began to scream and was killed. Her little dog stood yapping over her body, till they finished him, too.

It is vain to ask why such things are done. Nor is it easy to believe – and indeed no religious being can or will believe – that at this moment all consciousness of life was blotted out for them for ever. One can imagine them, indeed, as they stood there, risen in the astral light over their mangled bodies, bewildered, huddling together. For an awful instant, Anastasia was pulled back into the brutal moment, but they killed her, and she was safely back in the fold.

74

FRANCE THE COMPASSIONATE

The war – Proust noted – continued indefinitely, and those who had announced years ago from a reliable source that negotiations for peace had begun, specifying even the clauses of the Armistice, did not take the trouble, when they talked with him, to excuse themselves for their false information. They had forgotten it and were ready sincerely to circulate other information which they would forget equally quickly.

What he found so exasperating and harrowing was that every country said the same thing. Germany was using so many of the same expressions as France that one might think that she was copying her. She never stopped saying that she was fighting for her existence. When Proust read "We are fighting against an implacable and cruel enemy until we have obtained a peace which will guarantee our future against all aggression and in order that the blood of our brave soldiers should not have been shed in vain," or "Who is not with us is against us", he hardly knew if this phrase were Emperor William's or M. Poincaré's, for each one had used the same words, with variations, twenty times. The reasons given by the industrialist associations of Germany for retaining possession of Belfort as indispensable for the preservation of their country against French ideas of revenge were the same as those of French leader-writers exacting Mayence to protect France against the velleities of invasion by the Boches. How was it, Proust wondered, that the restitution of Alsace-Lorraine appeared to France an insufficient motive for a war and yet a sufficient motive for continuing it and for declaring it anew each year?

Proust's snobbish friend, the incredibly arrogant Comte Robert de Montesquiou (who in the great novel appears as the Baron de Charlus) judged the war from the feudal point of view or from that of a Knight of the Order of Jerusalem. His obvious deficiency of judgment, as exemplified by this nonsense, did not, however, disqualify him from showing uncommon sense when spotting other men's fallacies. For he was sincerely astonished, he said, that the public, though it only judged men and things in the war by the papers, should be convinced that it was exercising its own initiative. Completely detached where his compatriots were biased, and as though to vindicate his balance of mind by exposing the unreasonableness of ordinary men who considered him an oddity, Montesquiou was delighted to point out to his clever friend Proust how completely cockeyed was the reasoning of his fellow men. That the cathedral of Rheims itself, as asserted by French journalists, was less dear to Frenchmen than the life of a single one of their infantrymen, Montesquiou considered a very reasonable and moving statement, which, however, rendered absurd the rage of French newspapers against the German general who said that the cathedral of Rheims was less precious to him than the life of a German soldier.

Montesquiou was a French nobleman of an illustrious and romantic lineage in which he took more than a proper pride, not the least so in his semi-royal German blood on his mother's side, of which one like himself, so rooted in French history, could afford to boast even in the midst of a war with Germany. Proust, Jewish on his mother's side, and plain bourgeois on his father's, for his part could not afford to take the same intellectual liberties. Having exhausted his detachment in the Dreyfus Case, Proust during the Great War left no one in doubt about his patriotism. With a corner of his starved intellect, however, and while clearly leaving all the responsibility for such subversive views to the great scion of an ancient house of France who, if he so wished, could afford to pose as a traitor, Proust delighted to listen to Montesquiou disentangling the natural prejudices which, during a bitter national war, tie men up into knots of moral contradiction. Did, for instance, the Emperor William begin it? Montesquiou strongly doubted it. And if so, what act had he committed that Napoleon, for instance, did not commit? Acts he, Montesquiou, personally considered abominable. But he was astonished they should inspire so much horror in the Napoleonic incense-burners, in those who, on the day of the declaration of war, shrieked like General X, "I have been waiting this day for forty years. It is the greatest day of my life!"

For his part, Montesquiou enjoyed Proust's war philosophy ridiculing the imbecility of statesmen who spoke of the war as though it were a kind of train without brakes that, once started, could not be stopped.

On Proust's theory that the creation of the world did not take place once and for all, but that all things exist by virtue of a creation perpetually renewed day by day, the war itself was not, as generally supposed, an irrevocable decision. The truth was not the rhetorical "Now that Germany has wanted war, the die is cast"; the truth was that every morning war was declared anew. He who wanted to continue it was as culpable as he who began it, perhaps more, for the latter could not perhaps foresee all its horrors.

Proust and Montesquiou walked along the Paris boulevards, thronged with Allied soldiers on leave, and exchanged these views, Montesquiou not bothering even to lower his voice – a habit of his which alarmed Proust who, loyal with his heart if dispassionate in his mind, had no special wish that patriots should overhear his incisively indiscreet brain to the exclusion of his full and silent heart. But Montesquiou, reconciling both, wished that the just France, rightly trying to give voice to justice, should be also France the compassionate, making words of pity heard, if only for the sake of her children, so that when spring days came round and flowers bloomed again, they would brighten other things than tombs.

The war went on. The writer, some years later, when crossing a desert, passed two Arabs whose quarrel was a sort of reflection of the war. Each man hit the other at intervals across the head with a big long stick. Their heads were turbaned, but imperfectly, for the stick came down with a loud dry crack. The recipient staggered under the blow, then, slowly recovering as if from a trance, in turn brought down his stick with a sharp crack on his opponent's skull. Neither followed up his first blow with a second, but seemed to wait till the other was recovered sufficiently to deal him a blow on the head. The fight went on in the middle of the desert, far removed from any human habitation, from the League of Nations; went on leisurely, perseveringly, as though they were at work on something constructive, requiring concentration of mind. The motor-coach was approaching the gorges, but far away on the dim, sandy horizon the quarrel went on; one might almost have thought two blacksmiths were at work with hammer and anvil.

It was in these circumstances that they at last alighted on the idea of making Foch Allied Generalissimo. While the Marshal, ensconced in his warm steam-heated headquarters, was sending men out into the cold (warmth being a prerequisite deemed essential by another war-lord, Hitler, at his Russian headquarters), the tide began to turn against the Germans and in favour of the Allies. The Yanks were coming over, and Clemenceau urged Foch, as the Commander-in-Chief of the Allied Armies, to avail himself of this fine force. "What is the position?" he wrote to him. "Surely nobody can maintain that these fine troops are unusable; they are merely unused."

Foch, with his cavalryman's gait, ambled down the road as of a morning he returned from prayers at a nearby church, and his staff watched the Marshal coming, for he wore his kepi very straight when news was grave and tilted it at a rakish angle when there was success for

259

Allied arms. One morning Colonel Bentley Mott of the United States Army saw him swinging down the deserted little street of Bonbon, stick over shoulder and his kepi tilted right over his ear. There was no need to ask him how things were going. Another day the Colonel met the Marshal returning from the village church and, on being recognised, ventured the remark that the Germans were getting more than they could stand. "He came up close to me, took a firm hold on my belt with his left hand and with his right fist delivered a punch at my chin, a hook under my ribs and another drive at my ear; he then shouldered his stick and without a single word marched on to the château, his straight back and horseman's legs presenting as gallant a sight as one would wish to look upon."

On yet another occasion, when Colonel Mott had been directed by General Pershing to present certain matters to the Marshal in a manner which called the Colonel to exercise his gift of diplomacy, the Marshal listened and then beckoned him to the billiard-table on which was spread out a huge map of the Western Front. "Look at this," he said, "I am the leader of an orchestra. Here are the English basses, here the American baritones, and here the French tenors. When I raise my baton, every man must play or else he must not come to my concert."

Ludendorff, also conceiving himself as a conductor of orchestra, was studying the same map in his room at the German headquarters situated at the Hotel Britannique at Spa. It seemed a prophetic name. The realisation of the hopelessness of the German position, considered as a whole, overpowered him. Suddenly, having worked himself up into an impotent fury of resentment against his subordinates, his Kaiser, the Reichstag, and the navy, he fell, foaming at the mouth, to the floor. When in the evening Ludendorff recovered from his fit, he reviewed the situation, in no way improved by his own recovery, and advised the Government in Berlin to appeal at once for an armistice.

How Prince Max of Baden became German Chancellor on account of his well-known international reputation for moderation; how he lay for thirty-six hours in a coma from an overdose of sleeping-draughts after influenza while vital decisions hung in the balance; how the Kaiser, demanding that the German Foreign Office should protest through the Press against rumours of abdication, was told that already everybody on every street corner, including the best circles, was taking abdication for granted: all this followed as precipitately as the fighting had been drawn out. When the Kaiser was told by an official about his abdication being taken for granted, his reaction to the news was painful. "At this," he says, "I expressed my indignation." The official sought to console the Kaiser by observing that, should His Majesty go, *he* would go also; which, as a consolation, struck the Kaiser as ludicrous. "I went," writes the Kaiser, "or, to put it much more correctly, I was overthrown by my own Government, and – Herr Solf remained." Which struck the Kaiser as abominable.

The Kaiser was very certain of what was owing to him. "Seeing that we had the parliamentary form of government it devolved upon the political parties to bring about the change in the chancellorship and present me with a successor to Prince Max." Yes, present him! "This," he says, "did not occur." When Drews, the Minister of the Interior, suggested to the Kaiser that he might like to abdicate in order that it might not appear that the Government had exerted pressure on him, the Kaiser was appalled. How could he, he asked, looking Drews in the eyes: how could he, a Prussian official, make so infamous a suggestion? How could he reconcile it with his oath to his King? The Kaiser thereupon got Hindenburg and General Gröner to tell Drews off in his own presence, and was satisfied to see him 'very sharply rebuked in the name of the Army', by both these pillars of Prussianism. The Kaiser also was pained to learn that Drews, the reluctant mouthpiece of the sick Prince Max, had only undertaken to convey the suggestion of abdication after one of his own sons had been approached, apparently in vain. "My son," the Kaiser writes, "indignantly declined to suggest abdication to his father."

Finally, when everybody was pressing the Kaiser to abdicate, he decided that, while he might be asked to abdicate as Emperor, nobody could surely ask him to abdicate as King of Prussia. But no one wanted him, it seemed, at any price, and, after much heart-searching and, as he puts it, to spare further bloodshed, he betook himself out of harm's way across the frontier into Queen Wilhelmina's peaceful domains.

Before the Armistice, Marshal Foch convened at his headquarters at Senlis the Commanders-in-Chief of the American, British and French Armies, and requested them, in turn, to state their views. Of these, Haig's proved the most moderate, Pétain's the next most moderate, and Pershing's the most severe. Foch's own views proved more severe than those of the more moderate of the Allied commanders, and more moderate than those of the most severe. In particular he was liberal in his views relating to the German navy, on which subject the British were as drastic as they were prepared to be lax in other regards affecting the occupation or non-occupation of the left, right, both, or neither bank of the Rhine.

The first meeting of the heads of the Allied Governments, held on the last day of October, took place at the house of Colonel House in Paris. Foch was anxious from the start to dispel the idea, deemed by the whole war-weary world as beneficent but by him as nefarious, that President Wilson was to be regarded as an arbitrator between the stricken enemy and the conquerors. Colonel House was President Wilson's personal representative, and Marshal Foch, prepared to hear from him sentiments of moderation, was startled by the question of whether he considered it preferable to continue the war. To this he replied that he was not waging war for the sake of waging war. If he obtained, through the Armistice, the conditions sufficient to paralyse the enemy, nobody, he judged, had the right to shed one more drop of blood.

Of the Armistice negotiations with Germany in the office-car of Marshal Foch's special train lying on a siding built for heavy railway artillery in the Forêt de l'Aigle, near the station of Rethondes, Foch himself has published a detailed report included in his autobiography. The proceedings were characterised by a certain dour and snappy formality on the part of the Marshal, and a kind of owlish bemusement on the part of the German delegates. Marshal Foch asked them the purpose of their visit. Herr Erzberger, the head of the German delegation, replied that they had come to receive the proposals of the Allied Powers. Marshal Foch replied that he had no proposals to make. Count Oberndorff, another delegate, then asked the Marshal in what form he desired that they should express themselves. He did not stand on form; he was ready to say that the German delegation asked for the conditions of the Armistice. Marshal Foch replied that he had no conditions to offer. Herr Erzberger read the text of President Wilson's last note, stating that Marshal Foch was authorised to make known the Armistice conditions. Marshal Foch replied that he was authorised to make these known if the German delegates asked for an Armistice. Herr Erzberger and Count Oberndorff declared that they asked for an Armistice. General Weygand then read the principal clauses of the Armistice conditions.

This procedure continued for three days until the German delegation, who had unsuccessfully applied for suspension of hostilities three days previously, were asked on the morning of the fourth and last day how soon they would be ready to attend the plenary session, so that bloodshed might be stopped as soon as possible, now that the signing of the Armistice had been decided upon. On November 11th at 2.5 a.m. the German delegates stated that they were ready for the session, which was opened at 2.15 a.m. At 5.5 a.m. agreement was reached, and extraordinary haste displayed to save further bloodshed. The final page of the text, for instance, was typed before the others to get the signatures affixed to save time. Yet hostilities did not cease, for some reason, until six hours later. Notice of such things, apparently, is a prerequisite. Military technique is apparently not without its rituals and mysteries. Bitter indeed was the fate of those relatives who learnt that their sons were killed between 5 and 11 a.m. of that pregnant last morning.

75

CONGRATULATIONS

Firing ceased along the entire Western front on November 11th at 11 o'clock in the morning. After fifty-three months of battle there was a sudden silence. Next day Foch conceived his own monument in the words addressed as a General Order to the officers, non-commissioned officers and soldiers of the Allied Armies:

> After resolutely repulsing the enemy for months, you confidently attacked him with an untiring energy. You have won the greatest battle in History and rescued the most sacred of all causes, the Liberty of the World. You have full right to be proud, for you have crowned your standards with immortal glory and won the gratitude of posterity.
>
> F. Foch
> Marshal of France
> Commander-in-Chief of the Allied Armies

"But who," asked Kipling, sobered by four years of war, "shall restore us our children?"

London received the news of the Armistice, as H. G. Wells said, in a mood which only looked boisterous without really feeling it. People wanted to laugh and cry, but for the most part could do neither. Lloyd George was angry at having been anticipated by Admiral Wemyss, who took the thunder out of the Prime Minister's announcement of an Armistice by letting out the news to the Press. Henry and Margot sent telegrams of congratulation to the King and Queen and were later received at the Palace, when the King took Mrs. Asquith's hand in both of his and said that no man ever had a better or wiser friend then he had in her husband.

Followed speeches by Mr. Lloyd George, seconded in the House of Commons by Henry. One is not conscious of undue facetiousness in calling old Asquith Henry, an irresistible appellation for him, not the least so because nobody save his own wife called him that. With all his solid virtues, his dignity and port and old-world oratory, Asquith, though a statesman of finer calibre than our more rascally contemporaries, is no more immune from comic criticism than that Shakespearean figure he so resembles, Albany, whose sense at all times of the fitness of things springs from an inner poise altogether too imperturbable to avert the suspicion that the fine equilibrium he espies through his telescope in the outer world of pain and chaos is but the projection of his own stolidity. "When history," he said (betraying his favourite author as Balzac), "comes to tell the tale of these four years, it will recount a story the like of which is not to be found in any epic in any literature. It is and will remain by itself as a record of everything Humanity can dare or endure – of the extremes of possible heroism and, we must add, of possible baseness, and, above all, the slow-moving but in the end irresistible power of a great Ideal."

One is tempted to reverse a little Albany's closing speech in *King Lear* to adapt it to the situation at the Armistice. "The joy of this glad time we must obey; speak not what we feel, but what we ought to say. The youngest hath borne most: we that are old have never known so little joy, nor lived so brief a time."

76

WOODROW WILSON

A far greater document than the Marshal's was that of the President of the United States, who wrote:

> My Fellow Countrymen: The armistice was signed this morning. Everything for which America fought has been accomplished. It will now be our fortunate duty to assist by example, by sober, friendly counsel, and by material aid in the establishment of just democracy throughout the world.

The frenzy of relief felt at the Armistice in America had half spent itself four days before it came, owing to a premature report of the end of hostilities. But it did not lag behind London or Paris. In addition to the English delirium, New Yorkers accentuated their relief by draping themselves in American flags and smashing one another's hats. Pretty girls volunteered to kiss every passing soldier, and a girl sang the Doxology in Times Square from the platform of Liberty Hall, while crowds with sinister exultation trampled on the Kaiser's picture executed by a pavement artist.

Hugh Kingsmill, at that time a prisoner of war in Germany, found his guard bubbling over with mirth over the trend of events. "*Ja! Ja!*" he laughed. "*Deutschland kaput! Deutschland kaput!*" Germany's one aim, as he saw it now, was to please the good President who, if he heard that the Germans were no longer militaristic, would raise the blockade at once, and there would be butter and sugar again, *ach du lieber Gott!* and tea and soap and white bread! and no more army, no more discipline, no more rich and poor! And all nations at peace and friendly. A new world, a new world!

"The *Frankfurter Zeitung*," writes Kingsmill, "published leaders of an eloquence as impassioned as Cicero's, and more sincere. Especially fine was their attack on Ludendorff, as the author of Germany's ruin, the embodiment of the Prussian's blind insensate thirst for military domination. They published also an appeal to the young German poets to console the Fatherland in the hour of its agony." The *Daily Mail* wrote, "President Poincaré's stirring declaration at the great banquet to the King in Paris, 'We are united for ever,' marks the consummation of the alliance between Great Britain and France."

The American Army, two million in Europe, three million-and-a-half at home, still fizzing with do or die, was being decanted back into the jug of civil life. Disappointed at the suddenness of the German collapse, they felt they wanted to teach someone a lesson. The employer, restored to unhampered private enterprise, espied the Bolshevik bogey in labour, and meant to teach the unions a lesson. Labour, clamouring for higher wages in the face of a rising cost of living, in its turn decided that this was the time to teach the war-profiteer a lesson. There were strikes on the one hand, and lock-outs on the other.

Woodrow Wilson, whom to criticise during the war had been tantamount to high treason, was now being openly criticized by big business bosses as 'a dangerous radical', presumably for having ended without proper notice the war to end war, with all industries keyed up for maximum war production, and for having made the world safe for democracy without proper regard for the finer feelings of plutocracy. Three weeks after the Armistice, the *George Washington* took him to Europe where he toured France and England and Italy in godlike triumph. Nothing like this had ever been seen before. The full-throated acclamation of Londoners, Parisians and Romans was not the normal cordiality which crowds accord to a visiting monarch. The ovation surged from the depth of the wounded contrite universal heart to a deliverer, the shaper of a new world, the forger of new hopes.

With such a backing, how could the President, who had no mean opinion of his ability and no doubt whatever that his work was pleasing to the Deity, envisage for a moment the possibility of failure? But fail nevertheless he did. The old-world politicians, whose countries had been broken on the wheel of war, had more envy than love for Woodrow Wilson, little faith in mankind, and no charity at all for the defeated enemy, no disposition whatever to accept peace-terms from the head of a country barely eighteen months at war. The good-will latent in the hearts of men, and coming to the surface in these surging acclamations of the crowds at the sight of the President, did not impress Clemenceau or Arthur Balfour, and would only have impressed Lloyd George had he himself been the recipient. Human hearts were no concern of theirs and they knew that a mob could be made to shout and cheer at anything – for instance, at the sight of the Kaiser being strung up, or the triumphant progress of a Northcliffe who had achieved his aim, the final dismemberment of Germany and the parcelling out of its entire territory among the victors.

What Clemenceau, Lloyd George and Orlando were trying to achieve behind closed doors, where Wilson was no more than one in a Council of Four, was a compromise likely to satisfy the conflicting instincts of popular vengeance and benevolence vested in the political factions of the national states they happened to serve, with a steady eye on their own continued pre-eminence.

In America such a faction, at once retributive and wishing to wash its hand of the old world, crystallised around Senator Lodge, who was as distinguished and progressive in his way as Arthur Balfour. His way of looking forward was to discover endearing liberties in the past. So convinced was he that Wilson's ideas were baleful that he did not think it unpatriotic, patriot though he was, to supply the only Republican on the American Peace Commission, Henry White, with a secret memorandum to be shown in confidence to Balfour, Clemenceau, and Nitti, designed to undermine the President's position by substituting his own annexationist peace terms as being, in his opinion, the only terms the American people at home would support. He added, "This knowledge may in certain circumstances be important to them in strengthening their position."

It did indeed strengthen them. It put new heart into them. Again and again the President, exasperated by European cupidity and greed for snatching territories without regard to the wishes of their populations, retrieved a modicum of self-determination from the very teeth of the wolves howling for their share of the carcass. The only thing that could at all intimidate the old-world politicians was if he appealed to the conscience of the world. But the conscience of the world itself was being subtly changed by the organs of newspaper magnates describing themselves as the guardians of a free Press, and they sang in tune with the chief delegates, whom indeed they threatened to kick out when the ministers returned if they did not do as the Press lords told them to.

With this patched rag of a treaty the President sailed home at the end of June 1919, six months after he had left for France. And here indeed was the irony of his situation. Though he knew it to be a patchwork full of holes, he had, to get it accepted in the face of the rising opposition fanned by Senator Lodge, to pretend it was in all respects a fine document, a great charter of liberty, and his colleagues, Clemenceau and Lloyd George, noble men, sprung from the people and actuated by nothing so much as the welfare of common humanity.

On July 10th, 1919, the President laid the Treaty of Versailles before the Senate, which enjoyed, in Lodge's stressed view, an equal right with the President in treaty-making. In presenting to his own people this incompetent document which, while violating nearly every principle of his Fourteen Points, left the victors as defenceless against a repetition of war as it did the vanquished, Wilson, desperate to save his infant League from strangulation at the hands of Lodge no less than Clemenceau, swore black and blue that, far from bearing the mark of the cloven hoof, the babe had been the unassisted work of the Holy Ghost. "The stage," he orated, "is set, the destiny disclosed. It has come about by no plan of our conceiving, but by the hand of God who led us into the way. We cannot turn back. We can only go forward, with lifted eyes and freshened spirit, to follow the vision. It was of this that we dreamed at our birth. America shall in truth show the way. The light streams upon the path ahead and nowhere else." It was just the kind of rhetoric which Lodge, a meaner spirit but a finer scholar, so disliked. Readily he lent himself to the undoing of the Treaty – and the President.

Nor did God's Fifth Column, watchful lest any adulterated spirit be smuggled through into the Kingdom of Heaven on Earth, work only through the senile chauvinism of the old world and the senatorial patriotism of the new. It saw its main chance in the egotism, the personal ingratitude, the intellectual arrogance, the emotional aloofness, the spiritual pride of one who, having the temperament of a despot, exalted above his colleagues and Opposition statesmen the understanding of the lowest common denominator of mankind. Dedicating his heart and mind to 'the people', in the cause of the greatest good of the greatest number, the moralist had forgotten that none indeed is so conservative as the half-educated.

Lodge's Committee on Foreign Relations then settled down to tear the Treaty to pieces. It was short work. What could be easier than to appeal to the Americanism of Americans? "We would not have," Lodge contended, "our politics distracted and embittered by the dissentions of other lands. We would not have our country's vigour exhausted, or her moral force abated, by everlasting meddling and muddling in every quarrel, great and small, which afflicts the world." The much-patched Treaty was being unstitched by an infinite process of amendments and reservations which, among a multitude of other objections, disputed the British Empire's claim to six votes in the League of Nations, claiming six also for the United States.

President Wilson then decided to go to the people – the American people, surely more than an echo of the British, the French, the Italian people, who had so warmly acclaimed him and the new hope he voiced for a better world. Against the advice of his doctors, the worn-out man, never robust, who had all but broken down in Paris, now properly at the end of his tether, undertook a speaking-trip through the West. In forty speeches, mostly delivered at the rate of two a day, each a model of oratory, he represented that the heart of humanity beat in the Treaty of Versailles, that the good Clemenceau, the candid Lloyd George and the open-handed Orlando's hearts, God bless them, also throbbed through that great document with the pulsating heart of the people of the world. It was just then that Hitler, having received his card of membership, bearing the folio number seven, of the German Labour Party, was preparing to begin his debates in Munich beer-halls to expose that treaty as a document that would not bear comparison with its sister treaty, that fine example of Teutonic magnanimity enacted at Brest-Litovsk. A treaty which even the arch anti-nationalist Trotsky had thought too monstrous for a communist-internationalist Russian Jew to sign; nor would he have done so except on direct orders from Lenin.

From one town to another the President's train conveyed the sick and weary apostle of peace. Through city after city, standing up in a motor and waving his hat to the crowds, he was dragged to speak to multitudes in draughty halls without amplifiers, to go through all the paraphernalia of presentations and hand-shaking with city fathers and their wives, bouquets and a modicum of badinage which the free-born American expects even from the most austere of Presidents. Tossing sleepless on his swaying bunk night after night, suffering from indigestion, in the solitude of his mind he must have found it hard to reconcile a penal code with what he had to pretend to his countrymen was a new version of the Sermon on the Mount. The people, though, like the audiences in Europe, vociferous in their acclamations of him, did not support him in this view. They were against the Treaty not because of its shortcomings, but its idealism, of which, as well as his rhetoric, they had about had their fill. Here indeed was the same Athenian mob, at once proud of the eminence of their Pericles and derisive of his aloof schoolmaster-type of superiority which had, in turn, delayed them from going to war, dragged them into it, out of it, and now wished to drag them through the European mire, all in the name of some high falutin' moral principle. While on his last reserves of nervous strength he was campaigning in the hope of winning the country, news reached him that the Senate had voted against him.

And on the night of the next day, as he slept under a narcotic, his mouth drooled. In the morning he could hardly stand up to dress. Back he went to the White House, there a few days later to go down with a stroke. The stoppage of a blood vessel in the brain had caused partial paralysis. He could not move the left side of his body. The eager saviour of mankind had been struck down by Providence for an end that eludes us. An enduring world peace was within reach. "But it had not apparently been given to man to achieve it; and God did not seem to want it." Why did Providence strike down its most faithful servant? The universe moves its chess-pieces according to a plan that takes no account of human hopes and fears, and its Fifth Column agents counter, where deemed necessary, our own moves. Anyone may experience this in his own life. Resort by prayer to the Second Person of the Trinity, similar to an overdraft due to be repaid, may secure a delay of judgment. But it will have to be paid in the end.

So it must have been with Woodrow Wilson. In his collapse one espies the unseen hand sabotaging smugness and moral complacency, the lack of warmth and charity necessary to win his opponents. For eighteen months he still lingered in the White House, now transformed into a hospital, with its great gates closed and chained, locked and guarded by policemen. He refused to do any work. His mind seemed to rove in a dream world with a League of Nations living up to his ideal, an ideal that would become a reality when others too were fired by his faith.

Meanwhile the country, if it could be said to be governed at all, was governed by Mrs. Wilson. The President's influence, far from being heightened by a tragedy more poignant than Lincoln's, now waned. His last hope was that the 1920 election would serve as a 'great and solid referendum' in which the masses of the people to whom, he was confident, he could always appeal over the heads of their despoilers, would rise to vindicate his work on their behalf. They rose, by an overwhelming vote, against him and everything he stood for, confirming beyond any further doubt the verdict of the hostile senators. By first joining his supporters who objected to any change whatever in the Treaty, the hostile senators secured a majority against the long list of reservations sponsored by Lodge's committee, and then, by combining with Lodge, joined forces against what was left of the Treaty, approving only the cat's meat of reservations.

Wilson's bitterness at his enemies took the form of dropping his

269

friends. First he dropped House. Next he dismissed his Secretary of State, Lancing, for daring to call and preside over a Cabinet without presidential authority. Then he dropped his secretary of ten years' standing, Tumulty, for venturing to give an oral message misinterpreted as White House support of Governor Cox for the Presidency. When the aggrieved men wrote to him cordial letters in which they explained how the misunderstanding had occurred, he left their letters unanswered. They wrote again. There was no answer.

When two senators went to the White House for the purpose of ascertaining whether the President was in a fit state of mind to carry on his duties, since he no longer performed them (while refusing to delegate any of his powers to the Vice-President), they found him strangely lucid and in full possession of his faculties, though confined to his chair, and uncannily amused by their awkward mission to ascertain for themselves whether he was in his right mind.

So, without yielding his place or abating his ideals, Woodrow Wilson remained president to the full term of his office, until, on March 4th, 1921, now occupying but one half of his former body, a drooping jaw enhancing his lack of charity for his successor squeezed in at his side, he rode with the President-elect, Warren Gamaliel Harding, to the Capitol.

BOOK FOUR

THE NINETEEN-TWENTIES

77

THE AGE OF JOURNALISM

It was the custom of those unable to appreciate the subtle distinction between non-resistance to hypothetical, as against actual, evil to speak of Tolstoy as a great writer but a poor thinker. When Carlyle asked a carter whether his horse could draw inferences, the answer was, "Yes; anything in reason." And yet, Carlyle argues, in spirited defence of Coleridge's logic, men of genius are commonly denied the ability conceded to a carthorse! For his own part, he hastens to add, he had never come across a man of genius whose inferences did not accord immeasurably better with his premises than those of ordinary so-called practical men priding themselves on the logic of their very rudimentary type of reasoning.

"Every man," Coleridge says, "is born an Aristotelian or a Platonist. I do not think it possible that any one born an Aristotelian can become a Platonist; and I am sure no born Platonist can ever change into an Aristotelian. They are the two classes of men, beside which it is next to impossible to conceive a third. The one considers reason a quality, or attribute; the other considers it a power. I believe that Aristotle never could get to understand what Plato meant by an idea. There is a passage, indeed, in the Eudemian Ethics which looks like an exception; but I doubt not of its being spurious, as that whole work is supposed by some to be. With Plato ideas are constitutive in themselves.

"Aristotle was, and still is, the sovereign lord of the understanding; the faculty judging by the senses. He was a conceptualist, and never could raise himself into that higher state which was natural to Plato, and has been so to others, in which the understanding is distinctly contemplated, and, as it were, looked down upon from the throne of actual ideas, or living, inborn, essential truths."

The Age here contemplated is the tail-end of the Aristotelian conception of reason as power, carried to unprecedented lengths in personal dictatorship, and reduced to absurdity, and presently to universal contumely, in the illustration now before us of the world as 'great powers' blindly contending for power for power's sake, while reducing the sentient unit to impotent suffering.

It is by the touchstone of the Platonic conception of reason as a quality or attribute, as against the Aristotelian conception of reason as power, that this biography distributes its store of sympathy to the public figures of the last fifty years. The Platonic Idea is indeed the counter on which the sundry figures of the Age are thrown to find out whether they ring true.

The Aristotelian exploitation of reason for purposes of power can be traced in advertising, in politics, and particularly in journalism, which is a debased Aristotelian form of using human failings and weaknesses to extract power by deliberately exploiting these failings and weaknesses. Literature is an intuitive communication of the Platonic Idea of truth and beauty hiding behind the shadow of its material form. If journalism and modern advertising are debased forms of literature, propaganda is debased journalism.

But journalism as exploitation of suspense, trading as it does on human restlessness, is equally despicable whether it takes the form of detective fiction, films, plays or magazine stories. Art, communicating the eternal reality of the Platonic Idea which invests objects and persons alike with the breath of life, is constitutive, not conceptual, and as such it is independent of artificial stimulants. The criterion of a genuine work of literature is that you can open it at any page to savour each passage for itself, without the narcotic of induced excitement in the shape of knowing what has come before and speculating on what is to happen next, commonly called 'a plot'. If a book is worth reading at all it is worth reading more than once. Suspense is the lowest of excitants, designed to take your breath away when the brain and the heart crave to linger in nobler enjoyment. Suspense drags you on; appreciation causes you to linger. Detective-story writers, like opium-sellers, pretending to be giving the public what it wants, are driven by their own suspense of hoping to get out of it what they can. Goethe believed that an artist should not attempt to please anyone save himself: if so he would have a chance of pleasing other men of his own calibre. Crime fiction, on the other hand, consciously designed to fit the mentality of the lowest common denominator, and sometimes avowedly produced in response to a ballot held to guide the writer in his choice of theme, is something so divorced from sincerity that it strikes one as almost immoral.

This, then, is the exploitation of the Word for profit – the generic term of this remunerative if thoroughly un-Platonic pursuit being 'journalism'. But in no sphere was journalism so intellectually corrupt, the gang purveying this aesthetic drug so vast, so well and meticulously organised as in the films of the 'twenties. The initial stumbling of crude film melodrama before the First World War gave way to the un-

274

believably fatuous superstructure of a whole photo-magazine world upon the sordid and sorry realities of life on earth. The Hollywood city of cardboard and tinsel, pretension and fake and fatuity, and its eruption in the wide world on so vast a scale is so extraordinary that no generic term vast enough can be devised to give vent to one's feeling of mass inanity. It is – with negligible exceptions – an epidemic of the most pathetic pretence, and it speaks for the general level of humanity able to absorb – and with what relish! – such putrid cat's meat.

After this to the final deception – national propaganda – is not far to sink. Propaganda indeed is the last refuge of journalism – the avowed, bright and unashamed exploitation of the Word for power. In the hands of its most unscrupulous exponent it even resorts to a deliberate pogrom by way of getting the people into the desired alignment. Truth disappears, to give way to a synthetic truth made of ersatz material, cunningly compounded of lies to fill men's minds, craving for truth, with an impression of relative truth with which they must make do, as men indeed make do with banknotes redeemable at some indefinite date – beyond the veil? – by truth sterling. Hitler outlined to Rauschning his plan of presenting his own party, in juxtaposition to the Jews, as men of God and men of the devil. But, said the devil, showing him from a high mountain all the kingdoms of the world in a moment of time, "All this power will I give thee, and the glory of them: for that is delivered unto me; and to whomsoever I will give it. If thou therefore wilt worship me, all shall be thine." And Hitler did not apparently, like Jesus, answer, "Get thee behind me, Satan", but "Come right in front! Why, this is exactly what I do want: power from the nether world."

The Age of Reason as Power was swiftly moving towards its climax. The decline and fall was not far distant. Licence of power, abuse of reason were sure omens that the foundations had been undermined. God's Fifth Column had been already at work. The pillars were wormeaten. There were the first stirrings of Platonic wisdom manifesting themselves in men's minds and hearts.

Another field of Aristotelian 'journalism' reaping a rich crop of evil is the exploitation of nature for power. A further form of black magic. All 'inventions' are but discoveries of immutable occult laws. The Aristotelian prying into nature's secrets to apply them to a utilitarian end is making but a crudely complicated attempt to adapt them to the perverse, crippled and distorted necessities of physical existence.

The Aristotelian conception of life is to dismiss the Platonic reality of space and movement as interchangeable abstractions, and push on instead with the notion of conquering space by introducing the wheel, the train, the motor car (but also the tank, taking away with one hand what it gives with the other). It produces war lords and armament manufacturers, newspaper magnates, news editors, dictators, Foreign Ministers, and all manner of monstrosities of men who have no soul and cannot live on attribute, as fish cannot live on air. They have no lungs and must breathe through their gills, extracting from their element of power, out of which they are like fish out of water, such illusory life as they can contrive from preying on their fellows. They are a loathsome breed. They are the only valid category of distinction from the Platonists who, if fallen angels, are still the sons of God. Life should be reduced to the rudiments of simplicity as recommended in the New Testament, money abolished, quality substituted for quantity, attribute for power. But the Kaiser also in his Vatican speech to the Pope in 1903 ardently agreed with this! They will all swear that they are Platonists at heart, that sheer expediency in battling with the wicked world forces them to be Aristotelians. But one would hardly wish to dwell too long on the irreconcilable two categories of beings, lest they bring engines of war to bear upon their difference of outlook. Wars have been launched for less.

78

THE UNINHIBITED

The war to make the world safe for democracy had been brought, as the War Office presently informed its commissioned participants due to be thrown upon the employment mart, 'to a successful conclusion'. Equality of sacrifice was rewarded by a return to private enterprise with its assumed equality of opportunity in a Great Britain in which three-quarters of the entire population shared less than five per cent of the total wealth. Why? Largely as the result of accumulation of money manipulations by previous generations of ancestors. Young people so favoured and their more attractive hangers-on, disillusioned by inconsistencies of avowed ideals with palpable results, as exemplified by the behaviour of their parents, discovered a style of life for themselves which allied mature superciliousness about their elders with an insistence on the advantages of young years and limbs. This attitude was termed by films and magazines, betraying a commercial sense in excess of plain sense, 'sophistication'; in which terms those so described, with little or no notion of the origin of the word, espied a compliment and took a proper pride, trying their best to live up to it.

The 'sophisticated' 'twenties became a curious revival in modern dress of the Naughty Nineties. The solidly meaningless, grossly opulent Edwardians became the petulant, if no less meaningless, speed-addicted subjects of King George the Fifth, racing with an intense, determined inconsequence through the pleasure-resorts of the venal Continent of Europe in an attempt to mislay their money together with their identities.

They were served up to themselves, on a gilded platter of oriental make, as delectable confectionary by one Kouyoumdjian who, under the pseudonym of Michael Arlen, exploited the nostalgia of wage slaves at home, who could not race after those exquisites in pursuit of pleasure. In America the riotous cosmopolitan Wild Party,[1] which had its counterpart in London, struck the prevailing note of the 'twenties, mixing high spirits with mixed spirits and bodies moving in a floating melody, the girl doing more than her share:

> She brushed his lips with her hair:
> She arched inward:
> She clung:
> She pressed
> Her body on his from knee to breast.

Meanwhile, having changed partners, the other couple lay locked in a five-minute kiss, till

> Suddenly Kate had a moving thought:
> "Where's that cock-eyed bastard I brought?"

Presently

> The bed was a slowly moving tangle
> Of legs and bodies at every angle.
> Knees rose:
> Legs in sheer stockings crossed,
> Clung: shimmered: uncrossed: were lost.
> Skirts were awry.
> Black arms embraced
> White legs naked from knee to waist.

There is crossing and double-crossing in love, conversation like

> "Come here and I'll break your lousy head!
> You cock-eyed son-of-a-bitching scut!
> D'ye think you own this town, or what!"

[1] *The Wild Party* by Joseph Moncure March.

a bottle

> Flashed,
> Crashed
> On Eddie's head:
> Smashed,

Eddie's face turning white and going out like a light. And after a gun is fired and a man shot dead, the party's end is almost a foregone conclusion:

> A crash! –
> The chair:
> He almost fell.
> "Chris'" he mumbled: "What th' hell –?
> Jes's Christ! – I've hurt my shin –"

> The door sprang open
> And the cops rushed in.

However censorious the reader may be inclined to be of the situations so dexterously and faithfully recorded by the poet, he will think more kindly of these passages, descriptive at any rate of young people who are plainly enjoying themselves, when he compares their ecstasies with D. H. Lawrence's agonies in the same cause of propitiating the god of sex. Where the young people at the bottle party indulge themselves with some sincerity. D. H. Lawrence is plainly absurd in trying to fulfil what he considers to be his duty as *homme au moyen sensuel*. Walking one evening by the sea with a woman called, in the novel, Ursula, Lawrence, called Anton, was dismayed to hear her scream in a high, hard voice, like a gull, "I want to go." Inquiring, not unnaturally, where it was she wanted to go, he was by way of reply seized hold of by this woman and given a fierce, beaked, harpy's kiss. Back on the sand-hills, "she held him pinned down at the chest, awful. The fight, the struggle for consummation was terrible. It lasted till it was agony to his soul, till he succumbed, till he gave way as if dead, and lay with his face buried, partly in her hair, partly in the sand, motionless, as if he would be motionless now for ever, hidden away in the dark, buried, only buried, he only wanted to be buried in the goodly darkness, only that, and no more." Stealing an uneasy look at her, he sees her face in the moonlight, the eyes wide-open, rigid; he judges this a propitious moment for crawling off and plunging away into the sea, "on and on, ever farther from the horrible figure that lay stretched in the moonlight on the sands

278

with the tears gathering and travelling on the motionless, eternal face. He felt, if ever he must see her again, his bones must be broken, his body crushed, obliterated for ever."

The 'twenties were the decade not only of the libido, but also of the self-appraising autobiography. "Physically," wrote Margot Asquith, "I have done pretty well for myself. I ride better than most people and have spent or wasted more time on it than any woman of intellect ought to. I have broken both collar-bones, my nose, my ribs and my knee-cap: dislocated my jaw, fractured my skull, and had five concussions of the brain; but – though my horses are to be sold next week – I have not lost my nerve. I dance, drive and skate well; I don't skate very well, but I dance really well. I have a talent for drawing and am intensely musical, playing the piano with a touch of the real thing, but have neglected both these accomplishments. I may say here in self-defence that marriage and five babies, five stepchildren and a husband in high politics have all contributed to this neglect, but the root of the matter lies deeper: I am restless."

Henry James went silly when consulted by Mrs. Asquith about her memoirs. His mouth watered at the prospect of reading about actual duchesses and Foreign Secretaries and ambassadors, all enjoying a social eminence to which he had elevated his fictitious threadbare automations. One can only think for a parallel of Proust's mouth hanging open, after the manner of Professor Pavlov's dogs at feeding-time, were Mme. de Noailles to have apprised him of confiding in him the contents of her diaries relative to her encounters with the La Trémolles.

79

THE SPIRIT OF MODERN RUSSIA

The spirit of a country is nearly always divorced from the spirit of its literature. The artistic impulse springs from a vision of beauty essentially private. Art is a longing to salvage something for oneself, something individually precious, from the larger abstractions at the touch of which the poet instinctively tightens his coils of refusal. It is the ineluctable personal vision and memory which alone is transmutable into an acquisition for all souls. Such is the law of art. The poetry of literature is in this sense always the miraculous faculty of sifting the dust of the *temps perdu* for the sake of the few remaining gold grains of the *temps retrouvé*. Nor is it the poet, biased in his approach, who excels in sifting. What little there is of real abiding worth in any work of art enlightened posterity can pick out with a pair of pincers.

How has the tremendous upheaval, which has turned Russia socially inside out, affected this queer, nostalgic, envied but perpetually misunderstood creative energy that does not seem to spring from the same source but flows parallel with the river of life? For as long as there has been literature in Russia it has been free to express itself on all manner of subjects save one – the autocracy, upon which subject tacit consent has been the irreducible condition of publication. Catherine II, enjoying the reputation of an enlightened ruler, was vindictive to writers, like Kniazhnin, who attacked her personal regime, which she inevitably identified with the national welfare. All through the succeeding reigns poets freely attributed their own disabilities to a want of free expression. The more gifted writers overcame the artificial restrictions of censorship, the gifted writer having no need to identify 'seriousness of purpose', inherent in art itself, with utilitarian ends. Though the character of the struggle makes its own weapon of style, literature is not a scuffle, not an argument, but, as Schopenhauer has it, the mute unveiling of the Platonic Idea informing the common object. It is the scenting of a world-secret in the physiognomy of things.

The denizen of private universes, daring to hope that with the autocracy he has shed the debility lying heavily on his soul, was told that his deepest fulfilment lay in employing his art to extol the Soviet garden of which he might consider himself, if he fulfilled his set task, as being not the least of its flowers. The Soviet Government, exercised to create a new spirit, assigned to literature the task of serving as a model for life. It had a literary policy, which, however, it reversed every few years. Despairing of the political sincerity of existing writers, it invited the Futurists to carry the torch of Marx. The new was best served by the new. An independent proletarian culture was also being assiduously fostered in the hope that, if the Futurists sabotaged their loyalty to communism by becoming deliberately unintelligible, a new growth would by then have sprung from the native bed. In the new fashion of abbreviating a long string of designations typical of official nomenclature in old-time Russia, with commendable brevity, if without euphony, the new centres of proletarian culture were called 'Proletkults'.

Lunacharsky, the highly enlightened Commissar of Public Enlightenment in Lenin's Government, however, deplored the lack of reverence in the Futurists for the cultural heritage of the past and the literary excellence of existing writers. Trotsky took a gloomy view of proletarian literature, while proletarian writers, as their work fell below the standards of experienced old hands warily termed 'Fellow-Travellers', made up for a deficient power of words by raising their voice in the councils. Resenting the success of mere 'fellow-travellers' who had travelled ahead of them in the public esteem, and even that of the Government, the Proletkults began to agitate for full literary freedom to assert that communism was the vanguard of literature, and Communist literature the vanguard of communism and, as such, the vanguard of the Government. Such zeal alarmed Lenin who, though he might rate the virtues of communism above those of literature, was hardly disposed to rate above the communist Government a communist literature lacking literary virtue.

It must be owned that the Soviet Government showed considerable patience and tact in handling the various factions, and in 1925 it inaugurated a literary Magna Carta proclaiming such freedom of artistic expression as was not in open conflict with official policy. It extolled the fellow-travellers as literary specialists, and counselled the proletarian writers to suppress proletarian ruling-class snobbery inimical to art and literature. Whereupon the 'diehard' faction of the Proletkult, who, in an organ called *On Guard*, had asserted their political ideology as the first article of their literary creed, ceased publication and came out with a new journal called *On Literary Guard*. Tired of being told they could not write, they decided that it was their special task, as the ruling class, to command others who could. They started a movement of 'Social Command' which was to assign to the practised literary hand the task of merely giving expression in words, as other artisans do in bricks, to the creative ideas of the ruling class.

A tolerant policy towards literature and the arts on the part of the Government continued until 1929 when, perhaps a little jealous of the prestige of writers in a country that had its work cut out with a Five-Year Plan, the Government made known that, as it paid its pipers, it would call the tune. Weary of seeing the Proletkults laying claim to their superior ability to think, while assigning to the non-political craftsman the piffling task of literary execution, the Government told them all, proletarians and fellow-travellers alike, what they were to do and to go to it. An orgy of social commands, concurrent with the Five-Year Plan and designed to sing its praises, was released upon innocent literary pates, with the admitted result that seventy-five per cent of the literature of the period was fit only for the waste-paper basket. Finding that its bread depended on laying on thick the ideological butter, literature, robbed of its integrity, responded with a plethora of shameless unadulterated flattery, until, embarrassed by such transparent insincerity, the Soviet Government called a halt.

A new policy, sponsored by Gorky, begun in 1932 and continued to this day, was to merge all authors, futurist, proletkult and fellow-traveller, in a single homogeneous Union of Soviet Writers. A writer must still serve the Communist State, but confine his appreciation of the Government to an attitude of 'socialist realism', nothing being so suspect as flattery, now defined, in contra-distinction to 'socialist realism', as 'socialist idealism' and labelled – to warn off prospective customers – 'poison'.

In this spirit, then, of 'socialist realism', and in no fulsome 'socialist idealism', let it be said that the way they all rose to repulse the invader is evidence enough of their having, despite such diverting divisions, a broad enough principle for a united stand. What is the spirit which might be said to be the breath of modern Russia? It is of course the healthy absence of class-distinction, if not as yet entirely in fact, at least in principle. Far from making men uniform, it is in fact this classless uniformity which gives the modern Russian a chance to develop his individuality. For it is the corporate mark that substitutes, so lamentably, prestige for real values and makes a man pre-eminently a product of his school, corps, club, regiment, university, at the cost of anything else that might otherwise be in him. Having had it drummed into them for twenty-four years that they are the lords of creation, with their sense of importance fortified by a look at the map, is it any wonder that they are completely unselfconscious? No Soviet citizen could be conceived as going through the tortures, for instance, of a Proust threading his way gingerly through the social labyrinths of the Faubourg Saint-Germain, or of even understanding the morbid snobbery of Lermontov. Having exhausted his proletkult snobbery, there was nothing else for the Soviet citizen to be snobbish about but his ability to hold down a job. The Belgian conductor, Defauw, found the enormous open-air audiences lacking in every shadow of pretence. If they liked a thing their applause was spontaneous and tumultuous. If the piece left them cold, they sat taciturnly silent.

Imperial Russia tidied its desks and threw the social junk pell-mell into the capacious bottom drawers. In Soviet Russia, where the lower depths have been turned inside out, they have been tidying their bottom drawers first, neglecting appearances. Endowed with energy and a language supple, tender and sonorous, but saddled with an appalling style of journalism, they are forging a new ideal which, as Mr. Stalin has pointed out, is to raise the communal means to enable each to receive, not as at present according to his merits, but his needs. This ideal of economic liberty is the complement of the ideal of social liberty. Their joint realisation in the future political liberty must, it is argued, be forfeited in the present. For this they have fought. For this they fight again to-day. The only pity, as Bernard Shaw pointed out, was that men, agreed on setting up a new world, insisted on the prerequisite of disembowelling one another. Out of his garnered wisdom Goethe also marvelled that, since liberty, when crowned with authority, invariably turned into an oligarchy, it should have proved beyond the wit of man to devise a system whereby the balance between freedom and coercion could be adjusted automatically, and the violent swinging of the pendulum of politics perpetually neutralised. But apparently it was not given to man to achieve it, and God did not seem to want it.

80

THE DEATH OF PROUST

Persuading, but with difficulty, a publisher to issue even at the author's own expense *Du Côté de chez Swann*, the first two (and, in some respects, the best) of the sixteen volumes of the great novel, *À la Recherche du Temps Perdu*, Marcel Proust gained fame by a process of infiltration of the inlets of Bloomsbury and Greenwich Village, gradually to flood the whole world of hearsay. The cold, concise, urbane, polished prose of Anatole France that they had been taught to revere as a model of French expression blinded them to the merits of the new master. By the accepted standards of the first, the second was execrable. Among others, an English disciple, Clive Bell, was distressed "by those perplexing coils of dependent clauses which, instead of locking into each other as links in a chain, advance tentatively shoulder to shoulder or higgledy-piggledy".

But an Irishman, and by far the most penetrating if too tight-lipped, interpreter of Proust, Samuel Beckett, found the Proustian chain-figure of the metaphor a tiring style which, however, did not tire the mind. "The clarity of the phrase is cumulative and explosive. One's fatigue is a fatigue of the heart, a blood fatigue. One is exhausted and angry after an hour, submerged, dominated by the crest and break of metaphor after metaphor: but never stupefied. The complaint that it is an involved style, full of periphrasis, obscure and impossible to follow, has no foundation whatsoever."

Indeed, Proust's style assumes in the reader an intellectual breeding equal to appreciating his own which debars him from pausing to ram down your throat, as a vulgarian would do, an analogy, to Proust only valid collaterally, to be taken in your stride, while never losing sight of the goal he has set out to reach when he opened his sentence. In this he is most akin to Chopin, of whose method and style his matchless description of the '*beauté démodée de cette musique*' is perhaps the most perfect example of his own. The peculiar merit of this 'description', which is nothing less than a translation of musical into literary terms, is that it eschews all metaphor and symbol, strictly confining itself to movement and stress. The effort to render into English such a sentence of unalloyed lyricism, common to both poets, Chopin and Proust, is a labour of love to which one might with pleasure devote a year of one's life. I spent months in perfecting it; and if anyone can better it, I shall be pleased to receive suggestions. Here it is:

> In her youth she had first learned to fondle those long-necked sinuous phrases of Chopin, so free and flexible and tactile, which begin by essaying their steps outside and out of reach of their starting place, wide of the mark at which one might have hoped that they would attain their consummation, and that whirl away on their truant's flight of fantasy merely to return with more deliberation, a recoil more premeditated, with more precision, like some crystal bowl which will ring till you could scream, as they beat against your heart.

It is essential to remember that the complexity of Proust, reflected in his style, is the complexity of a modern, erudite spirit commanding a wide field of reference, but, like Chopin, never losing sight of the lyrical consummation of his opening phrase, while impatient to encompass the zest of life and commentary there and then, before he passes to his next sentence, with all the fulness he cannot curb poured into that. It is inevitably an orchestral style, writer and reader alike finding themselves in the situation of a practised conductor of orchestra so proficient in musical notation, the intellectual idiom of the culture of this age, as to take in at a glance all the simultaneous but separate instrumental parts.

Churchill's famous phrase about the R.A.F., "Never did so many owe so much to so few", applies equally to the overloaded Proustian plane. Considering the intellectual load it carries on its back, it is piloted with superb skill, for it never fails to make a perfect landing. Yet there is danger in cramming so much enthusiasm into a single phrase. As Voltaire has it, the secret of boring is to leave nothing out. "Tedious he is," Clive Bell complains, "but his tediousness becomes excusable once its cause is perceived. Proust tries our patience so long as we expect his story to move forward: that not being the direction in which it is intended to move."

Concurrent with his prose, his own life developed in a recumbent position, displacement in space not being the direction which his body was intended to travel. His life, like his book, unfolded in obedience to a law of inner necessity, like a flower. He was, Beckett observes, almost exempt from the impurity of will. "He deplores his lack of will until he understands that will, being utilitarian, a servant of intelligence and habit, is not a condition of the artistic experience. When the subject is exempt from will the object is exempt from causality (Time and Space taken together). And this human vegetation is purified in the transcendental aperception that can capture the Model, the Idea, the Thing in itself." Proust, in his new flat, wrote of that *tristesse* which afflicted him all his life, of which at all events his mother in her grave was spared the knowledge. (Alas, together with that of his great fame.) He was an invalid, and doomed to sorrow. But who, ill or well, has not experienced sorrow? That sorrow imbued with thwarted longings, be it unrequited love; a pending project deferred indefinitely for want of funds; separation in life or death from a being we love; anxiety in the face of pressing debts; the spectacle of Time-made flesh; or any other mortal grief.

Proust, desperately ill, was correcting his proofs in the same way as he wrote his books – lying in bed and balancing the sheets in mid-air on the palm of his left hand while manipulating a pen with his right. His asthma was choking him, his bruised and aching eyes were constantly failing him. The hardy printers, undaunted by his valiant corrections, were returning to him again and again a text which, on the most generous interpretation, might be described as an approximation to the author's intentions. After actors, printers are notoriously the worst misinterpreters of genius. Tolerably careful of sentences on their own level of understanding, they take liberties precisely where they are out of their depths, never so blithe and carefree as when they gallop over foreign words, or phrases foreign to them, deeming that any spelling will do in a language with which they are themselves unfamiliar.

That his work was not immediately appreciated at its true value, though it disappointed him, could not on reflection surprise Proust, who acknowledged that, in the nature of aesthetic perception, appreciation percolates only through the filter of memory. "Not only does one not seize at once and retain an impression of really great works, but even in the content itself of any such work it is the least valuable features that strike one first." "The public," said Chehov, "single out for admiration in art the banal and long familiar, that to which they have grown accustomed." André Gide, who on behalf of the *Nouvelle Revue Française* had rejected out of hand *Du Côté de chez Swann*, put off as he dipped into the two-thousand-page pile of manuscript lying for months and months on his table by a plethora of titled names, was struck by the work when he read it in print, and made hasty overtures to the author for the favour of publishing the entire work under the imprint of the house of which he was the literary director. Whereupon Proust, who had always wished to be published under that and no other imprint, with the help of several friends entered into tortuous negotiations to get himself released from his original publisher, who now professed a passionate admiration for the work published merely at the author's expense, and upon the successful result proceeding, as was his custom, to acquit his debt to his friends with the purchase of expensive if rather useless presents. Social climbers, dukes and ambassadors, espying in the work a world of dukes, ambassadors and social climbers like their own prosaic selves, but presented with a poetic nostalgia only damped by a merciless analysis, began to ask, "Who is this Proust?" They were astonished that, reading so intimate an account of their own doings, they had not apparently met him. They supposed that other dukes, duchesses and climbers had been in a better case. Proust, anxious to dissimulate his morbid snobbery, to some extent already disinfected in the process of analysis by the antiseptic of irony, wrote to his friend Charles Daudet of the contortions which he, as a man of the world, inured from early years to the lures of society, had to undergo to write of it naïvely and artistically in the spirit of a greenhorn new to it all and impressed by what he saw. In this he is suspiciously like Arnold Bennett who, far from having to dissimulate his perpetual astonishment at the ways of the great world, could never cease to write of the West End as a perpetual visitor from the Five Towns, indeed scarcely able to sit down to dinner without wondering why he wasn't standing behind his own chair.

As Proust's fame reversed a literary fashion which had decreed that high life was low literature, English aristocrats began to wonder why nobody had treated *them* to so full a dish of delicate appreciation garnished with such minute and exquisite observations on the cryptic significance of their ways, and the Duke of Marlborough, who said that if he hadn't been a duke he would have liked to be a Goethe (Goethe having once observed that, next to being Goethe, he would have chosen to be an English duke) made overtures to Proust to honour him with a visit to Blenheim. '*Monsieur de Marlborough*', so Proust wrote, had offered to indulge his invalidism to the last detail, vowing that he would be conveyed from Paris to Blenheim horizontally, carried on a stretcher from train to boat. Homage to a universally acknowledged master and pleasure in showing off a lion were mingled, perhaps, with the faint hope that in a future volume the master would treat an English duke *en* Guermantes.

But the Guermantes were a different pair of shoes from the Marlboroughs. Wrapped in the mystery of the Merovingian age, bathed, as in a sunset, in the orange light glowing from the resounding syllable-*antes*, they had been for Proust enormously distended, immaterialised, so as to encircle and contain all that sunlit *côté de Guermantes* of his childhood walks of which realm they were duke and duchess, evoking for him the course of the Vivonne, its water-lilies and its overshadowing trees, and an endless series of hot summer afternoons. What was there for him in the name of Marlborough? What indeed to evoke, save possibly the nursery jingle:

> *Marlborough s'en va-t-en guerre*
> *Mironton, tonton, mirontaine . . .*

Having exhausted his energy on the French counterpart of Shakespearean historical *dramatis personae*, he was utterly without strength to start the whole rigmarole all over again with the Westmorelands and the Worcesters, the Northumberlands and the Gloucesters, to say nothing of Lady Percy, wife to Hotspur and sister to Mortimer, Earl of March, and Lady Mortimer, daughter to Glendower and wife to Mortimer, with Mistress Quickly, hostess of the Boar's Head Tavern in Eastcheap for anticlimax. The visit to England did not materialise.

Few Englishmen, and not very many Frenchmen, had met Proust since he immured himself within the corked walls of his bedroom to keep out the sound of the street in his rue Hamelin furnished flat, with the bath, apparently in permanent disuse, serving as storage for potatoes. Clive Bell met the master after a first night of the ballet, when, at half-past two in the morning, up popped Proust, white gloves and all. Though Bell was impressed by his glorious eyes, Marcel Proust did not please him physically, being altogether too sleek and dank and plastered.

The last half of *Le Temps Retrouvé* abounds with the significant Bergsonian discovery which is the equivalent of Santayana's dictum that life as it passes is so much time wasted, nothing being truly possessed or recovered save in the form of eternity, which is also the form of art, together with the opposite discovery that he is dying and must make haste to write his great book. It is the pious fraud of seeing life on the surface, in a single file of 'facts' marshalled in a pretended chain of infallible cause and effect, an imagined sequence of fictitious logic regaling us in the result with but a miserable outline of chronology: the fallacy of seeing life through the impurity of the will, which Proust exposes as abject nourishment, inartistic vocation, un-Platonic philosophy. Our normal conception was as denuded of reality as that of a person listening to an orchestral recital who, conscious only of a somewhat arbitrary sequence of single notes, denied the existence of chords. Life, real and full, was akin to an actualisation of memory. In memory we could leap from one moment to another, or linger at will.

287

But our memory, he says in effect, is at best a pale shadow of the reality experienced, yet never tasted to the full. Contemplation of action in the very instant of action was needed for the full celestial nourishment denied us in life. Memory precluded action; action excluded memory. But if, by some corresponding scent or sound, touch, sight or taste which we stumbled against in the common day, we were involuntarily transported into the forgotten past, we rejoiced in it extra-temporarily precisely because we were no longer tied to it in Time. What else was this involuntary memory but an intimation of immortality?

A recluse from society, Proust, after carefully weighing arguments for and against such a venture, decided that he would go to an afternoon party at the Princesse de Guermantes. In her courtyard he had his first of several revelations of unconscious memory as the fulcrum of the lever of immortality and of art. He was strolling into her courtyard when a carriage, driving up at that moment, caused him precipitately to seek the refuge of the pavement, of which the worn edge was nearly on a level with the asphalt. The sensation suddenly plunged him, with extraordinary intensity, into a moment resurrected from the past, when as a youth he had paid his first visit to Venice, and in the Baptistry of St. Mark he had experienced the same effect of treading on the curb worn down to the level of the thoroughfare. This sensation, for a timeless moment, flooded his whole being. He felt himself back in the body of the youth of Venice. In his childhood he had conceived a magic idea of Venice and had cherished the thought of a visit which, however, had not sustained his illusions. On a subsequent visit, trying consciously to recollect the Venice myth of his childhood, he had not been successful. But now, in that Paris courtyard, thirty years later, he re-lived the authentic fragrance of a moment of his youth in Venice, fully and lustily, as he had not done at the actual time of his visit, because then he had been preoccupied with irrelevant considerations which now, free of their irksome and timely quality, merely certified the authenticity of a timeless moment of youth. The sensation was so overpowering that, for an instant which seemed eternal, the image of himself as a youth in Venice disputed the actuality of his standing, a sick and ageing man, in a Paris courtyard. If he but yielded to the timeless reality of the Venice scene hovering before him and flooding him with happiness, he would die. Then the Paris courtyard veered round into focus, and complacently he turned his steps towards the house.

But the feeling which remained with him was that a minute freed from the order of Time had come to live in him, that he might feel himself, while living in it, freed from the order of Time. He could understand why at such a moment he should be confident in his joy; he understood that the word 'death' had no meaning for him. Situated as he was out of Time, what had he to fear of the future?

Yet we may inquire – what was the precise nature of this timeless joy? What, apart from the realisation of immortality, conditioned it? Proust's answer in effect is this: In those rare moments, those entirely fortuitous moments which the conscious will could do nothing to evoke, our being, momentarily released from the one-dimensional Time to which in actual life it is tied, was 'real without being actual, ideal without being abstract'. Proust had experienced nothing less than a glimpse of himself in eternity. He had touched a point in the fifth dimension. He had re-lived an isolated moment in its crystal purity, free from the strain of anxiety and the blight of habit which had dulled the actual instant and made it nebulously unreal. He had re-lived it, this time, with insouciance because his being recognised it as real and ideal. Utterly real, with nothing in it to abstract from simultaneous realisation, the moment was also the ideal of contemplation. Man no longer stood in his own shadow. The duality had been bridged.

They were there, these essences of things and states of being, vases, each filled with a special perfume, its own climate, suspended each at its proper distance across the span of years, there sheltered and withdrawn from Time, perpetuated in eternity. And at a sound, a secret touch, we involuntarily tapped these vases, which released their fragrance to make us breathe a new air. The air of paradise it was, new only because we had already breathed it in the forgotten years. Forgotten, eternity had preserved it for us in its pristine purity, no longer cloyed over or distorted by our fears, habits or intentions, in the full beauty of its infallible proportions of light and shade, which vouchsafed its authenticity. These involuntary bursts of memory that assailed us so seldom but so powerfully were like sudden raids into the treasure-house of the resurrected life, where the transfigured body could tap all these moments at will, moving freely and swiftly over the network of memories. But while our feet plodded in the strait rut of Time, it strayed there but by chance when the attention wandered in a waking dream, or a forgotten sound or scent made it hover on the brink of a paradise it could not enter while the mortal body disputed attention.

It became clear to Proust that his art was more urgent than life, since it not only revealed life to itself but also resurrected its very essence. His duty as an artist was to translate these intimations of immortality into a medium which would resurrect dynamically through the magic of the Word. But side by side with the revelation of the magnitude of his discovery he was oppressed by doubt: would he have time and strength vouchsafed him to complete his work? One day, as he was descending the staircase, he clutched at the balustrade to prevent himself from fainting. The thought of a letter from an unknown lady, reading, "I have been astonished not to have received a reply to my previous letter", pulled him back from the brink of unconsciousness into stern reality and duty. Life was real, life was earnest . . . He postponed his lifework to force himself sit down and write to her in appreciation of her appreciation.

He was a dying man. His ineluctable snobbery (which some of his partisans vehemently denied, only by their protestations to establish it the more), by virtue of his integrity working against his desires, had dissected the foundations of French society, showing conclusively that nothing lasting could be built of such stuff. As a clever hand with the spiritual pickaxe, he was the effective agent of God's Fifth Column, claiming the spirit's right-of-way over the coruscated vanities of the flesh. Despite himself, he was having no truck with any attempt on this earth, vainly trying to model itself on the Kingdom, to set up an ungodly society. Although he fervently denied in his letters that his interest in fashionable society exceeded the interest of dissecting its body, and begged his correspondent who bluntly inquired whether it was true that he was, as reputed, a snob, to believe that, far from it, of the aristocracy, the bourgeoisie and the proletariat he preferred the last, and next to that the first, since the *grand seigneur* was more polite to the workman than could be said of the bourgeois, Proust nevertheless could not resist a great name with a family tree rooted in history. At a party given to him at the Ritz by an English writer, at which James Joyce had been awaiting his hero with a fervour he had not tried to curb, Proust, expected for dinner but arriving about two o'clock in the morning, took up his position as he entered the room at a safe distance from the guests who had been invited to meet him, observing to his host – like the giant who said "Fe! Fi! Fo! Fum! I smell the blood of an Englishman!" – that he espied the presence of the Duchesse de Polignac and would be glad to have a word with her. He was horrified when on his way home James Joyce, not to be denied the privilege of his acquaintance, forced his way into the private taxi (in which alone Proust could entrust himself to travel in Paris), and, crime of crimes, let down the window, when the night air was death to Proust. Arrived at the rue Hamelin, Proust, in a frenzy of anxiety lest Joyce force himself upon him, persuaded the author of *Ulysses* to depart in his taxi. As only the taxi-driver, a relation of Céleste, could work the lift, Proust, shivering in his fur coat, sat mournfully awaiting the return of the vehicle. His idea of 'back to nature' was to be driven in a closed car, muffled up to the ears in cardigans and furs, to observe through a pane of glass the hawthorn in bloom.

Nobody would believe that a man only fifty, who had suffered from asthma since he was a child, was going to die now at the height of his fame. His personal friends brought their wives to his bedside, unaware that their scent, more surely than the pollen, threw him into a welter of choking. Céleste, *alias* Françoise of the epos, who had been cook and maid to his mother, his aunt and his grandmother, and seemed to perform all these functions still, as well as tackling his manuscripts with the sewing-needle when he had insertions to make, though she had been complaining (in the novel) that, when he was but a child, her feet were already giving her trouble, was being sent backwards and forwards to the Ritz for iced beer, as though that was the only place where he could get it and Céleste the only one to obtain it. Although the doctor had insisted on his giving up all idea of work, Proust went on with his proofs and, to propitiate the doctor, as he thought, sent him expensive bouquets of roses to make up for defying his orders.

So he came to the day when his spirit was leaving a body that had become a whited sepulchre. In a panic he sent Céleste to the Ritz for iced beer, impressing on her that if she did not hurry she would, as always, prove to be too late. Knowing that he was dying, he impressed on her very earnestly that in no event was she to send for his brother. He wanted to die by himself, and at the approach of death called for his manuscript depicting the passing of his grandmother, *alias* mother, observing "*j'ai quelques retouches à y faire.*" His younger brother, Robert, was a doctor, and he was fond of him as far as it went, although they had little in common. Nor does one cherish at one's deathbed the presence of relatives with whom one has been out of touch. Now that he began to choke and struggle, Céleste, frightened, forgot all her promises, ran downstairs to a shop, from there to telephone to his brother, who arrived and began administering injections to relieve his brother's frightful pain, but succeeded only in prolonging it. As they lifted him to a sitting position to enable him to breathe better, an abscess on the lung burst, throwing Proust into a welter of mortal agony.

And the long struggle for breath began. When Robert understood that it was all over, heartbroken, he said, "*Mon pauvre frère*, I'm afraid I have caused you a great deal of needless pain." Marcel Proust, opening his eyes before he closed them for ever, murmured, "*Mon pauvre Robert*, I'm afraid you have."

He was dead. But for ever? Who can say? It is certain that neither spiritualist experiments, nor religious dogmas, bring us proof of the survival of the soul. What one can say is that everything happens in our life as though we had entered upon it with a burden of obligations contracted in an anterior existence; there is nothing in the conditions of life on this earth to make us think ourselves obliged to be good, to be sensitive, even polite; nor for the artist to feel himself compelled to begin a passage twenty times over again when the praise it evokes will matter little to the body devoured by worms. . . . All these obligations, which have no sanction in our present life, seem to belong to a different world, a world founded on goodness, on scruple, on sacrifice, a world entirely different from ours, and whence we come to be born on this earth, perhaps to return there and live under the rule of the unknown laws which we have obeyed here because we carried their principles within ourselves, without knowing who decreed that they should be; those laws to which every deep intellectual labour draws us nearer, and which are invisible only – and not even! – to fools.

So that [Proust concludes] the idea that Bergotte was not for ever dead was not without verisimilitude.

Next morning his friends came to look at him. In death, the man of fifty-one seemed to have regained his youth; as in Heine's poem, '*Im Sarge lag ein junger Mann mit leidend-milden Mienen*'. Piled in two rows on either side of him, as in his own description of the lying-in-state of Bergotte, were his works. Before he died, art had convinced him that life did not end in non-being. The unique, ineluctable accent to which each of the great poets of music returned despite himself, pointed, whatever science had to say against it, to the existence of the irreducibly individual soul. Spaced out by long intervals, mysterious intimations of immortality had come to him when watching a line of trees at Balbec, or the belfries of Martinville. But his deepest illuminations had been entirely fortuitous, as when his whole being was suddenly flooded by the ideal reality situated out of Time, because a moment in the present, identified with a corresponding moment in the forgotten past, had made him breathe the air of paradise and feel himself, for the space of that moment, an extra-temporal being, immune from death because immune from Time. So, in the tinkling of a spoon against a plate, he had heard the sound of a hammer testing a wheel of a train drawn up in a wood. The taste of madeleine dipped in tea had brought back all summer in a day contained in the promise of a morning sky scanned over a breakfast-cup in early childhood. Although seeming to cut him adrift from the visible world and all that made his life, these fortuitous '*correspondences*' had been the stepping-stones across the stream of Time, the stakes driven into the river-bed to serve as the foundations upon which he might build his real life. In the phrase that had spoken to him in the Sonata of Vinteuil, like a grave and gentle angel of Bellini, the promise had been an anxious appeal cast behind an empty sky. In the phrase of the Septuor it came again, this time like an archangel of Mantegna clothed in scarlet, trumpeting the vindication of its mystic hope of the life incorruptible risen from the body of this death into the ideal reality withdrawn from Time made flesh, whose bed is the grave.

81

POETS, PRINCES, PREMIERS, AND PIGS

After the war was won, the interest in it was liquidated by a millionaire avenue in Paris being named after the Marshal, and a statue erected in his honour in Grosvenor Gardens, London, bearing the one laconic word: Foch.

He had, after all, won the war for us, apparently a necessary preliminary to resuming our normal business by private enterprise.

When a few more years had elapsed, it even became a matter for debate whether it had been necessary to win the war at all in order to resume business by private enterprise. Admittedly, defeat at the hands of the Germans would have been bitter, even disastrous. But if a negotiated peace had been achieved, as advocated by Lord Lansdowne earlier in the day; if there had been a Stockholm Conference; if there had been peace under Asquith at Christmas of 1916, the wheels of international private enterprise might have been set rolling earlier, to the exclusion of a Bolshevik revolution in Russia, a Fascist in Italy, and a National-Socialist in Germany, with all the fresh havoc that these entailed. In 1929 Foch was dead and his world with him.

D. H. Lawrence travelled far and wide in search of a new life, defeated chiefly in his task of getting up a new society by having to take himself with him. Lawrence has seduced the minds of several writers who became his disciples. Catherine Carswell believed blindly that Lawrence was the prophet of a new way of life so remote that neither the disciples of Lawrence nor Lawrence himself could have any idea what it was. "One is reminded," Hugh Kingsmill commented in his book on D. H. Lawrence, "of the company promoter at the time of the South Sea Bubble who invited money from the public for a project to be communicated hereafter." Middleton Murry who, like Lawrence, stirred a protective feeling in others, was also a disciple. Aldous Huxley is yet another disciple who had reduced the occasional suggestiveness inherent in Lawrence's 'dark otherness' to a lucidity which makes plain nonsense. "Lean and mournful," writes Hugh Kingsmill, "a Don Quixote without dreams, he rode along keeping an eye open for a magician able to relieve him of his sanity." In addition, Lawrence attracted a number of female disciples thankful for his sunniness, so affecting in a state of alternate sunniness and cloudiness, the cloudiness predominating.

Lawrence had an uncouth charm, the persuasiveness, one imagines, of Hitler recruiting men for his cause before the Munich beer-garden *Putsch*, who, however, one felt in one's bones, was no earthly use to others, since his field of action did not exceed the expanding boundaries of his own conceit. While Hitler was – it seems an incredible scene, difficult to believe, but vouched for by the late novelist – discussing life with our Hugh Walpole on their perambulations around the hills of Salzburg, D. H. Lawrence was laying down the laws of his political credo. This credo uncommonly like Hitler's own, lays down that no man can be a pure individual; no State can be Christian; every citizen is a unit of worldly power and has his fulfilment in the gratification of his power-sense according to his place in the hierarchy.

If the citizen, Lawrence wrote, belonged to one of the so-called 'ruling nations', his soul was fulfilled in the sense of his country's power and strength. If his country mounted up aristocratically to a zenith of splendour and power, in a hierarchy, he would be all the more fulfilled. Lawrence was in fact toying with a sort of Nazi philosophy of his own, which, however, did not neglect the use of hereditary titles. Lawrence was in fact toying with a sort of Nazi philosophy of his own, which, however, did not neglect the use of hereditary titles. For his own part he had a measure of fulfilment in the gratification of writing letters on the crested notepaper of his German wife, running a pen across the crest, and explaining the reason for the deletion: Frieda's father was a baron. Dorothy Brett, who sailed with the Lawrences for the United States, Lawrence described as a woman who "paints, is deaf, forty, very nice, and daughter of Viscount Esher". Far from objecting to there being a House of Lords, he wrote to Lady Ottoline Morrell that indeed 'we' must also have, in his new scheme of life, a House of Ladies. Money and money differences seemed to him susceptible to liquidation in the liquidation of money; to which effect he merely issued his ukase in loose verse without specifying how it was to be done:

> Kill money, put money out of existence,
> It is a perverted instinct, a hidden thought
> which rots the brain, the blood, the bones, the stones, the soul.

> O! start a revolution somebody!
> not to get the money
> but to lose it all for ever.

On the divine rights of kings, he was even more summary. Beholding the Prince of Wales, with charming boyish diffidence accepting homage, perched high up in a pagoda, from a procession of elephants trained to crook the knee, Lawrence reflected how much better he would have

294

filled the bill. "I wish," he wrote in a poem, "they had given the three feathers to me." He visualised himself as reversing the motto *Ich Dien* into *Dient Ihr!*, expressing the conviction that he was meet to be served, and informing the elephants, first great beasts of the earth, that a prince has come back to them in his own person, in appreciation of which fact they should crook the knee and be glad, no doubt considering the presence of the Prince of Wales as rather irrelevant to the celebration organised in his honour.

But the Prince of Wales did not confine his goodwill ambassadorship to the beasts of the jungle. Wherever he went, bipeds crooked their knee before him – bipeds who were presently to tear him with their claws. At Oxford in the early 'twenties one saw him arrive to receive an honorary doctorate at the Sheldonian, and heard him declare, while nervously fingering his tie, that he was "proud to be an Oxford man". Before his arrival, the Public Orator solicited in old-fashioned Latin, with dulcet fingering of the consonants, permission of the Vice-Chancellor to open proceedings, which the Vice-Chancellor accorded with a sharp: '*Licit!*' uttered in the modern Anglicised pronunciation, raising in its trail a discreet storm of laughter. A little pleasing academic by-play, this, just to show that dons were still schoolboys merely advanced in years.

The next year Queen Mary arrived for a like honour, sponsored by the Chancellor of the University himself, the Secretary of State for Foreign Affairs, the Marquess Curzon of Kedleston, K.G., a nobleman who had collected, and was proud of, all the minor honours which had fallen to his feet like ripe fruit on his triumphal progress from the Viceregalship to the Premiership. Would he reach his goal?

In his impeccably arrogant pro-consul English, tinged with occasional native county Dorsetshire, as of a sire speaking the language of his own domains (which made him clip his vowels), he perorated to his Queen an address of welcome, and then, in consideration of her being a queen, read back her reply addressed to himself.

The English territorial oligarchy, as represented by rich dukes, like the Portlands and Bedfords, or peers who, without being dukes, are as good as dukes, like the Derbys and Londonderrys, play an uneasy game of mutual courtesy with prime ministers who, if more powerful while in office, are not in office long enough to withstand the power of the oligarchs who remain dukes year after year. Curzon who, as a territorial oligarch, was more than a cut or two beneath those others, owing his landed opulence to a rich marriage, and the rich marriage to a promising career in the Government, was, however resplendent, but a place-hunter in Lloyd George's Cabinet, enjoying high office which he occupied under perpetual notice of being sacked. His ambition made him a slave of one who had been only a solicitor in Wales and had worked himself up by means of an engaging oratory to a position of the powerful demagogue wielding the stick of supreme office, as it were, of the people, by the people and for the people.

Having imbibed the pleasure of rubbing shoulders with foreign statesmen in Paris and Geneva, Lloyd George gradually usurped the function of the Foreign Office, which he ran from Downing Street. Seeing Curzon, one day, attired in full gala dress, Lloyd George inquired why he was so resplendent. Suavely came the reply that he, Curzon, was attending the Levee in his capacity, he stressed, as though to remind the Prime Minister of the post he still held under him even if denied the practical opportunities of exercising his functions, of Secretary of State for Foreign Affairs.

Nothing in the affairs of men takes place according to expectation. There is no one so belligerent as a confirmed pacifist. The war-winner Lloyd George who had, after his stubborn pacifism during the South African War and his initial hesitancy at the outbreak of the Four Years' War, become an implacable belligerent leader pursuing war to the bitter end, was not rewarded by British progressives for his successful defeat of Germanic Caesarism.

Why? There is a certain instinct in the unreflecting masses, groping blindly for what is perhaps a sense of proportion. Without being capable of formulating their reasons, the people, after the initial khaki election, cooled towards their champion. You can be an out-and-out pacifist, hate war, champion the common people against the economic tyranny of feudal dukes. But you can hardly hope to expand these fine principles to include the same common people suddenly allied with the feudal dukes in a war to end war against a feudal German emperor without causing a moral inflation – a general depreciation of your currency of principle. The Tories chucked out their erstwhile War Chief, Ll.G., and the Liberals would not touch him with a forty-foot-long barge pole. He fell, and the common people would not even stop to pick up the fragments.

As he was leaving 10 Downing Street, exchanging an official for a private residence, a move that is always faintly invidious, Lord Riddell, a cockney millionaire, once a solicitor like himself whom he had made into a peer, shook his friend and companion by the hand. It was a hearty grip and a pregnant one. "It's been a grand time!"

But now it was over. Bonar Law, hitherto so loyal that he had caused tears to be brought to his chief's eyes by his overwork and illness, aggravated by the loss of two sons killed in the war, prompted by Beaverbrook and others to make a stand for the premiership, had suddenly declared that Lloyd George was all right, but he did not see why he should be Prime Minister for the rest of his natural life – only, however, soon to crack up in office and die of cancer of the throat;

whereupon Balfour, who had been both Prime Minister and Foreign Secretary, did not share Curzon's feeling that one who had been both Viceroy and Foreign Secretary could not be happy without becoming Prime Minister. Dear Arthur seems to have done dear George a deliberate bad turn. It almost seems that he awaited this opportunity. He put out his foot for Curzon to trip over, and thus break the neck of his life's ambition.

After Bonar Law's demise all the cards had now turned up, with his trump card on top. All possible rivals had walked out with Lloyd George. Curzon was the only considerable figure left in the Cabinet. He was, in fact, the only possible choice. His ambition had at last reached, as reach it must, given his potentialities, supreme success. That which he had dreamed of at Eton, prepared for at Balliol, was within his grasp.

He had retired to the country, there to await the royal summons. Kedleston, his luxurious country seat to which his two wealthy American wives had contributed their gold to keep their husband in velvet and satin, had no telephone. But when a local boy on a bicycle arrived with a telegram summoning the Marquess to London, he prepared for a triumphant journey. In the train he discussed the senior ecclesiastical appointments. He also wondered whether he was going to reside at 10 Downing Street or merely use it as an office, strolling over from Carlton House Terrace.

He lunched at Carlton House Terrace with his wife, and then they waited. From here he could see his sovereign's town palace. He had, when in India, reproduced his own Kedleston to live in it as Viceroy. But his London bedroom was spartan, though his wife's drawing-rooms were sumptuous. And his bedroom telephone was connected with the servants' hall in some way, enabling him to intercept the butler's private conversation. Here in this expensive Carlton House Terrace Arthur Balfour, too, lived.

It was nearing tea-time, and still no messenger from the Palace. They finished tea. And they went on waiting, as the hours went by, with growing inner agitation.

At last there was the fateful bell at the front door and Lord Stamfordham, the King's Private Secretary, was admitted, looking shamefaced and not a little confused; confused not at all, apparently, by having kept his friend on the rack of suspense. No. He had come on a much more onerous errand.

The King, on Arthur Balfour's advice, had in fact sent for Mr. Baldwin. The reason? Oh, some technical argument, deemed, however, vital in these changed times – the necessity of a Prime Minister being in the House of Commons,

Lord Curzon looked dumbfounded. He quite understood. It was, of course, in the concatenation of present circumstances, the outgoing Prime Minister being unable to advise on his successor, constitutional for the sovereign to seek advice from an elder statesman. Though he should have thought that, as Bonar Law's chief lieutenant, he was the natural choice. Still . . . Curzon betrayed little or no sign of his feelings.

But when the front door closed on the King's Private Secretary, he collapsed in a chair and sobbed, sobbed like a child over the ruin of a fifty-year-old ambition which had this morning been within his grasp and this evening had eluded him for ever!

His rich American wife, who had basked in his glories, put her arms around him, but he would not be consoled. Baldwin. Baldwin of all men! "A man of the utmost insignificance! But not even a public figure!" he sobbed.

But at the Carlton Club meeting he was already composed and austere. He was even suave. Mr. Baldwin had been called, he said, from his squire's duties so dear to his heart, to the graver duties of First Minister of the Crown. He must abandon the country life, however he might miss it, for the sterner task of leading the Government, although, if the truth were known, Mr. Baldwin would far sooner have stayed in Bewdley to tend his pigs. The moral, however, was clear. The pigs must wait.

82

POLITICAL PROTESTANTISM

Hitler's career is the triumph of the protesting commonplace. If you compare it with, say, Beethoven's, the protesting revolutionary mystic, you become aware of a striking difference. In Beethoven's case, it is a slow struggle through the Courts of Europe, notably the pumpernickel Courts of Germany, a solicitation of the favour of pumpernickel princes by letters addressed to their chamberlains and ministers. Goethe, as a man of genius himself, might have been expected to show willingness and understanding. But he showed only, at that particular period of his own development, a constitutional aversion to immoderation of sound, the fury of rebellion as expressed perhaps in the *Appassionate*, and the social aversion of the well-groomed courtier to Beethoven's gauche cockiness, and a personal aversion to his general uncleanliness.

In Hitler's case, the technique is radically different. It seemed to have consisted in aiming empty bottles at his adversaries, and in a certain quick erect decisiveness of gait in approaching your platform. Apparently it is the standard rule, for we have seen the same jerky pace and rather absurd un-English bearing in Mosley entering a hall with his bodyguard. No longer the slow pedestrian amble of a Cabinet Minister of the old school. Fighters all, apparently, and, chiefly, for fighting's sake.

Hitler – the overtone of everything – the *reductio ad absurdum* of all the creeds – patriotism, nationalism, my-country-right-or-wrong-ism, Realpolitik, materialism, masonry, even communism and Judaism – here they all were, naked and unashamed, personified in that unsmiling, rather imbecile face.

The rise of Fascism, Italian and German, was a form of Protestantism – political middle-class Protestantism against proletarian orthodoxy. It was also faintly irritated by old-family advantages, and in Germany positively goaded into fury by low-class Jewish wealth. Fascism gathered impetus from dissatisfaction of middle-class men who had tasted adventure in the Great War and who now returned to their office stools and ledgers, which they had left for foreign parts to enjoy some authority as non-commissioned officers or temporary officers during the four years of the struggle. Ne'er-do-wells, others out of luck, had not even an office stool to return to. They lacked either the hereditary seat of the aristocratic, or the dividends of the plutocratic youth who, coming home, willingly beat their swords into ploughshares. They lacked artistic vocations which are their own reward. The Fascists were the army of the disinherited, the unemployed, the non-artistic malcontents denied recognition.

Void alike of aristocratic traditions, regarding any inquiry into their unwritten privileges as in bad taste, and of a super-scrupulous attitude to property encouraged by those anxious to consolidate their gains, the Nazi-Fascists developed a cynicism to cover their sentimentality in desiring the trophies and trappings of a caste they admired while professing to despise.

The Fascist idea did not take root in England, where nobody (as King Edward VII had said when invited to become President of the French Republic) who was a doctor wished to turn veterinary surgeon. Aristocracy in England was too much the genuine thing for anyone to be fobbed off with a Nazi imitation.

The social struggle developing towards the end of the nineteen-twenties was also a conflict with Marxist orthodoxy – Moscow communism aspiring to the conception that all men are brothers, and finding it necessary in furtherance of this ideal to resort to the brutal practice of master and man – if only temporarily on behalf of the men.

Lenin and Proust, born within a year and dead within eighteen months of each other, each applied himself to the same essential task of abstracting from the common illusion this evil error of an imagined superiority of birth: the one practically, through revolution, the other artistically, through analysis.

Lenin was born in 1870, the year France, after Sedan, became a republic. Proust was conceived in Paris the same year. One passed a sponge over the evils of class distinctions over one-fifth of the earth's solid surface and left a clean slate, though what appeared on it since does not, to date, always make pretty reading. The other dissected and finally stripped bare, in a new psychometry, the social fabric of every self-delusion of hereditary nobility, and left the impression that our vanities are all irretrievably tattooed with the mark of the social beast. Snobbery he dissected to the bone and, but for the bone, all the social ills that flesh was heir to he traced to snobbery. It was not for Proust a question of whether we agreed with him about the superficial symptoms. It was a question whether we had eyesight keen enough to follow his dissection of human vanity to the bone.

That Proust, besides being a scientist of snobbery was, though he vehemently denied it, a snob himself has merely served his end in providing him with his own painful vanity upon which to perform a slow and full-scale vivisection. "Perhaps," he said, "it is only in really vicious lives that the moral problem can arise in all its disquieting strength. And of this problem the artist finds a solution in the terms not of his own personal life but what is for him the true life, a general, a literary solution. As the great Doctors of the Church began often, without losing their virtue, by acquainting themselves with the sins of all mankind, out of which they extracted their own personal sanctity, so great artists often, while being thoroughly wicked, make use of their vices in order to arrive at a conception of the moral law that is binding upon us all."

Lenin, a man of narrowly premeditated action, declared himself prepared, and indeed has travelled some distance towards that ideal, to exterminate three-quarters of the human race if only the remaining quarter survived to be communists. Proust, an artist testifying to the hopelessness of purging man of his social vanity, died commending – to such men as were able to analyse their vanities – the perusal of his new psychometry. Lenin, despairing of reforming predatory man by holding out to him like an ikon the ideal of a classless society, let loose the hungry rabble to pillage the stocks of the more provident peasants, and died fingering lovingly, with an imbecile grin, a gun, in the confusion of his mangled mind no longer able to identify whom exactly it was he wished to kill.

BOOK FIVE

THE NINETEEN-THIRTIES

83

THE COLLOCATIONS OF THE SUFFERING UNIT

Our common civilisation, instead of being built, as one would think it should be, on the innate common decency of the average citizen, rallies round place names and abstractions into inordinately large bodies – brainless monstrosities accommodating themselves to the mentality of the lowest gangster in their midst. We do so on the hypothetical and, in the circumstances, not entirely improbable assumption that the rival huge group is similarly placed. That is, it is in the same artificial position of having, for the sake of group loyalty, to subscribe to the sentiments of perpetual panic engineered by men of exceptionally low cunning amongst both them and us, and the defensively aggressive outlook, which goes with panic, of the lowest common denominator in the group – namely, of a murderer.

The world certainly did not want a second world war. It was, again, trapped into it, this time by the Nazis and Fascists revelling openly in their principles of violence and deceit. Our real fault was not that we were not armed, but that we failed to bring about a universal change of heart when, having won the First World War, we had the opportunity to do so between 1918 and 1930.

In the year of his death, 1910, Tolstoy observed, with reference to his wife and the state of the world at large, that periodically mankind was assailed by an attack of mass insanity, when, with few exceptions, in the general madness taking hold of whole populations, the individual succumbs to the epidemic without being aware of it. The time of the Inquisition must have been such a period. A complete aberration of a sense of proportion and of natural priority in human values seized the minds of masses of people. Torture and mutilation, blackmail, and confession extracted under duress, informers ready to betray family secrets, and the wholesale sacrifice of filial and natural affections, all this was being offered up in the name of some dogmatic notion which considered the sacrifice of all these things of small account in return for the Church's I.O.U. of eternal life.

The modern equivalent of the Inquisition, State worship, demanding instantly the supreme sacrifice from the suffering unit to avert some hypothetical future supreme sacrifice, is another form of the same mass aberration of elementary sense. Class warfare waged in the name of classless society is yet another. All these exact, and get, their fill of martyrs, whose fortitude under duress is extolled in the annals of human deeds. A curious predilection, this, for wanting to see men die 'honourably' for their opinions, when it is precisely this vexatious *difference* of opinion which is considered at all times as meriting a dog's death. No less curious is the historian's commendation of heroism on both sides, since it is this heroism on both sides in support of merely a contentious opinion which is to blame for deferring indefinitely the sweetness and the poetry of living in the present.

Of all mass insanities, the latest and most virulent is the *Führerprinzip*. When one considers that it is neither new nor proved sound or durable or beneficial in the past, and then observes the hypnotic enthusiasm with which whole masses of populations over large tracts of the earth are calling to be led, in the name of an outworn principle which decrees that they be so led, to slaughter, one begins to wonder whether they can really be 'all there'.

The idea of 'leadership' so often merely means the knack of ordering men about with an 'effortless consciousness of one's own superiority', and that ideal, by no means desirable, was fostered in the English public schools. The adage that whatsoever thou sowest, that thou shalt reap, is not confined to condign punishment following sharply on the heels of naked guilt. It is operative even in imponderables. The system of fags and prefects, of the team spirit, the idea of leadership, of playing for one's side – in a word, the collective spirit of our public schools, even the boy-scout movement, all patiently paved the way for the heavy-booted German conception. While the English were resting on their laurels, relaxing in their games, beginning to take it all with a pinch of salt, the Nazi movement was already at it, exaggerating into unconscious caricature our much-vaunted team spirit – in their hands, the *Führerprinzip*!

One knows the type so well: the prefect who in later life cannot find employment commensurate with the authority he exercised at school; a sad type, quiet at his humdrum job but, when drawn out in conversation, betraying a glowing loyalty to the collective principle, and with a latent wish to put everyone to rights.

Even Goethe, in the eighteen-twenties, deplored the habit of German young men to take refuge from life in studiousness for its own sake. All earnest, spectacled, from undue devotion to the printed page; interested only in the esoteric, the high falutin'; narrow-chested, wheezy; forever bowing from the waist, clicking their heels; over-deferential to authority and awkward in society. "Look at our young English visitors," he pointed out to Eckermann. "What splendid young men! Whatever may be said against them, they are, every one of them, complete, self-assured, life-worshipping youths imbued with fine physique and natural spontaneous manners. Every one of them is complete. Some no doubt are fools. Even so, they are complete fools."

With some acerbity, Goethe observed that while pale young Germans were splitting philosophic hairs, the young English barbarians were bestraddling the globe and, in their stride, annexing territories apparently in need of overlords. Goethe also commended to German attention the English habit of justifying their annexations on moral grounds, thus anticipating Kipling's stupidly sincere interpretation of this unconscious habit as 'the white man's burden', which Hugh Kingsmill later wittily defined as 'a sack of the black man's gold'.

Nothing that Goethe said would be lost on the painstaking German scholars. William II, too, looked longingly towards the playing-fields of England and deplored the German aversion to strenuous exercise in the open air. An incurably romantic nation, the Germans; when they finally did adopt the English ideas, it was with Teutonic *Tüchtigkeit*. The British absent-minded habit of regarding their own suzerainty of other continents as a providential trust on behalf of the native for the good of the native, the Germans interpreted as cynicism of the Machiavellian order. Romantically-minded to the last, they introduced, in pious emulation of the English, their *Realpolitik*, priding themselves far and loud upon their unashamed military policy of smash and grab, sustained in the diplomatic field by a sort of esoteric philosophy, the Will to Cheat, exercised in full daylight in the proud sight of Thor, the German God.

But, as in social climbing where dissimulation argues a certain sense of honest shame, while the frank intention 'to better yourself' revolts by its stark naked shamelessness, so in politics moral rhetoric (the English malady) is, if more irritating, less nauseating than the inveterate martial rhetoric of Germans. The German shouts that he is strong and therefore fine and right to take what and where he wants. The Englishman insinuates himself into the barns and warehouses of others with an air of coy protective shyness, in the sincere belief that he is too good to live.

84

THE FUNERAL

Chamberlain, knight of the woeful countenance, as somebody called him, and Chancellor of the Exchequer, was seen in a news-reel on Budget Day leaving his house, standing a minute or two on his step, with his wife and his despatch case, to pose and say a few sentences before motoring to the House of Commons.

And this is what he said.

You know Shelley's poem. 'O Wind! *If* Winter comes, *can* Spring be far behind!' The poetry, the longing, the nostalgia, compressed into this singing question!

This is not, however, how it struck the man from Birmingham.

He cleared his throat. He gave a knowing grin. "As the poet said" (as though there was only one poet), " 'When winter comes, spring can't be far behind!' " His mouth snapped to like a mouse-trap – the flicker of a crooked smile – and the Chancellor was gone.

A Member of Parliament came back with this story from Germany. They did not apparently think much of the run of British Cabinet Ministers out there. "*Aber der Ba-al-dwin, na! das ist ein Kopf!*" That was another story. Here we had a statesman of the highest calibre. And all the time, up their sleeves, they were arming.

Lord Beaverbrook's first visit to the Kremlin in the company of Lady Louis Mountbatten and Arnold Bennett, was followed by another team. Shaw and Lady Astor paid a visit to Stalin, Shaw reporting on his return that Stalin's quiet courtesy was that of a man essentially at his ease, not apparently at all, it seems, intimidated by . . . the sheer flashing brilliance of his interlocutors.

Wells once described Shaw as a jackdaw. And perhaps the term 'crow' would have occurred to many a newspaper reader made aware of Lady Astor's frequent interjections in the House of Commons. Why the master of the Union of Soviet Socialist Republics should not feel otherwise than completely at ease, confronted by two such alien political crows ignorant of his language, is not apparent. Any ready verbal repartee, moreover, for which Shaw is justly famous, was sure to be blunted, if not entirely deformed, in the handling of an interpreter more nearly intimidated by Stalin's power of life and death than by Shaw's force of words, to pay much attention to the niceties of an epigrammatic rendering, more satisfying to Shaw than to Stalin.

They returned from that home of experimental socialism to an England still the refuge of deposed kings. Alfonso complained to Castlerosse that George V had treated him coldly when he arrived here as a refugee from his own people. And perhaps the King had more sympathy for monarchs like Nicholas II, who preferred to die in their own country rather than seek refuge abroad.

England's was an amazingly gentle temper. Lights behind open curtains of enormous windows in West End clubs revealed to the gaping unemployed the sight of well-groomed gentlemen in evening dress sitting down to dine well. A unique sight, this, far too dangerous for the class-torn capitals of continental Europe, where wealth and opulence hid themselves behind heavy drawn curtains, shamefaced from hungry eyes.

But the day came when Britain went off the gold standard. This immensely rich country, which had been subsidising other nations and was the envy of Europe, suddenly, one morning in the autumn of 1931, found itself on the verge of bankruptcy. How it happened nobody could explain. That night a group of people were dining together, two or three immensely rich men, a financial expert, an economist, two ex-Chancellors of the Exchequer, a Rothschild, a Midland Bank director, a President of the Rolls-Royce Company, most of them now dead. And not one of them could understand or explain to his fellow magnates what had happened or what would happen next. The atmosphere was that of wealthy people on the *Titanic*, whose sense of doom was aggravated by what they had to lose in addition to their lives.

The request for French bullion to oblige us for this once by causing it to flow from that to *this* side of the Channel to prop up our wobbling currency, when it could only seem normal to them to see it flow towards them, to the French appeared almost obscene. But calculating carefully the profits and safeguards they, at last, still wonderingly, as though still in a dream, still marvelling at themselves and us, agreed.

The summer of 1935 saw the austere and sturdy London transform herself into a London of maypoles, to celebrate the silver jubilee of King George V. Piccadilly, illumined by strings of coloured beaded lights, all in garlands, was a leisurely promenade, every vehicle banned. The pedestrian had come back into his own. Englishmen lost their reserve. Gay chains of people overtook strangers and swept them along with them, galloped together down traffic-deserted Park Lane, sweeping along whatever fish was caught in the net. The Ritz was flood-lighted. Sounds of music and laughter. Soft illuminations under the tender spring sky. Venice carnival scenes. Bursts of song. They were dancing in Bond Street.

But a few months later, on January 20th, 1936, King George V, who had been astonished by his own popularity and had spoken from a full heart when, with a catch in his voice, he said, on the evening of his Jubilee, "My very dear people, how can I tell you what I feel . . .", was dying. "The King's life," read a late bulletin, "is moving peacefully to its close."

Before he expelled his last breath he inquired of his Lord President of the Council, James Ramsay MacDonald, "How's the Empire?" and on receiving from Ramsay, satisfied with his Stresa[1] the 'All's Well', nodded his habitual brief nod of royal dismissal, and gave up his soul to God.

His hands rested on the counterpane: Queen Mary put her own over his. Before midnight he was dead, the third English sovereign within living memory to mature, grow old and die.

The Prime Minister, Stanley Baldwin, stayed at his post in London, as though he and the prospective King, who flew to Sandringham and back, had the restive future in their trusty hands and could not risk letting go while the old King up there in Norfolk was being super-annuated from a perishable to an imperishable crown. It was not, however, long before Honest Stan was hatching his plot to demote the popular young sovereign from his royal prerogatives to a private life terminating in the governorship of the Bahamas.

It is the symbolic meaning of a royal funeral procession which strikes one most forcibly. The staff officer marching alone, at the head of it all, seemed conscious of the gravity of his position. He set the pace. And when people caught a glimpse of him at the bend of a street, they grew conscious of what he was leading. The superb slow dignity of his step suggested the measure of the increasingly majestic procession in his wake.

The same feeling was accentuated by the sight of the young Duke of Norfolk, hereditary Earl-Marshal of England, who, at a distance, led, as it were, the main body of the procession, the staff officer having served as an introduction. The most dramatic figure of all, of course, was the frail descendant of kings following immediately behind His defunct Majesty's coffin.

The contrast was complete. We had seen all the visible symbols of a great and mighty empire file past us in a contrast of colours and uniforms, and now, lying in a coffin, which implied our common mortality, was the monarch who had been the virtual head of all this pomp and glory. Following, stepping wearily, walked the new Sovereign. Such is the power of human imagination that it is a matter of indifference to us whether a king is tall, small, old, young, stout, or

---

[1] The Stresa Conference of April 1935, at which MacDonald and Mussolini united in condemning Germany's violations of her obligations under the Treaty of Versailles.

slender. Queen Victoria was a small woman. King Edward VII was of ample girth. The late King was of medium build. King Edward VIII, small and slim. In every case the popular idea of kingship is enhanced by the contrast to a previous monarch. The king is the repository of a nation's emotions; he is the personification of the aspirations and latent power of his subjects. "There he goes," we say as he passes, and whether he has a beard or is clean-shaven, whether he be old or young, he seems just right, just what he ought to be.

Each band as it passed contributed its quota of funeral music. And sometimes you heard the tail-end of one band while the next band already impinged itself on your aural consciousness. Funeral processions adhere strictly to tradition. How much more effective if, instead, orchestras of seasoned musicians had been stationed at selected points to receive the approaching procession with classic examples of the most poignant and shattering orchestral music. Though the procession was eloquent in itself, the music did not shake with sobs, did not break with love and pity, did not pierce with supra-human sorrow, as the best orchestral funeral music of Beethoven, of Mozart, of Chopin and Wagner would have done. But the situation was eloquent in itself.

The beautiful gold and red carriages of the Queen and the Royal Princesses, sheltering behind plate glass, symbolised, by their opulence and remoteness from common things, the rather tragic isolation of royalty from the ordinary joys of life. Queen Mary, as she sat upright in her carriage, must have remembered that on previous state occasions she had invariably sat by the side of him whom now she was following to his last solitary abode of stone and granite, from which there was nothing in royal power that could save him for a more kindly, human, more accustomed fate which might enable him, for instance, to come back at the end of a heavy day's work and have tea with her, as of old, in a warm room. No, it was as though he had walked out of their Norfolk home to where none could trace him and from where he could not find his way back to a wife, a kingdom and an empire in which all loved him and wished to serve him, and to all of whom he was devoted heart and soul.

85

ABDICATION AND CORONATION

The medieval heralds silver-trumpeted at the proclamation of King Edward VIII, only to trumpet again ten months and twenty days later to proclaim King George VI. If anything emerged from Mr. Baldwin's expert informality at presenting matters irrelevant to the issue, it was that the abdicating King (by virtue apparently of the mellowing sweetness in renunciation rendered more appreciative of honest Stan) and himself would be firmer friends than ever before. One is perhaps permitted to wonder, however, whether there is any regular exchange of mail between Bewdley and the Bahamas. The cold-shouldering of the Duke of Windsor by the British public has its parallel in the traditional attitude to romantic figures, such as Nelson and Byron and even Oscar Wilde, who, after a period in life when treated as though they were dead and buried, later, when properly in their tombs, become peculiarly live subjects for romantic biography. It is generally such neglected figures who later commend the Englishman to the attention of the Continent and the United States as not being quite so wooden as they might otherwise deduce from their experience of acquaintances in English trains.

The Coronation, following on the heels of the Abdication, was put over in a big way to cancel the painful impression caused by an adored monarch who in a moment had thrown on to the scrap heap all the millions of mugs and plaques adorned with his face. Now, to catch up, we had to pump, in four months, into the once Duke of York what had been pumped of popular affection into the Prince of Wales in the past twenty-five years. Indeed, there was not a minute to spare. The Archbishop of Canterbury, who had had a hand in speeding on his way hence one who, Queen Mary herself was said to have insisted before her other sons, was their King, turned from the Lords to the Commons with the solemn words, "Sirs, I present to you your undoubted King George."

At the head of the procession, when it came into sight at the bend of the Ring, was a mounted officer who could not manage his prancing steed. The horse sidled, refused to walk on, and finally about-turned altogether and for a while led tail forward; then he fell back and another horse took the lead.

The massed bands of His Majesty's Household Cavalry were pounding to the strains of the march 'Under the Double Eagle' and behind came the serried ranks of regiment after regiment, led by their own bands, a dexterous Scot turning, then throwing, a pole high into the air, catching it, all as if to stress by this seeming irregularity, even levity, the uncompromising effortless precision of his military step.

Troop after troop, band after band, they came up, piping and pounding, and passed out of sight. The armed forces of the Empire, as units of foot and horse, gun, sea and air passed before one, did not seem inadequate to our imperial commitments. White-capped sailors with a girl in every port went by and were cheered; and airmen as yet unloved, unacclimatised; and Canadians and Australians, with their wind-swept prairie and 'we're-*of*-you-if-you've-forgotten-it' look, marched lightly in their juvenility after the massed, cowed, uniformed and licked-into-shape lower orders of Britain. Came contingents from the subject races with that chocolate-and-almond 'proud-to-serve-you' look. All went by and more came, and again still more marched or pranced with their ensigns fluttering on their lances.

A trifle too many of them, perhaps; too many weapons. One might have wished to see thrown in a few painters and intellectuals, Bloomsbury types in loose flannels, even a golfer or two in plus-fours. Something more representative. Not all this *right! left! right!* It tired the eye.

But here came the carriages – rulers and bureaucrats, old, sedentary, seedy, bath-chair cases almost, in unfamiliar nautical headgear, and yet the real masters, they the arbiters of life and death over all these serried ranks of young and fit – and, paradoxically, *armed* – manhood. And here, now last, in inverse order of importance, Mr. Baldwin, Premier of Britain, with his indispensable escort, first lever on the keyboard of his power, the Metropolitan Police. Then bunches of assorted Royalty, foreign and home-grown, and then, and then – more troops, more heralds and trumpeters and –

There it comes. The fairy-tale golden coach as if hesitating on its course, nervously crunching the gravel, daintily picking its course, drawn by so many groom-bestridden horses and no proper coachmen to guide it, on its wooden, rather cart-like, royal wheels. The long-awaited climax – inside Their (newly-crowned) Majesties.

86

HOMUNCULUS

The Age had all the foibles of past ages served up for us anew, like a stale sausage and two veg left over, warmed up for our delectation.

In 1814 Alexander I and the King of Prussia had been carving up Saxony in the name of 'the New Europe'. The Germans had fought a War of Liberation against Napoleon, who, later on St. Helena, retrospectively conceived that what he had probably been doing in overrunning the map was – aha! – to attempt – that was it – to create a United States of Europe.

German students in Goethe's time had struck a blow for liberty of speech. Russian students in Turgenev's day, a generation later, had done likewise. The young, always keen to detect inconsistencies in the moral rhetoric of the old, canalise their overflowing energies into panaceas. Soberly, however, there are but two compelling courses of action open to human beings. They can either follow Christ's solution for the Kingdom of Heaven on Earth by respecting their nearest neighbour's interests as well as they do their own. Or they respect their own more than their neighbour's, with all the incessant groupings and regrouping of loyalties, all the shunting and shifting and manoeuvring for position that this entails, while putting as good a face upon it as their natural hypocrisy and civilised inclination to soft-pedal self-interest allows.

The strength necessary to resist Christ instead of the world is compounded of all the weaknesses. It is easily come by. Our limited liability in that *Société Anonyme* called the world makes each of us disclaim all personal responsibility for any crime incurred by the Joint-Stock Company as a whole. No shareholder of a limited company is likely to reproach himself for the death of colliers in the company's mine in which he merely owns a number of shares, and no national feels responsible for his country's aggression.

But out of this evil, which we thought was anonymous and had no face, at last a monster, with but an approximately human visage, a head, a nose, a mouth, a brain, and staring fixed eyes, materialised. In bawling stupidly, yet effectively, that he cared for nothing – nothing mattered – but the aggrandisement of his Deutschland, he merely reduced to absurdity, but an anguished absurdity for which living beings parted for ever from those they loved most, a theory that had already enjoyed a pretty wide run over the earth. In putting into renewed use the banal adage that all is fair in love and war, he merely, again, reduced to its complete logical absurdity a practice hitherto no less wrong-headed and absurd, if softened by more courtly ways, a slower tempo and more handicraft, if no less pain, in disintegrating the suffering unit. A pitiful anachronism to the sub-human Hitler, Moloch of our Machine Age!

Hitler is homunculus. He is not Frankenstein. He is the indictment of the Ape-Man for whom the Son of Man, despite intermittent clarifiers of the message, like Tolstoy of late, apparently laboured in vain: an indictment in ape-man language, ape-man deeds, a vision of himself and a throwing back in the teeth of the Ape Man the bottomless futility of ape morality; God's Fifth Column, again. It is as if, despairing, Providence had said to man, "If you cannot be made to see the salvation inherent in disinterested behaviour, if your ape's brain will not carry you to the higher view, then you shall have the ape philosophy demonstrated to you to the full *in action*, that you may assess it in the ultimate conclusions of its logic, gauge it well in working order, that the blindest ape among you may appreciate in practice its *reductio ad absurdum*."

Everything of that which was foolish, childish, wicked, caddish, hypocritical or openly deceitful in the centuries' long dealings between man and man, between group and group, faith and faith, nation and nation; every half-truth, insincere insinuation, veiled threat, concealed brutality, mere heartlessness masquerading as stern purpose and long view; every mental reservation, vanity, priggishness, small measure, petty larceny, bullying, strutting with the chest out and throwing about of one's weight, which has burdened the earth since after it had cooled to life, here paraded unashamed as bright scoundrelly virtue which hitherto had been decently hooded, not openly admitted, or, if admitted, tacitly understood as things that must shun the light of day. But here came homunculus, the product of mere chemistry, the Son of Ape in Man who could deduce anything he liked and turn to personal account everything he wanted from available data in the history of human behaviour, but who had no soul, and therefore no conscience. Here came the morose mad scoundrel, as indeed Napoleon, the bright scoundrel, had come before him, who, too, had had no difficulty in abstracting duplicity from the befuddled ethics of both Church and State and turn it profitably to his own account, while enjoying his consummate acting in the role of benefactor of the human race, its sublime, its heaven-sent teacher.

Here indeed was Napoleon brought up to date, made transparently absurd – humanity's greed and self-seeking standing naked and exposed and, this time, glorying in its shamelessness. Whatever you may reproach him with, that he will fling back into your face. When we sent missionaries with Bibles to convert black natives to Christianity, was it really the Gospel of Love or of profit we had in mind? The white man's burden? A sack of the black man's gold! Then kill and rob to glory and cut the cackle. When we advertised the use of sundry tooth-pastes as the sole alternative to contracting pyorrhoea, were we, or were we not, cashing in on human fear? Then why not the propaganda of frightful-ness, the war of nerves? When advertising beauty creams with pictures of our lovelies nobly sporting coronets, were we not deliberately preying on the snobbish weaknesses of the ignorant and the credulous? Then why not flatter a whole nation with their imagined Nordic purity and superiority of race on which, to defend, they will expend their life's savings?

The Spaniards believed they had a divine right to kill the Incas and burn their temples in the name of Christ. An error so cruel as that cannot end there, and comes home to Europe to roost in its nest. Hitler thought the Germans had a racial right to kill the Jews and burn their temples in the name of Thor. Like all other evil deeds, his crimes cannot cancel themselves. The cleverness of Hitler's idea of race was this – that every European of the middle, lower and upper distances, who was not a Jew, a Eurasian, a Eurafrican – that is to say, the vast majority – would dwell with pleasure on the thought of being a natural patrician. The second string to his bow was that every natural person – again the vast majority – would dwell with pleasure on the thought that he was a patriot, even though the love of one's country usually takes the form of hating two-thirds of the people who live in it. Like virtue, which is merely the salt in the dish of life and should be taken for granted, love of one's country and what is called patriotism should be seen but not heard. Patriotism is indeed the last refuge of a scoundrel. But so is any 'ism'. A love of communism, of fascism, of internationalism, of pacifism, mili-tarism, even deism is always the same bankrupt confession: 'As Smith, Schulz, Laporte, Popoff, I am nothing – nobody. But as an English-man, a German, a Frenchman, a Russian, a Conservative, a Nazi, a member of the *front populaire*, a communist, internationalist, left-and-right deviationist, I am the pride of creation!' Hitler had a third string to his bow. He offered a classless socialism to socialists; a class non-socialism to conservatives; a new hierarchical climbing ladder for out-classed climbers with class ambitions.

Here was the triumph of the lowbrow in politics – Lloyd George carried to a logical conclusion. Hitler admired Lloyd George for lower-ing his arguments to the mindlessness of the vulgar mob. As in the astral light all ideas become personified – bearing out the reality of the Platonic Idea – so Hitler, having by mistake got through the swivel door into our concrete world, could not again remove his silly mug. That is

314

exactly how they did look: vulgar, silly, menacing, cock-eyed, strident, yelling, raving – the sum of those Aristotelian exploitations of Nature for purposes of power. He was homunculus – he their personification. Yes, this was *it* in person. And when they greeted him they said at first, "How do you do?" and then, overcome by the feeling that he was the Idea, shouted "Heil Hitler!"

Fascism and National Socialism were a counterblast to Communism, whose harping on the exclusive virtues of the social scum in the end provoked the better-born to protest self-consciously, and in a language intelligible to the proletariat, their own middle-class merits, hitherto genteel in expression. The Nazis did not want to advertise themselves as social pariahs, having already, through their own or their parents' exertions, risen to the level of the lower-middle class. They had tasted social ambition, and did not fancy going back to their class origins; they wanted to march forward to complete social triumph.

But since they could get no kudos out of stressing their intermediate social status, their aristocratic nostalgia found common ground with the patricians in stressing pride of race. They were, if not patricians, Germans, Italians, Rumanians, and, identifying themselves personally with the generic term of the nation, they discovered they could pound their chests with the best of them. It was as though, unable to claim membership of Brook's or White's Club, and unwilling to belong to a trade union, they stressed for all they were worth that they were, as members of the Automobile Association, first, last and foremost *clubmen* who must have the right of way.

Man does not, apparently, live by bread alone, or he would not have espoused the rival systems of Communism and National Socialism, which have left him short of bread and butter. That captains of industry should reside in their mansions was one thing. That the workers, who resented this, should throw them over and institute a system in which, with more self-respect, in equal citizenship, they were to be badgered by party bosses was another conception of life. But that, again, the Nazi wasps should suddenly let fly over the space occupied by the Marxist ants, and be exterminated by flying ants in the process of exterminating ants they had never before seen, is, as a picture of some three hundred million human beings each endowed with a free will and a sense of good and evil, completely fantastic.

What everyone wants in his heart of hearts is not communism or capitalism, but a home of his own with no one to boss him, confining his love of gregariousness, not to a factory with its foremen, but to a club. What people want by and large everywhere in the world is to be left alone to find their own gaiety of heart, all having plenty of money to spend in well-lit crowded cities, shops working in two shifts and open half the night, restaurants, open-air cafés, plenty of leisure, and deep vistas of fragrant countryside to go to for holidays. They don't want to be badgered by party bosses.

87

SEPTEMBER

As the decade rolled on, one man, Hitler, became the sole pre-occupation of an anxious mankind. Every decision, whether a business venture or a projected holiday abroad, seemed to hang fire, depend on Hitler's mood, whether the cloud presently might lift from his scowl, a sob break his roar. One week he bellowed marching orders, told his army to stand on tiptoe, await his word – March! The next, he said mankind positively refused to be slaughtered again on the battlefields of Europe, and, for his part, he prophesied a long peace.

There was little enough that was appealing or even human about the man. He had none of Napoleon's endearing human weakness of appearing glamorously successful to his family. Such relatives as he had left were confined to a waiter-nephew settled in England, where Hitler had been vainly trying to move the bigwigs to a *rapprochement* in which Germany was to have a free hand in Europe.

Hitler tried to placate us by speaking of National Socialism as 'not for export', a product, he said, 'made in Germany', using the last words in English. One imagines him, who fancied himself as the acute political psychologist never failing to make a calculated impression on simple souls, chuckling to himself over these words: "That will strike an answering note in the black commercial hearts!" With that peculiar inanity typical of the man knowing only his own language, Hitler imagined he was conferring a pleasure on Englishmen in treating them to three words of their own tongue atrociously pronounced.

But, like so many things that have not the intended result deduced to be infallible by the laws of psychology, the Englishman at home did not even report the three words rendered in his idiom, dwelling instead with a sumptuous smacking of the lips on *Lebensraum*, which he fondly added to his store of German words already assimilated, of which

Aufwiedersehen was the favourite and *Weltanschauung* the most ambitious, passing over 'Made in Germany' as a trite and vulgar commercialism utterly cheapened by association with inferior German goods.

How came it that the ex-corporal Hitler, who didn't know what to do with his hands or how to hold himself in front of Prussian generals before whom he involuntarily quailed and all but clicked his heels by reflex action, came to be able to shout for one general, 'Keitel!' How came it about?

The answer is that man, like other living organisms, evolves by trial and error. When Hitler first called out, 'Keitel!', without, to his surprise, by way of answer receiving a clout in the ear, he gradually increased the volume: 'Keitel! Here!', until his own roar by acquired habit grew to be synonymous with Keitel's entry.

He really is the 'little man', the misfit, the dull man realising his thwarted nature in wishful thinking, laying heavily about him in a dream in which, brilliant, glamorous, powerful, he retraces the frontiers of Germany with his pen, and does all the incalculable things you can do in a dream, only to awaken again to the thwarted, subordinate, awkward and somewhat foolish figure he cuts in reality, the nonentity with the commonplace name, Adolf Hitler, groping with bare toes for his slippers, as he rubs his eyes and wishes the dream back again. Only somehow he never does awaken. There he is, not a brilliant adventurer, like Napoleon, grasping the crown by the sheer daring of superior brain-power, but just an average man of middling intelligence, indistinguishable in mind and face from all the millions of clerks whose longing for might, majesty and dominion would seem to have suddenly incarnated itself in him, and to be driving him on and up in a dream that will not end.

If the dream was a bit sketchy at first, showed loose ends, it soon tightened up. The vague figures solidified into Goering and Goebbels. One after another, German generals drew near and addressed him with cringing deference. He sat, clownish, absurd, nursing a top-hat on his knee, by the side of the veteran Hindenburg, saw him safely into his grave and installed himself in his place. Ambassadors sought audiences with him, and he felt awkward. His hero Mussolini, school prefect to him, a new boy, became first his pal, then his fag. Schuschnigg, hurrying to his summons, opened a portfolio crammed with memoranda showing how and where the Germans were interfering in Austria's internal affairs. '*Our* internal affairs, Herr Hitler! I have the evidence *here*! look, *here*!' An angry, impatient gesture, and, lo, Schuschnigg and his portfolio ceased to be. And Hitler was standing erect in a car that crawled slowly through the hushed streets of Vienna.

He had never wanted to be Austrian. He had left Austria in order to be German, but some people still said he was not German, but Austrian. So there was nothing for it but to take Austria and add it to Germany, and so be able to say that as an Austrian he was a German. 'I present *my* Austria to *my* Germany. I have brought my home home.' Perfectly simple.

The dream held on, held on. It would not break. Here was Mr. Chamberlain, Prime Minister of Great Britain, himself, actually here, on the doorstep.

Yes, there he stood, the British Prime Minister, in the rain – on the lowest of the garden steps leading up to the Berghof, in Berchtesgaden. And Neville, if one may translate him into canine terms, expressed his slightly sneaking curiosity about that big, spotted continental hound he had heard barking beyond the Rhine, by a friendly, somewhat apprehensive wagging of the tail. They sniffed each other warily and wagged. Sniff and wag again, walking round each other in circles.

> Do you remember
> that day in September?

Mr. Chamberlain, convinced that he could get what he wanted, as he had done in his commercial days, by going out in person to get it, even if this time the tender was not a boiler but world peace, had wired to the Führer that he was coming to see him to talk things over. Hitler's reply that he was *sehr bereit* to see him was inflated in translation into positive eagerness, and commented upon as a relief for the German Chancellor, who was thus enabled to retreat from an untenable position without losing face.

Upon his return to England, Mr. Chamberlain took his trusting fellow-countrymen aback by observing naïvely that he never *realised* before how much Herr Hitler had the German cause at heart, and that to that extent Britain was apparently the gainer by the Premier's flying visit to Berchtesgaden. The public, remembering his description of himself as 'a go-getter for peace', hoped that perhaps that was the way to go about it, by slow stages, the first stage, now over, having been a first-hand insight into Herr Hitler's complicated psychology, evidently swayed by a partiality for Germans over Czechoslovakians. The Prime Minister delivered himself of a reassuring statement, this time culled not from Shelley but Shakespeare (of whom it was said he was an assiduous student), and the line he delivered to the world was: "From the nettle, danger, we pluck the flower, safety." And Sir Philip Gibbs was quick to rush out with a best-seller, *The Nettle Danger*, from the nettle, journalism, plucking the flower, money.

318

At Godesberg, where, Chamberlain said, the Führer, mindful of an older man's fatigue, had offered to meet him half way, Hitler put up an artificial rage, had telegrams brought in at short intervals to intimidate his British colleague, screaming that he wouldn't, he positively wouldn't, stand these Czech atrocities any longer – no, he would not! – he'd had enough – he'd march at once.

After all this play-acting, having come out on to the balcony, Hitler, in a perfectly natural, yearning voice, said, "Oh, I *so* hoped I would be able to show you this heavenly unbelievably beautiful view. And now – look, *what* a pity! – the clouds have completely obscured those really magnificent mountain tops!"

The clouds also darkened the political outlook. Daladier and Bonnet were invited to London, sat, they said, with their British colleagues around the conference table in the Cabinet Room, just like one happy family, happy but for the steadily declining international situation. When, on the eve of Munich, war seemed imminent, Chamberlain that night in his broadcast address to the nation was dignified and moving. His voice, his choice of words, betrayed that he at least felt a collective shame burning in his breast at the renewed imminent breakdown of the completely inadequate international structure upon which reposed the dearest wish of mankind, the modest wish to be allowed to live in peace. His old heart was assailed by an incredulity that, after all that had been said for two decades about the horror and futility of war, mankind should find itself once more in this absurd, this ludicrous and, compared with its intellectual wealth, undignified situation, peace hanging by a thread dangled wilfully before the world by a loud-mouthed paranoic. Feeling what decent people everywhere felt, and expressing it with an admirable economy of language, his style and delivery that evening were as fine and fitting as his quotations from Shelley and Shakespeare on earlier occasions had been absurd. "Isn't it horrible, fantastic!" – he paused, and in his voice were incredulity, lament and indignation, "that here in London to-day we should be digging trenches, distributing gas-masks?" And he searched his heart and said we must search ours before we were sure we wanted to stake all we had and knew and loved, perhaps the whole of the British Empire, for a remote country in Europe of which we knew little, and for an issue that to some of us was obscure. And he told of his endeavour to find a solution, and he had to say that he thought the German Chancellor's attitude was unreasonable.

To most people the root of the whole predicament was: why were we not better prepared? To this question Ramsay MacDonald's answer would have been that he could not arm effectively while in fact working for universal disarmament, and Baldwin's lips seem still to be sealed. How Germany was allowed to arm in secret and steal a march on her conquerors in the Great War is a question best answered by military attachés and the whole hierarchy of official responsibility. Ramsay MacDonald's real failure, seeing what he stood for, was in not pushing universal disarmament far enough. There were too many defensive-offensive reservations in all directions, and, in any case, to disarm partially while retaining national sovereignties is to mock at God's Fifth Column and court early correction in kind.

Arming as the one and only way to deal with armaments still makes, in the face of the intellectual bankruptcy of the idea, an irresistible prima facie appeal to manufacturers of armaments. Others, too, who call themselves practical men, never get beyond ideas of parity and superiority in this or that arm or area to secure a precarious balance of power, ignoring the genesis of the First World War. To consider men who think tanks and more tanks and still more tanks a solution for civilisation, who pride themselves on their realism because they are 'tank-minded' or 'air-minded', and so invite the speeding-up of the same tank-mindedness in the potential enemy, is as though only those were realists who, impressed by the colossal industrialisation of production everywhere in our day, bearing as little resemblance to the handloom of their sires as the tank bears to the spear, presently conceived that the most effective use they could make of a captured enemy plant was, after all, to hurl by way of total frightfulness live prisoners into the whirling and clanking monsters of our marvellous machine age in a warfare more accurately described as totally psychological.

If the people who wanted to keep Germany down let her emerge ten times as strong as themselves, is it not perhaps safer to have those people make the peace who do not proclaim such initial intentions?

88

MUNICH AND AFTER

Munich is sufficiently described by the word itself, because when anyone now says 'Munich' all know what it means. Churchill perhaps summarised most succinctly the three conferences. Hitler had asked at Berchtesgaden, and been promised, a pound; held out at Godesberg for two pounds, and finally compromised at Munich for one pound, seventeen shillings and sixpence.

And the missing half-crown rankled with Hitler, so that, enraged at the ovations his Munichers had been giving Chamberlain and Daladier in their capacity of champions of peace, he accelerated his preparations for war, gave the Jews the taste of a pogrom, and prepared to attack Czechoslovakia and seize Memel. In a speech to his people he derided the French and English by imitating the way they spoke German. Why, he said, those fellows don't speak *our* German: they are not of us. An attitude so palpably stupid can only be explained by his boast that, while Goebbels could sway the intelligentsia, he, Hitler, like Lloyd George, possessed the unique gift of appealing to the lowest, almost entirely *emotional*, intelligence of the broad masses.

Nathaniel Gubbins later gave his idea of how Germans speak English – or German.

"Vot vos dot?"

"Dot vos anodder bompf."

"A lot of bompfs der Britisch haf must."

"Der Reich Marshal Goering say dot on her Sherman soil no bompfs vill drop."

"Der Fuehrer say dot last August der var will over be."

"Der bompfs drop and der var not over iss."

Hugh Kingsmill tells, soon after the Jewish pogrom with which Hitler expressed his own resentment of Munich, of two Bournemouth old maiden ladies, sisters, giving their opinion of Hitler. "I am sure," one of the sisters says, "that he is *much* more reasonable than people suppose. It is very sad about the Jews, but Mr. Chamberlain has said what he thinks about that, and Herr Hitler must realise he has made a mistake there."

But Hitler wanted a full stage, and all the paraphernalia of alarms, excursions, trumpets and the full cry of war, as a décor for his personality. Mussolini, too, deplored that, unlike those of Julius Caesar, his own triumphs had merely been civil ones.

Meanwhile Chamberlain was fulfilling an engagement undertaken at Munich to visit Mussolini who, in his time, had gone yachting with Chamberlain's brother Austen and presented Austen's wife with an enormous bouquet of orchids, all the Chamberlains thinking Benito rather a dear.

Mussolini, to impress on Chamberlain, on his passage through Paris on his way to Rome, that he had difficulty in keeping down Italian aspirations, had got his Fascist rabble to shout lustily for "Nice! Tunis!

Corsica!'' Chamberlain and Halifax, having taken tea with Daladier and big-nosed Bonnet at the Quai d'Orsay, dropping a hint that European stability called for give and take, France to do the giving, proceeded to Rome. Daladier the while, to discourage Chamberlain from making a present to Mussolini of the French Mediterranean as easily as he had given the Südetenland to Hitler, addressed a broadcast to Italy in which, manfully and sharply, he defined his concessions and rejections as coming into two distinct categories of *Oui!* and *Non!*

On the point of collaboration, whatever that might mean – *Oui!* Eventual discussion of differences with a view to possible minor readjustment – *Oui!*

As for being intimidated into anything definite or immediate – *Non!* Any cession of French interests – *Non!*

As all the concrete points were dismissed in advance with a *Non!* and only windy words made the subject of a *Oui!*, Mussolini instructed his rabble to augment their cries for 'Nice! Tunis! Corsica!', to which they added 'Djibouti!' and 'Savoy!'

Meanwhile Mr. Chamberlain and Lord Halifax were nearing Rome, wondering whether there would be anybody to receive them at the station, and were welcomed by Mussolini looking like a fat cinema porter, with Ciano, the melodramatic villain of an almost Levantine shadiness of expression: Chamberlain was wearing his funereal garb and false smile, more than ever the undertaker (or perhaps a mourner), and Halifax, a giraffe in a cartoon for juveniles, with a small bowler hat superimposed between his ears to invest the quadruped with nominal human qualities.

During the banquet Chamberlain, conforming to a plan forming part of the parcel of his general policy of appeasement, gave His Majesty's Government's sanction to the successful subjugation of 'leaping Ethiopians' by drinking the health of their new master as 'His Majesty King Victor Emmanuel of Italy, Emperor of Ethiopia'.

Maria Korda, speaking soft Italian to the Duce, inquired murmuringly, "Excellenza, why don't you become imperatore?"

Mussolini, taking her by the waist and looking into her eyes, 'Do you see any difference?'

They were taken to the Opera, appeared standing in a row, the four of them, at the front of a box, in sober evening dress, Mussolini and Ciano not lacking stars and ribbons across their shirt-fronts; Halifax embellished with the Garter and Star of India; Chamberlain without anything. Why is the British Prime Minister, who can make and unmake not only Ministers but even sovereigns, himself invariably despoiled of any visible honours and titles? It is merely in conformity with other left-handed English customs which make traffic keep to the left; dump the

Prime Minister's official residence, office and Cabinet Room in a cul-de-sac; call the most exposed and universally badgered cipher of the rank and file a 'private', though no one could enjoy less privacy, and a hundred other introverted habits of a shy, retiring people.

Hitler put matters in such a way as to enable Neville to draw the logical conclusion that, as Slovakia was no longer hyphened to Czechia, there was no longer any Czecho-Slovakia, and what was to become of Czechia was nobody's business. Neville spoke of the rape of Czecho-Slovakia in the tone of a chairman of a board meeting announcing to the share-holders the closing down for lack of custom of a provincial branch bank. But when he understood the force of general indignation in the country, it suddenly struck him how deeply he himself had been shocked, under-neath, though it had taken his emotions a little time to percolate to the surface, and in a speech at Birmingham he impugned Hitler's good faith. What interested him – what he wanted to know – was whether this was the end of an old series of adventures or the beginning of a new. We were, he felt, entitled to know.

But Hitler did not tell us.

Having given Prague the choice of his own trusteeship as an alter-native to being razed to the ground, the conquering hero returned to Berlin, to be acclaimed at the station by Goering as a man who had restored a priceless gift – decency – to Germans. The Berlin radio com-mentator, beside himself with ecstasy, regaled his listeners with word-pictures of the ceremony on the arrival platform. "And now," he said, "the Führer has approached the Diplomatic Corps . . . *und drückt dem Japanischen Botschafter so ganz bonsonders herzlich die Hand.*"[1] He then did a sort of solitary goose-step between cheering crowds lining the streets. He was badly put together; nothing seemed to fit anything else. The nether parts of his legs did not seem to fit the upper parts; the upper parts were not properly joined to the hips; he took unduly long strides, about three inches more than was natural. He seemed to wobble on his legs but maintained a kind of artificial athleticism, making up for his wobble by being deliberately martial, as though to charm himself into precarious equilibrium.

After taking the call several times from the Chancellery balcony, he retired, it was explained, to attend to the situation which had (this was not explained) meanwhile taken a turn for the worse, Mr. Chamber-lain's indignation having had time to work itself up from the depth to the surface of his being, where it had found vocal expression.

---

[1] ". . . and shakes the Japanese Ambassador's hand with a quite peculiar heartiness."

89

THE AMOEBA OF WAR

Having slipped up over the Südetenland and allowed Hitler to roll up Czecho-Slovakia to its entire disappearance from the realm of dialectical politics, Neville, now bereft of continental responsibilities and in a position of espousing Lord Beaverbrook's very sensible policy of Splendid Isolation by capping it, moreover, with an offer to America of full union, was instead looking about him for another crown of thorns with which to wrack the sleep and vigil of his countrymen with a septuagenarian's groans and sighs. He found it in guaranteeing, overnight, Danzig and the Polish Corridor, and, guaranteeing countries having gone to his head, he quickly guaranteed the rest of Poland, Rumania, Turkey and, somewhat against her will, even Greece. All these were guarantees against German aggression, with the result that it made them even more frightened than before of Germany.

How came it that, lamentably below strength ourselves, we took on these new commitments? How came it that one so cautious, so well-trained in conservative business methods, as Mr. Chamberlain, should have, overnight, become a reckless gambler? Chamberlain's excessive meticulousness suddenly running riot in recklessness is a feature not unknown to psychologists. It would have been far better for him and the world to have made up his mind quickly that he was not going to have a war at any price. Germany would then have attacked Poland and Russia (which she did in any case), allowing Britain and France time to bring their armaments to the required strength, and sparing the ordeal of Norway, Belgium and the Netherlands. If Russia was not as strong in 1939 as in 1941, nor was Germany herself, and the tug of war, less destructive to either side, would have been relatively the same in the result. Instead, Chamberlain, having after exhaustive hesitation and misgivings, once got under way of guaranteeing countries right and left (enough, indeed, to make Lord Grey of Fallodon turn in his grave), he threw discretion to the winds, driven on by sheer force of momentum and as though defying the British Left Wing to call him an appeaser. The governments Chamberlain and Halifax were guaranteeing were at the time chiefly Fascist dictatorships which, one would have thought, might have known how to get on with their largely ideological neighbours without requiring a free democracy to take them under her wing. Russia, with which it would have been profitable to have made an early alliance (at any rate, before distributing guarantees to smaller countries) was being rubbed up the wrong way for not conforming to British public-school standards.

Compared with the endless trouble taken by trustees in, for instance, eliminating risk by insuring and re-insuring the property of wards in chancery, and the caution with which the whole financial edifice is propped up on all sides against contingencies of every kind, the fool-hardy hazard, with which Mr. Chamberlain and Lord Halifax alone staked the existence of the whole British Empire on the question of Danzig and the Corridor, reveals that the higher the stake the bigger the risk which men of affairs, whose instinct for caution has been exhausted in the smaller cares of business and private life, are prepared to take.

But just because their private patience and caution had been exhausted by months of tension and humiliation, and they were weak and hollow now, the amoeba of war espied them as an easy prey: it flowed round them, incorporated them, and oozed on.

Colonel Beck arrived in London dressed unconventionally in a canary-coloured-cum-teddy-bear sort of British warm, with his wife, said to be the best-dressed woman in Warsaw, and was met on the arrival platform at Victoria, as prescribed by diplomatic protocol, by his opposite number, Lord Halifax, replete in astrakhan coat and small bowler hat set between his protruding big ears. He had a vacant, wondering expression, as though half aware that he had been wholly incorporated by the amoeba and must ooze along now, flowing round anything that might turn up, incorporating that, and oozing on.

They were, the pair of them, Chamberlain and Halifax, implementing a hasty and, by all considerations, most ill-advised unconditional guarantee they had given Poland, suddenly over the week-end, on the spur of the moment. Hitler had made a laughing-stock of Chamberlain, pocketing what they had all so cordially guaranteed together. And, when tempers in Westminster ran high, Halifax had put his foot down and goaded Neville into ill-considered action. And Neville, just to show he was not afraid of Hitler, guaranteed some more.

When on Good Friday Mussolini attacked Albania, in Berlin it was emphasised that this was indeed a *démarche* for which the German Government had *ein vollkommenes Verständnis*.

Having taken Memel in his stride, with the world too agape at Axis robbery with assault to notice a mere piece of shop-lifting, Hitler turned his 'sickening technique' upon Poland.

Beck said in a soft even voice, very quietly and without emphasis, in the Polish Diet, that it was not compatible with the dignity of a sovereign nation to give up something for nothing. There is a Mr. Dad in one of H. G. Wells's novels who thrusts his hands deep in his trouser pockets, "an indignant man, a business man asked to give up something for nothing". Only Beck was not a recalcitrant business man, but a Polish diehard, one of the 'Group of Colonels' with the idea ingrained in their natures that they formed the backbone of Poland, which usually means a Poland with themselves in the saddle and intent on sticking to all they have got, and to all intents and purposes this attitude, whether in business or in politics, is sufficiently the same.

90

BEFORE THE BOMBS

In the summer of 1939 Lebrun came to London to return the visit of the King and Queen to Paris. There is something strangely moving about national exchanges of civilities. It is probably the punctilious politeness, eloquent of good breeding, a sensitive eagerness to do right, which astonish the decent citizen, whether of France or of this crowned republic, hardly attuned to expect such expression of sensibility from the dull and gross Moloch, representative of the lowest common denominator at home, which is the national State. We are filled with a tender yearning as if over somebody we had misjudged who turns out to be good: the visual correction of the mind overwhelms the heart.

The President's white yacht is steaming to a point in mid-Channel, accompanied on each side by French warships and overhead by French aeroplanes. And as they reach the middle of the Channel, the white yacht with the President steams on, and is taken under protection by British warships, with British planes circling above, wheeling round to escort the President to England, while simultaneously French planes and warships wheel round on their lone way home, having entrusted the head of their Republic to their ally's care.

There was a command performance at Covent Garden, Sir Thomas Beecham conducting the more weighty part of the programme, Mr. Constant Lambert the lighter ballet pieces. Mr. Harold Nicolson, partnered and out-distanced by a resourceful lady brought in to fill the gap, was describing the gorgeously coloured audience of king and queen, president and wife, princes, statesmen and courtiers, ambas-

326

sadors, generals and admirals in red and gold and blue, with tiara'ed wives in full force, almost the last full-dress pageant of the *ancien régime* before the Second World War and presumed social collapse. And per- haps to recoup himself for having, so to speak, through a peephole to observe and report into the microphone scenes such as he had once himself attended, Mr. Nicolson side-tracked into a pardonable if some- what irrelevant description of his own father's life as one-time ambas- sador at Madrid.

Right in the centre of the boxes crammed tight with the *corps diplo- matique*, and very much to the fore, was little Monsieur Maisky, Ambassador of the Union of Soviet Socialist Republics at the Court of St. James, at which Court he had had his ups and downs. Upon this old-world scene he now seemed to bestow the full if subtle smile of his benediction. At the moment, his diplomatic position, after years of neglect, was sharply in the ascendant, divided only by weeks, days, from the signing of the Nazi-Soviet Pact and the consequent relapse to ignominy, and, at the outbreak of the Russo-Finnish War, to sink to the lowest depths of degradation, only to rocket up to unprecedented heights of honour and consideration upon his country coming in and winning victories for the common cause.

At the time of the command performance, Mr. Chamberlain was being goaded into courting Russia's favour by Mr. Churchill, then a private Member, who was urging the Prime Minister not to look a gift horse in the mouth. Mr. Chamberlain had at last despatched, by a circuitous sea-route, a mixed Military and Naval Mission to Russia. They seemed to be a long time on the sea, as though cruising for their health, and when they at last reached Moscow there was not much that the Russians had to tell them, even though it was, in the light of later events, feared that they might have told the Russians more than it was good that the Germans should get to hear. The Soviet Government had required our consent to their taking over, as part of a general plan for their own defence before they could venture to champion other nations against Hitler, the Baltic States which had once been Russian provinces. But Don Quixote Chamberlain's idea was that Russia, alongside Britain and France, should be the big fearless brother ready to take risks to champion his own and other little sisters against the big bad wolf, rather than begin by swallowing them himself to augment his strength in facing the big wolf with confidence.

Then, while individual officers of the Mission, who bore compound double-barrelled and, to the Russians, unpronounceable names, were being photographed alongside nervous-looking Red Army colonels who have been shot for less, the German-Soviet Non-Aggression Pact burst upon the western world. Our potential ally against the big bad wolf, the gift horse, had signed a pact of friendship with the big bad wolf himself. "We don't want to pull *their* chestnuts out of the fire," Molotov declared amidst vociferous approval before the Supreme Soviet, called to hear an explanation of the *salto mortale* in Soviet foreign policy, and indignant with the British who were apparently trying to get the Red Army to do their fighting for them. "Let us see," he said amidst jeers, "what kind of warriors they prove to be who want to push us into bloody battle against our German neighbours."

It was a muted company of military and naval officers of the British Mission who got into the train at Moscow on the first lap of their homeward journey, and there was nobody much, apart from their French colleagues, to see them off. When the last whistle had blown and the train was almost under way, there came in a half-hurried waddle along the platform a rotund and ample, red-faced figure, a fairly senior Vice-Deputy General Somebody, blowing and puffing up, but in not too great a hurry, accompanied by his aide-de-camp and just in time to wave a jaunty goodbye to the homing double-barrelled members of the British Military and Naval Mission which Mr. Chamberlain, much against his inclination, had been goaded into sending to Moscow, from which terminus they were now slowly, if rapidly, gathering speed, steaming out: puff-puff-puff-puff-puff . . .

But when the train had drawn out of the station and the Vice-Deputy General slowly turned back to walk away, he stopped, and his aide-de-camp with him, dropped his arms, threw back his head and abandoned himself to an orgy of broad Moscow mirth: 'Ha! ha! ha! ha! ha!' he roared, and, leaning forward to embrace his girth, 'Ho! ho! ho! ho! ho!'

91

THE STRUTTING MALE

The war seemed set. An afterthought struck the Führer as the British Ambassador was about to take his leave. Hitler cast a cloudy look of inquiry at Nevile Henderson: "Would England care to have an alliance with Germany?" Nothing would have suited him better. He did not care for his Russian pact. Henderson, like all ambassadors unable to say yes or no, shuffled. Well . . . perhaps . . . it was not impossible. Mr. Chamberlain might succeed in carrying Parliament with him.

Hitler's watch was set, the time-table scheduled. He was conscious of the British consciousness of his own enormities. Mr. Chamberlain would never carry Parliament with him in a projected alliance with Nazi Germany, who had just raped Czecho-Slovakia guaranteed by England and France and, in the event of such an alliance, would, with, or more probably without, their consent, rape Poland. He did not believe that even Henderson could believe what he was saying. His cloudy look of abrupt inquiry relapsed of itself into the dyspeptic cast of features natural to the Hitler face in repose.

Hitler's answer to Chamberlain's move to guarantee Poland was a *rapprochement* with Russia. This had been the urgent business for which he cut short his repeated appearances on the Chancellery balcony upon the night of his return from Prague. A *rapprochement*, an alliance, a guarantee, growing distrust, a reshuffling of allies and of enemies, a bi-lateral agreement, a non-aggression pact, balance of power, crisis, war – these large and windy inanities, these dismal insincerities are about all that statesmen and diplomatists, old or new, seem to be able to contrive out of their banal repertoire. Were you to ask them whether they hadn't anything else – something to provide man with a loophole to escape being caught in a situation in which he has to choose the least of two evils: to kill rather than be killed – they would consult their White Books and Blue Books and Yellow Books and say, "No, we have nothing else." And they have not, not even the newest and maddest of totalitarians: they least of all.

The anarchists alone have a loophole. They turn out their pockets at night and share out their contents, and if one of them is fired by an idea for which he thinks they ought to be prepared to die, the others follow him, fired by his eloquence. But overcome midway by common sense they shoot him in the back. That is the only way to deal with potential Führers, in a civilised state, as distinct from a civilised State, which provides no loophole.

All profundities are simplicities, profound only because they have to be dug up for morons who had buried them beneath the débris of their own crudely complicated experiments in living. The real questions are the childish ones. The adult's attitude to life is crusted over with inanities. It is demonstrably plain that, were the whole matter of victualling the world on a non-national footing taken right out of the hands of the strutting male and handed over to a dozen sensible women who do not want to have their children killed, politics, which are nothing but a glorified form of housekeeping, would long since have been deflated to the problem of running a canteen.

But that was not how Ribbentrop and Molotov viewed their pre-destined stations in life. Molotov and Ribbentrop each broadcast to the world that they both, in fact, read history in the identical sense – namely, that whenever in the past Germany and Russia had been friends, both were at peace and so happy that they were the envy of all other nations. Instead of treating the world as *united* philologically by language groups, each having borrowed, and paying back in words, and literature and culture, men, being men, had to strut and thrust out their chests and regard the world as *divided* into antagonistic groups of sovereign 'nations'. From all this pretence followed pretentiousness and insincerity and double meaning and mental reservations and plain stark lies. The solemn punctiliousness in signing the non-aggression pact between Germany and Russia belongs to the larger international absurdities, comical not merely in retrospect. Molotov, seated, head inclined, carefully reading the text of the various clauses lest he sign away something; a secretary lifting the blotter, then the Stalin-Ribbentrop handshake, the steady eye, the vow of two men of oak.

The Western Powers were shocked. "But come," said Russia in effect, "don't you know that a non-aggression pact means non-aggression just so long as there happens to be no aggression?" And Russia cited more than one non-aggression pact since resolved in aggression.

The Western Powers reflected, found it to be true, if sad.

The West End was opening with a new play about the last war, *Only Yesterday*, which ended in a moving scene – the tragedy of human nature rising in pain and sorrow above artificial national hatred. A young German officer, just released from a British prisoner-of-war camp, as he visits the bereaved parents of his English friend killed in action, stands rigidly to attention as from a passing military band come the strains of *God Save the King*. Then the new war broke out.

"Never," said Lady Oxford, "have we had to fight for a more noble cause."

Too true. But it is the attitude of merely partial, qualified horror – Hitler, Mussolini, but not Napoleon, not Charles XII, not Peter the Great, not Frederick the Great, not even William II – which is the womb in which a Hitler is conceived. And it is the temporising eupepticism that wars in principle are respectable, manageable and inevitable, that 'defence will always keep pace with attack,' which is the sperm that fructified the womb from which a dragon with neither heart nor soul rears its head and whom we have no option but to fight, or die.

92

HITLER AND GERTRUDE STEIN

With his reiterated grievance of Versailles, and the genesis of the National Socialist movement, and how he was a simple *Front-Soldat* in the last war, repeated ad infinitum and introduced into every new speech, Hitler reminds one of Gertrude Stein with her 'groping for a *continuous present* and for using everything by beginning again and again', and who confesses, "Having naturally done this I naturally was a little troubled with it when I read it." In dressing up the belligerent past as a beginning as well as an end, since even the millennium dominated by the ultimate pure race did not appeal to him without continuous sabre-rattling, Hitler might have described his own 'sickening technique' in the words of Gertrude Stein:

> It was all so nearly alike, it must be different and it is different, it is natural that if everything is used and there is a continuous present and a beginning again and again if it is all so alike it must be simply different and everything simply different was the natural way of creating it then.

Hitler reminds one of Gertrude Stein also in his fanatical worship of mindlessness, in which respect, alongside D. H. Lawrence, he is the child of his generation. Her work, Gertrude Stein said in a lecture she delivered at Oxford, would have been 'outlawed' in any other generation than the post-war one. True. After writing

> Not as yet and to ask a question and to ask a question and as not yet. As not yet and to as yet and to ask a question and to as yet and to wind as yet and to as yet and to ask a question and to as yet ask a question as not yet, as not yet and to ask as not yet, and as not yet to ask a question as yet, and to as yet to wind as not yet, as not yet to wind please wind as not yet to ask a question and to and not yet. Please wind the clock and as yet and as not yet. Please wind the clock and not yet, to please not yet as not yet.

she says, "Enough said."

Hitler, like Gertrude Stein, 'naturally a little troubled with it' when he surveys his plan of getting everyone now living to sacrifice themselves for the doubtful benefit of the planet of millennium ahead, and with every-thing by then 'in a continuous present' and appreciably the same, unable to resolve the contradiction, theorising himself silly, his moral sense completely in abeyance, his brain jabbering in a circle:

> and as not yet to ask a question as yet, and to as yet to wind as not yet, as not yet to wind please wind as not yet to ask a question and to and not yet please wind the clock and as yet and as not yet,

"Enough said!" he cries and grasps a gun to silence any further in-tellectual opposition.

To the Reichstag he convened on September 1st he bawled about the wicked Poles who had kept him waiting two days in Berlin! "For two whole days I waited!" he wailed in his fruity adenoid voice. "I came over specially from Berchtesgaden to Berlin, and there I waited. *Und da habe ich gewarted und gewarted und gewarted!*"[1] he raged, a rich sob choking his throat. His patience had, as usual, been exhausted.

For *two* whole days the poor pet waited. Two whole days spent in Berlin away from the balmy air of Berchtesgaden – perhaps of all men dear Arthur, were he still alive, alone could have appreciated the extent of the Führer's sacrifice.

Having set the guns going in Poland, which action, he had been warned over and over again, would bring England and France into the war against him, he reassured his Reichstag audience, "I have offered England and France my hand of friendship."

Hitler was quite capable of saying to an anxious Reichstag, after having ransacked the Soviet Union and brought disaster on the German Army, "I have offered Stalin my hand of friendship."

When, nevertheless, two ultimatums had been served upon him he bawled to the Reichstag that, if Germany was to take any notice of ultimatums, then she might as well relinquish once and for all any idea of playing a decisive role in the power-politics of Europe!

Where outside Bedlam has one ever heard such language? Where outside Bedlam has any citizen empowered his government to 'play a role in the power-politics of Europe'? That mature old Europe was but a playground for homicidal lunatics with the mentality of boys of fourteen wanting to 'play a role' in the old style, and dress up for it, sword, bandolier and all, came as a mild shock from a man who was believed by many to be consumed with but a single, if fanatical, passion – human justice. It will be said that the notion of Europe as a field of Mars could only lodge in the brain of a Prussian junker. But Hitler was not a

---

[1] "And there waited and waited and waited."

Prussian, not even a German, but an outcast and an oddity to whom it had occurred that the Prussian military caste was not playing its cards to full advantage.

93

THE PERPETUUM MOBILE

How is mankind to rid itself of adolescents who contrive to climb into the signal box? By abolishing the signal box. All that indeed is necessary by way of government is a sense of general fair play. People, it has been proved, will stand even rationing so long as their sense of fairness is not impaired. The sun shines and the rain drops on the unjust and just alike; there is no favouritism, nor is there any rancour in our grumbling at the weather. In the same way, if science could contrive an automatic economic register, demonstrated to be flawlessly exact and fair to all, all would submit. What men object to is to be 'ruled' over by homicidal lunatics, interested blackguards, nincompoops, or even great good men. There is no occasion to 'rule' or be 'ruled over'. Mankind, left alone, has already travelled some little distance towards recognising that toleration of all views, parties and factions variously interpreting toleration is a tolerable alternative to the more intolerable compulsory toleration of the intolerant.

A government elected by the people is the only kind of government that people want. Which would be true if electors knew what they were electing; if those elected had not wangled to get elected and wangled to get into the government, and if it were necessary – the craziest of delusions – to have a government at all. Everything that is most tiresome and crippling today proceeds from men who, unable to think themselves into a state of tranquillising coma, translate their imperfectly digested thoughts into political action. It should be clear to the meanest intelligence that, to achieve the peace of the world, nothing more radical is required than the abolition of centralised government in countries which have already achieved an inter-urban habit of amity. Supposing the Government of Great Britain were rescinded, it would be unlikely that the city of Manchester would march on the city of Sheffield. Such

333

passions for rivalry as may exist have already found their expression in organised competition in the sporting fields.

Is the opposite system of bilateral international agreements really rooted in human nature? Consider. Human beings of the same nation so hate and suspect each other that it is a wonder why certain householders in London should not have formed bilateral agreements with other householders in order to ensure a defensive arrangement against the concerted attacks by other groups of householders. But the fact is that no such groupings and alliances are contemplated, because the thought of doing so has very reasonably failed to occur to anyone. If we could induce the same forgetfulness and negligence in regard to the larger groupings of units by lulling ourselves, through the hypnotic effect of profound thought, into a benignant inactivity, we should reap the same fruits of subtle, vivifying peace.

The common level of the ordinary decent citizen the world over has outstripped the good will of his government, still that of a stalked and stalking beast of prey. The trend of a raw and frightened populace clustering behind king and government, who muster it in arms against a like-minded actual or potential foe, has become a trend in the opposite direction – of mankind, as represented by the average citizen of any country, so closely united as to be able to afford to dispense with central governments in order to avoid the focus of international friction. That scheming men, like Hitler and Mussolini, consumed by their personal adolescent ambitions to 'play a role in the power-politics of Europe', have attempted to put the clock back (and all but succeeded) does not disprove the trend in men's hearts towards a loose national de-centralisation, on the one hand, and a loose world centralisation, on the other. The half-heartedness manifest everywhere in France and England, and even in Germany at the outbreak of hostilities, the dismal lack of all enthusiasm with which men rallied to the colours when their respective governments informed them they were all once more at war, reflected a bewildered incredulity in men and women that governments, who had arrogated for themselves so much attention and importance, had been photographed and news-reeled on their comings and goings, should, at the end of a mere interval of twenty years or so, again proclaim their utter impotence to 'save' the world – from what? – from that which the world positively did not want to do.

People of adult intelligence, mature and mellowed in the experience of living, have long felt that politics should be bereft of all emotion, and run by nondescript bodies and persons, like the Water Board or Miss Margaret Bondfield or the Metropolitan Railway, hardly likely to arouse violent emotions of partisanship. Emotion should be reversed for love, nature, friendship, religion, and the poetry of life. Were this the accepted pattern of human life, there would not, on September 2nd, 1939, mature out of a chimera of personal ambitions this ridiculous thing – a time-fuse – called respectably 'a crisis', and a match lifted to its wick called by another respectable diplomatic term, 'an ultimatum', placing the vast majority of hard-worked fathers and mothers of families in the position of rabbits sent scuttling for the nearest hole.

But was there no kind of safeguard to ensure that, if a lunatic did climb into the driver's seat, he could at any rate not start the engine? No, we have to say, there was no safeguard of any sort or kind. The safest thing that we could think of in that case was for our own elected engine-driver to climb into the engine of *our* train, replete with our own passengers, and set it going with the intent of colliding at full speed with the train now coming up, driven at a breakneck speed by the homicidal lunatic, in the good hope that, in the collision that must presently ensue, the lunatic would be knocked off the driver's seat. But if that did not happen, if our carriages, as was to be expected, got badly mauled and twisted in the impact, it was to be hoped that the occupants of the other train might meet with relatively heavier casualties than even our own, each side, however, seeing to it that the next of kin was speedily informed.

94

OLD FAVOURITES

That is as far as pooled political wisdom had managed to carry the passengers entrusted to its care, and paying for it by 1939. Further than this our wizards in Parliament were not to go, did not indeed consider it politic, or as they preferred to put it 'practical politics'.

To Mr. Amery, one out of many, the war did not seem to get under way soon or quickly enough. Mr. Chamberlain, who still felt that, while there was life there was hope that, while the war had not begun, the calamity might still be averted, hedged and dallied as he waited for news from Paris, from Rome. Not so Mr. Greenwood who, carried away by his own appalling imitation of Pericles, had also lifted little Amery off his feet. "Speak for England!" Amery shouted to the Deputy Leader of the Opposition who, whatever he was speaking for, was in favour of taking an irrevocable decision.

Chamberlain, again goaded into ill-considered action by men presuming to impugn his patriotism, in his turn goaded Paris into agreeing with him upon what, when resorted to by honest men, is always a counsel of despair: the despatch of an ultimatum with a time-limit.

It was, of all days, a peaceful Sunday when, at eleven o'clock in the morning, the aged Chamberlain's weary and too self-centred broadcast, with the stress upon *his* (rather than our) disappointment, the ruin of *his* hopes, *his* life-work, informed a dazed and even wearier British public that they were once again at war. Mr. Kennedy, the American Ambassador, went in to see the Prime Minister who had just delivered himself of this heavy day's work, and they talked a little in the Cabinet Room, both suddenly unable to continue. The sense of the appalling tragedy, the futility of it all, choked them: they stood there and both openly wept.

Churchill's House of Commons speech, an hour later, about the 'sunshine in his heart' jarred on our taut sensibilities. Sidney Maiden, the brilliant caricaturist, had in 1937 represented him as an elderly man persistently revolving in a swivel-door because he always came out when he thought he was going in. And now he *was* in.

The first War Administration was duly photographed. There were two rows: lean cadaverous Halifax with his unduly narrow trousers seated in the front with mourner Chamberlain in the middle, somnolent Simon, the all gone-to-seed Kingsley Wood, and dapper lynx-like Sam Hoare well to the fore and seated on each side of their Chief, and rotund rosy Churchill with Hore-Belisha and the lesser fry all standing behind like good dutiful juniors. Here they were, old favourites and new, none apparently capable of averting a war. For a historian writing of our epoch from the vantage-ground of a thousand years hence, the incredible discovery that early in the eighteenth century there had been a war for the Spanish Succession might assist him to believe that, in 1939, there was a War for the Definition of Freedom, in which slaves of State and slaves of Private Enterprise disembowelled each other, until a gradual addition of belligerents, variously professing to adhere to either theory, obscured the issue, and the war became, on all hands, frankly a war for survival.

The war aims, on our side, tended to stress the fight again as one for democracy, even intransigent employers of labour becoming strangely left-wing, exalting personal liberty as an ideal inextricably bound up with the survival of interest payment on capital.

On the enemy side, the National Socialists stressed their socialism, more national, however, than socialist, presented themselves to our plutocrats as right-wing patriots whose fastidiousness was strained by the Soviet pact, and to our workers as brothers of the Russian proletariat whom it pained to see British Labour exploited for profit by a Jewish plutocracy. They stressed that, in being joined in a common intolerance of opinion, they were delightfully free and equal, were not anti-capitalist, and not, though the State seemed to absorb the lot, in principle against payment of interest on capital.

As both in England and Germany there were people who had invested money, the disparity of war aims during the initial months of stalemate seemed as though it might eventually narrow down to – *What rate of interest?*

95

LOCUSTS

'We have,' said Mr. Chamberlain in Parliament, 'no quarrel with the German people except that they allow themselves to be governed by a Nazi Government.'

Why did they? Why do they? The amoeba of war, when Mr. Chamberlain made this statement on September 1st, 1939, had already flowed round him, incorporated him and oozed on with him, and the amoeba of war was gradually to do this with the rest of the sullen and half-resentful population of Great Britain and finally the world. But it did not seem to need the slimy persistence of that mindless amoeba of the collective human free will, devoured by its own directionless necessity of least resistance to individual greed, to flow round Germans and ooze on with them to Mars. For they seemed in many ways to be more like locusts. David Garnett ends one of his novels with a masterly description of the characteristics of these brown insects:

When they fell in waterless desert places they died; where they passed they left desert; they sprouted wings and flew. Their seed sprang again in wingless armies from the earth. They had no reason and little that might be called instinct. All their movements are due to the heat of the sun. They are thermotropic.

Germans, too, seem to be thermotropic, but their movements are due not so much to the heat of the sun as to that of Mars.

The *Deutschlandsender* broadcast a sermon in which the preacher called upon the Lord to bless 'His golden host', the Nazi Army. "*O Herr!*" he called, "*gesegnet sei dein goldenes Heer!*" and held out to the Germans who fall in battle the prospect of "*das ewig' Morgenrot*". And the B.B.C., not to be outdone, but shy of Lord-of-Hosts panegyrics, reciprocated with the military history of the Gloucestershire Regiment.

All Germans brought to the microphone and invited to give a first-hand account of themselves, invariably began with: 'Ja . . .' long pause. A German soldier on patrol, extolled to the public by the radio announcer as a proficient marksman – '*schiessenausgebildet*' – and prompted to tell of his exploit, said, '. . . ja . . .' he had shot down fifteen Frenchmen. Was that because he was so perfectly *schiessenausgebildet*? He thought, and said, 'Ja', and, feeling more was expected of him, added, "*Das hat mir grosse Freude bereitet.*"[1]

The war on land, on our part, opened with an attack on a German outpost. As though a British football team – so friendly is the spirit – advanced on a goal held by Germans. Why? In conformity with the policy evolved by officials that, after we had beaten them, we could all be boys together once more. Sir Eric Phipps, a former British Ambassador in Berlin, resented this idea of being all boys together, and advocated hatred in perpetuity, which, if less amiable, was more logical, and not more stupid than the first stage in which we fought not Germans but Nazis, as the Russians fought White Guards, not Finns (all the while friendly with Germans, and keeping quiet about Germans being not Germans but White Guards).

There followed the bombing of Scapa Flow. It seemed as though some malevolent spirits, a race apart from the human and devoid of all kindred feeling, were, in a dream, disclaiming their hitherto assumed kinship and letting themselves go – a pop at Aunt Sally at a mechanical-table.

After all this, one was perhaps disappointed not to hear of the Man in the Iron Lung, who did not seem prevented from doing anything at all in it, joining up in the war, his iron lung made to fit into a specially constructed tank.

As Gogol says, "It's a dull world, my masters!"

---

[1] "That has given me great pleasure."

EPILOGUE

96

THE FUTURE

God's Fifth Column, sabotaging all inconclusive formations, works towards the building of human society resting upon the only foundation acceptable to God. Having considered the self-satisfied physiognomy of the Age during the last five decades, foaming at the mouth in the present sixth, the question naturally poses itself: Do you want to go back to it? The answer will probably be that, in so far as the preceding five decades have caused the explosion of the 1940s, they must not be repeated. Everyone, save people living deceptively on their memories, wants a new world. What kind of a world is it to be?

The most striking feature in this demand for a new world is that it is unanimous, and that there is more agreement than disagreement about the kind of world it should be, the disagreement being largely one of superficial misunderstanding caused by a too pedantic adherence to names. Never before in history has there been this opportunity for securing so wide a margin of universal consent for a truly democratic principle of reconstruction. Would-be converts are rapidly shedding their prejudices against social systems they had previously abhorred; adherents to established systems are as rapidly shedding their illusions. Men of business are uncoiling to receive the blessings of socialism; communist war-horses, impatient of ideologies, are becoming great captains of industries. It would seem that here was the opportunity for building a new world by salvaging the best from all systems, while dropping the red rag of obsolete nomenclature.

We want a new world that will include with the noblest and sanest elements of communism the vitalising fundamental principle of individual enterprise, while eschewing the names associated in the opposite camp only with the noxious aspects of the conflicting economic systems. We want a world in which the gold standard is replaced by the human standard, the dollar unit by the human unit. We want a world in which every adult human being receives as his birthright, in universal currency, say, one dollar a day, that dollar being so regulated in relation to world-market prices as to form the irreducible standard of his daily subsistence, the inducement to work springing, not from abject necessity, but from the common human wish to augment his comfort and embellish his existence. This modicum of absolute necessity is to be deducted from the annual total world output before private enterprise earns its extras from the superflux, the heavy incursion into the fruits of production providing production itself with a steady market of consumption, the very basis of its financial stability. We want scientific world control on the one hand, and personal liberty on the other. We want socialism in Geneva, and the fruits of private enterprise in our own cities. We want the League of Nations palace to expand into a World Academy of scientists and economists instructed so to balance the housekeeping accounts of the planet as to encourage, within an adjustable framework of world control, the free play of private initiative. We want them to do precisely that which made Goethe wonder why so comparatively easy an equation should have been beyond the wit of man to work out and maintain: the balancing of an automatic system by which the violent swinging of the pendulum, whether of politics or economics, is perpetually neutralised, and the defeat of liberty by oligarchy perpetually obviated. The demand is for stability ensuring mobility; uniformity of educational prestige ensuring individual diversity; the economic revolution of universal endowment ensuring a contented conservatism; the pooling of national sovereignties in a supra-national order accentuating, far from obliterating, the true cultural development of individual nations. We want the common people to come into their legacy of leisure and culture in order to shed their commonness and become uncommon. We want the meek to inherit the earth. We want our nations to inherit and cherish their cultures.

How is it to be done? The conclusion of the Second World War will leave the world in such a chaos of conflicting cross-sectional stresses, interests and impulses that to reconcile and satisfy them even approximately will prove far more difficult than to supersede them by a supra-national solution. The imperative need is to satisfy, not national abstractions, but the elementary instincts of mankind; the folly is to thwart them. Security of property, Voltaire's final recipe for happiness – *cultivez votre jardin* – is fairly easily achieved within a supra-national framework which, while abolishing the shadow of national economic offensively-defensive territorial sovereignties grants the substance of the natural affections for the local, ancestral or cultural ties on one's own land.

The scramble for world markets which, as Lenin insisted, was the root cause of the last world war, and which again crystallised around national sovereignties, is even more obviously the root cause of this [written in 1942]. It will not stop with the cessation of the war and will not fail to cause another.

World communism is the solution advocated by those who, without forfeiting their intellectual savings sunk in a theory to the study and exposition of which they have devoted so many years, cannot welcome a more elastic alternative. We must get away from the fatal fascination and repulsion of mere names. Our only concern should be to satisfy man's major instincts in a way which will reconcile conflicting differences. Nearly all the trouble and unhappiness of the vast majority in the last fifty years was rooted in the dearth of markets, the incapacity of the many to buy the goods they were being sweated to turn out as fast as they could. In the past this capacity to buy rested on a totally irrelevant and rather useless metal called gold. As machines increasingly dispensed with human labour, the capacity to absorb production has become the indispensable condition, absurd though it seems, of making the wheels of industry turn.

If the wheels of production could be induced to turn for something so nominal and arbitrary as gold, on the basis of which convention industry was perfectly content to receive banknotes of paper for which other industries were content to go on turning out goods, then the human unit, each worth the spending power of three hundred and sixty-five dollars a year, cannot but constitute a more reliable prerequisite for toil: a stomach, a market, ready to consume the output.

Industry in the broadest terms will carry the population of the earth, gratis, on its back. Why should it wish to do so? For the opportunity of sharing in the superflux of what money can buy after the subsistence of the suffering unit, lifted everywhere above want and anxiety, is assured. What that share may be of the total output must be computed with unimpeachable impartiality on the basis of the difference between total maximum inducement for production (compounded of employers and employed) and maximum unearned consumption (rising with the increased mechanical ability of industry to dispense with human labour). The ideal is to provide the population of the world with an unearned daily increment, never to fall below a living standard, but capable of rising in proportion to the total world output of which, as it increases, the enterprising and industrious, at last forming but a fraction of the total population, will be getting commensurate profits without appreciable incursion into the total provisions.

This is, broadly, what people want when they speak of wanting a new world but not wanting communism or capitalism or socialism or any other 'ism' because they think it will rob them either of personal freedom or a sense of security, or saddle them with unemployment, or produce

343

strikes or lock-outs, or make them a cog in the State machine, or turn them into food for powder. What certainly nobody wants after this war is a glut of goods with no purchasers to absorb them, a scramble for overseas markets, and a dumping of goods sorely needed at home in some economically contested virgin area in Africa or Asia, and an increasingly long row of unemployed young men in our cities ringing at your front door and depositing encyclopaedias and vacuum cleaners on approval. None of these things do we want. We do not want the fatuities of another Faubourg Saint-Germain. We do not want slums. We do not want playboys. We do not want racketeers.

Nothing save dire unimaginativeness has so far prevented the United Nations from trumpeting aloud this obvious expression of what, on our side, should surely have argued a noble imagination, had we proclaimed this Economic Charter as our ideally practical war aim. Mankind is over-ripe for pooling those absurd militant sovereignties in an economic world merger, establishing as an act of faith in man's political wisdom the long-overdue and in any case inevitable World Federation, abolishing not merely sovereignties and national independencies but the last vestiges of defensively-offensive national systems with all the Bedlam of inter-*national* relations, by rescinding all frontiers and citizenships, the populations of the world clustering in a certain instinctive pattern around the nuclei of language groups, ancestral ties, habits and cultural leanings, chiefly of course in their own countries, with only local government to keep the peace, and a world police air force to prevent any militant groupings overriding the profound desire and right of men and women everywhere to be left alone. Against the magnet of such beneficent creative forces, no single country, least of all a Germany badly mangled by the Russian bear, could have stood out long. All suspicion of an aggressive capitalist imperialism in the outside world would quickly dissipate in Russia. Threatened by nobody, she would soon mellow at the edges and, who knows, perhaps later merge into the World Federation. A World Economy satisfying the heart and mind and stomach of a cheated humanity, would no longer be tempted on its donkey-round by the carrot of 'national sovereignty and independence'. Problems, alike of 'encirclement' and '*Lebensraum*' dispensed with, men free to live their own lives in a world of plenty, the whole green earth their garden – how long would it be before an essentially culture-loving Germany, made pregnant by a cheap drivelling and out-moded superman, was brought to bed with a *fausse couche*?

If we just tinker with sundry nationalisms and imperialisms and various combinations of what are already being fatuously described as 'the peace-loving nations', and feebly accept the artificial dearth of money with its intermittent booms and depressions and stock-exchange crashes and class struggle and strikes and lock-outs and slumps, low wages and slums, bitterness and want as the sorry and ugly physiognomy of our capitalist society, then we are obviously doomed to another world war. If we take leisured independence as the epitome of life, the standard of human well-being, we shall come through. No very novel idea, this, of course. It is implied in the parables of Jesus: it is the essence of modern economics. Spiritually, it postulates a certain transvaluation of values – the lifting of the money fog which darkens counsel and clouds the brains of bankers, least able of anyone to rationalise the needless intricacies of finance.

It is difficult to conceive a more vivid representation of hell than a tank full of eels, all twining and creeping over one another. Add a hundred varied fish, water-beetles, tadpoles and such-like creatures, and the picture of a living hell will be complete. Life on earth is not unlike this crowded hell-in-a-tank. Not a few spiritualists are inclined to regard it as the real hell from which, at death, we rise into less congested regions. If, however, our present life is hell, we seem largely unaware of it and are capable even of enjoying it in part. Yet the analogy is complete. It is, indeed, doubtful whether the eels and the other creatures in the tank are acutely unhappy. It is doubtful whether they are more than dimly conscious of any discomfort. Their state corresponds to our own.

Seen from outside the tank, our life is a congested hell. But we are too dim, altogether too dazed, to realise our condition, least of all to be able to find a way out of the tank. The water in the congested tank is money; the tank the rigid credit system within which suffering humanity is unhealthily confined. The tank is sorely in need of expansion, and could do with a few bucketfuls of fresh water to relieve the pressure and congestion within. In other words, man has reached the stage at which he needs cheap money, cheap leisure, cheap goods, and more and more clever machines as his slaves.

The objection most likely to occur at this point is: too difficult; or: it will not work. To this it might be retorted that the existing capitalist system of production, labour, distribution, finance and reward, based on neither reason nor justice, and so complex and chaotic that *nobody* even pretends to be able to explain it, even so seems to work, at least in the intervals of wars which reverse it, when, in obviously unsound, completely fantastic conditions, it is *made* to work again. If *that* can work, anything will work; we need have no qualms on that score.

It is contended that there are conservative forces, as well as very radical forces, at bay, who would invariably oppose a solution running counter to their established traditions. For – it had better be breathed – the prerequisite of the working of the controlled New Capitalism is the abolition of usury and speculation. But is it rational to permit statesmen and politicians, who will soon be dead, and who are not a little responsible for the jeopardy into which they have flung the whole of human society, to perpetuate their prejudices into a future in which they will have no share. M. de Charlus, half paralysed and near the end of his span of life, informs Proust of the ravages Time has wrought in the rolls of his contemporaries. "Hannibal de Breaute – dead! Antoine de Mouchy – dead! Baron de Talleyrand – dead! Sosthene de Doudeauville – dead!"

Of the figures who have enriched these pages without advancing the art of living on this earth, one could echo the dirge of Montesquiou's sepulchral whisper, falling like clay from the gravedigger's spade: "Bismarck – dead! Moltke – dead! Count Berchtold – dead! Georges Clemenceau – dead! Raymond Poincaré – dead! Northcliffe – dead! Ludendorff – dead! Senator Lodge – dead! Nicholas II – dead! William II – dead! General Conrad – dead! General Suhomlinov – dead! Arthur Balfour – dead! Leon Trotsky – dead!" The future must not pledge itself to the prejudices of the past, of men who will soon lie under the turf.

It is the English-speaking nations upon whom it will devolve to be the trustees of the new world liberty embodied in personal economic freedom, such initiative clearly being beyond the strength of General de Gaulle or General Sikorski. This must be so since, after victory, the supra-national defensive forces will of necessity at first reside in the signatories of the Atlantic Charter. But as a pledge of good will, as a sign that no prejudicial attitude whatever is contemplated, the Soviet Union must be free to go its own way unmolested, and not again be driven underground by a hostile and predatory capitalism. More, as a safeguard, a political investment for our future, a guarantee against the possible failure of our new benevolent supra-national capitalism, a safety-valve for the hot steam of rhetoric at home, communism, far from being feared, should be considered as a ready alternative if, after a stated period, the Soviet system prove, after all, to be the better of the two. For all these reasons, there must be trade and intercourse and understanding between the two rival but friendly social-economic groups. In this way bitterness will be obviated, partisanship reduced to a single benevolent comparison, and, in the fulness of time, either the one or the other or the best of both systems will be freely adopted by the entire world.

This should be our declared war aim to remove suspicion, clear the future, and put new heart into the citizen increasingly despairing of the sagacity of statesmanship. It would win us a walk-over victory over the forces of bigotry and race discrimination. Who can doubt it? The appeal of it – security – is the secret wish of nearly everyone today, every man and woman not merely politically free, but economically independent, a world citizen, his unearned living assured, additional income awaiting him in free employment or as the fruit of his own enterprise, with an assured uncongested and expanding market in which to develop it. It will be a world of peaceful leisure and culture for all, not excluding the few already in possession of such privileges. The sanctity of the person as the first article of a new civilisation; and this for all, without discrimination of nationality or race, without the least imposition on the industrious, the clever, the talented, the enterprising. Is that not everyone's real war aim? Would you have them lay down their lives for less?

When this war is over, the social criticism released against the older order will be overwhelming and bitter. And just because there will be opposition, the peace-war will fritter away all the benefit, the same professional politicians again jockeying for position, and, as in 1919, an opportunity to reconstruct society will be missed. The solution is to say now what we will do, and so obviate post-war war, while shortening this war.

Then let us proclaim it as our war aim, reanimating with its spirit the over-cautious, well-intentioned but only half-filled balloon of the Atlantic Charter to date, which flags a little for want of boldness, zest, explicitness, and faith in man. Afterwards let us broadcast it unceasingly on all waves which span this tragic blood-soaked earth to reach those misguided dupes or victims of an insensate sovereign nationalism carried to its logical conclusion, whom we fatuously frighten into closing their ranks by impressing on them what is coming to them, until we take the wind out of their sails, the stuffing out of their New Order, and see how long the badgered and hungry enemy citizen will hold out against this beckoning of a new life, this imminent rebirth into a new world

Was it possible, Hitler long ago asked himself, to eradicate ideas by force of arms? His conclusions were that ideas, philosophical systems and movements based on spiritual values, whether sound or not, could not, after they had taken root, be broken by the use of force, save when force itself was in the service of new spiritual values.

If he is right, our own conclusion in our struggle against him should be to take a leaf out of his book and turn the principle against him. If so mean an ideal as his can take root, how easy it should be for us to uproot it with the peerless ideal of a world republic.

The structurally admirable United States should serve as the world model. According to Osbert Sitwell, "The Pilgrim Fathers, when they left England, were most surely essaying to run away from themselves, to elude the strength of their own passions, that, pent up, had distilled them into so gloomily bitter and cantankerous a minority, quite as much as to escape a problematic religious persecution. As well attempt to avoid your own shadow." It is the United States of America which is the solvent. They can no longer hope to exist, or even subsist, withdrawn unto themselves, must return to their destiny, their roots in old Europe, to their inheritance of seekers after a simple truth, not in escape from their own fate, of which they carried a shipload to found a new world with, but in forging the unity of the human family, to find their heart's content in that which they themselves have made a Land of Promise, of all the world.

It is the first sign of good organisation that one is not conscious of the wheels of organisation, as it is a sign of health that a man is not conscious of his organs. What would we think of a housekeeper who carried on her work by fits and starts in response to the vociferous acclamation or denunciation she managed to enlist from among the occupants she was engaged to serve by inviting their emotional confirmation of her views on how to carry on her duties?

In the same way the World State should so run the economic life as to make the suffering unit unconscious of it; so serve the individual's needs that none of his emotions or even interest should be engaged. He is, after all, the only one who feels and suffers; he is the sentient being in a mechanism which should have no other purpose than to keep house for him.

H. G. Wells's *Outline of History* was widely read, but changed nothing. It did not avert a new war, did not produce a world state. "The only thing that man learns from the study of history," says Hegel, "is that men have learned nothing from the study of history." There are no facts, properly speaking, giving birth to principles because, as Coleridge insisted, unless an investigator first had a principle of selection he would not have taken notice of those facts upon which he grounded his principle. You had to have a lantern in your hand to give light, otherwise all the materials in the world were useless, for you could not find them, and if you could, you could not arrange them. To the objection that any principle of selection came itself from facts, "To be sure!" answered Coleridge, "but there must have been again an antecedent light to see those antecedent facts. The relapse may be carried in imagination backwards for ever – but go back as you may, you cannot come to a man without a previous aim or principle."

The capacity, the range, of a historian's thought was, according to Coleridge, determined by the variety, sustained order and originality of his associations. But, if so, why should the writer of history pick out an arbitrary order at his own discretion rather than sit back and wonder at the human chaos? It is an old-maidish pedantry to pick out of this

348

universal chaos and confusion a few selected threads and call it sense and order.

Homo sapiens is like a water-mill-wheel which new men constantly leap on to, to weigh down and slip off into the spume, eventually to vanish in the ocean. Nature may show a questionable partiality for homo sapiens, but Providence, one gathers, is not concerned with him as such. Abstract Man of the Species is for ever turning on his own axis. And the sole purpose of this otherwise unnecessary perpetuum mobile seems to be that the mills of God grind something, something secret, something having no relation to the motions of Man or the energy and purposes of men, something evidently very precious, grind finely each single grain: yes, every human heart. For the thoughts and deeds of living beings are as nothing beside their griefs!

The future of mankind would seem to lie between two extremes. Our salvation is in attaining universal nobility of heart and mind through a standard education introduced to abolish the last vestiges of class distinction in anticipation of the complete subjugation by science of the world of matter to minister to man's material needs. Falling short of such vision, towards which education should direct the heart and mind, it is abject compromise: the compromise of an Al Capone at the helm, extending as a by-product of his larger activities a protection to culture – as he indeed did to the labour unions. This, briefly, represents our choice. Which shall it be?

There is, failing a belief in the sanity of man, even a belief in life, still a belief in God, in the sense that one could hardly believe in the omnipotence of material forces. For to believe that there is nothing in the universe beyond material causes and effects is as though a blind pit pony, conscious only of drawing a load in the dark, assumed that this was the Alpha and Omega of all existence, while knowing nothing of light, or of Beethoven, or of the flight of human thought. Reduced to its rudiments, the materialist conception is confined to something which is being pushed, pushing something else, while explaining the queer exotic flame of culture kindled by mankind as a surprising by-product of material causes – a pretty light given off by the phosphorescence of putrefaction.

Surely if there was this light within the brute material microcosm it was because this microcosm itself was steeped in the light of the macrocosm; that the microcosm was not a self-contained universe but a reflection in a crooked mirror of the macrocosm *plus* the microcosm. Together, and in the clear straight mirror of the soul cleansed of impurities, they made a satisfying self-explanatory whole, in which all contradictions were reconciled. In the deep serenity of the soul, time and space and numbers, in whose distorting mirror all life had seemed a broken and lopsided caricature of paradise, now leapt into place. And everything was everywhere and always.

As early as 1869 Helmholtz observed that the final aim of natural science was to discover the motions underlying all alterations, and the motive forces thereof; that is, to resolve itself into mechanics. To Spengler this meant a reduction of all quality to quantity; that is, the referring of the *seen* nature-picture to the *imagined* picture of a single numerically and structurally measurable order. That is what, reduced to simple terms, the scientific 'biological' outlook amounts to.

Whereas nineteenth-century science believed that nothing was as it was seen to be, twentieth-century science went further, and asserted that in the last resort things were in fact just as we might wish them to be. That is to say, the previous century prided itself on its realism in supposing that things were not at all what they looked, but what they could be reduced to. Our own century, on the contrary, believes that they are in fact as suggested by their visible physiognomy, the universe being a multi-imaged appreciation of feeling, in obedience to which the minute fluctuating particles of nothing, which compose the substance of things, shape themselves according to the laws of a largely unknown morphology responsive to some aesthetic principle in life.

The astronomist, Sir James Jeans, likened the universe to a thought in the mind of a great mathematical thinker. And Sir Arthur Eddington ascribed natural laws of the external world to some creative impulse that no science seemed able to circumscribe. In exploring his own territory, the physicist came up again and again against the influence of some wider reality that he could not altogether shut out, but which seemed to point to a reversal of the hitherto accepted scientific principle that material forces had caused a refinement of the brain power we called the mind, by postulating a primary reality, a mind behind the world of matter, which, by its selection of values, may indeed be said to have created its physical environment.

The Aristotelian mind, believing nothing it could not prove to the satisfaction of its own perceptions, has, after subjecting man's perceptions to a scientific scrutiny leaving in doubt both the competence of the perceptions and the jurisdiction of the scrutiny, come round full circle to the Platonic Idea of the reality of the unseen informing the seen.

Life is always in a state of transition. While we are battling for the right to mass-produce and undersell internationally, we are already impinging on a new era which, by broadcasting the vibrations composing matter, will re-enact the miracle of the loaves and fishes. And that means not only a luncheon broadcast from the Savoy Grill, but also houses to live in, trains, buses, even beautiful ballet dancers re-enacting for your private delectation the dance of the dying swan on your own drawing-room carpet, all for an inclusive radio licence of ten-and-six a year. That means the end of the invidious necessity of 'earning a living', the beginning of life freed of material care.

The age of transcendent miracles looms behind that. The triumph at last of the Platonic Idea: the re-incarnation of the ego in a new natural body when the old is wasted by disease beyond all practicability of further medical tinkering. Chehov prophesied that one day mankind would not only overcome the fear of death but would also overcome death itself. And that is one way of overcoming death – in the flesh. The Platonic Idea will have met the Aristotelian extraction of Nature's secrets: truth will have become apparent to the naked eye and to the soul alike, and men will know the truth, as Chehov said, as clearly and self-evidently as they know that twice two are four.

The fallen youth, mowed down like grass, might not be deemed to have died altogether in vain if, we say, a new order of peace and justice is in consequence to reign on earth. The unhappy millions whom death had snatched before their time, gone for ever, might well have wondered whether their dying was so positively necessary in order for a better world to be built upon their bones as those who urged them into battle seemed to think it was. "They will forget us, forget our faces, voices, and even how many there were of us . . ."

"But who shall restore us our children?" That is the indelible scar, the deepest and abiding sadness, against which no consideration of gain, no eupeptic writing off of casualties, balancing of numbers from the ledger of the quick and the dead, dare measure themselves. Priests and laymen alike, seeing in the sacrifice something to put to the credit of the temporal account, merely wallowed in rhetoric. Consolation indeed there was, but it was not of this world.

The antithesis was between those who regarded the material world as a self-contained universe, and those others who felt it to be an undue simplification of our limited five senses, a lop-sided view of a mysterious whole, a reality akin to our own but freed from the shackles of Time and truly self-contained, no longer transient. The collective acceptance of disease and death and war, and means as justified by the end, and nations and classes, and sacrifice squared with a village war memorial, hung like a black cloud over mankind choking in its own effluvia of accrued sin. It hung heavily, surrounding the earth with a poisonous yellow fog. Beyond and hidden from us was the shining face of Divinity.

The sense of its unseen proximity informing our spirit, like some blinding light of perpetual day, a full and blazing truth percolating but dimly through our sluggish time-bedraggled senses, is at once the source of illumination of all great art, art being, as Schopenhauer truly says, but

351

the communication in phenomenal terms of the Platonic Idea: of that unseen reality hiding behind its material shadow (alone visible to the bodily eye), a mysterious whole unfathomable to our mortal state; Man's highest apprehension of the unknown whole, being, as Goethe puts it, a sense of the miraculous.

Such intimations are present in Wordsworth's poetry. Only rarely, in the purest work of genius, as in Mozart's 'Concertante Sinfonie for Violin and Viola', in the concluding bars of the second movement of the Andante, is there that abrupt transition from the yearning of an imprisoned angel for lost paradise to the state of being in heaven, a cessation of weeping semi-tones, infinitely lovely, yet of a doleful sensuous expression, groping after resting-places which cannot be sustained but needs must precede the heavenly coda. Then, quite at the end, suddenly – it is heaven. The full noontide of the unimaginable day. Not sad, not yearning now: *pure ardent being*. Where now the fear, and where the waiting? Where the wishing, sorrowing, hoping? A timeless striding out to a new measure, a free but self-retracing step, a joyous but unearthly swing. A hymn to everything now, everywhere and always. It was, after all, so simple.

INDEX

T. 179 !!!

Moncure March 277-8.